It was a long way from the slums of Philadelphia to the superstar stratosphere of international jet set glamour—but Eddie Fisher made it by the time he was twenty-five.

It was a long way from wild longing for unobtainable girls to possessing the most beautiful women on earth—but Eddie Fisher made that, too.

It was a long way from the public image of a baby-faced, dreamily romantic entertainer to a man trapped in a private nightmare of drugs and desire, but Eddie Fisher had to make that masquerade go on and on.

Now that masquerade is over—as Eddie Fisher goes all the way to reveal what even the most lurid rumors never hinted at—

EDDIE
My Life, My Loves

Eddie
My Life, My Loves

EDDIE FISHER

BERKLEY BOOKS, NEW YORK

This Berkley book contains the complete
text of the original hardcover edition.
It has been completely reset in a type face
designed for easy reading, and was printed
from new film.

EDDIE: MY LIFE, MY LOVES

A Berkley Book / published by arrangement with
Harper & Row, Inc.

PRINTING HISTORY
Harper & Row edition / August 1981
Berkley edition / December 1982

ISBN: 0-425-05656-2

A BERKLEY BOOK ® TM 757,375
Berkley Books are published by Berkley Publishing Corporation,
200 Madison Avenue, New York, New York 10016.
The name "Berkley" and the stylized "B" with design are
trademarks belonging to Berkley Publishing Corporation.
PRINTED IN THE UNITED STATES OF AMERICA

Acknowledgments

A performer may walk out on stage alone, but there are always others, backstage and standing in the wings, who have helped him get there. I am indebted to many people for that same kind of help in writing my book. Here I can only list them by name with my thanks and deep affection.

Bob Abrams, Sheila and Bob Bandier, Rona Barrett and Bill Trowbridge, Greg Bautzer, Helen and Dan Blackstone, Milton Blackstone, Judy Burstein, Georgia and Ramsey Clark, Pat Colecchio, Peter Cohen, Warren Cowan, Betsy Crawford, Dr. Stephen Gushin, Penny and Ron Dante, Janine and Joey Forman, Tim Fowler, Kurt Frings, Dick Fox, Lenny Gaines, Kathy Green, Grossinger's, Willard Higgins, Dr. Tom Jacobson, Jack Kelly, Keith Levenson, Marion Logan, Gloria V. Luchenbill, Dr. Donald Naftulin, Tom Schiller, Liza Shulman, Marilyn and Bruce Schwartz, Dr. David Serota, Bob Steinberg, Jane Bushell, Bill Feeder, Howard Thaler, and Linda and Rudi Unterthiner.

I am particularly indebted to Arlene and Howard Eisenberg for their help and friendship.

I owe special thanks to Warren G. Harris, the writer whose

research and tape-recorded interviews with me and others were essential to the creation of my book.

I am also indebted to the many people who have shared in the process of its publication: Harvey Ginsberg, the editor who first undertook the project; Buz Wyeth, vice president and executive editor of Harper & Row, whose support and encouragement were invaluable to its completion; and Bonny Fetterman, who served as the picture editor. For their own special skills and contributions, I am also grateful to Harriet Stanton, Florence Goldstein, James Fox, Maarten Kooij, Kathleen Hyde, Marjorie Horvitz and Edmée Reit.

Contents

To Lyn
who arrived just in time

If writing a book can be compared to recording a song, I am indebted to Burton Beals for arranging my words, capturing on paper the sound of my voice and the expression of my thoughts and feelings.

Prologue

My wife finally came home about five o'clock that morning. She had been out all night with another man and I was lying awake, waiting for her. This was the first time, but I knew it wouldn't be the last, and when she entered our bedroom I told her I was leaving. Our marriage was on the brink of destruction and I felt powerless to do anything more to save it.

A few hours later, on March 19, 1962, I was so drunk that friends had to help me board a flight from Rome to New York. One of them had given me a gun a couple of weeks before and said, "Why don't you kill that son of a bitch, Eddie? In Italy a crime of passion is considered justifiable homicide." I put the gun in the glove compartment of my car but never thought seriously of using it. Shoot Richard Burton? Why? Who could take that scruffy, arrogant buffoon seriously? My wife and I had made jokes about him when they began working together in 20th Century-Fox's extravagant production of *Cleopatra*. Burton was always supposed to have affairs with his leading ladies, and that was the biggest joke of all. Obviously Elizabeth Taylor would be the exception.

I wasn't laughing now. What began as whispers on the sets at Cinecittà and rumors circulated by the crowd that hung out along the Via Veneto had blown up in my face. Reporters called them "Liz and Dick." God, how I hated that nickname for my wife. And where the hell was I supposed to fit in? There were hysterical scenes, confrontations. I had to leave. It had happened once before, but I got only as far as Lisbon before rushing back to Rome. Elizabeth was in the hospital and no one would tell me why.

Now I had to get out. I was the fall guy, the patsy, in this triangle, and the humiliation was too great. If Elizabeth and I separated, I thought she would wake up, realize that Burton was merely manipulating her. "You don't need her," he told me one afternoon as I fed him brandy at our house on the outskirts of Rome. "You're a star already. I'm not. She's going to make me a star. I'm going to use her, that no-talent Hollywood nothing." How could Elizabeth throw away all we meant to each other for a man like that? We had been so happy; I was still deeply in love with her and thought she loved me. When they finished this picture, Burton would go back to his wife; he always went back to his wife. Then Elizabeth and I might be able to pick up the pieces of our marriage and go on with our life together as if he had never existed.

I drank even more as soon as the plane left the ground— straight vodka. I seldom touched liquor, but I was angry, despondent, desperate. I just wanted to pass out, to forget. But representatives from 20th Century-Fox met me at Idlewild; reporters shouted questions as I ducked into a limousine. Who'd told them I was coming to New York? The studio had a huge investment in *Cleopatra*—something like twenty-five million dollars, and production was far from over. A romance between its stars would be great publicity for the film, money in the bank. I had sacrificed my own career for Elizabeth's. Did the studio expect me to sacrifice my marriage too?

Milton Blackstone was waiting for me in my suite at the Pierre. He looked as he always did: weary, concerned but cautious. He was my manager, my partner, my friend—the man who had guided my career from almost the moment I arrived in New York in 1946, a green, awkward, eager kid with only one ambition—to become a singing star. Milton had helped make that dream come true, and even though we had disagreed in the past, I trusted him completely. He stood by me when my marriage to Debbie Reynolds ended in a blaze of bad publicity. I knew he would stand by me now.

"I'm glad you're here," he said. "Are you ready to go back

to work?" He was smiling, but his eyes evaded mine. Always wary of becoming too deeply involved in my personal life, he didn't ask me what had happened in Rome. Work: that was his solution to every problem.

"Jesus, Milton, look at me. I'm exhausted, I can't work."

"Hmm," he said. "Well, we'll talk about it tomorrow."

Max Jacobson walked into the room carrying his big black medical bag. He and Milton were exact opposites. Loud and arrogant, Max didn't care how he looked or what he said. He clapped me on the back. "Well, you dumb bastard, you've sure got yourself into one hell of a fix this time."

How long had I known this man? I met him when I was twenty-three years old, singing five shows a day at the Paramount packed with screaming fans, cutting records, doing interviews, staying up late, riding the crest of my first popular success. It was too much. I lost my voice and was taken to see this German doctor who gave me a shot of something called a vitamin cocktail. Dr. Max Jacobson's Magic Elixir. My voice came back and I sang better than I had ever sung before. Since then—for the past eleven years, whenever I had to perform—Max was never much more than a phone call away, with his black bag and hypodermic needles. And here he was again.

"Milton thinks I should go back to work," I said.

"Everybody's after you," Milton said. *"What's My Line"* wants you as the mystery guest. They're waiting for me to give them a date."

"That's work?" Max said in his thick, guttural accent. "Just let me know when you're going on and I'll mix something up for you."

Milton and Max, my two Svengalis. I was back in their capable hands.

The program was a disaster. What *was* my line? Cuckold? Dorothy Kilgallen, a regular on the panel, guessed my identity immediately. She made it her business to know who was in town, and my arrival certainly hadn't been kept secret. There were a few barbed questions and remarks. Kilgallen had often cut me up viciously in print. I was the world's number one heel for "abandoning" Debbie and our two children to become Elizabeth Taylor's fourth husband. As far as Kilgallen was concerned, I was getting exactly what I deserved.

The press reported that I looked "ravaged" on the show. I

probably did. Stories from Rome were making headlines and every standup comedian had a routine about "Liz and Dick." There was even a sketch on one of the television variety shows about Cleopatra and her slave Eddie. The destruction of my marriage was being turned into a media event—and I was the butt of the jokes. Maybe I should have expected that, and ignored it. But the derision was tearing me apart, stripping me of whatever self-respect I had left.

Reporters were clamoring to interview me, and Milton wanted to give a press conference. "No," I said. "Absolutely not. There's nothing I can say."

"Come on, Eddie," Max chimed in. "You're a big boy now. Let the people take a look at you."

"Max, I can't sleep. I can't eat. I'm a prisoner in this damned hotel."

"Okay, okay. You need a little rest, a little privacy."

Max was not accredited to any hospital, but through friends he got me into Gracie Square. No one knew where I was, and at last I was able to relax. I started to eat, and my third day there, I sank into the first decent night's sleep I had had in weeks.

"Eddie, Eddie! Wake up!"

Max was shaking me. I rolled over groggily, and as my eyes began to focus, I saw Milton standing behind him, holding a copy of the *Daily News*.

"Read this," Milton said, showing me the paper. "There's a story in here that says you're locked up in a psychiatric ward getting shock treatments."

I sat up and looked around. This wasn't a padded cell. Gracie Square had a psychiatric ward, but I wasn't in it. I was in a regular hospital room.

"It's only a matter of time before they find out where you are," Max said urgently. "Put your clothes on. We're getting you out of here."

It was four in the morning and I just wanted to go back to sleep, but Max opened his black bag, pulled out one of his famous golden needles, and gave me a shot. Suddenly I was wide awake and ready to go.

They put me on a stretcher, covered my face, and smuggled me out of the hospital. A photographer snapped my picture as I was being loaded into an ambulance. The whole thing was like a grade B movie. Then I found myself in a room in Max's apartment, so tiny it seemed worse than a padded cell. "Please, Max," I begged him, "there has to be some other place I can go."

He took me to the East Side house of friends of his. I had a nurse and the press wasn't able to find me. I felt safe. But my disappearance only added fuel to the fire and people really were beginning to believe I had been carted off to a mental hospital.

"You've got to talk to the reporters," Max told me over the phone.

"Since when have you become an expert on how to handle the press?" I said.

"*Ja*, I'm glad you've got some of your fighting spirit back. But Milton says they're going to keep on calling you crazy until you talk to them."

They kept up the pressure until I finally gave in, as I usually did. A press conference was scheduled at the Pierre and that afternoon I walked to the hotel with a plan. If I had to show myself, if I had to prove I wasn't crazy, fine. Let them see me, let them take my picture, and that'll be it. I wanted to avoid the questions I knew would be asked. I looked around the front entrance of the hotel. No reporters, no photographers. I walked back and forth through the lobby: somebody take my picture, please. No one saw me. No one was there. I had to go through with the press conference.

I took the elevator up to my suite, where Max was waiting to fortify me with a shot. Then I tried to reach Elizabeth in Rome. Before I left, studio executives had urged me to say that I was in New York on business for *Cleopatra*. It was only a temporary separation. There was nothing to all the reports of a romance between my wife and Richard Burton. To protect Elizabeth I agreed, but now, as I was about to face the press, I had to find out if she still wanted me to stick to that story. I couldn't reach her. She was not available.

At least a hundred people were jammed into one of the hotel banquet rooms, waiting for me with pencils poised. Lights blazed and flashbulbs popped as I walked in. There were television cameras and more microphones than I had ever seen in my life. Smiling, trying to appear at ease, I fielded a barrage of questions and stuck to the story. No, I hadn't left my wife. I was in New York on business. Yes, I admired Richard Burton as an actor. No, he and my wife were not having a romance.

"The only romance I know of," I said, "was between Mark Antony and Cleopatra."

One of the reporters stood up and said, "There's a picture of your wife and Burton in an offstage embrace on the cover of *Oggi,* Eddie."

I was stunned. "Oh," I said lamely. "I'd like to see that myself."

The press conference was interrupted when I was called to the telephone in the manager's office. It was Elizabeth, returning my call. "We have to change the story," she said.

"What do you mean, we have to change the story?"

"Something's happened here. We have to change it."

"What's happened?"

"I can't tell you."

"For God's sake, Elizabeth, I'm talking to the reporters right now."

"All I can say is we can't keep that story."

"I'm sorry," I said, and then hung up. Until that moment, I think I really believed I had been telling reporters the truth. Elizabeth loved me, not Burton. Our marriage could still be saved. Now I knew I had been lying to them, lying to myself. It was over.

I went back to the press conference in a daze. The reporters knew the call had been from Elizabeth. "What did she say, Eddie?" they shouted at me. "Tell us what she said."

I stared vacantly around the room, blinded by all the lights. Their faces a blur, the reporters leaned forward in their seats. Television cameras whirred. The world was waiting for my answer. "We're still in love," I said softly. I didn't know what else to say.

The press conference was featured on all the news shows and there was a huge headline in one of the papers: "People Will Say We're in Love." For the first time since I had left Rome, public opinion seemed to be swinging in my favor. I was no longer the pitiful husband with horns. Elizabeth and I were still in love. And I knew it was a lie.

I had to live that lie. A few days later, the Friars Club gave a testimonial dinner for Joe E. Lewis at the Waldorf. Lewis was a show business legend, a talented and generous man who had helped me in the early days of my career, and the Friars asked me to say a few words about our long relationship. I didn't want to do it. Certain that reporters would badger me with more questions, I just wanted to disappear until the whole thing with Elizabeth was settled, or people got bored reading about it. But Milton and Max urged me to go.

"It'll be good for your image," Milton said.

"I'm tired of hearing about my image," I replied.

"All right, then. Think about your career."

"I'll give you a shot right before the dinner," Max said. "And I'll make up another syringe, one and a half cc. Put it in your pocket, and if you begin to feel bad, just go to the men's room, pat yourself on the behind, and push the needle into your buttocks."

The evening of the dinner, I was sitting on the dais between Phil Silvers and Dr. Ralph Bunche, America's ambassador to the United Nations. Phil told jokes, trying to make me laugh, and Dr. Bunche asked how I was able to hold up under so much pressure and publicity. Their words simply didn't register. Max's first injection seemed to be wearing off and I began to panic. This is trauma time, I thought. In all the years I had taken Max's magic elixir, I had never injected myself. Now there was no alternative. I got up and went to the men's room. Twenty or thirty reporters who had been standing behind the dais crowded in after me, so I quickly locked myself in a booth, pulled down my pants, and sat on the toilet. I took the syringe out of my pocket and looked at it. The needle was an inch and a half long. How the hell was I going to do this? Max had tried to show me many times in his office. We practiced on grapefruit. But injecting a grapefruit wasn't the same as grabbing your own ass and sticking a needle into it.

Somehow I did it. I stabbed myself. To death, I thought. I didn't feel the needle go in. There was no physical pain. Yet at that moment I knew I had turned a corner in my life. I felt the pain of dying. I was killing myself.

When I got back to the dais, my hands were trembling as I waited for the injection to take effect. Nothing happened. Had I done it wrong? Was the preparation less powerful than the ones Max usually gave me? In desperation, I looked for him in the crowd. He and his wife were sitting at a table with Milton. Trying to attract his attention, I kept shaking my head, hoping he would see me. He didn't look up.

The room was beginning to close in on me. I started to sweat. I couldn't let all these people see me like this. In a panic, I got up and ducked through the curtain behind the dais.

I ran, ran like a crazy man, stumbling down a flight of stairs and dashing through the lobby of the hotel, with reporters running after me. I didn't stop. Jumping into a passing cab, I went to the Pierre and collapsed on a couch in the living room of my suite, gasping for breath. I thought I was going to die.

The telephone rang. It was Max. "What are you doing, you fucking idiot? Get the hell back here!"

"Max, I'm sick. I'm out of it. They don't need me."

"I'm coming over," he said.

"I won't go back."

"Stay there. I'll give you something."

A few minutes later, he came in the door, dressed in a rumpled tuxedo and carrying his familiar black bag. Opening it, he fixed the shot and my arm went out automatically. I was like a Pavlovian dog.

It worked immediately. I was up. Max and I returned to the Waldorf, I slipped back into my seat on the dais, and when it was my turn, I gave a little speech. I don't remember what I said, but even as I spoke, I felt the shot beginning to wear off. I had to get out of there. After acknowledging the applause and embracing Joe E. Lewis, I turned and just left. Back at the Pierre, I crawled into bed and tried to sleep.

For the next couple of weeks, Max wouldn't let me out of his sight. If I wandered too far away from him, he bawled me out: "You stay around, stick with me, you idiot!" Where else could I go; what else could I do? First I had to divorce Elizabeth. There was no other way to ease the pain of being tied to her, no other way to end all this insanity. Still I was haunted by her rejection—would be haunted by it for years—and Max was giving me as many as three or four shots to keep me going during the day and a massive dose of tranquilizers to help me sleep at night. We were seldom apart, even when he went to the White House, with two brand-new black medical bags, to give John F. Kennedy the benefit of his special medical treatments.

One day we were in my suite at the Pierre, 5807. Unable to sit still, I stood up and looked out a window. There were skaters on the rink in Central Park fifty-eight floors below. "You know," I said to Max, "I feel like I could jump out this window." I was trying to be funny, or maybe a little theatrical. I didn't really mean it, but Max pulled me away from the window and pushed me roughly into a chair. The cigarette in his mouth dribbled ashes down his chest. "When did you first feel this tendency?" he said, staring at me intently.

I burst out laughing. "Max, I'm kidding. Where's your sense of humor?"

"This is something you don't kid about," he said solemnly.

If I never considered suicide, I was deeply troubled by other thoughts. Every time I looked in a mirror, I could see that exhaustion, anxiety, fear had etched new lines on my face. I was thirty-four years old, with two disastrous marriages to my credit, two children of my own who barely knew I was alive, two more children whom I had adopted and might never see again, and a career I had ignored for more than a year. Whatever money I had would be tied up until Elizabeth and I were divorced. And I was becoming more and more dependent on shots from Dr. Needles.

Facing Max, I was speaking seriously now. "I didn't ask for any of this. What am I supposed to do now, Max? What the hell am I supposed to do with the rest of my life?"

"Your life isn't over just because of some woman," Max said. "Forget her. Listen to Milton. Listen to me. Have we ever failed you? Take my advice. Go out and work. Go out and fuck."

Max was right. This wasn't the end of my life. It was the beginning—a new beginning. Just yesterday, it seemed, I had the world by the tail and my life had been measured in millions. I was the idol of millions of teenage fans; I had sold millions of records, earned millions of dollars. Everybody had loved Eddie Fisher. Now I would have to start all over again to win back that love and regain my own self-respect. And this time I wouldn't let everything slip through my fingers. I was going to grab it and hang on. Sure, I was unhappy and scared, but I knew I could do it. I had done it once before.

1

We were very poor, and poverty either drives you up or drags you down. It destroyed my father. He was a defeated man and took out his frustration and anger on my mother, shouting at her, insulting, ridiculing, and humiliating her. He never beat her physically. The way he beat her mentally was worse. He was a tyrant, who treated my mother like a slave.

A small man with sharp eyes and an even sharper tongue, he started yelling the moment he got home from work. My brothers and sisters and I had stations at the windows, which we slammed shut hoping the neighbors wouldn't hear. My mother took his abuse without protest. If she uttered a word, he went berserk. All we could do was wait patiently until he calmed down, and then open the windows. I wanted my mother to fight back, to stand up for herself, and because she never did, I thought she was weak. Now I realize she was the strongest of us all. With everything my father put her through, she had to be strong or die.

I once heard my mother say, "Joe, I'm going to divorce you when our children are grown up." And she did. But I felt that my father had destroyed whatever love there was between them long before I came along, the fourth of their seven children. How could she have lived with a man like that for so many years, how could she have borne him so many children? Had she ever loved him?

We were talking together not long ago. We spoke often over the phone, but I hadn't seen my mother for a while. Eighty now, she seemed smaller and stouter than I remembered. Only her smile hadn't changed over the years, the smile everyone said I inherited. If I had changed in her eyes, she didn't mention it. I was still her son.

"Sure, I loved your father," she told me. "He was a rough boy and a hard man. But he was educated. He went to school in Russia before he came here, you know, and that was very unusual for a poor Jewish boy in those days. He was smart. He read books. Tolstoy. He never lost his Russian. Russian books and American books. History. He read the papers, listened to the news. Once upon a time, I loved your father very much."

His family name was originally Tisch or Fisch, and my mother didn't know why or when it had been changed to Fisher. His father was a tailor who emigrated from Russia to America, found work in Philadelphia, and then saved up enough money to send for the rest of his family. Joseph, my father, was a boy of thirteen when he arrived. With three younger sisters, he had to leave school to help support the family, probably the first of the many disappointments in his life. He found work making and repairing trunks and suitcases, a job he did off and on for the rest of his working life.

My mother's maiden name was Monacker, but that, too, was changed, to Minicker. Her father, Zelick, was also a tailor in Russia, whose first wife died, leaving him with three small children, when my mother, Katherine, or Katie, as she has always been called, was just a year old. He remarried six months later. "Your grandmother Ida," my mother said. "Legally she was my stepmother. But I never thought of her that way. She was my real mother as far as I was concerned. An angel from heaven. She raised us and gave us a good life."

My grandmother owned land in Russia, which she sold after marrying my grandfather, and they used the money to bring the whole family to Philadelphia, where they had relatives. She and my mother remained very close. Buba was always around, helping out, taking care of my brothers and sisters and me if my mother was sick or went to the hospital to have another baby. She was the first one who encouraged me to sing.

"You were the apple of her eye," my mother said. "She made you a playpen out of a crate because we couldn't afford to buy one. And whenever you stayed with her, she taught you little Jewish songs. I would come to pick you up, and she would say, 'Sonny Boyele'—that's what she always called you—'sing your mother that little song I taught you last night.' And you would sing. You weren't more than two years old. 'Did you hear that?' your grandmother would say. 'That boy is going to be an *oisnem*'—a hit, something special."

My mother was three years old when she came to America, and like my father, she never finished high school. She left at the age of fourteen to help out at home, and met my father that same year. "I have to laugh when I think about it now," she told me. "I had a girl friend, I don't even remember her name, and we wanted to go to the social club, a Zionist club, but you had to be sixteen to get in. So my girl friend put a big bow on me to make me look older and we got in. Right away I saw your father looking at me and I guess I was a little nutty because I started talking and laughing and you weren't allowed to do that. Your father kept looking at me so sharp and serious, you remember how he could look, and finally he came over and said, 'Katya Monacker, stop talking!' He seemed to be the leader of the group, but I just turned away and kept right on. Then he said, 'Katya Monacker, leave the room!' So I had to go, but he followed me out and said he didn't mean to punish me, but if he let me talk, everybody else would be talking too. After that he helped me get into the club even if I was too young. And that's how your father and I got started."

Two years later, when Katie was sixteen and Joseph seventeen and a half, they crossed the border into Maryland, where they could get married without their parents' consent.

"We came back that same day and I said, 'Pop, we went off and got married. Here's the papers.' Well, my father took one look and tore them to pieces. 'This is no marriage,' he said. So he and your father's father gave us their consent and we got married again at Philadelphia City Hall. Then we had a private little ceremony at a rabbi's house. That was our wedding."

I had a lot of aunts and uncles and cousins around Philadelphia. But it was a very strange family. Most of the time, my mother's side and my father's side just didn't speak. And after my mother divorced my father and married his best friend, there was no communication at all. I literally had to force my relatives to pose together if someone wanted pictures of my family. It was terrible and I never understood why until my mother told me that it went back to the days when she and my father had eloped. The Fishers were poor, but the Minackers were *very* poor, and my father's family could never forget that he had married a girl who was beneath him.

Their life together was hard from the very beginning, and it never got much easier. They started out renting a room and sharing a kitchen in the apartment of friends. Then they moved back in with my mother's parents for a while. They didn't have an apartment of their own until my brother Sidney was born, in 1921. My mother was only seventeen years old.

Sidney, or Sol as we called him, used to be my idol when I was growing up; we slept in the same bed until he joined the army just before the war. He was stationed at Pearl Harbor at the time of the Japanese attack, and after I heard about it on the radio, I rushed out into the street shouting that my big brother was there, so bursting with pride that I didn't even stop to think he might have been killed or wounded. Sol came back from the war safely and seemed to have trouble finding his way. He was still my brother, but no longer my idol.

After Sol, my sister Annette—Nettie—was born in 1923, and my sister Miriam in 1926. I came along in 1928, number four, and then Janet in 1932, Alvin in 1934, and my baby sister Eileen in 1939. My mother was always pregnant, always cooking and cleaning and scrubbing the floors, always washing, ironing, and mending clothes. And always taking care of Nettie. Although she lived to be about fifty years old, Nettie had the mental age of a little girl of five or six.

"What happened to Nettie?" I asked my mother. "Why was she like that? I never knew."

"How could you know?" she replied. "It happened when you weren't even born. I was pregnant with your sister Miriam, and Nettie was about two. Such a clever little girl, talking and everything. We had a woman living with us, a cousin of mine boarding so it would be easier with the rent, and she came home one day and went upstairs to her room. Nettie was playing in the kitchen, where she couldn't hurt herself. She had little bells on her shoes and I could hear her running around. But all of a sudden I didn't hear the bells anymore and I called, 'Nettie, Nettie.' What happened was she followed my cousin upstairs and when I called to her, she turned around to see if I was coming and fell down fourteen steps. Her head hit every single step.

"I was scared to death, but the doctor came right away and thank God everything seemed to be all right. A little later I went to the hospital to have your sister Miriam and when I got home Nettie had a little cold. She was lying in her crib near me one night and Miriam was in a basket. Look how many years ago and still I can't forget. Nettie was crying, so I touched her and half of her was hot and half of her was cold. I took her into my bed, covered her to warm her up and she quieted down. But then the next thing I knew, my child was in convulsions."

Tears filled my mother's eyes as she remembered the story. "Again the doctor came and told me what to do, but two more times it happened and we took Nettie to the hospital. She got pleurisy and then pneumonia and the fever went to her head. We brought her home and right away I knew she was different. She was a healthy child. Any one of you could have any kind of disease and Nettie never caught it. But she wasn't the same, and when it came time to go to school, I knew they wouldn't take her. They said to wait until she was older. So I went with her to the Board of Education and this man asked her a lot of questions and then said to me, 'Mrs. Fisher, there is nothing you can do with her. My advice is to put her in an institution.'

"'Why?' I said.

"'You have more children,' he said, 'and they're going to be ashamed of her.'

"'I'll raise my children that they have a sick sister and not to be ashamed.'"

That's exactly what Mom did. We teased Nettie a lot, as kids always do. She loved attention even though she was shy and would run away and hide. But we were never mean or spiteful. Mom took her to other doctors, specialists. They told her there was nothing they could do. So we kept her at home and Mom taught her things—cooking, washing and ironing, how to thread a needle. "I started with one of those big needles like they use to sew up potato sacks," she said, "then smaller and smaller. It took me about a year, but I had patience. And afterwards, when my eyes began to go and I couldn't see to do it, Nettie threaded my needles for me."

No one could have taken care of Nettie the way my mother

did. Nettie worshiped my mother and my mother worshiped her. She was more of a companion to her than both her husbands. I think she was more necessary to my mother.

"You remember all she did for me," Mom said. "You remember how she loved you, how she played your records over and over until they wore out. 'My brother is the best singer in the world,' she always said. How she saved everything you ever gave her, all the clothes she folded up in the dresser drawer that I couldn't get her to wear because they came from you."

I once gave her a little dog, Gittel, a Yorkshire terrier. It was after Mom's second husband had died and she and Nettie were living together in an apartment. They didn't know pets weren't allowed until somebody complained and they got a notice to get rid of the dog or move. Mom was frantic. She said Nettie would die without that little dog. So her neighbors got together and signed a petition to let her keep Gittel.

"Everybody loved her," Mom said. "Whoever invented television, God bless him, because we had happy years. Television was the whole world to her, and that little dog was her pleasure, her baby. She was so clever. She was so good. 'Don't worry, Mommy, don't worry,' she said to me when I lost my husband. 'I'll take care of you, you'll take care of me, we'll both be together.' And we were. We enjoyed each other, every hour, till God took her."

Nettie died of cancer and I thought it was going to be the end of my mother. But she survived. Whatever happened, my mother always survived.

Miriam was my favorite sister. Almost three years older than I, she was the one who took care of me when I was little. Mom reminded me that she had once saved my life.

"How could you forget?" she said. "Well, you left home. You went into a new world. And you know, when you really recall the past is when you get old. Now I can remember people and things that happened years ago, but when you're young, your life isn't occupied with such concerns. So you were maybe eight years old and Miriam was eleven. You both had your supper one night and I told Miriam to watch you on the street. I was inside the house serving your father when I heard a screech, you know the screech of a car stopping fast, and everybody started screaming. I ran out and I saw them carrying my Miriam. Her shoes were gone and her socks were hanging, both socks, and I thought, My God, her legs are cut off! They told me what happened. You crossed the street and Miriam saw a car coming, so she ran and pushed you out of the way and the wheels went over her toes. She was lucky. They just pulled off the nails, all the nails on one foot and about three on the other. You would have been killed, definitely."

I was born August 10, 1928, at Northern Liberty Hospital in Philadelphia. The name on the birth certificate read Edwin Jack Fisher, but my family never called me Edwin and most of the time not even Eddie. To them I've always been Sonny Boy or just Sonny. The story of how I got the name has been told a thousand times, but my Mom swears it's true. Eleven girls were born in the hospital that day, no boys, so when I came along the nurses made a big fuss over me. If I cried they picked me up and sang "Sonny Boy," the Al Jolson song that was popular at the time: "Climb upon my knee, Sonny Boy . . ." My father heard them and went home and told everybody the nurses had named me Sonny Boy. That's what I've been called ever since.

My brother Alvin was born six years later, and for some reason he was nicknamed Bunny. Every once in a while my mother would call me Bunny and then correct herself: "Bunny— I mean Sonny Boy." I guess she had so many children she forgot who was who. She used to forget even after I had grown up, and once, to tease her, I said, "Mom, don't you know Eddie Fisher is Sonny Boy, not Bunny? Don't you know who I am? I'm famous. I'm a star."

She just looked at me and said, "I have seven stars."

One of my earliest childhood memories is of carrying my brother Bunny—who's now six feet tall—in a royal-blue knitted woolen suit my mother made him. Only his face was showing. It was in the middle of the night, a horse and buggy down on the street was loaded with our furniture, and we were skipping out because we couldn't pay the rent. Mom told me we moved about twenty times for that reason, from one dirty little house to another in some neighborhood where we weren't known. In one place, she said, she kept a broom handle by the door and swore she'd use it if anybody came to throw us out. But eventually we always had to move, and as a parting gesture to the landlord, we flushed a couple of apples down the toilet.

Times were hard for everybody during the Depression. My father always had a job, but it was piecework and he never made much money. Never enough, anyway. And once, during a strike or some trouble at the place where he worked, we had to go on relief.

"I had pride," Mom told me. "I tried to stay away from relief. But one day you kids came home from school and all I could give you was tea and a piece of bread, some jelly. There was no food in the house, no money to pay the rent. Your brother Bunny was just a baby, so I asked my neighbor to watch him and I walked all the way to the place where you signed up for relief. Thirty-two blocks. Standing in line, I said to myself, Why am I embarrassed? Everybody's here for the same thing. But then I just passed out. I hadn't eaten. They took me to the main office and gave me a cup of water and a piece of pretzel—my first pretzel; I remember that. Then they said, 'Go home, you'll get a check tomorrow.' That's how I got on relief: seventeen-fifty a week, for everybody."

We had to go to the abandoned railyard of an old station to pick up the food and shoes and clothes distributed to families on relief, and Mom used to make me come with her. She rigged up the baby carriage with a pillow and a cover and a net, so people would think there was a baby inside. And when we got to the railyard, we put flour and potatoes and beets and whatever else they gave us in the carriage, covered everything up again, and wheeled it home. I always pushed the carriage through the alley while Mom went in the front door and met me at the back, where we unloaded it so nobody would see. I hated every minute of those trips, overcome with fear that people would find out we were on relief.

The clothes were the worst. Mom used to dye the shoes and take the trimmings off the girls' dresses to disguise where they came from. But there was no way to hide the blue-and-yellow sweater worn by both boys and girls, and the gray-and-white-striped shirts. That's what I had to wear to school and I was so ashamed.

"You wouldn't drink the powdered milk they gave us," Mom said. "So what did I do? I picked up the glass milk bottles on the doorstep that people left for the milkman to collect, and when you were asleep, I made up the powdered milk and put it in the bottles. You drank it. You didn't know the difference. Oh, Sonny Boy, how much I could tell you. Those were terrible times."

I guess like most kids I was too concerned about how I felt

to feel sorry for my parents. It's funny, but I don't have any remembrance of being poor. I just remember being embarrassed, ashamed that this was the way we had to live. The houses we rented were like matchboxes. The cellars, where the coal was supposed to be but wasn't, were always full of junk left by the families that had lived there before us, the backyards were piled high with garbage. Why do poor people never have time to clean up? Secondhand furniture. Broken dishes that didn't match. All the boys slept together in one bedroom, in one bed, and the girls in one bed in another room. One tiny bathroom for the whole family, with leaky faucets, a toilet that didn't always flush, and not enough hot water. My mother washed our clothes in the bathtub and I would climb in and use the same water.

We shared our food and our bodies with bugs: cockroaches, lice, bedbugs. I had lice in my hair and was always afraid the kids who sat behind me in school would notice them. One day, walking to school with a cousin of mine, I looked in a mirror and saw a bedbug on my face. Certain my cousin had seen it too, I thought I was going to be sick. There seemed to be no way to get rid of those bugs wherever we lived. We squeezed them with our fingers, and the sheets on our beds were always spotted brown with dried blood. We even tried to burn them out. After taking the mattresses off the beds and spreading newspapers underneath, we lit a penny candle and ran the flame around the springs. The bugs dropped off by the hundreds and we squashed them on the paper.

My mother did her best to keep us clean. She got us up in the morning, and made us wash and brush our teeth. But what I remember is being dirty. My hands were always grimy, my fingernails black. And when you're dirty, you smell, you stink. Somehow, though, cleanliness was less important than just learning how to survive, and I think we used poverty as an excuse, a cover-up for anything and everything that was wrong in our lives. If we were dirty, it was because we were poor. But I was lucky. I was born with a voice. Who knows why? Nobody else in the family was musical at all. The only music we heard was on the radio. And who knows when I first started using my voice? I just opened up my mouth and sang.

"You don't know?" Mom said. "Wait, I'll tell you. They were putting on a show, some kind of concert for Christmas or Chanukah, and Miriam was in a little group that sang. She went to rehearsals every Friday night and you pestered her to take you along. You were four years old. So she finally said, 'All right, come on, you brat,' and she took you. But when you got there, still you pestered her. You wanted to sing. Mr. Grossman, the master of ceremonies said, 'Miriam, honey, what is the matter with your little brother?' And she said, 'He's bothering me because he wants to sing.'

"'So let him sing,' Mr. Grossman said. 'Then he'll sit still.'

"Well, you got up and sang 'Santa Claus Is Coming to Town,' 'Animal Crackers in My Soup,' some Jewish song, I don't remember. And right away Mr. Grossman said, 'Tell your mother to dress him up and bring him to the concert.' Well, when Miriam came home and told me that, I said, '*Oy*, everything happens to me. I should be bothered dressing him up.' But I did. See these two hands, Sonny Boy? They sewed, they knit, they crocheted, they did everything. All your clothes I made. So I made you little white pants, short pants, and a white shirt, and the night of the concert I dressed you up all in white, little white shoes and socks. You were a handsome little boy.

"I couldn't go. I had babies to look after, so your brother Sol took you. There were three hundred people there; you sang and the whole place went crazy. You won first prize, a big cake, and they all wanted to eat you up. 'Oh, let me touch him,' everybody said. 'He won first prize.'"

I have no memory of that night. I only remember that if my parents asked me to sing for their friends, I would run away and hide under the bed. But as I grew older, I guess I wanted people to pay attention to me, to love me, so I stopped hiding. I sang in school, in synagogues, in churches. Whenever and wherever anybody wanted me to sing, I sang. Nobody taught me how to do it, nobody forced me. I loved to sing, and I knew I loved it.

My first dream was to become a cantor and sing in the temple. The music of the temple and the cantorial style had a profound effect on me. The sound the cantor made and the way he used his voice were my greatest influences. Singing in temples at a very early age, I didn't understand the words, but I could tell what they meant by the feeling in the cantor's voice. I wanted to sing with that kind of feeling. I wanted to move people with my voice. But when I discovered I could do that, I got very upset. Singing for the High Holidays at the synagogue in our neighborhood, dressed up in a robe and standing on a box, I remember seeing the men downstairs and the women upstairs, and everybody was crying. I wondered why and Mom said, "Sonny Boy, they were crying because they love you." That didn't make any sense. I wanted people to love me, but I didn't want to make them cry. I wanted to make them happy.

Although we lived in tough neighborhoods, I wasn't a tough kid. Small and skinny, how could I be tough? I was a good kid, a likable kid, who did what he was told and tried to stay out of trouble, which wasn't always easy. All the kids I grew up with ran in packs; the Jews stuck together and so did the Irish, blacks, and Italians. One time my buddies and I were in the street next to the schoolyard, around a fire we had built to roast some potatoes. We were putting them in and pulling them out when this other gang of kids climbed over the school-yard fence and started beating the hell out of everybody. All my buddies scattered, but I got stuck with my back to the fence, unable to get away. The leader of the gang came up to me and asked if I had any money, and I said, "Money, ha!" I had to open my big mouth. So they started pushing me around, I pushed back, and they got hold of me and asked if I wanted to fight their leader. I said no. Then they said go home, but again I said no. So this big kid came at me, and I didn't know what the hell I was doing but suddenly I was on top of him, crying and my nose running. I thought I was bleeding, but I wasn't. It was just snot and tears. And somehow, I don't know how I did it, I beat that kid up. Then I was terrified to go to school for the next week or two, scared out of my pants that he was going to get revenge. Years later, that same kid was put in jail for murder.

My voice saved me. Because I was little, the guys always made fun of me. And anybody who wanted to be a singer had to be a sissy. But when they heard me sing on the radio, they seemed to respect that. Or maybe it was envy; I don't know. If kids have nothing, they're impressed by somebody who's got a little bit extra, no matter what it is. He's different, he's a person.

Even my father was impressed. Otherwise he was a great shrugger. So what? He didn't care what I did. He had more important things to think about, other standards of success and failure. In grade school, after winning the marbles championship of South Philadelphia, I changed my shooter from a small marble to a big marble and lost the city-wide championship to a girl. My father never let me forget it. It was rare that he showed affection openly. He loved his daughters, but if he had any love for his sons, I never saw it. To me he said, "Just sing." I knew he was proud of me when I sang in the temple, and he once asked me to sing for his social club. But usually all I got was a shrug, so after a while I didn't care anymore. I became indifferent to everything he did, except the way he treated my mother. I hated him for that. Or resented him. I didn't know much about hate then. Now I realize how tough things must have been for my father. His only break was some money he received from an insurance company. But he had to damn near die to get it.

"Let me think," Mom said. "I was in the hospital having Bunny, so it must have been 1934. Eight pounds, eleven ounces—a beautiful blond, blue-eyed boy. He was gorgeous. Your father came to see him, that was Sunday, and on Monday he went to the country for a job and the car he was in had a collision with an ice truck. All the ice fell off the truck and the driver got killed. They had to pull your father out of the car. It turned over three times and he was covered from head to toe in blood. Broken ribs, broken nose, broken pelvis, and nobody told me. I was still in the hospital with the baby and the rabbi didn't want to name him. He thought I'd want to call him Joseph after your father and they were waiting for him to die. But finally the rabbi performed the ceremony, I left the hospital and went to my sister-in-law, who was taking care of all of you. Still I didn't know about your father, but I suspected something was wrong because they didn't want me to go home.

"So a day or so later, my sister-in-law said to me, 'Katie, what would you do if you got a lot of money?' And I said, 'I can't tell you what I'd do because I don't have a lot of money.' Then she said, 'Well, you might as well know. Joe had a little accident, and it looks like he'll get a lot of money.' And I said, 'Oh, my God!' I'll never forget it.

"I went to the hospital to see him every day for the next four and a half weeks and took care of him when he came home. I'm not going to tell you the whole story. It's too much to know. But we got five thousand dollars. It took two years before the case was settled, but we finally got it."

They used the money to invest in a business—Fisher's Delicatessen. They opened up the store in a better neighborhood than we usually lived in, and we rented a nice house about a block away. It was my father's big chance, the one opportunity he ever had to catch lightning in a bottle. He was the proprietor, selling the fruits and vegetables, while Mom cooked the corned beef and made her own potato salad: Mrs. Fisher's potato salad. Not much more than eight years old, I arranged the cans and helped clean up. I was so proud of that store. We owned something and everybody worked very hard, but the business only lasted about a year. "The way I figure," Mom told me, "is we bit off more than we could chew. Times were hard, business wasn't good. It didn't bring in as much as we thought. It wasn't run good."

That was the end of the store, the money, and the nice neighborhood. We moved back downtown and went on relief again. Then my father became a peddler. He bought an old LaSalle for fifty dollars and when that broke down, an old Packard took its place. Removing the back seat, he went down to the wholesale market on the wharf and loaded up with fruits and vegetables. My brother Sol and I had to go with him. We were the hucksters. He'd pick a neighborhood, a nice neighborhood, but not a rich one because rich people didn't have alleyways; their houses weren't tied together. So we went where we got the maximum number of houses on each side, and my father sent Sol and me into the alleys to sell his wares.

"You were called the singing salesman," my mother said. "People felt sorry for you. You were such a skinny little boy, they used to bring you out cake and milk."

I hated it. I hated the way my father poured out the strawberries, put the rotten ones on the bottom and made three and sometimes four quarts out of two. And he treated Sol and me like slaves, sending us into the alleyways while he sat in the car counting the pennies we brought back to make sure we weren't cheating him. Finally I couldn't stand it anymore and refused to get out of the car. My father didn't hit me or even yell at me. Maybe he knew I could be just as stubborn as he was. But he made me sit there for the rest of the day until it was dark and we had to go home

"Some vegetables were left over," Mom said. "That helped because you couldn't get along with seventeen-fifty from the relief. It hurts to remember these things, Sonny Boy. So much has happened in this life. I wasn't a run-around. I was a quiet woman. I didn't know about leaving baby-sitters with you kids and going out, or anything. I didn't know. All I knew was my children. My children were my whole life. Outside for me was only my children."

My father went out. We weren't sure where: his social club, or sometimes he just disappeared on the weekends, and my mother says there were other women. "Sonny Boy, why do you make me tell you these things?" she said. "But maybe this you should hear. No money in the house, I'm feeding you kids bologna and watered-down milk, and then your father comes home and wants a meal from A to Z. With all that, he likes to bet the numbers. He wraps up two dollars, three dollars, in a piece of paper with the numbers on it and sends one of you kids a few doors down the street, where they bet. Usually I didn't say a word because it made him mad. But one day I spoke up: 'Joe, believe me, if you give me that money, how I can use it. What a help it would be.'

"'What's the matter with you?' he said. 'If you can't manage with what I give you, I've seen finer women than you go to work.'

"'I don't claim I'm any nicer or any finer,' I said. 'I've carried all our children.'

"'So what—dogs and cats carry too.'

"'But I want to raise them right, Joe. That's my work.'"

It wasn't like my mother to complain about the past or anything else, but she said, "I don't know how I ever lived through it. You were a good boy. All my children were good children. That was my reward. Only once was I called to school on account of you. You came home and said, 'Mom, my teacher wants to see you tomorrow morning.' And I said, '*Oy, vey is mir*—tomorrow morning, with my schedule.' I was always a busy mother. I never sent anything out. I washed, I ironed, I sewed, and I was pregnant with your sister Eileen at the time. Nobody was allowed to interrupt my schedule. But I said all right. So the next day I went and the teacher told me, 'We don't know what to do about your son Edwin, Mrs. Fisher. He has a lovely voice. Just the other day in assembly, we put him on a chair and he sang "God Bless America." But now, just because he can sing a few songs, he thinks he's a big shot.' You had to go to the bathroom, the teacher told me, and you didn't raise your hand. You just got up and walked out and the other kids started doing the same. You had a big head on yourself. I listened to all that, then you came in the room and I smacked you. 'My God,' I said, 'don't you ever have me called to school on account of things you're not supposed to do.' 'Oh, Mrs. Fisher,' the teacher said, 'you shouldn't have smacked him.' And I said, 'I can't afford to be called to school on account of misconduct. There is no reason. My children are not brought up that way. If it's important, I'll be right here to help them.' And you know, Sonny Boy, I was never called back to school again."

Mothers sometimes have their own way of remembering stories about their children. That wasn't the real reason for her visit. I found a two-by-four my brother Sol had left in the bureau drawer. That's what we used to call those little books that showed comic strip characters—Popeye and Olive Oyl, Tillie the Toiler—doing dirty things. They were exaggerated and really filthy. Tucking the book in my pocket, I took it to school and sold it for two cents to a friend of mine. The teacher caught him reading it, and standing him up in front of the whole class, she asked where he got it. "Edwin Fisher," he said. "All right, Edwin," the teacher told me, "bring your mother to school tomorrow."

I was terrified. My mother came to school the next day, slapped my face, and then said, "Now wait till your father gets you"—which terrified me even more. That night, after we all had dinner around the kitchen table, my father was reading the paper as usual and one by one everybody drifted out. Just my father and I were left and I didn't know what was going to happen next, because he had a terrible temper. He looked up at me, then took his chair, moved it around the table, and sat down. Suddenly he hit me. "Who are your friends?" he yelled, and hit me again. "Who are you hanging around?" *Boom!* Another hit. "What is this? Where do you get this nonsense?"

I jumped up and ran, but he caught me in the living room, threw me down on the floor, picked me up again, and threw me down again. My mother ran into the room. "Joe, stop!" she cried. "You're killing him!" He couldn't stop. He got carried away. I tried to run up the stairs, but he tackled me and pulled me down.

I lived. But it was the worst beating of my life. And the most attention my father ever gave me.

2

Skipper Dawes was a small man with a receding hairline, horn-rimmed glasses, and a warm, reassuring smile. As educational director of station WFIL in Philadelphia, he put on radio shows. And he was the one who first discovered the little kid with the big voice, even if I wasn't too hard to find. It was 1940 and I was twelve years old when Skipper came to Thomas Junior High School looking for talent. He auditioned piano players, violin players, singers, actors. I already had experience singing in synagogues and at school. But I was terrified to audition for Skipper. I don't know why. I just wouldn't do it.

Ida Schwartz, one of the girls from school, was called to the radio station for a second audition, and she asked me to go with her. I didn't think she had any idea of tricking me, but as soon as we got there she said, "Mr. Dawes, my friend sings too."

"What's your name, son?" Skipper said.

"Eddie Fisher."

"Okay, Eddie," he said with one of his big smiles, "let's hear what you can do."

I stood up and sang "The Army Air Corps Song." "Off we go into the wild blue yonder, Climbing high into the sun..." No accompaniment, top volume, and if Skipper was tempted to put his hands over his ears, he didn't do it. He listened to every note and his reaction was more than enthusiastic. "That's wonderful, Eddie," he said. "How would you like to sing that song on the radio tonight?"

Tonight! I said yes, but all I could think of was a little girl I had once seen singing into a microphone who was so terrified she peed in her pants. And it wasn't only a microphone that scared me. Radio was something very special. We had a big set at home—the one piece of furniture with any value. And my father monopolized it. After supper he would put his ear right up to the loudspeaker and listen to the Yiddish news about the war in Europe and the terrible plight of the Jews in Germany. If we made a sound we would be killed. But then the whole family gathered around to listen to Eddie Cantor, Jack Benny, Fred Allen, Bing Crosby on the *Kraft Music Hall.* I loved the sound of Cecil B. De Mille's voice on the *Lux Radio Theater:* "Good night to you from Hollywood." There was another world out there, where people sang and made jokes and led interesting lives. It was better than my world, and now I had a chance to be part of it.

That evening, Skipper Dawes stood me up in front of a microphone at the WFIL studio, I sang "The Army Air Corps Song" again, and somehow I got through it without peeing in my pants. "That was even better than this afternoon," Skipper said. "How would you like to be a regular on the show, Eddie?"

I just nodded, certain even then that I wasn't destined to work in a luggage factory or hawk vegetables like my father. I was destined to be a singer. I had never been taught manners: how do you do, nice to meet you, hope to see you again soon. If anyone spoke to me, I hardly said a word because I didn't know what to say. But even though I was painfully shy, I was confident about my singing because every time anybody heard me sing, something out of the ordinary happened. Ever since I could remember, I had had one dream: to become a singer. Without knowing how or where or when, I was just waiting for that dream to come true.

The *Magic Lady Supper Club* was a fifteen-minute children's program that was broadcast three evenings a week at six o'clock. The kids on the show sang a few songs, accompanied by Skipper on the piano or Milt Spooner on the organ. And then Arvene Livonia, the Magic Lady, transported us to the "Kingdom of Natar" for a five-minute adventure. I played a character called "Boney," Bernie Rich, who talked like he had a frog in his throat, played "Cough Drop," Joey Forman was "Slick," and Fred Bonaparte, a black boy, was called "Napoleon." It was a serial, and we always got into some terrible predicament so the kids would tune in next time to hear how we got out of it. The scripts, which Skipper wrote, were pretty corny, but as far as I was concerned, the *Magic Lady Supper Club* was the *Kraft Music Hall* and the *Lux Radio Theater* all rolled up into one.

I was very timid at first about reading lines. I was a singer, not an actor—or so I thought. As it turned out, I didn't know much about either, but Skipper was patient with me. I talked like a dumb kid from a poor Jewish neighborhood, which is exactly what I was, so when I rehearsed my lines, Skipper would correct my pronunciation and inflections. He never made me feel stupid or inferior; he just said it would sound nicer if I spoke a certain way, and it did. He helped me with my singing too. I thought all I had to do was open my mouth and out would come this beautiful voice. Skipper taught me there was more to singing than that.

One afternoon we were rehearsing the song I was going to sing that evening on the program. Skipper was at the piano, chain-smoking as always, and he said, "Eddie, you know who Al Jolson is, don't you?"

"Sure," I said. "That's how I got my nickname, from his song 'Sonny Boy.'"

"Then you know that Al Jolson sings from his heart. You do too, Eddie. It probably comes from your Jewish background and the way you sing in the temple. Don't ever lose that quality. If you can keep it, someday you may be a great singer. You have the voice, but it's an instrument and you've got to learn how to *use* it."

I'm not sure I understood what Skipper was trying to tell me. All I heard were the words "great singer" and that was enough to make me trust him and try to do everything he told me.

Just after I began singing for Skipper, I entered a contest sponsored by the *Horn & Hardart Children's Hour*. I won first prize—a chocolate cake—and a spot on the program. But it was on KYW in Philadelphia and I would have to choose between that and Skipper Dawes on WFIL. I chose Skipper because he was teaching me how to sing. More than that, he took a great personal interest in me, and I cringe now to remember how much I had to learn. My clothes were hand-me-downs and I had a big mop of curly hair which I wore in a pompadour, topped off with a wool cap which I even slept in. Skipper taught me how to dress, and how to be clean. He was very frank about it. "Look, Eddie," he said, "you've got to wash your hair and your neck and your ears. Brush your teeth. Blow your nose in a handkerchief, don't wipe it on your sleeve." He gave me a comb and told me to use it, and if I came to the studio with a dirty face and grimy hands, he made me go to the bathroom and wash. I was terribly embarrassed, but I began to care about how I looked and dressed. The other kids on the program were clean, and the studio was the cleanest place I had ever seen. I loved it. I wanted to belong in a place like that.

Skipper knew my family couldn't afford to pay for music lessons. He was going to have to teach me, but when my voice began to change, he wanted a professional opinion. He was afraid if I kept singing I would ruin it. He spoke to my mother and she took me to a music teacher in downtown Philadelphia. "He was a very famous professor from Germany," Mom remembered. "Wolfe, I think his name was. I heard about him and told Skipper Dawes and he said, 'Fine, Mrs. Fisher, take him. Find out what we should do about Eddie's voice.' Well, it was twenty-five dollars a visit, which I didn't have. So I went to the office and spoke to the receptionist, and I cried. I said I have a little boy, he's got a beautiful voice, everybody says so, but I'm worried about the change. I've got to see this professor. So the receptionist went inside and came back out and said, 'Bring your little boy around.'

"I brought you on the trolley and the professor looked at you and said, 'Do you really want to sing?' 'If I can't sing,' you said, 'I'll be a street cleaner.' Then he says, 'Do you want to give up baseball playing? Snowball playing?' And you said, 'Yes, I'm ready to give up anything if I can only sing.' 'All right, let's hear it,' the professor said, and if I'm not mistaken you sang 'Prisoner of Love.' Just a few notes before the professor stopped you. 'Mother,' he said, 'your son has a golden throat in there but it's got to be wrapped in cotton because he's going to have his ups and downs. He should continue singing, but somebody has to watch him when the voice changes.' Well, you can imagine I cried when I heard that, Sonny Boy. But

I told Skipper and he said, 'That's all I want to know. I'll watch him.'"

Skipper arranged all the music we sang on the program, and if my voice cracked on a high note, he lowered the register or let one of the girls sing the song. When everything settled down, the voice was still there, and Skipper continued teaching me how to use it. I listened to Bing Crosby records. He was Skipper's favorite and my idol, but I don't think I consciously imitated him. I picked up some of his tricks of phrasing, but the expression was always my own. And my greatest influence remained the music of the temple and the cantorial style. My favorites were David Kusevitsky, Kipov-Kagan and Yossele Rosenblatt. I began to collect their records as soon as I had a little money in my pocket, and I listened to them over and over again. I went to hear the good cantors who were singing in Philadelphia; thrilled by what they could do with their voices, I tried to do the same when I sang popular songs.

Skipper encouraged me to sing in churches and synagogues around town for the experience and the exposure. I even sang at my own bar mitzvah. "It was at Alec's Restaurant," my mother recalled. "Your thirteenth birthday. You were singing on the radio by then. You were well known. So Mr. Mandell said he'd be master of ceremonies as a present to you and we didn't have to pay him. And he spoke to Alec to give the dinner a little cheaper. It was just the immediate family, about fifty of us, and you sang. It was the nicest little bar mitzvah that poor people could ever make."

I wore a green double-breasted jacket whith orange stripes that my mother had made over from another suit, a green necktie with a tie pin, white flannel pants, white shoes, and a little white yarmulke. The song I sang was called *"Kabad es ovekha"*—"Honor thy mother and father," the Fifth Commandment, ironic because honor was the last thing I felt for my father. He pocketed the money and all the other gifts my relatives gave me for my bar mitzvah, just as he always took the few dollars I made singing in synagogues. And if I asked for some of my own money back, he would toss me a dime or a quarter and say, "Now get away from me, you little bastard."

There were never more than a few pennies in my pocket, and when I first started singing for Skipper I didn't have enough money for the trolley and had to walk halfway across Philadelphia to get to the studio. Before I left home, my mother put pieces of cardboard in my shoes to cover up the holes, and she gave me two pieces to put in for the trip back, because the cardboard didn't last both ways. I was always late, and when Skipper found out why, he began to slip trolley fare in my pocket. Later he paid everyone on the show fifty cents a week, then it went up to a dollar, a dollar-fifty, three dollars. We all sat around while he counted out our money from a pack of a hundred brand-new dollar bills from the bank. We thought we had discovered King Solomon's mine.

I gave the money to my mother. "Sonny Boy," she said to me, "don't ever tell your father about this money because he'll take it from you or deduct from what he gives to me, so let's keep it a secret. I'll hang on to it and you'll have money to buy whatever you need, go wherever you have to go." Of course, my father found out, but my mother managed to keep some of the money, and for the first time in my life I could buy new shoes or a new pair of slacks or a sweater if I needed it. As far as I was concerned, money was meant to be spent, not saved. I had no conception of its value. More often than not, I wasted it on Cokes and candy just to impress my friends—and to prove to myself that for a while at least, I was no longer poor.

The *Magic Lady Supper Club,* which was sponsored by Lit Brothers department store, was really a pretty terrible show, but all the kids listened to it, and the department store people asked Skipper to do another program, called *Junior Music Hall.* It was broadcast every Saturday night at seven-thirty; Joey Forman was the announcer, and I, at fourteen, was supposed to be the star. But I didn't use my real name because the night before on the *Magic Lady Supper Club,* Eddie Fisher was trapped in a cave or hanging over a cliff in the Kingdom of Natar, and Skipper decided I just couldn't reappear on Saturday; it would spoil the suspense. I was called Sonny Edwards, but I don't think anybody was fooled. It was the same voice. Then came another program, *Teen Time,* on Saturday afternoons, sponsored by Breyer's Ice Cream, and advertising posters with my picture were plastered on trolley cars all over Philadelphia. When Joey Forman told me he'd seen lipstick smears on my face, I got pretty excited and started chasing trolley cars to see if I could find out who was kissing my picture.

I knew who at least one of my fans was: Marion Hollingsworth, a nice goyish name, and that appealed to me. The only sexual advice my parents ever gave me was stay away from shiksas. So naturally I disregarded it. A beautiful brunette with fine teeth, which also appealed to me, Marion, who played a character on the *Magic Lady Supper Club,* literally ran after me. She obviously had a crush on me and I really couldn't understand it. She invited me to a party at her house in the suburbs and I went without knowing what to expect. I had never been in a house that wasn't attached, let alone a gentile home. Anyone who came from my part of Philadelphia was made to feel like an outcast in that world, and I was acutely self-conscious because I was Jewish and because I was poor. But Marion's parents were very polite to me, and I couldn't believe the way they lived. Nobody yelled and screamed. The house was clean and nicely furnished, and there was a big yard with grass and trees. Marion and I took a walk outside and for the first time in my life I felt real physical desire. But we didn't do anything more than just hold hands.

I learned about sex on the streets of my own neighborhood. I was about fourteen, and all the guys I hung out with, who had already had some kind of sexual experience, figured it was my turn. They fixed me up with Tootsie Stern, a girl with a reputation for fooling around; she invited me to a party at her cousin's house and we ended up in the kitchen with the lights out. First I discovered she was wearing falsies, which was a shock. Then when I got an erection, I didn't know what to do about it. I didn't know anything. The whole thing was over before it started, and I thought to myself, I'm not going to have any more sex. Sex is out for me. I'm going to sing. That's how I'll get my thrills.

I avoided Tootsie after that, and the day she came to the WFIL studio to see me, I hid in Skipper's office for a couple of hours, hoping she'd go home. She didn't. Still waiting for me by the elevator, she looked me straight in the eye and said, "Eddie Fisher, you can kiss my lily-white ass." At that moment, the elevator doors opened, she got in, and they closed. That was the last time I ever saw Tootsie Stern.

The next girl in my life was Angelina Costellano, the soprano on the *Junior Music Hall.* Again a beautiful shiksa, great teeth, and a little chubby—*zoftig*—and I liked that. Joey Forman had a crush on her too, and after the show we used to hang around Marty's Candy Store, play the pinball machines, and talk about Angelina. We called her Angel Eyes. One day we got into a big argument. Joey said Angelina loved him, not me. And I said no, she loved me. Finally we both crowded into a phone booth, called her up, and asked her. When she said she loved me, Joey had tears in his eyes and I felt terrible, because he was my best friend. It was a very, very serious thing. But even though we were both hopelessly in love, Angelina never got any closer to me than just sitting on my lap in a car.

Joey grew up in my part of Philadelphia. We were about the same age and went to the same schools, but we didn't become friends until we both started working for Skipper Dawes. Joey's father owned a soda fountain in a mixed black and white neighborhood and we used to hang out there, eating ice cream and candy on the house. Our personalities couldn't have been more different. I was serious, quiet, almost paralyzed with shyness. Joey, who was a sharp dresser with the reputation of being a "bad kid" was funny, outgoing, friendly with everybody. My ambition was to be a great singer, his was to be a great actor. He was handsome too, which was one reason I was so surprised that Angelina said she loved me and not him. But Joey took it in his stride, and pretty soon, as far as experience with girls was concerned, he had left me far behind.

I must have been fifteen or sixteen when Joey came to me with a proposition. "My Uncle Sam wants to give us a present," he said.

"What kind of present?" I asked suspiciously.

"He's got a couple of girls he wants us to meet."

"What kind of girls?"

"Nice girls," Joey said. "You'll see."

Joey thought he was doing me a favor. His uncle had introduced him to these girls before, and now that he had made this great discovery about sex, he wanted to share it with me. They took me to an apartment on North Broad Street, where we met the two girls, only they weren't girls exactly. They must have been about thirty and seemed like old women to me. Joey and his uncle were very relaxed. I was a little nervous, especially when the women started showing off their wares. Nice girls just didn't get into such positions. But overcoming my shyness, I went into another room with one of them and did what was expected of me. Joey swears that I came out singing "Ah, sweet mystery of life, at last I've found thee" at

the top of my lungs. And I probably did. Often when words
failed me, I would just start singing.

I was growing up fast—too fast. Never a very good student,
I just got by, and after I started singing on the radio, I completely lost interest in school. I listened to every kind of music,
but I read radio scripts, not books, and my only interest other
than singing was baseball. All the kids in my neighborhood
played stickball in the streets and I was captain of my grammar
school baseball team. Later, in high school, I didn't have time
for even that. And like everybody else, I was concerned about
the war, but all I could talk about, all I really thought about,
was singing.

Teen Time was the most important kid show in Philadelphia,
and I was becoming a hero around my neighborhood. People
started treating me as if I were some kind of star. Kids my own
age seemed to be in awe of me, and I even got grudging
recognition from older guys. I had always liked to hang around
with older kids, and now they let me do it. I was a celebrity,
the Philadelphia Flash, and naturally I began to have dreams
of glory.

It was the time when Frank Sinatra was being mobbed on
the streets and bobby-soxers were screaming and swooning in
the aisles during his performances at the Paramount Theater
in New York. I sang all Sinatra's hits on the radio, and when
the girls in the audience sighed and screamed, my ego soared.
I started thinking of myself as the next Sinatra, even though
there was absolutely no similarity in our musical styles. He
was a crooner and I was a belter. But he was a skinny little
kid from Hoboken who had made it big. Why couldn't a skinny
little kid from South Philadelphia do the same? It was more
than a dream. I was convinced it was going to happen. In the
audience when Sinatra sang at the Earl Theater in Philadelphia,
I saw myself, not him, up there on the stage. And after the
show, watching his bodyguards muscle him through a huge
crowd of teenagers who just wanted to touch him or get his
autograph, I promised myself I wouldn't treat my fans like that
when *I* was a star.

I soon suffered my first taste of disappointment. Skipper
got a show on ABC, the Blue Network, and the manager of
the station didn't want to use me because he didn't think I was
good enough. Then Eddie Cantor came to the station on a
publicity tour and I was sure this would be my big break. At

the height of his popularity on records and radio, Cantor was famous as a discoverer of new young talent, and he was the one who would make me a star. But when Skipper asked him to listen to me sing, he refused. He had a cold. After posing for some pictures with us, bugging his eyes, which was his trademark, he left and I was almost in tears. I had to wait quite a few years before Eddie Cantor heard me sing.

I did sing for Perry Como. In New York, I got a single ticket to his radio show and sat in the audience, again dreaming that I was the one there on stage, not Como. After the show, he asked if anyone would like to sing a song, and all of a sudden I found myself jumping out of my seat, waving my arms. He called me up on stage and I had the nerve to sing his own song, "Prisoner of Love." Then, pressing my luck even further, I sang "Wrap Your Troubles in Dreams," a Crosby hit. The audience probably applauded my guts as well as my voice, and Como said with a smile, "Well, I guess I'll have to sharpen up my barber tools again."

Skipper never lost faith in me. I don't know why he was so kind. He had two young sons of his own, but he treated me like a son too. And the first time he and his wife invited me to their home in Swarthmore, it was a revelation. The snow out there was white, not the black slush I was used to seeing in the city. They gave me a bed of my own, with clean sheets and a quilt. Skipper's wife tucked me in, and when she opened the window, fresh air came in the room. We always kept the windows closed in the city. It was one of the most marvelous nights of my life. I stayed there often after that, while Skipper and I worked on songs together or just sat around and talked. He was disappointed that I wasn't more interested in getting an education. I would regret it later on, he said, and he was right. But he told me if I really wanted to be a singer, that's what I should be. His advice and encouragement were invaluable, and if I ever had doubts, all I had to do was think about his house in the suburbs. I wanted to live in a house like that. I wanted a bedroom and a bathroom all to myself. And I knew the only way I'd ever get them was by becoming a successful singer. I didn't realize then that Skipper had a drinking problem, perhaps because he had never been able to fulfill his own dreams as a musician. And perhaps he hoped he could live out his dreams through me.

In a sense, I left home when I started singing on the radio.

I ate and slept there, but I couldn't wait to leave for good. My mother understood and encouraged me. She wasn't a pushy backstage mother; she had her other children to worry about and didn't play favorites. It was just that she wanted what I wanted, and knew that if I was going to make something of my life, if I was going to get the things she had never been able to give me, I would have to do it by myself.

My father didn't seem to care. He had seen so many of his own dreams go down the drain, he didn't believe in them anymore. He was proud of me when I sang in the synagogue, those great Jewish cries, "Why me, Lord? Why?" because that's the way he felt about his own life. But even though I brought home about twenty-five dollars every week for my radio work, singing as a career was another matter. "You want to make money?" he told me. "Get a job." He wanted me to follow in his footsteps, and took me one day to the luggage factory where he worked. "This is what a job is," he said. "This is work. What can you make as a singer? What have you got if you fail?" The place was oppressive with heat and the smell of sweat, leather, and glue. I had to stay there the whole day. I didn't want to hurt my father's feelings; this was his trade. But I swore I would never work in a place like that.

Joey and I got a job together. Another one of his uncles owned a concession at Franklin Field and hired us to peddle hot dogs and soft drinks during the football games. Too embarrassed to sell anything, I hid under the stands. I didn't have to do this. I was a star on the radio. Then I got a job working in a pants factory, sorting them into their sizes—small, medium, large. I lasted one week, just long enough to pick up a sixteen-dollar paycheck. I gave my father the money and never went back.

After that experience, I was more determined than ever to become a singer. I couldn't work in a factory. I couldn't live the way my family did—the poverty, the dirt. I had to get out. I was thinking of myself, but my thoughts were of my family too. If I succeeded as a singer, I'd buy my mother a mansion and hire a maid. My kid brother and my sisters would have toys and clothes and get an education. I'd give them all the things I never had. And I'd prove to my father that I could make money as a singer.

The opportunity came in 1945, when I was seventeen years old, and I grabbed it. After Skipper got his network show on

ABC, song pluggers started coming to Philadelphia to try to get their songs on the air. Among them was Lester Sacks, who ran one of Frank Sinatra's publishing companies and was the brother of Mannie Sacks of Columbia Records. Skipper asked him to listen to me sing, and Mr. Sacks seemed to like what he heard. He told Skipper to make a demonstration record and he would see what he could do. We cut the record and sent it to him, and on his next trip to Philadelphia he told us that Buddy Morrow was forming a new band and needed a male singer vocalist. "You got the job if you want it," Mr. Sacks said. "The band opens at the Lincoln Hotel in New York in one week."

If I wanted it? It was the break I had been waiting for; my dreams really were coming true. Frank Sinatra had sung with Tommy Dorsey's band. Now I had the same kind of job, and it would only be a matter of time before I stepped into Sinatra's shoes.

I told Joey and he was happy for me. But I think he was a little jealous of my luck. "New York," he said. "I wish I could come with you."

"Why not? Listen, I'll be making seventy-five bucks a week. We'll share an apartment and you can get a job too. We'll both be famous."

He didn't believe me. I'm not sure I believed myself. It all sounded like some MGM musical, with Mickey Rooney making it big on Broadway in a show he produced back home in a garage. I didn't care. That's exactly the way I felt. And it wasn't happening to Mickey Rooney; it was happening to me.

Skipper was pleased, but he warned me to be careful. "Singing with a band isn't like singing on the radio," he said. "Listen to what Buddy Morrow tells you. He's a good musician and he's got a good band. I know you'll be fine, Eddie, but if you ever need anything, if there's anything I can do for you, just let me know."

We shook hands and I started to mumble my thanks. Skipper had been like a father to me, but I couldn't find the words. He gave me one of his big smiles. "Forget it, Eddie. You've always been much better at expressing yourself with music."

When I told my family, all I got from my father was the usual shrug. Everybody else was excited, and Nettie, my biggest fan, gave me a hug. She had listened to every radio broadcast I ever made. My two younger sisters and my brother Bunny wanted to come hear me sing in New York. They were all happy for me; only my mother seemed a little sad. She didn't say much until, a few days later, it was almost time for me to leave.

There was nothing to pack. I don't think I even had a bag. I was wearing everything I owned: a sports jacket, a fancy tie, slacks, and a pair of shoes. That was it. That was all I took with me. My mother gave me the money she had saved. It wasn't much, just whatever I had given her that she had been able to hide from my father.

"He's proud of you, Sonny Boy," she said, "even though he doesn't know how to show it. I'm proud too, but a little worried. A mother is worried about her son, so what else is new? You're a good boy, you've always been a good boy, and I know you'll never do anything to make your mother ashamed. Just promise me one thing. Promise me if this job doesn't work out, you'll come home. You'll finish school."

"Mom, it's going to work out. I know it. I'm going to be a great singer."

She took my face in her hands and kissed me. "I'll settle for good, Sonny Boy. A good singer and a good person."

On the way to New York, all I could think of was what I was leaving behind, not what was ahead. I had a job in show business, that was the only thing that mattered, and it meant love and money and acceptance. All the good things. The nightmare was over. Philadelphia was through with me and I was through with Philadelphia. I'd never have to go back. I had my wings. I was on my way.

3

New York, with exactly a dollar and a quarter in my pocket. As soon as I got off the train, I headed for Times Square and walked up Broadway to the Paramount Theater. Standing there in the middle of the sidewalk, oblivious of all the people streaming by me, I saw my face on the posters, my name in giant letters on the marquee: "The Paramount Theater Proudly Presents EDDIE FISHER." The Lincoln Hotel was only a block away, on Eighth Avenue. I was practically there.

That one-block journey was one of the most difficult and frustrating I ever had to make.

Just three nights after my New York debut in the Blue Room of the Lincoln Hotel, Buddy Morrow, unimpressed by a scared seventeen-year-old kid who could barely read music or keep time with the band, fired me. But luck was still running with me. Charlie Ventura was in the audience my last night and asked me to sing with his band at the Boston Post Lodge, a big dance hall in Larchmont, New York. I took the job, even if it was a long way from the Paramount.

In Larchmont I found a place to live with an older couple who owned a laundromat, and spent my first week's salary—seventy-five dollars—to buy the band uniform, a powder-blue one-button suit with padded shoulders, rolled lapels, and pegged pants. If I looked like the other members of Ventura's band, that was as far as the similarity went. They were musicians and I wasn't. Ventura was patient with me, and I tried to learn, but we both knew from the very beginning it wasn't going to work.

When Joey came up from Philadelphia to stay with me for a couple of days, he was impressed by the hall and the size of the audience. "So it isn't New York," he said. "A lot of people will hear you sing."

"Who listens to me?" I said. "People come to dance. I just stand up, sing a chorus or a couple of bars, and then sit down again. It's boring."

Sitting on the bandstand night after night in that ridiculous zoot suit, I felt as if I were in prison. I was miserable and showed it. Then one night during a band break, a man asked me to join him at his table. His name was Manny Mangel and he said, "You've got a good voice, kid, and I can see you're not too happy up there. How would you like to sing at the Copa?"

I thought he was crazy. It was the answer to a prayer. Ventura had already told me he was going to have to let me go, and I had no idea what to do next, or even where to look for another job. Working at the Copacabana, the most famous nightclub in the world, was beyond my wildest dreams. "Are you kidding me?" I asked Mr. Mangel.

"No, I'm not kidding," he said. "I've got connections. My brother Ira is a captain at the Copa. If you want an audition, I can arrange it."

I said yes without stopping to think that I was hardly ready to sing at the Copa. Naturally I saw myself walking out on stage as the star of the show. Even if I had to start in some smaller job, it had to be better than being a band singer. And I would be back in New York.

Skipper came up from Philadelphia to help me rehearse and to play the piano for my audition. The day we went to the Copa, we were directed down the steps to the cellar. Chairs were turned upside down on the tables. The place was dark and empty. Skipper went to the piano and struck a few chords. Standing nervously in the light of a single spot, I started to sing my old standby, "Prisoner of Love," followed by three or four other pop standards and a piece of special material Skipper had written for me: "Just because my hair is sort of curly, 'cause I'm underweight, as you can see, some folks think I'm copying Sinatra, but Sinatra's even skinnier than me...." There were verses about Crosby and Como, and then for my big finish I launched into *"Vesti la giubba."* Corny, but I was showing off the range of my voice and the different kinds of songs I could sing.

There was nothing but silence when I finished. That's it, I thought. I've struck out again. Then this dapper, portly little man emerged from the shadows, Monte Proser, the owner of the Copa. "Will one-twenty-five a week be enough?" he said.

Almost choking on the words, I said, "Yes, sir, that's just fine. When do I start?"

"First rehearsal in two weeks," he said. "By the way, son, how old are you?"

"Seventeen," I said.

"I thought you looked pretty young. You can't sing here until you're eighteen, son. It's the law. When's your birthday?"

"August."

"Good. Come back in September for the fall show. Joe E. Lewis is the headliner. You'll be the production singer."

September? What was I going to do all summer? How was I going to eat?

Proser saw the look on my face. "I take it you need a job. And you certainly could use a little more experience. Well, let me see what I can do."

Monte Proser sent me to see Milton Blackstone. I didn't know it then, but it would be the most important meeting of my life. I didn't even know who Milton Blackstone was. In fact, he ran one of the most successful theatrical advertising agencies in New York, and Blackstone himself was called a promotional genius. The Copa and the Latin Quarter were only two of the many hotels, cafés and nightclubs he handled, but his most famous account was Grossinger's. Working with Jennie Grossinger in the thirties and forties, he had transformed a sleepy little boardinghouse in the Catskills into the biggest and most exclusive resort hotel in the Catskills. In the early days, the Catskills were known primarily for front porches and rocking chairs, and as a place where one recovered from tuberculosis. Blackstone changed all that by persuading famous boxers to train at Grossinger's. Notables of show business and politics soon followed and Grossinger's was on the map. A man with ideas, a builder, Blackstone was willing to take chances even if the odds weren't always in his favor. Once, during the war, he jumped on the running board of the open car that was carrying Franklin Roosevelt in a motorcade and persuaded the President to make a detour to the nearby shipyard owned by Blackstone and his brothers to boost the workers' morale.

His office was on West Fifty-seventh Street near Carnegie Hall; the sign on the door read: "The Blackstone Advertising Agency." Inside, the place was crowded with desks and people, phones were ringing, typewriters clacking, and in a small office of his own sat the man in charge. Milton Blackstone. He was the puppeteer, and everyone danced and sang at his command. I expected him to be imperious, high-powered, theatrical. Instead I met a man of about my father's age, with a round face, a lightly balding head and a ready smile. He was kind, polite, and as shy as I was. He could have been Walter Winchell's double, but his only theatrical touch was the gray felt hat he used as a prop.

I liked Milton Blackstone. A great listener, he made me feel that what I had to say was important. But when I finished telling him my story, he gave me that bemused look that would become so familiar to me. He was not an impetuous man. Everything was deliberate, cautious, calculated, until he suddenly came up with one of his brilliant ideas. But at the moment he wasn't quite sure what to do with a seventeen-year-old kid who had nothing going for him but a big voice.

"Well," he said finally, "I guess I could send you up to Grossinger's for the summer. You could sing there. Do you think you'll be lonely?"

It was a peculiar question. With all the people around in a resort hotel, how could I be lonely? Skipper and his wife drove me up, but they didn't want to come in. We said our goodbyes in the parking lot, and as I watched the car drive away, tears started streaming down my face. I *was* lonely. Milton Blackstone was right. He was always right.

Grossinger's was part enchantment, part disappointment to me. The buildings, the grounds, the tennis courts, the golf course, the private lake—it was a long way from the slums of Philadelphia. I had never seen anything more beautiful. But

I can remember those first moments, standing alone in the parking lot, looking down at the cracks in the cement. Somehow I expected that a place like Grossinger's would be paved in gold.

No one knew what to do with me. As Milton Blackstone's protégé, I was something special. His word was law at Grossinger's and I wasn't asked to sing or do anything else until he had made his pronouncement. I ate in the staff dining room and slept in a room underneath the playhouse, with a rabbi, a tennis pro, and a waiter. The rabbi scared me to death, and a tennis pro might as well have come from another planet. Later they moved out and two six-foot-six basketball players moved in. I had nothing in common with any of them, and nothing to do but just wander around and consume three enormous meals a day. I was being paid twenty dollars a week to eat and sleep at Grossinger's.

When word finally came down from Milton Blackstone, I was allowed to sing a couple of numbers every night with Eddie Ashman's band. The first time Jennie Grossinger heard me, she gave me a warm, motherly hug. A caring, gracious woman—the First Lady of the Catskills—she made room in her hotel and her heart for everyone. Milton Blackstone beckoned me over to the bar. He always came up on weekends to keep an eye on things and play golf with his celebrity friends, but he had never heard me sing before. "I can see why Monte Proser has so much faith in you, Eddie," he said. "Would you like a drink?"

"Just a Coke, Mr. Blackstone. I don't drink."

He nodded. "Do you smoke?"

"No, sir."

He nodded again, and then said, "Well, it's late, Eddie. Don't you think it's time a young man like you should be in bed?"

I had been given the Blackstone seal of approval. My salary was raised to fifty dollars a week and I became the featured singer with Eddie Ashman's band in the Terrace Room—still a band singer, but people actually stopped dancing to listen, surprised that such a little kid had such a big voice. And I was surprised by the way they reacted to me. They wouldn't let me leave the stage. Every night my audiences and I discovered each other all over again. I stayed at Grossinger's through the

Labor Day weekend and then came back to New York, happy, well fed, a few dollars in my pocket, and ready to take the big city by storm.

I reported for rehearsals at the Copacabana, expecting instant stardom until I found out just what a production singer does—and doesn't do. I would never appear on stage alone. There was a girl singer, who was my partner, a male dancer and his partner, and if that wasn't distraction enough, it was the Copa chorus line—eight of the most beautiful show girls in New York City—the customers really wanted to see. We rehearsed three production numbers, all original songs and all terrible. I was just supposed to stand there singing some silly lyric to my partner while the Copa girls paraded around the stage dressed in huge hats and glittering costumes. My costume was a bolero jacket and a pink scarf.

That costume, I later discovered, was dry cleaned once a week, when it began to smell. And God, the dressing rooms! All the girls were crammed into one room, and I shared an airless little space right next to the kitchen with Joe E. Lewis and the male dancer. The odor of the Copa's famous Chinese food was overpowering, and we could hear the man who ran the kitchen screaming at the waiters: "Move it, you lazy bums! Get the hell in there!" Lewis appeared the day before we opened, and the first thing he did was hang up his jock strap on the wall. It was supposed to be a joke. He was rumored to be the most well-endowed man in show business, but he said he had given up sex for alcohol, which may have been true. He was seldom sober, on stage or off, but he was a star, the "king of clubs"; more than just a comedian, he could make an audience laugh and love him like no other man in the business. He was polite to me but otherwise indifferent. I was just the production singer.

Opening night, I was so nervous I sprouted a big pimple on the end of my nose, and when the music started for the first number, I walked on stage before my cue. After standing there a moment, completely flustered, I stuck my thumb in my mouth and walked off. Somehow I got through the rest of the show and it was a magic moment in my life. The Copa was such an exciting place, an intimate room where the audience seemed to be right on stage with you. We did three shows a night; the hours were long, the work was hard, and I quickly learned that the glamour of the Copa was all facade. The place was crowded and too expensive; the girls in beautiful costumes were just great window dressing. And by the third show Joe E. Lewis was always completely intoxicated. But something happened on that stage. Lewis became a pixie, a Jewish leprechaun; the production numbers were done with style and taste. It was my first real exposure to show business, and even if it wasn't everything I expected, I loved every minute of it.

Variety was not particularly impressed by my talents. I was called "an okay looking lad who'll be a good bet for a Broadway musical when experience gives him greater presence and a knowledge of selling, which he now lacks." That hurt, but it was true. I didn't know how to sell a song, or myself. On stage, I really hoped nobody would notice me until I could open my mouth. Then I just clutched the microphone and sang from the heart.

Because I was so green, the Copa girls started mothering me. They fussed over me and brought food to fatten me up, and we all went out together after the show. They were older than I was, all except Joan Wynne, who was just eighteen and fresh from parochial school in Brooklyn. A beautiful girl with perfect features and auburn hair, she was even shyer and more inexperienced than I was. The other girls decided that Joanie and I were meant for each other, and it wasn't long before we were going out by ourselves, talking, dreaming, making plans. I'm afraid I did most of the talking, but whatever I hoped for myself, Joanie hoped for me too. We fell in love, a Jew from Philadelphia and a Scotch-Irish Catholic from Brooklyn. It began as a friendship, and grew into a love affair that lasted off and on for almost seven years.

When I realized I was in love with Joanie, I didn't know where to go from there. She was everything a girl was supposed to be, lovely, pure, and I had great respect for her. I used to take her home to Sheepshead Bay on the subway and we smooched on the couch in her parents' living room, but we were both afraid to go any further than that. Finally I persuaded her to come up to the room I rented from a married couple in an apartment on Forty-fifth Street. We were lying on the bed, fully clothed, just talking, and suddenly the wife burst into the room. "What are you two doing?" she screamed. "Get up! You can't do that in our house. This is terrible, terrible!"

Joanie and I were petrified. We thought the woman was going to call the police and have us arrested. I moved out and got a room at the Edison Hotel, and one night when we were there together, I said, "This is really ridiculous, Joanie. Everybody thinks we're having a mad, passionate affair and we're scared to even touch each other." We laughed and then it happened, easily, naturally. We were in love the way only teenagers can be in love.

Everyone thought we were a perfect couple—except my mother. When I told her I wanted to marry Joanie, she said, "Over my dead body"—the instinctive reaction of a Jewish mother. Then she and my father came to New York to hear me sing and met Joanie. She won my mother over completely and they grew very fond of each other. There was everything to like about Joanie, everything to like about my mother.

Joanie's mother was a different matter. One night she called me up on the telephone. "When are you going to marry my daughter?" she shrieked. I hung up on her, and for several days after that I was certain she was going to have me put in jail. Joanie was very important to me and I wanted to do the right thing. I've always wanted to do the right thing, sometimes so badly that I wound up doing it wrong. But I couldn't give Joanie very much, only my love, whatever I had, whatever I was capable of at the time. I really wasn't ready for marriage. I had a big dream, and the dream came first.

Every so often after the third show on Sunday, Monte Proser staged a "Celebrity Night" at the Copa. The headliner introduced celebrities from the audience, who sometimes came up on stage and gave impromptu performances. I was standing in the wings on one of those nights as Joe E. Lewis introduced Frank Sinatra, Jackie Gleason, Vic Damone, Eddie Duchin. Then suddenly I heard him say, "And here, ladies and gentlemen, is a kid who's going to cut 'em all." He couldn't mean me; he didn't even introduce me by name. But in his own quiet way he had planned this. The girls shoved me on stage and that night I sang as I had never sung before. Just me, no distractions, and there was pandemonium in the audience. I stole the show. I was crying with excitement when I bowed off, and Joanie and all the other girls started kissing and hugging me. Monte Proser shook my hand and said he wanted me to stay on as the production singer for the next show.

It was pretty heady stuff for an eighteen-year-old. Frank Costello, the Mafia godfather who was then supposed to be a silent partner in the Copa, was in the audience that night and offered to be my manager. So did the famous and powerful press agent George Evans, who had been instrumental in Frank Sinatra's early success. I asked Milton Blackstone for advice and he told me not to sign anything. I wanted him to be my manager, but he refused; he was too busy with Grossinger's and his other accounts. Still, people were paying attention to me at last, and that made me cocky enough to turn down Monte Proser's offer. My days as a production singer were over. I was a star.

Proser hired the tenor Bill Shirley to replace me in the next show at the Copa. I was backstage opening night when Bill sang Jerome Kern's "All the Things You Are" and stopped the show. "See, kid," Proser whispered in my ear, "that could have been you." Even so, I didn't regret my decision, not then. I got an agent, Val Irving, who booked me at the Glen Casino outside Buffalo. My name was at the bottom of the bill, but I was such a hit that I went immediately to Buffalo's Town Casino, the biggest nightclub in the country, where I shared top billing with Eleanor Powell. Back in New York, things began to get tough. Bill Shirley went on to star in a Broadway musical. I began a gradual slide into obscurity, washed up at the age of eighteen. It was worse than being an unknown, much worse because for a few brief moments I had come so close.

For the next two and a half years, from the spring of 1947 to the summer of 1949, I served my show business apprenticeship, the basic training almost every performer goes through on his way to becoming an "overnight sensation." I saw it all: the indifference that hurt even more than rejection, the small successes that kept hope alive only until the next failure, a string of jobs, any job, just to keep working, just to keep eating. I sang at a club called the Rio Cabana, where they made me change my name to Skippy White and then Dick White because someone said I would never make it with a name like Eddie Fisher. It was a dive, a cheap imitation of the Copa, and the management was even cheaper. My contract called for one hundred dollars a week; I was paid seventy-five. I got fifty for my first recording—I sang a chorus with the two Marlin sisters on a single for Columbia Records called "You Can't Be True, Dear." Mannie Sacks, who continued to take an interest in my career, got me the job. I used to haunt his office at Columbia

Records, hoping he could find something else for me to do. He introduced me to Lou Levy of Leeds Music and for a while I demonstrated his new songs with a piano accompanist for stars like Dinah Shore, Jo Stafford and Buddy Clark. I got ten bucks a song and compliments on my voice, but that was all. My first theater audition was at the Winter Garden for *As the Girls Go,* a musical that was being produced by a flamboyant character named Mike Todd. I sang a couple of songs while he sat in the back of the theater fooling around with his wife, Joan Blondell. He came up on stage, told me to sing this or try that, and called me back six times. But finally he said, "Go home, kid, and get a little older." Another disappointment, and I thought that Mike Todd was close to the bottom of the show business barrel, a crude, insensitive man.

Joanie stood by me. She was still working at the Copa and we used to hang out in the drugstores and Automats along Broadway. I couldn't afford to take her anywhere else, and I was ashamed to bring her to the places I had to live. For three months I rented the back room in Buzzy Goff's apartment in a terrible building called Hildona Court on West Forty-fifth Street off Eighth Avenue. Buzzy played the trumpet at the Copa and his wife was expecting a baby (who grew up to become the singer Gloria Loring). My room didn't even have a door.

I shared another apartment with a man named Ken McSarin who was notorious for his consumption of Lindy's cheesecake. It was a fourth-floor walk-up over the Famous Door, a strip joint on West Fifty-second, which was called Reefer Street in those days because the musicians who played in the jazz clubs were heavy marijuana smokers. McSarin, a seedy character who sold hot watches among other things, used to wake me up at two in the morning and make me walk the streets. I didn't know why until I found out he did a little pimping on the side. The bureau drawer in my room was full of French ticklers and McSarin's girls and their customers used my bed while I hung around a White Tower eating crackers and sipping an orange drink.

One day just before Christmas, someone rang the bell, and leaning over the railing, I saw Joanie struggling up the stairs with a big red ease. I was so surprised I didn't even run down to help her. She was bringing me my Christmas present, an expensive Webster wire recorder. I don't know where she got the money; she must have saved it up. I was completely over-whelmed because it was a gift for my voice, my career. I've never forgotten that gesture of thoughtfulness.

Milton Blackstone came to my rescue. Although he still refused to be my manager, I could always count on him for help and advice. When I told him I was paying fifteen dollars a month to share my bed with prostitutes he said, "You're welcome to go back to Grossinger's, Eddie. They like you up there."

So I spent another summer in the Catskills, singing with Eddie Ashman's band and eating the first decent meals I'd had in months. Joey Forman remembers that summer. After graduating from high school in Philadelphia, he had come to New York to find a job as an actor and his luck was even worse than mine. So when I went to Grossinger's I brought him along as a stowaway.

"We shared a room with a masseur, a waiter, and a trumpet player," Joey recalled recently. "Four guys on the staff, including you, and only four beds, so you and I had to sleep together. You used to smuggle me food from the dining room—chicken wrapped in a napkin, seven days a week. Finally I said, 'Eddie, I'm tired of chicken, for God's sake. Can't you get me a steak?' And you said, 'Chicken is easy to steal. They count the steaks.'"

They soon found out Joey was there, he was put to work on the athletic staff, and we spent the whole summer together. With nothing to do during the day except an occasional re-hearsal, I acted more like a guest than an employee. I tried golf and discovered quickly it wasn't my favorite sport. And I took a couple of tennis lessons, but I didn't think tennis was a game for Jews, especially Jews from South Philadelphia. Handball I knew about, and baseball. Joey and I played on the celebrity teams of sportswriters, columnists, and athletes who were stay-ing at the hotel.

I felt at home at Grossinger's. I was accepted as part of the family. It was comfortable and safe, the audiences loved me, but it wasn't the real world. Most of the well-known guests who came there were from New York and that's all they talked about. Broadway, that was real, and that's where Joey and I wanted to be. We were both going to become stars—it was as simple as that—and when the summer was over we were eager to get back.

"How many hotels did we live in?" Joey said. "Ten, twenty?"

I started counting. The Taft, the Empire, the Capitol, the Lincoln, the Edison, the Dixie. Even the Luxor Baths. Whoever had money checked in and the other would sneak by the desk and share the room. Bernie Rich had come to New York too, and he joined us. There were others—Al Cernik, who became Al Grant who became Guy Mitchell and wanted to be a singer too. And Robert Effenbach, a dentist's son who had changed his name to Robert Evans and seemed to be hanging around just for the fun of it. We all moved like Gypsies from one hotel to another. There were four of us living in one room at the Victoria until the management caught on and kicked us out. I slept on the bed, Joey slept on the mattress on the floor, Guy slept in the bathtub, and I don't know where Bernie slept. Hope was the only thing that kept us going. And odd jobs here and there. We shared whatever we earned, usually just enough to rent another room or buy the next meal.

"I remember Bernie and I had an apartment together when you were singing somewhere out of town," Joey said. "It was Thanksgiving and Bernie won a turkey in some kind of raffle. We didn't have a kitchen, just a closet with a couple of little gas burners. So I dissected this enormous twenty-five-pound turkey and cooked it one piece at a time."

I was convinced all my troubles were over when I tied for first place with a girl violinist on the *Arthur Godfrey's Talent Scouts* program. Godfrey was famous for giving young people a chance, and winning usually meant a week of appearances on his morning radio show. That's all I got, but I did land a job as the male vocalist in a road show edition of *Stop the Music*. Guy Marks, who also happened to be from Philadelphia, was the featured comedian on the show and we became lifelong friends. We played in theaters all over the country and I hated every minute. In the few months I traveled with the show, I don't think I ever sang more than six or eight bars before the bell went off and the music stopped. But I would do anything for "exposure." That was Milton Blackstone's advice, and I took it because I was young enough—naive enough—to believe that if I got just one chance to really sing, my luck would change. Even after more than two years of scratching out a living on the sleazy fringes of show business, I still had faith in my voice, and in myself. If I had swallowed my pride, somehow I had kept my innocence. It was the only armor I had left.

And Joanie. Her love, her belief in me, were essential to me and I clung to her selfishly. I knew she didn't want a career in show business for herself, but still I expected her to make the same sacrifices I was making. I wanted her to keep her innocence too, and I was truly shocked to find out she had been going to the racetrack with some of her friends. I was a puritan. To me, going to the races was the first step to hell. "How could you do that?" I said. "You're my girl. You belong to me. How can you got to a racetrack, where people drink and bet on horses?"

"Because I like it," she said, laughing.

It was no laughing matter to me. Dead serious, I had no sense of humor, no sense of proportion, about my career or Joanie. I *had* to succeed as a singer. Joanie *had* to love me.

We were separated for several weeks when I went on the road with *Stop the Music* and Joanie left the Copa to work at the Beverly Club in New Orleans. Someone told me she was seeing another man and I couldn't believe it. An old man! A bald-headed man! Here she had a nice-looking boy her own age with a glorious voice and a glorious future, and she was going out with an old man. I didn't know who he was, but I was outraged and deeply hurt. On top of everything else, I couldn't hold on to my own girl.

I was just about ready to quit, until Milton Blackstone told me he had persuaded Bob Weitman, the manager of the Paramount, to give me a job. I was elated. The Paramount! That long journey was over. I had made it at last. Then I found out what kind of job it was.

"I couldn't talk Bob into hiring you for the stage show," Milton said candidly. "He doesn't think you're good enough yet. But you can work as the intermission singer."

As far as I knew, the Paramount had never had an intermission singer before. It was a Blackstone invention and I was grateful, but I couldn't conceal my disappointment.

"Look at it this way, Eddie," Milton said. "It's experience. Any time you can get on your feet and sing before an audience is experience. No matter where, no matter how bad, it'll be good for you. Hard knocks are good for you."

More than just another hard knock, the job was a humiliation. For seventy-five dollars a week I sang a couple of songs between every show, accompanied by George Wright, the organist who had been at the Paramount for years and resented me because the spotlight was supposed to be on him. I stood in front of a big curtain that must have been a thousand years old, choking on the dust. The houselights were up in that cavernous theater and people shuffled in and out, looking for seats, talking, impatient for the next show to begin. Someone in the audience always threw pennies at me.

That was the end. Sinatra had been the star attraction at the Paramount and bobby-soxers swooned in the aisles. My name was listed last on the program and as soon as I started singing the aisles were filled with people walking out. I remembered the days when my father sent me into the back alleys of Philadelphia to hawk vegetables. I was still begging for pennies.

Twenty years old, and I felt I had nothing to show for my life. No money, no career, no future. Why should I keep chasing some ridiculous dream? I had lost my girl, and now I had lost faith in myself. Without that, there was no place to go but back home to Philadelphia.

4

Nothing had changed. My family still lived in the same dingy little house. My father had the same job in a luggage factory; my mother, with Nettie and my younger brother and sisters to take care of, was still struggling to make ends meet. I walked in the door and it was as if I had never left home.

My mother knew something was wrong. "I could tell just by the way you looked," she said. "When you came home after you won the *Arthur Godfrey's Talent Scouts*, you were so happy you burst out singing 'I'm Sitting on Top of the World.' This time you weren't singing. You didn't say a word."

I had left that house full of so much hope; I came back empty. Thinking about what my father would say when he found me there, I just flopped down on the sofa in the living room and stared into space.

"So?" my mother said.

"I'm home for good, Mom," I said finally. "That's it. I'm not singing anymore."

Mom looked at me. "You're not what?" she said.

"Two years, Mom. I've been knocking myself out for two years and I'm nowhere. You don't know what I've been through."

"I don't know?" she said. "I don't know about that place

43

where you lived with a pimp and the people were lying out on the pavement smoking marijuana? I don't know sometimes all you have to drink is a bottle of Coke, and a little box of crackers to eat? No money, no jobs. I know."

I shared only the good things that had happened to me with my family, and I wondered how Mom found out about Reefer Street. "Joey told Skipper Dawes and Mr. Dawes told me," she said. "My heart ached for you, Sonny Boy. But what could I do? I had nothing to give you, no money to send."

"It doesn't matter," I said. "It's over. I'm never going back to New York. I've had it. I'm not singing anymore."

"Oh, yes you are," she said.

"How? What can I do that I haven't already done? Just tell me how."

"Sonny Boy, you remember that man we met when your father and I went to see you at the Copacabana. Mr. Blackstone. I heard what he said to you that night. He said, 'Eddie, if you ever find yourself in a predicament or if you need somebody to talk to, come see me.'"

I tried to explain that Milton Blackstone had done everything he could for me. I didn't want to ask him for any more favors. But Mom kept after me, so I called him in New York and he said exactly what I expected him to say: "You're welcome to come up to Grossinger's for the summer, Eddie."

Grossinger's. I didn't want any part of it. Two summers there and nothing happened. Why put myself through that again?

Joanie was the only reason I decided to go back. I'd learned she was working in the chorus line at Young's Gap, a small resort hotel a couple of miles from Grossinger's. We had parted in anger after an argument about the older man she was seeing, Nat Brandwynne, the orchestra leader. Now I wanted to see her again, confident we could patch things up.

As soon as I got to Grossinger's I called her. She was very cool and said she couldn't get away because of rehearsals. But finally she came and we danced together that night in the Terrace Room. She was the most beautiful girl there, absolutely breathtaking, and I was so proud and happy with her in my arms. For those few moments at least, I forgot that all I had to give her were promises for the future even I didn't believe anymore. My illusions were gone. Singing no longer mattered. When the summer was over, there would be nothing to do but go back to Philadelphia and get that factory job my father was always talking about.

Eddie Cantor was scheduled to perform at Grossinger's on Labor Day weekend of 1949. Because of his great influence as an entertainer, every young singer dreamed of being "discovered" by Cantor. And as the weekend approached, I was no exception. Maybe I had a chance after all. Performing with Cantor would be a golden opportunity, far better than being on *Major Bowes and His Original Amateur Hour* or *Arthur Godfrey's Talent Scouts*. Deanna Durbin, Bobby Breen, and Dinah Shore were three stars who got their start that way. A nod from Cantor was not an automatic guarantee of success; you had to have talent. I knew I had that, but when I began to imagine I might become the latest of his discoveries, I reminded myself that just a few years ago in Philadelphia, Skipper Dawes had been unable to persuade Cantor even to listen to me sing. Why should it be any different now?

I underestimated Milton Blackstone's powers of persuasion. That weekend he literally begged Cantor to come to a band rehearsal to hear me. It was like pulling teeth. He came and didn't seem particularly impressed. But Milton persisted. He knew I was popular at Grossinger's; he knew what happened between me and the audiences there, and he was counting on that to impress Cantor.

I sang two songs in the show that night and the response was fantastic. The applause shook the rafters of the playhouse roof, and as the commotion finally died down, Cantor bounded on stage and said, "Believe me, ladies and gentlemen, this boy is really going to be something." For a moment I thought it was a kiss-off. He had let me sing as a favor to Milton Blackstone, and that was the end of it. But then he said, "I've heard many a crooner in my day, ladies and gentlemen, but this boy isn't a crooner, he's a singer. I want him to join my show on our cross-country tour. Is that okay, Eddie? And when we get to Los Angeles, I'm going to take you home to meet my five daughters."

The audience roared its approval, while I just stood there in shock, grinning from ear to ear. Eddie Cantor had indeed "discovered" me. He even thought I would be a good catch for one of his girls.

Several years later, someone wrote that Milton Blackstone

had rigged the audience's response that night. Members of the staff at Grossinger's were stationed throughout the playhouse and told to applaud wildly when I sang. I didn't want to believe it, but Joey Forman, who was there that night, said, "It's possible, Eddie. You know the way Milton did things. I saw him strolling around the grounds with Cantor, probably talking about you, and if he persuaded Cantor to let you sing in his show, do you think he would have left the rest to chance? Milton was a manipulator. He had an angle on everything."

Milton didn't operate that way. It wasn't necessary. That night the playhouse was jammed with so many paying customers, they had to stand in the aisles and even outside the doors, along the sides. The only room left for the staff was up in the back of the balcony where the spotlights were. If anything was rigged, the people in the audience did it themselves. They wanted Cantor to discover me as much as I did.

Just twenty-one when I went on tour with Cantor, I was still incredibly naive and idealistic about show businesss, even after my experiences in New York. I idolized Cantor. He was a legend, and part of that legend was his devotion to his wife, Ida, and their five daughters. I was deeply shocked to discover he had a mistress. I learned, too, from other members of the troupe, that Cantor had once had a longtime affair with the comedienne Joan Davis. Ida had been looking the other way for years. It was one of my first encounters with the legends versus the realities of show business, and it seemed to me that any performer, Eddie Cantor in particular, had an obligation to live up to the image he presented to the public.

I was also bewildered by Cantor's behavior on the tour. He was not always the happy-go-lucky man he appeared to be on stage. Demanding perfection, he was extremely tough on Cookie Fairchild, his conductor, and the other members of the troupe. Yet he was very kind to me. Once, as I was waiting, with an anxious look on my face, to go on stage, he said, "Don't worry, kid. After I introduce you, you can go out there and pee and they'll still love you." Cantor paid me five hundred dollars a week, which was a lot of money for someone who had been living on Coke and crackers, and he gave me clothes and an expensive wristwatch. But as a seasoned performer, a veteran, he was skeptical of a kid who had so little experience, no matter how talented he was.

The show toured several Eastern cities and I had to prove myself night after night until, finally, in Chicago, Cantor was convinced. There, after audiences had responded very enthusiastically to my performances, he offered to be my manager. And again I was puzzled. My opinion of managers and agents was not very high, and the picture of Cantor actually making money off his latest "discovery" didn't coincide with his image as the man who supported and encouraged young newcomers. I called Milton Blackstone to ask his advice and he said, "Don't sign anything. Just do what Cantor wants you to do, but don't sign anything."

I looked up Uncle Jack, my mother's brother, while we were in Chicago. The only member of the family who had been graduated from college, he was a left-winger and one night his son and daughter took me to a meeting to hear Paul Robeson speak. The place was so crowded that we had to sit on the stage, and suddenly Robeson entered from the rear of the auditorium, singing without a microphone, a handsome, powerful, dynamic man with an incredible voice. It was one of the most electrifying moments I had ever experienced and I couldn't wait to tell Cantor about it. He was horrified. "You went there, with those people?" he said incredulously. "Don't tell anybody, or your career is finished."

Cantor's reaction was, of course, typical of that time. My Uncle Jack had already lost his job in Washington for his left-wing affiliations. Robeson himself, in spite of his genius, was also vilified for his beliefs, and for me that was another lesson. It was becoming clear that a performer's politics, as well as his personal life, had to conform to his audiences' expectations or they could destroy his career. Image.

In Chicago, Cantor was in the process of negotiating a contract with the Bluebird label of RCA Victor Records. He came to me, threw his arm around my shoulder, and said, "I'm not signing unless they take you too." This time I wasn't suspicious of his motives. If he had overreacted by offering to be my manager, here was genuine proof of his generosity and faith in my talent. I auditioned for Bluebird and made my first solo record, "My Bolero," with "Foolish Tears" on the other side. The string section of the orchestra gave me a standing ovation, RCA Victor signed me to a contract, and naturally I thought the record would be an instant hit. But in the weeks that followed, it barely made a dent. I was so eager, so impatient. I knew I was going to make it someday—but when?

Our tour ended in Omaha, and Cantor took a plane to Los Angeles, leaving the rest of us to drive on to the West Coast in the car we had been traveling in, a Cadillac convertible. I had taken out a learner's permit for the tour and enjoyed doing some of the driving—until we got to Kearney, Nebraska. There I hit a soft shoulder on the road and when I jammed my foot on the brake, the car swerved to the other side and turned over in a ditch. Five of us were in the car—the writer Sid Fields, Cookie Fairchild and his wife, Vivian, Cantor's secretary, who also did comic bits with him on stage, and me—all upside down. Everybody was shaken up but no one was hurt. We scrambled out and I just walked away, laughing. I must have looked like a smart-ass, a cocky kid who thought it was funny to wreck a car and almost kill five people, including himself. It was nervous laughter. I was terrified of what Cantor would do to me. I'd heard him bawl out other people for the most trivial offenses. He would kill me for this.

I called him on the phone, told him what had happened, and waited for the explosion. There was a pause. "Well," he said finally, "it's a good thing nobody was hurt. Why don't you all stay overnight where you are and take the train in the morning? Don't worry about a thing." I hung up the phone with one more reason to be grateful to Eddie Cantor.

I fell in love with Hollywood, but not because it was the movie capital of the world. I knew I would live in a Beverly Hills mansion someday when I was a star. But now I would settle for a park bench if I could get a job singing on the radio. And strolling past the NBC and CBS studios where all the great comedy and variety shows were broadcast, I said to myself, "I'm here. I'm actually here." Cantor introduced me to Jack Benny, George Burns, Edgar Bergen, Bob Hope—the royalty of radio—and I was too awestruck to mutter more than a couple of words in their presence. I had no illusions about my own status. I was just another in a long line of Cantor protégés, some of whom had made it to the top, some of whom had not. From now on it would be up to me.

Cantor continued to be more than kind. I was booked to perform at the Orpheum Theater in Los Angeles and the Golden Gate Theater in San Francisco. And he made a record introducing me as "a new boy who is destined to become the most important singer of popular songs in America," which was played from the wings if he couldn't be there in person. He also found me a place to live in a small, inexpensive hotel in Brentwood and encouraged me to stay around to see what might develop with my career. His business manager paid me an allowance, which was less than the five hundred dollars a week I had received on tour, but enough for me to live comfortably and still send money home to my family.

I auditioned for shows on both NBC and CBS, but nothing clicked. When was it going to happen? I wanted to be another Bing Crosby—overnight. He was the master, whose great success was due as much to his personality as to his voice. Wise, friendly, funny, human, Crosby was another of my idols, different as we were. He was Catholic, I was a Jew; he was the Groaner, I pulled out all the stops. But I admired everything about him; to me he was living proof that even in the fiercely competitive world of show business, a nice guy can finish first.

I'll never forget the day I met Bing Crosby. I was having lunch with Eddie Cantor and some of his business associates at the Brown Derby when Lester Gottlieb, an executive with CBS who liked me and had tried unsuccessfully to get me a job with his network, came up to our table. "How would you like to meet Bing Crosby?" he said. "He's sitting right over there with some friends."

I almost fell through the floor. Of course I wanted to meet Bing Crosby. Gottlieb took me to his booth and said, "Bing, I'd like to introduce a new and up-and-coming young singer, Eddie Fisher." Crosby raised his eyes for just a second, said "Hello," then turned away and went right on talking to his friends.

That was it. No smile, no handshake, no acknowledgment that I was still standing there. I walked back to Cantor's booth completely disillusioned. Obviously I had expected too much of my idol, but he hadn't even taken the trouble to be polite. Later encounters with Crosby confirmed my first impression. He was a cold man—so cold, as someone said, that he pissed ice cubes. He himself told me that nothing had ever come before his career—not his wife, or his sons, or his friends; nothing. Here was another chasm between image and reality. Glimpsing that for just a moment in Bing Crosby at the Brown Derby, I wondered if it was true of every great performer.

Cantor, good as his word, invited me to his house for dinner one evening to meet his family. My usual shy and speechless self, I just sat there drinking it all in, a poor kid from Philadelphia actually having dinner in the home of Eddie Cantor. Yet I was disappointed again, because everything wasn't quite what I expected. Ida Cantor was a charming, dignified woman, but she and her husband didn't seem like a loving couple to me. As for the five famous daughters, they were attractive and very nice, but they weren't beautiful. And the house was just a house, not a castle. It didn't even have a swimming pool.

Why was I so reluctant to admit that Cantor was only an ordinary man, a human being, not a god? His study impressed me the most. There, lining the walls, were at least a hundred plaques commemorating his contributions to various charitable causes. Looking at those plaques, I vowed that when I became successful I would be as generous with my time and talent as Cantor had always been. But I wouldn't be a hypocrite; there would be no contradiction between my public image and my private life. I wouldn't put my career ahead of my family. When I was a star, I would keep the best of it and throw all the bad away. I honestly believed I was going to be perfect.

Years later, Cantor and I performed together, singing songs and doing old vaudeville routines. A man who could make people laugh and cry and love him, he had touched millions in his long career. I went to see him after he had a heart attack. He was dying and could barely speak. I had to do all the talking and I tried to express my gratitude for what he had done for me. He just took my hand, nodded, and smiled. Tears came into my eyes as I realized, at last, that if Eddie Cantor was not a god, he had always been a great entertainer, a great man. I was older and wiser then. At twenty-one, my head was full of schoolboy ideas. I still had a lot to learn about show business, about people. I still had a lot to learn about myself.

One evening, just walking the streets in Los Angeles, I passed a theater and recognized the name of the play on the marquee. I knew it was something about a prostitute and I walked quickly by. But then I turned back, intrigued, looked to see how much it cost, and bought a ticket. I was embarrassed as I went in; it was like going to a porno movie and I prayed nobody would see me, Eddie Cantor's protégé, the clean-cut kid destined to become the most important singer of popular songs in America, sneaking into a play about a prostitute.

I have completely forgotten the play, but I thought the woman who played the prostitute gave an excellent performance. When the curtain came down, I went backstage to congratulate her, telling myself it was a show business tradition; actually, I wanted to meet a person who dared play a role like that on stage. She was an older woman—thirty or so, which was older to me—and somehow I found the words to compliment her and tell her who I was. I was stunned when she asked me to have dinner with her. An actress of the legitimate theater wanted to have dinner with me!

She said she knew a restaurant at the beach; why didn't we have dinner there? What beach? I had been to Atlantic City and visions of a boardwalk and thousands of people went through my head. I drove her car and the beach wasn't like Atlantic City at all. It was beautiful, and the restaurant was small and quiet. I wasn't the greatest conversationalist in the world. She did most of the talking and after a while I realized she was making a pass. I was being seduced and it was very exciting. There was a wonderful place, she said, farther on up the coast near Carmel, a motel where we could spend the night. That scared me, but I didn't refuse to go.

We checked into the motel and that was the end of the polite conversation. She meant business and immediately took off all her clothes, expecting me to do the same. Embarrassed, I turned away from her and started to fumble with my trousers, thinking to myself, Why am I here? Why am I doing this? I had enough experience to know there was more to making love than just jumping into the sack with a complete stranger. The woman on the bed looked ugly to me now. I wanted to get out, to run away. But I stayed and it was all over in an instant.

The next day, we had breakfast and then lunch together. We walked around the little shops in Carmel and I bought her a few inexpensive things, trying to be a gentleman, but all I could think of was what had happened the night before. Why had I done something I didn't really want to do? Was it just sex, or something more than that? Whatever the reason, I was deeply disappointed in myself, and even though I knew it wasn't her fault, once we drove back to Los Angeles I couldn't wait to get that woman out of my life.

I wasn't perfect after all, and never would be. But remembering my mother's words, I still wanted to be a good person, in public and private. And I thought then that there would be no conflict between those two parts of my life. I had yet to find out how difficult it is for any performer to live up to his public image—how much more difficult it would be to live up to my image of myself.

5

Los Angeles was another dead end. I loved the city, loved gawking at celebrities, but I felt like a tourist, a spectator. The doors I wanted to open just wouldn't budge, even if I was Eddie Cantor's latest discovery. Singing in nightclubs and theaters seemed to be the only thing left for me, which meant New York, and I was reluctant to go back. My memories of that town were not particularly happy. But Joey and all my other friends were still in New York. At least we could starve together. Joanie was there too. And so was Milton Blackstone.

If I made a nuisance of myself hanging around the Blackstone Agency, Milton didn't appear to mind. He was one of the kindest men I had ever met. And the wisest. It's tempting to think I knew he would be the key to my eventual success. I didn't have that kind of foresight. In fact, I already had a deep distrust of theatrical agents and managers; to me they were the epitome of bloodsuckers and flesh peddlers. But I had an instinct about Milton; an inner voice told me he was above all that. He was interested in me, not the money I might make for him. Because I was somehow certain he was the one man who could help me, I continued to beg him to be my manager, and he continued to refuse until I suggested he give me just one day out of his busy week. Maybe it was my eagerness and determination that won him over, or maybe he could see into the future. "Okay, Eddie," he said finally. "One day a week, and we'll see what happens."

There was no mention of money, no contract; just a handshake. Milton knew I had talent and was putting me to some kind of test. And at first the jobs were few and far between: a week in some small New York club like the Bagatelle, a weekend at the Blackamoor Room in Miami where I was on the bill with Harry the Hipster and stood on the bar to sing. I was always available on short notice for a benefit, any benefit. Milton invested thousands in my career and wrote me one-hundred or two-hundred-dollar checks out of his own pocket. I never kept track of how much I made, or how much Milton gave me. I picked up my New York life just exactly where I'd left it off, moving from one hotel to another, usually with Joey or Bernie in tow, hanging around with other singing hopefuls like Guy Mitchell and Al Martino—all of us still scratching, still waiting for that one big break.

Ironically, my big break was already in my pocket—my recording contract with RCA Victor. Even if the sales of my first record were less than spectacular, everyone was impressed by the way I sounded. The big voice was beginning to replace the big band as the dominant sound in popular music. The crooners—Crosby, Como and Sinatra—were still enormously popular. But teenagers were looking for something different, new idols and a new kind of music they could call their own. Johnnie Ray, Tony Bennett, and Frankie Laine were at the top of the pop music charts, and RCA Victor decided to take a chance on Eddie Fisher. In quick succession I cut two more singles for Bluebird, which did well enough so that when that label was discontinued, I was the only performer transferred to the Black label. Three more singles followed, each climbing a little bit higher on the charts but falling short of the "Top 50," which would qualify it as a hit. Then I recorded "Thinking of You," without much hope that it would become a hit either. Guy Mitchell had recorded the same song for Columbia, it was doing well, and my version was intended as a "cover"—just to pick up any left-over sales. Everyone hoped, including me, that my next record would be the one to make it. We didn't have to wait.

Things started to happen all at once in the spring of 1950,

beginning with one of those unpredictable last-minute substitutions that occur so often in show business careers they have become a cliché. I got an urgent call to come to Milton's office. "Eddie," he said, "how would you like to sing at the Riviera?"

Bill Miller's Riviera, a popular nightclub across the George Washington Bridge in Fort Lee, New Jersey, was a world above any place I'd played recently. Next to the Copa, it was the best. "You're kidding," I said. "When do I start?"

"Tomorrow night."

I stared at Milton in disbelief.

"I know it's short notice, Eddie, but Fran Warren is sick. She can't sing, and I told Miller you just happen to be available."

"How can I be ready in time?"

"You've got to be," Milton said. "You know who's opening there tomorrow night? Danny Thomas. This isn't a one-night stand, Eddie. This is a two-week engagement with Danny Thomas, one of the biggest draws in the business. Reviewers from every paper in town will be there."

That wasn't very reassuring. So far New York reviewers hadn't paid much attention to me. I agreed to go on, but I was scared. And skeptical. How many times had I been on the threshold of something big, only to have it fizzle out? Still, hope dies hard; this time, I thought, maybe something really will happen.

Joey and Bernie were just as excited as I was, racing around New York the next day to buy me a new tux and have it fitted. I wanted Joanie in the audience that night to give me moral support, and I called all over town but couldn't find her. By the time I got to the Riviera, I had about one hour, amid the usual chaos and confusion of an opening night, to run over my music with the conductor, figure out my entrances and exits, work with the lighting and sound men. It was hopeless, so when I heard the introductory bars of my first number, I did what I always did—just walked out on stage and sang.

The Riviera was a spectacular club. The roof was open to the stars and the lights of the George Washington Bridge and Manhattan twinkled in the distance. The place was packed, but I wasn't aware of the lights or the people or anything else. I was in a kind of trance until the end of my first song, when a great burst of applause jolted me back to reality. I couldn't believe my ears. These people were here to see Danny Thomas, not me. The response to my second song was even more enthusiastic, and the third.

The audience wouldn't let me off the stage. I sang every song I knew, and still the audience wanted more. I remembered a song I had just recorded, "Where in the World." The orchestra didn't have an arrangement, so I sang it a cappella. It was not a very good song, and singing without even a piano to back me up could be ridiculously unprofessional. But I followed my instincts and somehow it worked. It brought the house down. Like the audiences at Grossinger's, the people weren't merely applauding me; they were rooting for me.

Danny Thomas was waiting impatiently in the wings for all the commotion to die down so he could begin his act. When I finally walked off stage, he gave me a sour look and said, "Take it easy, kid." But even that little bit of professional jealousy couldn't dampen my spirits. I started dancing around like a lunatic, hugging everybody, phoning all my friends.

It was about four in the morning before I found Joanie, and I was still flying high. "I was terrific!" I yelled into the phone. "I stole the show from Danny Thomas." On and on I went, telling her how marvelous I was, until she promised to come to my next performance. I invited Guy Mitchell too, and he and Joanie sat together in the audience.

I thought I was terrible that night, just awful. The magic of the night before wasn't there, and I was almost sick about it. "Eddie, you know the second night is always a letdown after an opening," Joanie told me. "Besides, you weren't terrible. You were wonderful."

I didn't believe her, positive I was in for another slide into obscurity. The Copa, Grossinger's, and now the Riviera. Fortunately the reviewer agreed with Joanie. *The New York Times* said I had a "sensational singing voice and style." *Variety* called me "really one of the fine young singers to carve a niche for himself in the swooner sweepstakes." *Time* magazine ran a short piece about me. I carried those reviews around in my pocket long after my two weeks at the Riviera were over.

To my even greater surprise, my version of "Thinking of You" began to outsell Guy's and suddenly my name appeared on *Billboard's* chart of best-selling records. "Thinking of You" was listed forty-eight out of fifty, but it was a hit! I rushed out and bought copies of the paper for all my friends. The song was played everywhere the summer of 1950, and I would stop dead in my tracks to listen to my own voice coming from a radio or a jukebox, or blaring from the record stores along Broadway.

The Eddie Fisher "sound" was beginning to catch on, and more than anyone else, Hugo Winterhalter was the man responsible for that sound. He chose all the songs I had recorded so far, made the arrangements, conducted the orchestra, and produced the records. Our recording sessions were held in a big, musty old studio in Webster Hall, on East Eleventh Street. I still couldn't pick up a piece of music and sing it on sight. Hugo went through every song with me, and we rehearsed it over and over again until we got what we wanted. Hugo was above all a musician, and in our early recordings he used French horns, cellos, violins, with my voice soaring over a full orchestra. The words of the song didn't particularly matter, just the music, and as a result my first solo records—and even many of my later hits—never really became pop standards. The way a song was arranged was always more important to Hugo than anything it had to say, and that proved to be both an advantage and a disadvantage in my career. Together Hugo and I created a recording style that was both distinctive and exciting, but it was done with a disembodied voice, a musical instrument. It would be up to me alone to find a way to express the personality, so important in live performances, that would be uniquely my own.

Hugo and I remained professional associates for several years, and friends for many years after that. I loved the man. He was so serious and dignified that it was a challenge to make him smile, but if you could get him to laugh, tears came to his eyes. He gave so much of himself and his talent to me and the other recording artists on the RCA Victor roster, like Perry Como, Tony Martin, and Dinah Shore, that he left a permanent stamp on the music of the 1950s. Inevitably, styles and tastes began to change, and Hugo's contribution was all but forgotten. When he lost his son in Vietnam, I think he also lost his will to live. I had met the boy only a few weeks before, on a tour to entertain troops, and Hugo asked me to go to his funeral. The next time I saw him, he had become an old man, a broken man. We were reminiscing about the long string of hits and personal appearances we had made over the years and Hugo said, "It's about time you and I got together again, Eddie." I thought it was a marvelous idea. But we were never reunited. He was making plans for a tour when he died.

RCA Victor moved quickly to capitalize on the success of "Thinking of You," which had soared to the number one spot on many lists. Hugo and I recorded "Turn Back the Hands of Time" and "Bring Back the Thrill," both of which had an almost identical Fisher-Winterhalter sound, and both of which went to the top of the charts. There were others, and at one point in late 1950 and early 1951, I had three or four best-sellers. That was like having your name up in neon lights. It was called saturation, and it meant I had become not only a top recording artist but a very valuable property. My contract with RCA Victor provided for the 5 percent royalty on the sale of each record that was standard for beginners—with all the production costs deducted from my earnings—so I had never made much money on my early recordings. Now I was growing rich. And I was in demand everywhere. Milton persuaded Tom Rockwell, head of General Artists Corporation and Perry Como's agent, to handle me, and I sang in theaters and night-clubs from New York to Los Angeles. Monte Proser, who had finally been induced to sell the Copacabana, had opened two new clubs in New York: La Vie en Rose and the Cafe Theater. I packed the Cafe Theater for several weeks and just stood up and sang at La Vie en Rose whenever I happened to be there. But obviously my only appeal was not to older, well-heeled nightclub audiences. It was the teenagers, the bobby-soxers, who were saving their allowances to buy my records and were clamoring to see me in person. Realizing that, Milton made a shrewd decision.

"Eddie, I've booked you at the Paramount," he said.

Shocked at first, I saw myself standing in front of that dusty old curtain again, with George Wright drowning me out on the organ and the audience throwing pennies. "Oh, no," I said "I don't care what they pay me."

"As a matter of fact," Milton said, "they're paying you five thousand dollars a week. And you won't be the intermission singer, Eddie. You're the star."

I wasn't *the* star. The Mills Brothers headed the bill. But the day I opened at the Paramount, my dreams of following in Frank Sinatra's footsteps, as crazy and unattainable as they had always seemed to everyone but me, came true. All of them—my name in big letters on the marquee, my picture on the posters, teenagers behind barricades in Times Square waiting to get in, fans screaming and swooning in the aisles, autograph hounds thrusting matchbooks or bits of paper at me to sign, mobs of people at the stage door clamoring to see me, touch me. The same scene was repeated day after day, all day and into the night. One of my friends got out of the subway at Times Square and thought there had been some kind of major disaster. It was exciting and it was frightening. Once, as the moving stage descended at the end of one of my performances, a girl leaped out of the audience, grabbed my jacket, and ripped the whole back off. Another time, mounted police were trying to hold back the crowd as I came out the stage door, and I was almost trampled by the horses.

I had been recognized often in public, ever since I started singing on the radio in Philadelphia, and even later in New York. But this was something different. When anyone spotted me on the street, the cry went up and I was mobbed instantly. If I enjoyed it at first, I quickly grew very apprehensive, always glancing out of the corner of my eye, waiting for someone to start screaming, and planning a way to escape. I can remember waving out a fourth- or fifth-floor window of the Paramount and watching all the people on the street below crying, yelling, going crazy. I loved it. And I was exhilarated by their screams and sighs during my performances. I could overcome my shyness and stage fright when they were at a distance. But when that distance was eliminated, I became even shyer than usual, and often terrified that I would find myself in a situation beyond my control. The experience was overwhelming, overpowering. I was like a kid on a roller coaster, my emotions swooping up and down from sheer joy to near panic.

It was Milton who directed the course of that crazy ride from the very beginning. Milton who created order out of the chaos that erupted almost overnight in my life. He was not a dazzling showman but he was a great innovator. He wanted my career to be built on a solid foundation. Howard Eisenberg, who worked at the Blackstone Agency as a press agent for Grossinger's, became my press agent, scheduling interviews, writing publicity releases, traveling with me wherever I went. The first fan mail I got in any significant quantity came with the success of "Thinking of You," and the Blackstone Agency took on the job of handling that too. Originally Milton used volunteers, young fans, to answer letters and requests, send out autographed pictures, and write thank you notes. One of them, Arlene Scharaga, was sixteen when she came to the agency, and as Eddie Fisher fan clubs began to emerge spontaneously all across the country, she persuaded Milton to hire her full-time to organize and charter them. Nothing was more important, Milton told me, than making my fans happy, meeting them in person, smiling, chatting, posing for pictures, signing autographs. So I did it, and really wanted to do it, even though the adulation of teenage girls made me a little uncomfortable.

Selling my records was also a responsibility I couldn't ignore. One hit can be largely a matter of luck, but after a whole string of them, and with the Blackstone agency and RCA Victor behind me, I was swept up in a whirlwind of newspaper, magazine, and radio interviews, my picture began to appear in the papers and my name in the gossip columns, all in the name of publicity. That's the way it was done. Only a recording session, a rehearsal, or an actual performance took precedence over the business of keeping my name and face in the public eye. I sang "Thinking of You" in my first appearance on Ed Sullivan's new variety show, *The Toast of the Town*. And I performed my hits on stage, of course, but I was also sent out to plug them on radio shows all over the country. A disc jockey could make or break a record just by the frequency with which he played it. People had to hear a song and like it before they started feeding nickels into jukeboxes and buying the record. So disc jockeys were among the most important men in the business, and the most ardently courted. Personal gifts and favors, and large sums of money—payola—sometimes changed hands, but in my case, as far as I knew, I was the only payola. I appeared on Martin Block's *Make-Believe Ballroom*, and spent all day with Jack Clayton in Boston, Brad Phillips in New York, Dick Clark in Philadelphia, Johnny Grant in Los Angeles, and Ed McKenzie, known as "Jack the Bellboy," in Detroit, talking and answering questions about myself between records. Other recording artists did the same thing, but I always tried to do just a little bit more.

I felt much more comfortable behind a microphone in a radio station than I did in front of a huge audience or in the middle of a mob. And the contrast between my speaking voice, which was soft and tinged with a South Philadelphia accent, and the big, booming voice on my records always came as a surprise. I went everywhere, did everything that Milton and RCA Victor asked me to do. And gladly. I was told that Mario Lanza, who also recorded for RCA Victor and was then at the height of his popularity, had refused to make appearances with disc jockeys. In retaliation they stopped playing his records and sales began to drop. That would never happen to me. I was eager to please everybody, from the chairman of the board of RCA Victor right down to the kid who asked me to autograph a candy wrapper. And it seemed to be paying off.

At twenty-two years old, I was a "star." And even though I had worked for it for years, made solemn resolutions about how I would behave when it happened, it hit me with such bewildering rapidity that there was no time, no thought, to be anyone other than just myself. It has been said that Milton Blackstone "created" Eddie Fisher, the shy, likable kid from Philadelphia, the boy next door whom any mother would be glad to have her daughter marry. That was the image beginning to emerge in the publicity and all the stories written about me, but it wasn't the invention of some promotional genius, Milton or anyone else. I wasn't playing a part. That was me. What Milton did was sell me to the public, and at this stage in my career, when image and reality were one and the same, he managed me brilliantly.

If Milton's primary object was to promote my career, he also seemed anxious to protect me and shield me from the crass world of show business. "Be like Rocky Marciano," he said to me. "Go out there and knock 'em dead. I'll take care of all the rest." We seldom talked about money, contracts, deals; most of our discussions were about what I had to do to live up to my image: how to dress, how to behave. But Milton never said do this or don't do that; his advice was always offered politely, with a smile. I worshiped the man, listened to his every word, followed his advice to the letter. At his suggestion, I went to one of the best dentists in New York and began the long and expensive process of having my teeth capped. He reminded me to be respectful to everyone, including stagehands and waiters in restaurants, but above all else the public. Milton's god was public opinion, and although he never said it to me in so many words, his motto might have been: "Be what the people want you to be."

It wasn't hard. I had a big smile, a kind of awkward, boyish charm. I was a good listener; I made friends easily and had a humility and modesty that were totally genuine. My background in the slums of Philadelphia, my lack of even a high school education, were too fresh in my mind for me to move with self-assurance, let alone arrogance, in the stratosphere of stardom. If it's true, as has often been said, that nothing about me, except my voice, ever really belonged in show business, it was because in Milton Blackstone I found a combination of my father and my mother—a father who had once said to me, "Just sing," and a mother whose greatest wish was for me to be a good boy. Milton asked nothing more of me—just sing and be a good boy; he would take care of everything else. He did, and I was more than willing to let him do it. In the excitement of having everything I had always wanted, I never stopped to think that I couldn't remain a boy forever.

It took only eight months, from my engagement at the Riviera to my opening at the Paramount, for my life to change completely. And with Milton in the background, smiling his approval, or shaking his head in disapproval, those changes were always measured against my boy-next-door image. I said goodbye to Broadway drugstores and Automats and ate only in the popular theatrical restaurants—Lindy's, Sardi's, Toots Shor's, Lüchow's, "21"—where I sat and listened deferentially to the show business greats who hung out at them. I was hot at the moment, but Milton was smart enough to know that if my popularity was going to last, I would have to find acceptance in that elite fraternity. He also saw to it that I was available—for nothing—for benefits and testimonials. But again I wasn't playing a part. I genuinely admired these men, particularly the work they did for their favorite charities. I wanted to be like them and wanted them to like me. I wouldn't be some snot-nosed kid spoiled by sudden success.

I didn't regret leaving the cheap hotels I had been living in for years. I moved into a small suite at the Park Sheraton Hotel, a suitably modest step, so Milton thought, and my friends came with me. If they didn't actually live there, someone was usually sleeping in the guest room or on a couch. Milton didn't approve. He had a million friends, but essentially he was a loner who had built a wall around himself. I couldn't live like that. I had to have people around—old friends like Joey and Bernie, Al Martino, Guy Mitchell, Bob Manning, who also wanted to be a singer, and all the new friends I was making. Surrounding myself with people probably reflected my own insecurity, but I didn't think I was buying their friendship. Of course I paid the bills; I was the only one who had any money.

Besides, I could afford to do anything I wanted. I was rich. I didn't know how rich, and didn't really care. As eager as I had always been for success, it was recognition, not money, I really wanted. And now that I had reached my goal, money just seemed to be a natural part of it, unimportant, almost dirty. I thought I had higher concerns. So once again I let Milton handle everything. He continued to give me pocket money— only the checks were larger now—he paid my bills, sent money to my parents, opened bank accounts. No one was more surprised than I was when a headline in *Variety* announced that in one brief period I earned $365,000 in record royalties alone.

Milton was very sparing in his comments about the way I began to spend my money, thinking perhaps that a little extravagance wouldn't tarnish my image—or hoping that, like a kid in a candy store, I would eventually get my fill. I didn't. After so many years without a dime, I relished the security, the power, of spending money—a lot of it. That's what it was for. The more there was, the more there was to spend, and I thought there would always be an endless supply.

The number of available girls was suddenly endless too— overwhelming—but Milton had quite a few suggestions to offer in that department. "Eddie, could I see you for a minute?" he said one day, beckoning me into his office. He was nervous about something as he sat down behind his desk. "Hmm," he began. "I really don't know how to put this. You're a normal, healthy boy, Eddie, with normal, healthy desires, but what I want to say is, well . . ."

I saw what he was driving at and was a little amused. That was one thing I thought Milton didn't know much about. But I respected him too much ever to make fun of him. "You mean girls," I said solemnly.

"Well, yes, girls. There are certain girls in this town who like nothing better than hitching their wagons to a star. Well, you know the kind I mean. They'll do anything to be seen with you, have their pictures taken and their names mentioned in the columns. That may be good publicity for them, Eddie, but it's terrible publicity for you. Your fans don't like it. You're a nice boy, and I'd like to see you go out with nice girls."

The only really nice girl I knew was Joanie and we were

drifting apart. It was my fault. We had talked about marriage all the years we had been going together, with the understanding that my career came first. Now I think Joanie was waiting for me to propose, but once success hit, real success, marriage was the farthest thing from my mind. I remembered Eddie Cantor telling me that when you're in show business you're already married. And there was always Milton in the background to discourage any such idea; marriage, no matter how nice the girl was, would be disastrous for my image. Beyond all that, I was selfish. I enjoyed my new celebrity and freedom too much to give them up. Joanie was happy that I finally had what I wanted, but it wasn't really what she wanted for herself: a home, a husband, children, a quiet, normal family life— ironically, the very things I couldn't give her now. In many ways, she understood me better than I understood myself, and I will always think of Joanie with gratitude and love, glad that she, too, eventually found what she was looking for.

Milton's warnings about star-hitchers came too late. Even before my opening at the Paramount, I had met a show girl in the chorus line of the Cafe Theater. Her name was Joan Olander, a beautiful blond Southern belle who, I was told, had been married at fifteen and was now being seen around town with Jack Dempsey. I was very flattered when she showed an interest in me, and we started going out together. Never a movie or a quiet restaurant; our dates were always a production—the most expensive and popular places in town, with Joan, provocatively dressed, hanging on my arm, smiling and waving to make sure she was seen. After a while I stopped taking her out. When we met again, some time later, her name was Mamie Van Doren and she invited me to a big Hollywood party at the Mocambo. She was still up to her old tricks. *Life* was doing a story on her and there were photographers all over the place, but I refused to let them take my picture with her. "I'm going to get you for this," she said furiously, "if it's the last thing I do." I offered to drive her home, but she wouldn't wait for my car. With a remark very similar to what Tootsie Stern once told me to do, she walked out and took a taxi.

I couldn't help being attracted to beautiful women, almost always women who were not Jewish, because they were forbidden. And I was excited when they responded to me, whatever their motives. Going out with a pretty shiksa, going to bed with her, was like spending a lot of money—a way of proving I was no longer a poor Jew from the slums of Philadelphia. I was somebody. Yet I had sense enough to know that mere physical release proves nothing, and once it was over I was always sorry and disappointed. I was looking for something more—an intimacy, a sharing, a relationship. Paradoxically, my celebrity made sex too easily available, and the kind of relationship I wanted almost impossible to find.

There were, however, other aspects of being famous that I found totally gratifying. One was a trip to Grossinger's that I can describe only as a triumphal return. I was welcomed as a conquering hero, the kid who had started out singing with the band and had risen to become a star. Jennie Grossinger was especially warm and affectionate, as proud of me as if she were my mother, and proud that Grossinger's had been part of my success. She was a wonderful woman—a lady—simple, dignified. She never forgot a name or a face, never uttered an angry word to anyone. I grew to love her very much.

It was a novelty to be given one of the best suites and treated like royalty at a place where I had once slept under the playhouse and stolen chicken from the staff dining room. If Milton thought it was past my bedtime, he didn't say so. I was a big boy now, meeting as an equal men I had hardly dared speak to before. One of them was John Garfield, an idol of mine since childhood. I had seen him at Grossinger's before. Following him around at a discreet distance, I watched him pinch girls' asses and once heard him say to a waitress, "Hey, sweetheart, you want to fuck?" Another idol shattered. But when we finally met and I heard him talk, my admiration returned. He was dressed in a white shirt open at the neck and even with a cigarette dangling from his mouth, the sound of his voice was poetic. That's the way I'd like to look, I thought, the way I'd like to talk. I could identify with Garfield because he, too, was a poor Jewish boy—his real name was Julie Garfinkle—who had made good. But there was another thing about him I wanted to emulate: his honesty. Whatever else he may have been, he was not a phony, and people accepted him for himself.

If anything could compare to my reception at Grossinger's, it was my return in March 1951 to my old high school in Philadelphia to celebrate "Eddie Fisher Day." I should have been embarrassed by the whole idea, but I wasn't. Who hasn't had a fantasy like that? I had been the smallest kid at school; now the kids sitting in the auditorium looked like they were in kindergarten and I was a giant. And I had a special reason for wanting to be there—Dr. Jay Speck, the music teacher who once told me I would never have a career as a singer. When my voice changed, he said, I'd be finished. He was a little fellow, like a penguin, and that day he was sitting on the stage with the principal and some of my other teachers. When I sang, I really let him have it, full volume.

My parents still lived in the same little house near the school. They had become celebrities too; photographers took their pictures, reporters asked them for interviews. My mother loved it; she was always happy to talk about her Sonny Boy, embellishing stories of my childhood each time she told them. But my success never went to her head, even when the name of a street near their house was changed to Eddie Fisher Street. As for my father, he boasted about me to his friends, but I think he had a secret suspicion that the whole thing was a fluke. Someday the bubble would burst and we would all be right back where we started.

How could it ever end? My records were selling by the millions; hailed as the biggest sensation since Sinatra, I was singing five shows a day to capacity crowds at the Paramount. But the bubble did burst; my roller coaster ride came to a sudden jolting halt. Overnight, Eddie Fisher, the idol of a million teenagers, became Private Edwin Jack Fisher of the United States Army.

6

"**I** know how you feel, Eddie, but it's something you've got to do," Milton said. "I'll take care of business here, and if you're the boy I think you are, everything will work out fine."

I didn't want to go into the army. Who did? Right up until the day I was sworn in on Whitehall Street, I thought, This can't be happening to me. I was a star. Besides, it just wasn't fair to snatch away everything I had worked so hard to get. Two years is a long time and I was afraid people would forget all about me. Yet in a funny way I wished they would forget. Just let me do what I had to do without any fanfare. It was not to be. The day of my induction, the headlines read "Eddie Fisher Goes to War," and when I reported to Fort Devens, Massachusetts, a pack of reporters and photographers were on hand for the ritual haircut. Some of the other draftees swept up the clippings and mailed them to their girl friends.

Things were better as soon as I got to Fort Hood, Texas, for basic training. The army is a great equalizer. Assigned to a barracks with guys from the Deep South who had never heard of me, I felt more uncomfortable as the only Jew than as a celebrity—until I started getting phone calls from Milton. "Private Eddie Fisher, report to the orderly room!" the loud-speakers blared. "Will you please not call me quite so often,"

I asked Milton. "It's very embarrassing." Then the fan mail began to arrive, potato sacks full of thousands of letters every week. The other guys didn't understand what was going on, so I decided to let them read the letters. They went crazy, with hoots of laughter and a lot of wisecracks, but behind the Southern drawls and mean looks, there was a certain amount of admiration. A few of the guys pulled letters out of the pile and began corresponding with my fans.

Eventually everybody knew who I was, officers and enlisted men alike, and everybody was watching me, a tough and awkward situation to be in. I couldn't goof off, even though most of the other guys did. I had to be a good soldier just to prove I was no better than anyone else. On KP I usually got the grease pits, but I did what I was supposed to do—with one exception. During grenade training, the instructor told us to pull the pin and count three before we threw it. I thought he was nuts. When he handed me a grenade, I didn't count anything. I just pulled the pin and got rid of it. I was certain my gas mask was going to leak, and I wasn't too happy about the infiltration course either, crawling on my belly under tangles of barbed wire with machine gun fire whistling over my head. We had to get up at 4 A.M. for our first fourteen-mile hike. It was freezing, so I put on long johns under my fatigues, shouldered my rifle and a full field pack, and off we went. By afternoon the temperature was up to at least 105 degrees; half the guys had dropped out and were being taken back by truck. Not me. I was exhausted and miserable, but I couldn't quit. I was the last one to stagger in, all alone, my fatigues crusted white with dried sweat. The whole company was there waiting for me, cheering me on. I made it!

"Eddie, it's all set," Milton reported in one of his phone calls from New York. "I had to pull a few strings, but you're going to be assigned to the army band as a soloist for the rest of your tour of duty."

Was nothing, not even the United States Army, beyond Milton's power? Pulled out of basic training a week before completing the course, I was sent to Washington, D.C., relieved, naturally, not to be going to Korea. But I could see resentment in the eyes of the men in my company who were. After knocking myself out to gain their respect, I was hurt to lose it because I was being given special treatment. But the army wanted me to be a singer, not a soldier, and I suppose that made a certain amount of sense. Singing was the thing I did best. Later in the 1950s, Elvis Presley was drafted into the army with a lot more hoopla than I'd received, then spent the next two years driving a truck in Germany. Even when generals asked him to sing, his manager, Colonel Parker, later told me, "I said, 'Sure, but it'll cost you fifty thousand dollars.'" Presley was probably a very good truckdriver, but it wasn't what he did best.

Milton's only advice to me was: "Be a good boy, Eddie. Do what they tell you to do. Cooperate." What he meant, of course, was "Don't act like a star," and I tried to follow his advice. When I reported for my new assignment at U.S. Army Band headquarters at Fort Myer, Virginia, and discovered that band members were not required to live on post, I rented a small one-bedroom apartment at the Dorchester in Washington. I drove back and forth in a little khaki-colored Ford which Milton bought and urged me to use, with the reminder that Vic Damone got himself in trouble in the army by driving a big Cadillac convertible and parking it in spaces reserved for generals. Gone were the days of spending money like water. My army pay went into insurance and savings, and I lived on a small monthly allowance from Milton. My one extravagance was having uniforms custom tailored in New York by the man who made General Eisenhower's uniforms. But there was no way to become completely anonymous, no way to escape reporters and photographers, or the people who insisted on treating me like a star. I was assigned to the army band precisely because I was a popular entertainer, and it wasn't always easy to walk the fine line between Eddie Fisher the celebrity and Eddie Fisher the army private.

I couldn't have spent more than three or four nights in my Washington apartment. I was traveling with the army band or appearing on radio and television shows on behalf of army or air force recruiting. I sang everywhere. At one performance for patients at Walter Reed Hospital, I met a pretty little Hollywood starlet named Debbie Reynolds. Standing with me in the wings watching her perform, her mother whispered in my ear, "Isn't she wonderful? Debbie can do anything." Audiences for regular Friday night concerts on the Capitol steps grew from the usual crowd of a few hundred to a few thousand after I started singing with the band. And at a Fourth of July concert given by all the service bands in front of the Washington Monument, I sang for more than a quarter of a million people. My fears of being forgotten were obviously groundless. I was getting more publicity and exposure than ever before.

Not all the publicity was good, however. How is it, some people asked, that Eddie Fisher, who is supposed to be serving his country, has a new record out almost every month? The answer was simple. As my commanding officer, Major Hugh Curry, told me, "What you do on your own time is none of our business, Eddie, just as long as you don't disgrace the army or your uniform." Like any other soldier, I had occasional off-duty weekends and leaves, and went to New York for recording sessions. I could cut as many as three or four songs in a three-hour session, and the records were released at a later date.

I don't know how many songs I recorded for RCA Victor while I was in the army, but almost all of them were hits. When I first heard the music for "Wish You Were Here," the title song of a Broadway show, I hated it. The record became a best-seller and was credited with saving the show. I picked "Lady of Spain" myself after I saw the music lying on the piano at one of our recording sessions and asked Hugo Winterhalter if we could do it. The lyrics were corny and the song was old, but it was perfect for my voice. I could really belt it out, and with one of Hugo's extraordinary arrangements, it too became a hit. And with "Anytime," I had my first million-seller—a gold record. I remember driving one day through Washington in my little khaki Ford, twirling the dial on the radio. "Anytime" was playing on three different stations, and letting out a yell, I almost drove the car right up on the sidewalk.

My father paid me a visit one weekend in New York. A crisis in my family was coming to a head. While I was still in Texas, my mother had written to tell me that she had finally decided to do what she'd threatened to do for years: divorce my father. Shattered, I called her on the phone and said, "Mom, you can't do this. The king and queen of England can get a divorce but not my family, not my mother and father."

"Sonny Boy," she said, "this has nothing to do with kings and queens. It's between your father and me. So don't worry, and save your money on long distance. I've made up my mind."

I went to see her the first chance I got, hoping to talk her out of it. She was living with my sister Miriam and her husband in Baltimore, which was one reason she had left my father: for the first time in her life she had someplace else to go. I begged her to change her mind, but she said, "Think about what you're asking, Sonny Boy. I should stay with that man for the rest of my life? Enough. I've always said I'd go when my children were grown up. Now is the time."

"Eileen is only twelve," I said.

"Twelve is old enough to understand."

"What about Nettie? Who'll take care of Nettie?"

"Who always takes care of Nettie?" Mom said. "She goes wherever I go."

Now my father had come to plead his case. He paced around my hotel room, shouting, shaking his fist in anger, crying, "Sonny Boy, you've got to talk to her. She can't do this to me. I won't let her. My whole life I've given to that woman, and this is my reward. I love her. I can't live without her. You've got to do something."

He was a broken man, and even though I could never forget, or forgive, the way he had treated my mother, I felt sorry for him. I decided I could bring them back together by buying them a new house, a car, sending them more money. Maybe if my father didn't have to work, if my mother didn't have to worry, everything would be all right. But there was no love left between them. My mother went ahead with the divorce and later married Max Stupp, my father's best friend. He was a kind and gentle man, and they had fourteen good years together before he died.

Not long after the divorce, my father started seeing another woman and eventually they married. She loved him, but I wondered if anyone could have made my father happy.

Around Christmas of 1951, after completing a tour of army camps all along the Eastern Seaboard from New England to Florida, I ended up in Palm Beach with a few free days on my hands. Mike Todd was there, divorced the year before from his wife Joan Blondell, alone and looking for excitement. At Milton's suggestion I gave him a call, we met, and this time he didn't tell me to come back when I'd grown up. He virtually adopted me. We drove back and forth to Miami and went everywhere together—restaurants, parties, the beach. Once we walked into a nightclub and Mike said at the top of his voice, "Make way, ladies and gentlemen, make way for Eddie Fisher." On the beach, he made me stand on a pile of sand and sing while he strode around and shouted, "Step right up, ladies and gentlemen, and hear the one and only, the great Eddie Fisher." I was embarrassed, fascinated, flattered, and finally overwhelmed.

With Mike, there was always *tummel,* always action. Part huckster, part magician, he was above all a showman. Everything he did was a production: his Broadway musicals, his marriages, his friendships, his life. He was then in his forties, with dark piercing eyes and a jutting jaw, not much taller than I was, forever brandishing or chewing on a cigar. The direct opposite of the solemn and cautious Milton Blackstone, Mike was flamboyant, impetuous, and totally unconventional, a combination of chutzpah and pure genius. He was broke when we met, but as he said, "You're not rich unless you owe at least a million." Rich or poor, his extravagant life style never changed. He had already made and lost several fortunes, and his brain was always teeming with ideas to make another. At the moment, he was planning to revolutionize the entertainment industry with Cinerama, Todd-AO, Cinestage, and something he called "Smell-O-Vision."

I soon discovered that Mike's tough-guy behavior was a pose. He was a very gentle and sensitive man. But he never hesitated to say just exactly what he thought. I loved the way Mike treated people. He worshiped talent and detested pretension. Women were attracted to him on sight, but he could dismiss a Palm Beach socialite with a vulgar remark and make a streetwalker feel like a queen. He treated me like a buddy, a pal, an equal, and our feelings for each other would grow into something even deeper than friendship. Mike may have thought of me as a kid and was certainly free with paternal advice, but ours was not a father-son relationship. I was not conscious of the difference in our ages. He made me feel older, I made him feel younger. We became like brothers. It seemed as if we had been waiting for each other all our lives.

Coincidentally, I had recently met Elizabeth Taylor at a party in New York given by Merv Griffin. Elizabeth was perhaps twenty, just divorced from Nick Hilton after a very brief and unhappy marriage, and a full-blown Hollywood star. After we were introduced, she smiled and said a few words, and then spent the rest of the evening sitting in a corner with a drink in her hand, talking to her friend Montgomery Clift. We spoke again briefly as she left the party. Just hello and goodbye: nothing to remember, really, except her extraordinary beauty.

The army had a curious way of not showing its favoritism for me. I was promoted to private first class after basic training, and remained a PFC until I was discharged. My salary was roughly $100 a month, which I earned by making as many as fifteen appearances a week. I got goose bumps whenever I sang the national anthem, but I failed to see how singing at a luncheon for congressmen's wives was helping win the war. If I couldn't be a soldier, I wanted to do something for the men who were. I wanted to go to Korea.

"Absolutely not," Major Curry said. "You're doing a great job right here."

I persisted and put in my request through official channels, but nothing happened until I met General Harry Vaughan, President Truman's military aide. He set up an appointment with the President and the afternoon I was ushered into the Oval Office, I was more nervous than I had ever been in my life. President Truman stood up, shook my hand briskly and said, "How's my favorite PFC?"

"Fine," I managed to stammer.

Then the President turned and walked to a window. Looking out over the White House lawn, his back toward me, he said, "You know, Eddie, I don't know what the hell I'm doing here."

It was a moment I'll never forget. Too stunned to speak, I just stood there, wondering what he meant. Perhaps he wanted me to know he was only a man, not some superhuman being just because he was President of the United States. Or perhaps he was telling me that all of us, Presidents included, sometimes find ourselves in situations for which we are not prepared.

Finally he faced me again and said, "So you want to go to Korea? Well, not only am I going to send you to Korea"—and the tone of his voice was so serious that I thought he was about to say something terrible—"I'm going to send you all over the world."

The interview ended after we posed for some pictures, and

the following day the newspapers announced that President Truman was sending his "Favorite PFC" on a world tour to entertain American troops.

In 1952, American troops were indeed stationed all over the world, and for the next several months I was on special assignment, performing with groups of other entertainers at military bases in England, Scotland, Germany, France, Austria, Iceland, Greenland, Alaska, the Aleutians, the islands of the South Pacific, Japan, and of course, Korea. The trip to Korea was a nightmare. The flight from Washington to Tokyo took fifty-four hours on a plane full of generals, and because you had to sit according to rank, I was in the tail section, chilled to the bone and nauseated by the turbulence. To make matters even worse, I had a toothache all the way from Seattle to Seoul, and when I finally got to an army dentist, he told me, "That cap has to come off, Private."

"Wait a minute," I said. "My mouth cost me fifteen thousand dollars!"

I put in a call to my dentist in New York, who said, "For God's sake, don't let them touch your teeth!" So my entire time in Korea, I took two A.P.C.s every four hours, washed down with Coca-Cola, to kill the pain.

Memories of Korea are still vivid in my mind. Soon after my arrival, I was invited for tea and cookies with General Christenberry, head of the Far East Command. And I had my first glimpse of enemy territory while flying in a helicopter with another general. But I was there to entertain the troops, not to socialize with generals, and once our show traveled so close to the front lines that we came under direct enemy fire. We were driving up Mount Baldy in a small convoy of camouflaged jeeps, when I heard a series of whizzing sounds. It was mortar fire, and all of a sudden everybody disappeared. I didn't know what was happening or what to do, so I stood up and started yelling until someone shouted, "Get the hell down!" I jumped out of the jeep and crawled into a ditch until the firing stopped.

We entertained everywhere—staging areas, base camps, hospitals. Sometimes I sang for just a handful of men on forward patrols; sometimes there were thousands in the audience. Once I performed inside a huge, empty swimming pool, the same place where Al Jolson had entertained a couple of years before. Jolson had died in 1950, not long after returning from Korea, and I recorded "Good-bye, G.I. Al" as a tribute to him. His example was one of the reasons I wanted to go to Korea, and I was proud to follow in his footsteps. At another camp, I sat with a group of soldiers watching a movie. Outside, rain was pounding on the tent; inside, we saw *Singin' in the Rain*, and there she was again: Debbie Reynolds. A lot of the guys in Korea dreamed of coming home to a girl like Debbie, and they were very impressed to hear I had actually met her.

I was moved by the bravery and sacrifice of all the men I met in Korea, shocked by the suffering I saw wherever I went. Once, on the road from one camp to another, I watched helplessly as an empty truck swerved around a corner and side-swiped another truck, full of Korean men, women, and children. Bleeding and mangled bodies were scattered all over the road. I almost lost my own life in another accident. At the front lines we were always looking for a place to bathe, and even the Yalu River, with United Nations forces along the southern bank and North Korean and Chinese forces on the opposite side, was too tempting to resist. I jumped in and started splashing around, until I suddenly realized the current was pulling me downstream away from the bank. I would either have drowned or been swept to the enemy side if Lou Tulianello hadn't dragged me back to shore.

Lou was a member of a singing quartet called Three Sharps and a Natural, which performed with our troupe. Nobody liked the name and I usually introduced them as "The Four Joes" because we couldn't think of a better one. For one performance the boys suggested I call them by a new name. The Four Muff Divers. That was all right with me. Believe it or not, I had no idea what it meant, so in front of one of the biggest audiences we had ever had, maybe forty or fifty thousand people, I walked out and said, "Here they are, The Four Muff Divers." A great roar went up from the crowd.

The next day a major serving under the colonel who headed up the Special Services unit in Korea came to see me. "Eddie," he said, "the rest of the tour is being canceled. The colonel is sending you back to Washington."

"Why?" I said. "What's the matter?"

"The colonel isn't too happy with the show, Eddie. There

were nurses and chaplains in the audience last night, and you said something that was very offensive to them." Then he explained what a muff diver was.

I was appalled. The humor in our show was sometimes a little blue; we weren't entertaining at a Sunday school picnic after all. But I thought I had committed a court-martial offense and ruined my clean-cut image forever. Without Milton Blackstone to intercede for me, I didn't know what to do, until I remembered something General Christenberry had said to me: "Eddie, if there's anything you ever need while you're in Korea, don't hesitate to call me." The last thing I wanted to do was call up a general, but I was desperate. After waiting three hours to reach him over the one line in operation, I said, "General, I don't know if you've heard about it yet, or what you've heard, but if I did something wrong, I'm sorry, and it'll never happen again."

"Forget about it, Eddie," General Christenberry said. "Don't give it another thought."

That was all. I wasn't sent back to Washington and the tour continued.

When we left Korea, our troupe was given a few days of R & R in Tokyo before returning to the United States. My records were very popular in Japan, and I was invited to go to a place that I think was called Myoshi, a special geisha house reserved for generals and other visiting celebrities. The invitation came from an army sergeant who claimed he had arranged similar visits for Jack Benny, John Wayne, and a lot of other celebrities. I refused to go unless I could take my buddies with me, so there were fourteen of us that night. After changing into kimonos and sandals, we all sat around a long, low table while the geishas entertained us and prepared traditional Japanese dishes. Then Lou Tulianello rushed out to get his accordion and we sang for the geishas. Finally it was time to choose, and blushing with embarrassment, I picked a very pretty girl who spoke a few words of English. Once we had paired off, we all walked through a garden full of beautiful flowers and trees to another building, where we undressed, showered, and then bathed in a large pool. Yelling and laughing and splashing around, we must have been quite a spectacle in a place of such dignity and decorum. Then the girls led us across the garden again, into tiny separate rooms to spend the night. The prophylactic on a low table beside my bed had a picture of Susan Hayward on the wrapper.

By an odd coincidence, a couple of years later, when my brother Bunny was in the army, he also spent a few days of R & R in Tokyo, where he met a Japanese girl and took her dancing. When he told her he was my brother, she opened a bracelet she was wearing and showed him my picture. She was the girl I had met at Myoshi.

Touring military bases in Europe came as something of an anticlimax after Korea. And for the last month or so of my term of service, I found myself back on the luncheon circuit in Washington. Like every other GI, I started counting the days until discharge. My two years in the army had gone pretty fast, but the last few weeks were torture. Then, with about a week left to go, I heard a rumor that the army planned to send me on one final tour—to military bases in the Arctic. Even after logging thousands of miles over both the Atlantic and the Pacific, the thought of flying to the Arctic sent me into a panic. I went to Major Curry and said, "I've gone everywhere the army wanted me to go, but please, sir, don't send me to the North Pole."

"How much longer have you got in the army, Eddie?" he said.

"Eight days, sir."

"In that case, I think you can forget about the North Pole. Unless, of course, you want to reenlist."

I did not want to reenlist. It was time to move on. But looking back on them now, the two years I spent in the army were the greatest years of my life. I had put on a few pounds and was healthier than I had ever been. And I had earned my high school diploma, although my army experience was more like graduating from college. It was a period of tremendous growth, tremendous learning, tremendous exposure to the world and to all kinds of people—my education in how to handle many different situations, how to handle myself. I felt I had earned the respect of my fellow soldiers, something that was very important to me. I had worked hard and was proud of the job I had done. And with that pride came a feeling of confidence in myself, a new sense of independence. I wasn't a kid anymore. I was beginning to grow up.

7

Milton had my future planned right down to the last detail, and there was no time to waste. Discharged from the army one minute after midnight on April 10, 1953, I was due to reopen at the Paramount at 11 A.M. that same day, just exactly where I'd left off two years before. My train from Washington arrived in New York at 6 A.M., Milton and a slew of reporters and friends met me at Penn Station, and I rushed directly to the theater for a three-hour rehearsal before the first show, with barely enough time to change into civilian clothes.

That bleak morning it was pouring rain and I thought this was going to be the end of my career, my farewell performance. Nobody would come out in weather like that. I was wrong. The first show was packed, and all day thousands of kids stood in line outside, wet and shivering, waiting to get in. I started my first song offstage, "Thinking of You," and when I made my entrance, the audience broke loose with screams and cheers. I sang for about thirty minutes, and nobody heard a note. It was bedlam five shows a day for the next three weeks.

Joey Forman was on the bill with me, doing his comic impressions of Hollywood stars. "I was absolutely panic-stricken," he told me. "Sure, I had spent a couple of summers at Grossinger's developing my act, but this was one of my very

78

first jobs in show business. From total obscurity to the stage of the Paramount, that narrow little ledge God knows how many feet over the audience, no footlights, playing to thousands of teenagers there to see you. The first show, my act got a great reaction, the second show, just pretty good, and by the third, the audience was reciting the jokes right along with me and throwing back the punch lines. I died. Hundreds of kids stayed all day."

Milton had already arranged the next step in my career. The movies could wait; in fact, he had a deep distrust of what he called "Hollywood types." But he wasn't opposed to the idea of television when Sonny Werblin, the agent at Music Corporation of America who handled many of the big bands, proposed to star me in a live fifteen-minute twice-weekly show sponsored by the Coca-Cola Company on NBC. The only hitch in the negotiations was my agreement with General Artists Corporation. MCA bought out my contract.

Milton had told me, just after I went into the army, that he wanted the Coca-Cola Company to be my sponsor.

"Why Coca-Cola?" I asked.

"Well," he said, "it can't be a cigarette, or Cadillac. They wouldn't be right for your image."

Coca-Cola was, and the first show would be telecast on April 29, just after my run at the Paramount. In May, I had to fulfill a prior commitment to perform at the London Palladium, and then back to New York for more television, theater, and nightclub appearances, in addition to recording sessions that sometimes lasted until two or three in the morning.

Young, healthy, eager to make up for lost time, I didn't question the wisdom of such a frantic pace. If Milton said go, I went. The first sign of trouble came while I was still at the Paramount, giving my all at every performance, trying to make myself heard over the screams of the audience. My voice began to crack on the high notes, and finally it was gone. I couldn't utter a sound.

Nobody knew what to do. Milton paced back and forth in my dressing room wringing his hands, while I just sat there with a helpless grin on my face. Hugh Martin, my pianist, came up with a suggestion. He had heard of somebody called Max Jacobson, a doctor who specialized in cases like mine. With just one injection, this doctor could clear up my throat and my voice would come back. A lot of Broadway stars went to him for the same problem. What did I have to lose?

Milton and I took a cab to Jacobson's office on East Seventy-second Street. A lot of people were waiting to see him, but I was ushered right in and Dr. Jacobson, pointing to an examining table in the middle of the room, greeted me with a brusque "Sit down." The place looked more like a laboratory than a doctor's office. It wasn't even clean. Glass-fronted cabinets were jammed with boxes and jars; a wastebasket in the corner overflowed onto the floor. Dr. Jacobson peered at me for a moment through his thick, horn-rimmed spectacles and then began to mix up something from a lot of different bottles. I jumped when he cracked one open on the edge of the table. He was in his shirtsleeves; his fingernails were stained black with chemicals. He's no doctor, I thought; this man is some kind of mad scientist. I watched, horrified, unable to move until he filled a syringe and came at me with a needle. Deathly afraid of needles, I held up my hands in protest. Once, in a doctor's office, I had passed out when a nurse took a sample of my blood.

"No nonsense," Jacobson snapped. "Roll up your sleeve." I didn't feel the prick of the needle. The only thing I felt was a hot flash in all the openings of my body—my mouth, my nose, my ears, my ass.

Jacobson stood back and with a flourish tossed the syringe into the overflowing wastebasket. The man was an actor. He was giving a performance.

"Sing," he said.

I shook my head.

"Sing!" he commanded.

I opened my mouth and sang. My voice had never sounded better.

"So?" Jacobson said, with a satisfied smile.

Dr. Max Jacobson, a Jewish refugee from Hitler's Germany, was in his early fifties when we first met. He was not a quack; his medical credentials were impressive, and apart from his general practice, he was well known as a specialist in the treatment of physical and psychological stress. The list of his patients read like a theatrical Who's Who: Cecil B. De Mille, Zero Mostel, Margaret Leighton, Johnny Mathis. A big, barrel-chested man with dark hair and a deep, rich voice, he spoke with great aurhority in a thick German accent that always made him difficult to understand. His moods were mercurial; one moment he might be mumbling softly, the next shouting at the top of his lungs. He was not afraid of anyone. His rudeness and bad temper, his dictatorial personality and eccentric behavior, kept his patients continually off balance. Even so, he could be a very charming man. You either loved or hated Max Jacobson; there was nothing in between. I loved him.

In the cab on the way back to the Paramount, I was seething with excitement. "My God, Milton," I said. "It's a miracle. I can sing. I feel terrific. That man is a genius." My mind was racing. My whole body was charged with energy. I couldn't sit still, and I couldn't stop talking.

"All right, Eddie," Milton said. "Just calm down. Save your voice."

That day I thought I sang as well as I had ever sung. But after the last performance, my energy had somehow disappeared. I was tired and slightly depressed, my appetite was gone, and I had trouble sleeping that night. The next morning my throat felt scratchy again, and when I complained to Milton, we went back to Dr. Jacobson's office. The routine was the same. I was ushered in immediately and watched with fascination as he drew some mysterious combination of chemicals into a syringe and plunged the needle into my arm. Again I felt the hot flash, the instant lift.

"What is this stuff?" I said. "I feel great."

"Shut up," he said. "Don't ask. Who's the doctor here, anyway? Can you sing?"

I sang a couple of notes.

"*Ja,* good," he said. "Now get the hell out of here."

After that, Dr. Jacobson came to my dressing room at the Paramount at least once a day, striding through the doorway with supreme self-confidence, carrying a big black bag full of enough chemicals to stock a drugstore. After injecting me, he would look at the other people in the room and say, "Anybody else? You, *ja?* You want it in the arm or in the ass?"

Eventually I found out what was in Max Jacobson's shots. Vitamins made up the major part of the injection, but the most active ingredient was methamphetamine in varying amounts, buffered by calcium and the painkiller procaine. The initial reaction, the hot flash, was triggered by the calcium; the methamphetamine did the rest—the sudden surge of energy, the feeling of confidence and well-being, the racing thoughts. The nickname it later acquired was very appropriate: speed.

The compounds Jacobson used were experimental and certainly controversial, but they were not illegal or widely abused. Not then. This was 1953, long before the term "speed freak" entered our vocabulary, and Jacobson looked upon himself as an innovator, a medical pioneer. He always injected himself to test the effects of some new combination of drugs. But his patients were his real guinea pigs. There was no set formula for his shots; he increased this or decreased that according to what he thought was needed. He prided himself on being able to diagnose his patients at a glance, and his injections were designed to treat them for fatigue, nervous tension, vitamin deficiencies, or anything else he thought was wrong with them. Whatever was in those injections, they seemed to work. Even more impressive was his ability to handle the anxious, neurotic, insecure people who populate the world of show business. If you were receptive, Max Jacobson's personality, no less than his "vitamin cocktails," could make you his slave.

I was receptive. With Max's injections, I had found a way to get through my murderous daily schedule. The loss of appetite didn't bother me; I never had time to eat anyway. Nor did I worry about the fatigue, the depression, or even the slight tremors that developed as an aftereffect of an injection. To me, all that was just the normal result of the hectic life I led. And if I couldn't sleep at night, well, Max had a shot or a pill for that too. Of course, the momentary high after the injections felt terrific. But that wasn't the reason I took them. I needed the extra energy and self-confidence I got from the shots, not instant exhilaration. Vitamins were good for me. Max was good for me. He gave me the feeling that he could fix anything. Max and his magic elixir were made for me. This man had saved my voice. He could be saving my life.

Max was called a variety of nicknames by both his admirers and his detractors—Dr. Feelgood, Dr. Miracle, Dr. Needles, among others. When I first saw him and the thick-lensed glasses he wore, I thought he looked like Dr. Cyclops. A lot of the famous people he treated didn't want it known they were getting shots. I was proud to be his patient, and his friend. My regular doctor, a prominent Park Avenue specialist, warned me about pumping my body full of unknown chemicals. And Mike Todd said, "Stay the fuck away from that man. He'll kill you." He said it only once; if you didn't take Mike's advice, that was your worry. I not only ignored him, I became Max's most devoted disciple, a Saint Paul, spreading the word to everybody I knew about this marvelous man.

When did Milton start getting injections too? I don't really remember. Maybe he tried one once while Max was shooting up everyone else in my dressing room. If so, he apparently approved of the results, because, like me, he became a regular customer. Why not? After all, Milton's schedule was just as frantic as mine. We were in this thing together, Milton and I. And with Dr. Needles there when we needed him, we were on top of the world.

The premiere of *Coke Time* was broadcast live from NBC's Studio 6B in Rockefeller Center, and with three cameras, TelePrompTers, and cue cards all over the place, I didn't know which way to look. The experience was totally new and very different from a recording session, where I could stop and do it over if I made a mistake, or even a live theatrical performance, where rapport with the audience is so important. Television itself was so new that no one really knew what he was doing. The show could have been terrible, but to my surprise the reviews were universally good. No one expected a slick professional performance from a young kid who just happened to have a good set of pipes. I was called a "natural."

The sponsors were surprised too. During contract negotiations, they had not been at all certain I could perform successfully on television, and Milton agreed to a starting salary of only $1,250 a week. That was the way he operated. Money didn't matter; it was the "exposure." He didn't want to make waves; everybody was supposed to love Eddie Fisher. The sponsors were also wary of using a "teenage idol" to sell Coca-Cola, and hired Don Ameche to act as host and do the commercials. Once one of the most popular and highly paid actors in Hollywood, Ameche would lend the show greater prestige and respectability, as well as appeal to a more mature audience. He was the spokesman, I was just the singer, and his salary was probably double mine. But I was soon given a huge raise and Ameche left the show. The sponsors had simply miscalculated their audience, and in me they found by accident what they were looking for: a performer who could be immediately identified with their product. With Fred Robbins, the popular disc jockey, I started doing the commercials on the show, then I began to appear in their print advertising, and in short order I became their official spokesman: Eddie Fisher, the Coca-Cola Kid. Teenagers in drugstores all over America ordered Eddie Fishers, not Cokes.

Selling Coke posed no particular problems for me professionally. Dinah Shore sold Chevrolets, Perry Como sold Chesterfields; that's what television was all about. And I liked Coke; I probably drank at least twenty bottles a day even before I was on the show. Now whenever I went into a restaurant, a bottle of Coke was waiting for me at the table. But the company already had a spokesman, Morton Downey, the Irish tenor, who was being paid $300,000 a year as Coca-Cola's Ambassador of Good Will. My contract provided that Downey appear every so often on *Coke Time,* especially on Saint Patrick's Day, but our performances together were an embarrassment for both of us and it was decided to ease Downey out. That triggered a reaction from the columnist Jack O'Brien, a friend and frequent companion of Downey's. O'Brien usually wrote very favorable comments about the show, but as soon as I became a threat to Downey, he began running items in his column that always cast me in an unflattering light. They were the opening shots in a battle that O'Brien waged against Milton and me for many years.

Another columnist who had taken a dislike to me, even before *Coke Time,* was Dorothy Kilgallen. I don't remember when she began to criticize me in print, but she unleashed one of her more vicious attacks against my recording of "Goodbye, G.I. Al," which she said was in the worst possible taste and a crassly commercial attempt to cash in on Jolson's reputation so soon after his death. Friends told me to chalk up her venom to anti-Semitism. But whatever the reason, I was very upset. I wasn't sure how to react to hostile criticism. My skin was still pretty thin. I knew I wasn't perfect, but bad publicity was new to me, and if I thought my intense desire to please everyone made me invulnerable, I was mistaken.

London, in June 1953, was caught up in all the color and pageantry of the coronation of Queen Elizabeth. And I was part of the excitement, top of the bill at the Palladium, a show business pantheon. To make sure of giving my best, I brought Max Jacobson to London with me. His shots had the desired effect, and my English audiences were just as demonstrative as American teenagers. One day a phalanx of fans battered down the huge double stage doors at the theater and police had to call in reinforcements to hold them back.

Even Princess Margaret was a fan. At a benefit she sponsored at the Savoy, the Red, White and Blue Ball, she sent a note backstage to request her favorite song of mine, "Outside of Heaven." Afterward, I was asked to join her at her table, and when she rose to greet me, everyone else in the room stood up too. I didn't know what to do or say as she extended her hand and graciously thanked me for my performance. But I had been told she was a collector of American pop records, so I finally blurted out, "I hear you like American singers."

Caught by surprise, she said, "I beg your pardon?" And realizing what my remark implied, I blushed with embarrassment. Later she asked me to dance, and I was still so flustered that I stammered, "I don't dance." From that brief and awkward meeting, both the British and the American press fabricated a romance between "The Princess and the Pop Singer."

After one of my performances at the Palladium, Noel Coward came backstage, introduced himself, and promptly began to give me advice. Referring to the spot in my show where I called out to the audience for requests, he said, "A terrible mistake, dear boy. You see what can happen. Chaos, pure chaos, and suddenly you've lost control. You must always keep a curtain between yourself and your audience, an invisible curtain. You are the entertainer and you must never let the audience forget that."

He invited me to see his current production, a play he had written himself and virtually a one-man show. He sat me on a chair in the wings and proceeded to play the whole show to me. It was a masterful performance. "There you see," he said after the curtain came down. "It is simply a matter of keeping the proper distance."

I respectfully disagreed. Although I admired Coward as a writer and performer, his style was not my style. "I have to feel close to my audience," I told him. "I'm a fighter. I love to go out there, reach right across the footlights, and meet the people head-on. I need their reactions. Without that, I might as well be singing songs in an empty theater."

I suspect that Coward had an interest in me beyond giving professional advice, but it wasn't until a few years later, when we found ourselves as fellow passengers on the *Queen Elizabeth,* that he made an actual advance. We met in the steam room one day. I was flat on my stomach getting a massage and he said, "Let me just pat you, dear boy, let me just touch it." He was referring to my bottom and I broke up with laughter. That wasn't my style either.

Back in the United States, my popularity seemed to grow greater with every passing month. *Coke Time* was among the top-rated shows on television, pictures and stories about me appeared regularly in all the magazines, and every new song I recorded became an instant best-seller—"With These Hands," "How Do You Speak to an Angel?" "I Need You Now," "Downhearted," "Many Times," just to name a few. And with "Oh! My Pa-Pa," I had a record that was a huge international hit. As soon as I heard the title of the song, I said, "I'll do it," and after listening to the music and reading the lyrics, I knew it would be a great success. Pure schmaltz, but somehow it touched everyone, including my own father, who thought I had recorded it just for him. More than once in Philadelphia, with both my father and my mother in the audience, I felt very guilty about singing a song that expressed sentiments I didn't really feel. I always dedicated the next song to my mother: I had to give her equal time.

My income from television, radio, personal appearances, and records was skyrocketing to an estimated $25,000 a week—over a million dollars a year—when Milton and I finally entered a formal financial arrangement. With so much money coming in, the accountants demanded something on paper, and I suggested we become equal partners, fifty-fifty. Milton refused at first, but I insisted, and we became the Fisher-Blackstone Corporation, and later Ramrod, the nickname given to Milton by Hot Lips Page, the famous black trumpet player. Milton designated himself president and treasurer of the corporation, which I considered appropriate. He had always made the major decisions; he had always signed the checks. It never occurred to me that I was being too generous and maybe even foolish. I owed Milton everything.

I don't know what he did with his share of the money. I spent mine. Just after *Coke Time* began, I moved into Eddie Cantor's apartment at 36 Sutton Place South, where, ironically, the view across the East River from my windows was a huge neon sign flashing "Pepsi-Cola." Then I went to Hampshire House on Central Park South, along with my valet, Willard Higgins, whom I inherited from Milton Berle. More than a "gentleman's gentleman," Willard was a man of great charm and consideration. I chose the Hampshire House to be near Mannie Sacks, who had left Columbia Records and was now high in the ranks of RCA Victor. More than a mentor, he had become a friend, and when he moved next door, to the Essex House, I moved too. One day Mannie summoned me to his office and announced that RCA Victor had sold more of my records that week than all their other recording artists combined, popular and classical. I forget what the number was, but it was a lot of records. Mannie was yet another older man who played an important role in my life. Milton Blackstone, Max Jacobson, Mike Todd, Mannie Sacks—all M's.

Wherever I lived, in New York or on the road, I always insisted on space—a reaction to the cramped rooms of my childhood—and at least one guest room for relatives or friends. My entourage was growing larger: Joey and Bernie, of course, Bob Abrams, whom I met in the army, and Lenny Gaines, an actor and comedian with a sharp wit and a gift for mimicry, our court jester, the funniest man in the world. If I gave them money, I didn't consider that a luxury; my friends were a necessity. I didn't think I was buying their friendship. I had always been generous, even when I was poor. And I loved their company. Others came and went: Julie Chester, Marvin Kane, Mickey Addy, Jack Spina—songwriters and pluggers, musicians, guys who knew much more about the business than I did. There were things I could do for them and their careers now, things they could do for me too. We shot the breeze together, swapped stories about show business, or just joked around. They were real people, a welcome relief from the unreality of celebrities and screaming fans. I could always count on them to knock me down a peg or two if I started acting like a "star." They helped me keep myself and the incredible things that were happening to me in some kind of perspective.

I had very little perspective, or even common sense, about clothes. Once I bought a dozen custom-made seersucker suits, identical except for the color of the stripe. I accumulated drawers full of shirts and closets full of expensive shoes, slacks, and jackets, most of which I wore once or twice and then gave away. Lenny Gaines, who was exactly my size, inherited a lot of my suits. "For years," Lenny told me, "my dry cleaner thought I was you because everything I brought in had a label that said 'Made Expressly for Eddie Fisher.' I buried my father in one of your suits." I bought jewelry and watches I never wore, pipes I never smoked, gold cigarette lighters I never used, extravagant gifts for everyone I knew. Milton presented me with a blue Cadillac convertible, probably as a reward for my using that little khaki Ford while I was in the army. I drove it around town happily for a few weeks until I spotted a white convertible in a Park Avenue showroom. I walked in, paid cash, they opened the showroom window, and I drove it right out into the street. It was a Mercedes. I had no idea what happened to the Cadillac.

Still in the offices of the Blackstone Agency on Fifty-seventh Street, Milton was now commanding an organization that almost amounted to an industry. There were accountants and bookkeepers, secretaries, writers—an army of people working for me and my career. Arlene Scharaga had become "secretary-general" of a world-wide network of 65,000 fan clubs with names like Fisher's Well-wishers, Bodies by Fisher, Fish-erettes and Fisher Fleas. She and her staff published a fan magazine for them and tried to keep up with the four to five thousand letters they received every week. Howard Eisenberg's job as my press agent had grown too. He became my Boswell, following me around and recording my every word and move-ment. More often than not it was a lock of his hair, not mine, that was sent to an eager fan. But somehow he and Arlene found time to fall in love and get married.

Fans trailed me everywhere I went. They serenaded me from the street under my window at the Essex House at eight o'clock in the morning. I found one under my bed, and once I went into my bathroom to discover a girl hiding in the laundry ham-per. Even if they sometimes turned up in unexpected places, I was very grateful to my fans. They bought my records and bombarded radio stations with cards and letters requesting that they be played. They packed my performances and carried signs around in the streets. Their enthusiasm was infectious, and one of the most enthusiastic was a young fan named Rona Burstein.

"We were living at the Essex House the first time I saw her," Joey recalled. "This chubby little girl with a nice smile who looked about thirteen years old, just sitting in the lobby day after day waiting for you. Every time she spotted me, she would rush up and say, 'How's Eddie? Where is he? When is he coming down?' She became president of one of your fan clubs, working in Blackstone's office as a volunteer. And then I lost track of her until she reappeared as a Hollywood gossip columnist under the new name, Rona Barrett."

I reminded Joey that Rona and I had another connection. She is very happily married to Bill Trowbridge, a great friend who worked for me at one time as my road manager. Rona later told me that I had been the first love of her life, and she would always be grateful to me for introducing her to Bill.

Barney Ross, once both the lightweight and the welterweight champion of the world, was another member of my organization who became an important part of my life. He and Milton had been friends for years; in fact, Barney was the first major sports figure Milton persuaded to train at Grossinger's, the idea that proved to be the turning point in making it such a popular and well-known resort. His days as a boxer were long over when I met Barney, and I never saw him in the ring until I watched an old film of his fight with Henry Armstrong. Barney was past his prime even then; everybody knew he was through, and Armstrong tore him to pieces. He took it for fifteen rounds, as great in defeat as he had been in victory.

Barney was a hero at Guadalcanal, but after contracting malaria, he became addicted to morphine. I just thought he drank too much until I learned that Milton had taken him to the hospital in Lexington, Kentucky, for a cure that didn't work. By that time, all the money he'd made as a boxer had disappeared, so Milton hired him at the Blackstone Agency and then gave him a job as my bodyguard.

Barney was far from the conventional punch-drunk pug. He was a good husband and father, a beautiful man. He never just hung around; he always had something to talk about, something to do, someplace to go. I've never known a man who had so many different circles of friends. "Eddie, baby," he would say, "if anybody ever bothers you or if you ever need anything, just call Barn-Barn." The times were very rare when I really needed a bodyguard, but on one occasion, after a performance at a big auditorium in Cleveland, I decided to walk the couple of blocks to my hotel. Barney came with me and some guy in a passing car yelled out, "Jew bastard!" Taking off like a shot, Barney caught up with the car and smashed his fist into the guy's face.

Everyone respected Barney. My feelings went deeper than that. He tried to teach me the gentlemanly art of self-defense, which was a losing battle, but I did learn to love boxing. It became my favorite sport and many boxers became my friends: Joe Louis, Rockey Marciano, Sugar Ray Robinson, Floyd Patterson, Muhammad Ali, Ingemar Johansson. But my greatest friend was, and always would be, Barney Ross. Even though I had yet to learn what it's like to be on top and then on the bottom, and had no idea what any addiction can do to a man, I loved Barney. We were together for fifteen years, until he died of cancer.

With two *Coke Time* shows a week, plus personal appearances on other television shows, theater and nightclub performances, and a long list of benefits, I hardly had time to pursue any serious relationship. But I did have dates and the gossip columnists linked me romantically with every girl in town. Ignoring Milton's advice once again, I became involved briefly with another starlet who wanted very much to become a star. Terry Moore had a refreshing girl-next-door look about her, though even she didn't deny she had been around, married to and divorced from Glenn Davis, and one of Howard Hughes's many romantic interests. Terry was fun to be with, but as soon as I realized she cared more about publicity than she did about me, I tried to back off as graciously as I could, which wasn't easy. I was good at getting into things, not out.

Audrey Hepburn was playing on Broadway in *Ondine,* and after seeing the show one night, I fell hopelessly in love with everything about her. The next day I sat down and wrote her a letter, printing it out carefully like a schoolboy and sending it to her with some flowers. I have no idea what I said— something about being her number one fan, hoping she would suggest we meet. But all I received in return was a very formal and ladylike thank you note. Years later we did become dear friends, and at the premiere of *My Fair Lady,* when Audrey already suspected she would not win an Academy Award for her performance because everyone felt that Julie Andrews should have been given the part, she turned to me with tears in her eyes and said, "Are you still my number one fan?"

When I was introduced to Hope Lange, I thought she was one of the nicest and most beautiful girls I had ever met. She was doing commercials on *Coke Time,* and I didn't even know she wanted to become an actress. She wasn't a publicity seeker. Our dates together were always very quiet, very intimate. I brought her to Grossinger's once, and that was like taking her home to meet the family. I often dated the girls who appeared as guests on *Coke Time.* In Jane Morgan I found someone much more than a girl; she was a marvelous performer and a very sensuous woman. One evening in her apartment, she said, "You know, Eddie, all the homosexuals who hang around me think you're homosexual too."

She was smiling, but I was surprised. How could anyone believe the Coca-Cola Kid was homosexual? "Who thinks that?" I said. "Get him on the phone."

She picked up the phone, dialed a number, and when someone answered, she said, "Eddie Fisher is here with me. He wants to talk to you."

I grabbed the phone and shouted, "I am *not* a homosexual!" All I heard was laughter on the other end of the line.

Marlene Dietrich came to see me one night at Bill Miller's Riviera. I was the last person to perform at that beautiful club before it was torn down to make room for a highway. After the show I went to her table and we began to talk. She was preparing her own nightclub act, she told me, and when I said I thought of her as an actress, not a nightclub performer, she laughed and said, "Eddie, I was singing in cabarets before you were born."

Marlene was fifty-five and I was twenty-five, but to me everything about her was youthful—her face, her figure, the way she spoke, the way she moved. Even though there were a lot of other people at the table, we became completely engrossed in our own conversation, and in each other.

I had seen Marlene once before, at a cocktail party for Adlai Stevenson, but we didn't meet. I was there to meet someone else, Margaret Truman, who was supposed to be my date. Columnist Leonard Lyons had invited me. I was barely out of my teens when he befriended me at Grossinger's, and one day, sitting beside the pool, he summoned me over to show me a magazine article entitled "Never Marry an Actress." "Take a look at this, Eddie," he said. "It's good advice." The article had been written by Marlene Dietrich. I read it, but in case I was still tempted, Lyons arranged my date with Margaret, who I thought was very nice. That night I also met Virginia Warren, the daughter of Earl Warren, the Chief Justice of the Supreme Court, and I thought she was even nicer. Virginia and I had several dates and she even flew with me in the small private plane I used to make one-night appearances. She was a marvelous girl, but since then, it seemed I had dated no one but actresses. And if I had not yet married one, contrary to Marlene's advice I soon would—three of them, in fact.

That night at the Riviera, I had introduced Marlene to the songwriters Jerry Ross and Dick Adler, who were helping me with my act; I thought they might help her too. She called a few days later to thank me and invite me to supper. I went to her Park Avenue apartment, which was furnished in perfect taste, and came as a very pleasant surprise to someone accustomed to living in hotel suites. We were alone and Marlene was dressed in a beautiful and very revealing beige gown. She asked me to open a bottle of wine, we drank, and then she disappeared into the kitchen to prepare supper. She served it herself and we ate by candlelight. She was the sophisticated older woman and I was the inexperienced boy, just like in one of her own movies, and I was both excited and a little scared. But Marlene knew how to make me feel like a man. After dinner she sat at my feet and we talked about our lives, about love. The ceiling of her bedroom was mirrored, which was also a surprise. And that night, I discovered the aura of glamour and mystery that always surrounded Marlene was not a trick or an illusion. Her beauty, her charm, her humor, her generosity were real.

We began to meet often and our evenings together always ended in Marlene's apartment. She was aware that ours was an unusual relationship. "You know, Eddie," she said, "I *am* old enough to be your mother."

"No, no," I said. "You're much younger than I am." And she was. What the hell did I care about the difference in our ages? She was a marvelous conversationalist, a very warm and unselfish woman who knew how to enjoy life. She *was* life. The nights I left her to go back to the Essex House, I was walking on air. She was the most stimulating woman I had ever met.

My friends were cynical about my relationship with Marlene, but behind all the innuendoes there was a certain admiration, even jealousy. Everyone knew what a truly remarkable woman she was. Their wisecracks didn't bother me, but I couldn't ignore Milton Blackstone. I had invited Marlene to come with me to a heavyweight championship fight at the Polo Grounds, she accepted, and the day before the fight, my phone rang. It was Milton. "You cannot be seen with that woman," he said. "It will ruin your career."

I scarcely recognized his voice. This was not Milton's usual polite suggestion; it was a command. "But she's a wonderful person, Milton," I said, trying to reason with him. "How is my career going to be ruined? We've been seen together before."

"This is different. The Polo Grounds is different," he said. "Just do what I tell you." And he hung up the phone.

I called back but he refused to speak to me. And calling again later, I was told he wasn't there. No one knew where he was. I had learned to expect some kind of reaction from Milton whenever I became involved with a woman. After the familiar warnings, he usually withdrew into a kind of shell. This time, he completely disappeared.

He had never acted like that before. I was angry and part of me was tempted to tell Milton Blackstone to go to hell. But there was another part, the part that had always followed his advice about my image and my career. I couldn't disobey Milton. I called Marlene, told her what he had said, and canceled our date.

"Well, Eddie," she said, "maybe he is right." She was a wise woman. She understood, and when we met again at a party a few weeks later, she was as gracious to me as ever. I was the one who didn't understand. Because of Milton I had acted like a foolish kid *and* a coward. Even if he was managing my career, did that give him the right to manage my life? I still trusted him more than I trusted God, but I was beginning to have doubts.

There were other things about Milton's behavior that annoyed and puzzled me. If he wanted something from me, it had to be done instantly, no questions asked. But if I, or anyone else, wanted a decision from him, he would vacillate, procrastinate, even forget. His favorite response was, "Hmm, we'll talk about that tomorrow." I often kidded him about his clothes. If I had too many, he didn't have enough. Whenever we traveled together, he bought what he needed along the way, and left whatever he was wearing behind. He was becoming careless about his appearance. And he was beginning to drink a lot, frequenting several nightclubs around town, where he would lean up against the bar with a glass of Chivas Regal in his hand; that was his station and he waited for people to come to him. I knew nothing about his personal life other than that he was unmarried and lived with his mother. He had never invited me to their apartment.

I didn't hear from Milton for several days, and I refused to call him until Max Jacobson made peace between us. "Eddie," he said to me in his familiar rasping voice, "everything Milton does is for your own good."

"I know," I said. "He tells me that often enough himself."

"So don't be a fucking idiot!" Max shouted. "He wants to talk to you."

Milton and I finally got together again and nothing more was said about Marlene. It was forgotten. But there would be other disagreements, and Max was often called upon to intercede. "Milton wants . . . Milton says . . ." his lectures always began. And from Milton, "Max says . . . Max thinks . . ." until both of them were making suggestions, offering advice, giving orders. They were becoming a team: Milton and Max, the masterminds of my career, collaborators in my life. All they asked in return was my soul.

8

Some performers can separate their professional and private lives, lower a curtain or shut a door between the public and the private. My door was always open, the curtain always up. I had no private life, nothing I wasn't willing to give or share. Somehow it was always hard for me to say no.

During my run at the Paramount, I had to get up at six in the morning for the first show at eleven. I hated that. I was a night person and liked to sleep late. Even after *Coke Time* began, a typical day started as early as seven. The first thing I did was walk through my suite, just to enjoy the feeling of space or to find out who was there. Breakfast was delivered on a cart by a waiter. I never used the kitchen. Room service had become a way of life. With the exception of the clothes in the drawers and the suits and shoes in the closets, nothing in the suite was mine, not even the pictures on the walls. It all belonged to the Essex House. I lived in a hotel, not a home.

Every day I had a printed schedule from the corporation telling me when to be where: a meeting at nine, publicity pictures at ten, an interview at eleven, another meeting at twelve, a fan club at one, a recording session for the rest of the afternoon. Rehearsals for my show or for a guest appearance on another program took up most of my time. Lunch was a hamburger, a Coke, and french fries, which I usually ate standing on my feet. Or if I happened to be in a restaurant, a cheese omelet, double on the cheese. Even dinner was geared to business. Around the table there were always men from the corporation, RCA Victor, the Coca-Cola Company, or MCA, sometimes people I scarcely knew who were involved in my career. After that an appearance at the Cub Room of the Stork Club, the Colony, El Morocco, or some other place where you were supposed to be seen. And finally, in the early hours of the morning, Lindy's for strawberry cheesecake.

From the moment I woke up until I went to bed, I was surrounded by people who steered me in one direction or another, or simply trailed along in my wake. I didn't resent the pressure and the lack of privacy. On the contrary, I was so conditioned to them that if there was a moment or two with nothing to do, I felt a little lost. Even if I wasn't actually standing before a microphone or a television camera, I had to be "on."

I also spent a lot of time working for charity, as did many other celebrities. Benefits, testimonials, telethons—I did them all. If some children in a hospital, dying with blood diseases, asked to see me, I went. It had nothing to do with building my image. I sincerely wanted to help in any way I could. With my background, my lack of education, all I had was a voice. But that gave me the ability to communicate, the power to do things for people. And that was one of the most fulfilling parts of my career.

It never occurred to me to slow down, relax, take time just for myself. I had to say yes to everything. And the only way I thought I could do that was with Max's help. I became completely dependent on his injections before every performance, and sometimes simply to get me through the day. He never sent me a bill, as far as I know. I used to pay him in cash— one hundred dollars, five hundred—whatever I had in my pocket. His patients were among the richest people in the world, and not all of them in show business, yet he was continually broke. With an income of $500,000 a year, he spent money extravagantly, but never on himself. It all went back into his practice—thousands of dollars' worth of chemicals, equipment, magnets, rocks for his laboratory, a dirt shack out on Long Island, where he cooked things in pots and experimented with his formulas.

I was as addicted to Max himself as I was to his injections. He was my friend. If Milton was evasive, I could always get a straight answer from Max. And if Milton's eccentricities were beginning to trouble me, Max's did not. I often found him standing on his head in a corner of his office. "So?" he said, glaring at me upside down. "It's good for the circulation." He could fall asleep anywhere; sometimes he dozed off right in the middle of giving me a shot. Odd as he was, he was funnier than most of the comedians I knew. I enjoyed his company, and he made me the prince of his court. He loved to hear me sing in his office, no matter how many people were there or how sick they were. *"Ja!"* he would cry. "I did that." He asked me to come to his office on Thursday nights when he treated patients with multiple sclerosis free of charge. I spoke to them, trying to make them comfortable while Max prepared injections that apparently gave them at least temporary relief from their pain. He was doing good for everybody; wasn't I the living proof of that? I was his prize pupil, his number one exhibit—his prize number one sap.

Milton finally agreed to entertain movie offers. Paramount wanted me to do a musical Western called *Red Garters* and one day Jay Cantor, my movie agent at MCA, met Milton and me at Toots Shor's with a standard seven-year studio contract. Milton said no; it had taken him months to renegotiate my contract with RCA Victor so that I wasn't responsible for recording costs. And I agreed. The contract was ludicrous—and so was the script. I couldn't see myself as a cowboy riding a white horse. My friend Guy Mitchell eventually got the part, and the movie was a disaster.

There were other offers. Dore Schary at MGM wanted me for a musical remake of *Dead End,* and on a trip to Hollywood I was treated like visiting royalty. The answer was still no. I wasn't playing hard to get; there were serious doubts in my mind about my abilities as an actor. Even with so much experience on television, I was ill at ease whenever I stopped singing and had to speak lines. And if I was uncomfortable playing myself, how could I be convincing as somebody else? I wanted to learn how to act. I went to Lee Strasberg, who sent me to a drama coach. I was very excited about the prospect of studying with her until she started chasing me around her apartment. That was the end of my acting lessons.

I was back in California in June of 1954 for an engagement at Hollywood's Cocoanut Grove. Again the movie studios rolled out a red carpet, and Joe Pasternak, who was trying to interest me in making *Hit the Deck* for MGM, took me on a tour of the lot. A musical called *Athena* was in production. Pasternak knocked on the door of a dressing-room trailer on the set, and a very pretty young woman opened it. Debbie Reynolds. We were introduced and I don't remember what we said after that, probably something about having met before at Walter Reed Hospital in Washington. And I asked her, either then or that evening on the phone, if she would like to be my date for my opening at the Cocoanut Grove. She said yes.

I was attracted to Debbie. She was bright, pretty, funny, very talented. I don't think MGM knew what to do with her. In her early twenties now, she was growing too old for the cute-teenager roles she usually played. And even after scoring a personal triumph in *Singin' in the Rain,* she was still a contract player making $1,250 a week—more than a starlet, not quite a star. Born Mary Frances Reynolds on April Fool's Day in El Paso, Texas, she grew up in Burbank, just north of Hollywood, where she was a high school cheerleader and won the title of Miss Burbank in a beauty contest. She had been making movies since she was sixteen, and if anything, her public image was even more wholesome than mine. As the "All-American Girl," she was the perfect match for the "Boy-Next-Door." Not even Milton could find fault with Debbie Reynolds. And she was well enough established in her own career so that she wouldn't have to use me for publicity. Even more important, she seemed so natural to me, real—rare qualities in other girls I knew in show business.

Our relationship got off to a hectic start. Because I would be rehearsing right up to the last minute, I asked Mike Todd and Evelyn Keyes to bring Debbie to the Cocoanut Grove, and she sat with them until I was free to join her between shows. Then I discovered that Pier Angeli was in the audience and thought *she* was supposed to be my date. I had met her at MGM too, and invited her to come to the opening. I had invited everyone, and tried to explain that to her, but she was so upset she walked out of the club. I followed, still trying to explain, and she stopped only long enough to put something in my hand: half a gold coin on a key chain. "When you find the other half of this coin, you'll find love," she said, then turned and ran away.

The Grove that night was overflowing with hundreds of prom kids sitting on the steps leading up to the stage, displaying their usual enthusiasm for my performance. The second show was even more crowded than the first, and Debbie had to sit through all that too, until we were finally able to get away together. We went to a party that was being given for me, and after that I drove her home to Burbank.

It was late but we sat in the car for a while and talked. We made plans to see each other again and I kissed her on the cheek. She kissed me back, opened the car door, and ran quickly into the house. Driving back to Hollywood, I thought to myself how sweet and unspoiled she was, just like the parts she played in the movies. No exaggerated makeup or fancy, low-cut gown. Her mother had made the dress she was wearing. She lived with her parents, and even in the dark I could see their house was small and unpretentious, no different from all the other houses on the block. I had found a really nice girl—in Hollywood, of all places.

We saw each other often during the six weeks I was playing at the Grove. Debbie sat in the audience or waited for me in my dressing room until the show was over and I could drive her back to Burbank. I met her mother, Maxine, again, her father, Ray, and her brother, Bill. Maxine was all over me at first; she practically dusted off the chair before I sat down. Debbie was obviously very important to her; almost every sentence out of Maxine's mouth was about how wonderful her daughter was. I was embarrassed, but Debbie didn't seem to mind. And I suppose her father was used to it. He usually sat in a corner reading a newspaper. I don't know when it occurred to me that Debbie and her mother were too close, that perhaps Maxine was living her life vicariously through her daughter and Debbie was letting her do it. But Maxine and I didn't get along very well from the start. She had a way of putting people down. She had no humor. And I got the impression that this woman would not sit still for anything or anyone who got in her daughter's way.

Because we were both celebrities, there was a fuss whenever Debbie and I appeared in public. The only time we had alone was driving to Burbank, and once or twice I spent the night in a little guesthouse in the back, beside the pool Debbie had built for her family with the royalties from her record "Aba Daba Honeymoon." We had fun together, there was a lot to talk about, and soon we both knew we wanted to be more than just friends. I was shy, but eager too. Debbie would go only so far. She told me she had never been really involved with another man; her previous romances were nothing more than studio publicity. I didn't think she was trying to tease me. She said she was a virgin and I respected that because I was beginning to think seriously about marriage, something I had never done before. But the feelings I had for Debbie were completely new.

Neither of us knew what we were doing, what we were getting into. We were two very immature kids who needed more time to be alone together, to get to know each other better. On the surface at least, marriage just didn't make sense. Debbie was Protestant and middle-class; I came from a Jewish working-class background. She was a movie actress in Hollywood, my career as a singer was centered in New York. We weren't even sure we were in love. Those were the realities that should have been sorted out before we went any further. But fantasy is the stock-in-trade of show business. And it was fantasy that began to take over our lives.

"Debbie and Eddie" became an item in gossip columns right after our first date, and soon every move we made was covered by the Hollywood press. Debbie was probably far less surprised than I was to read that we had been someplace we had never been, or to see a quote of something we had never said. She was, after all, a creation of one of Hollywood's most powerful studios, a "good property" with a reputation for being very cooperative with the press. I knew the stories about us were not coming from Milton or anyone else in New York; they had to be coming from MGM, Debbie, and Maxine.

I went along with it. With Milton as my mentor, I was no stranger to publicity myself. And this was good publicity—for both of us. I consented to an interview with Louella Parsons, who knew Maxine and took an almost motherly interest in Debbie and me. I was amazed by the way she operated. She asked me one or two leading questions. That was all; she didn't even take notes, and from a few minutes of conversation, she wrote a five-page article. I didn't see how she could write all that. Well past the days of her real power in Hollywood, she was getting old and seemed ill and a little fuddled to me. People laughed at her behind her back. But I liked her and agreed to appear on her radio show. "Hello to all of you from Holly-wood"—it was really very funny, the way she read her lines. Even so, she was a good gossip columnist, and unlike her rival, Hedda Hopper, a kind person.

Was it Louella who first called us "America's Sweethearts"? Whoever it was, the label stuck. "Debbie and Eddie" were billed as an ideal couple and our romance grew from Hollywood gossip into a national preoccupation. The press was uniformly favorable and sympathetic, and that kind of attention is always flattering. But many reporters were predicting marriage long before Debbie and I even thought about an engagement. It was as if we had no choice in the matter. We were public property. And although I had never cared about privacy before, I did now. First Milton, then Max—and now the press was telling me how to run my life.

Debbie loved all the publicity. She was an actress and liked nothing better than being in the spotlight. I could understand that; it was her business. But when we went out together, I thought she was sometimes too animated; she tried too hard to be bright and funny. And even among her close friends, she always had to be the center of attention. One evening she gave a party for me at her house, invited all her friends, and went to great lengths to entertain us by putting on a show about me. First she strutted around in army fatigues, swigging from a bottle of Coke; then, dressed as a señorita, she mouthed my recording of "Lady of Spain," exaggerating the way I per-formed. It was funny and playful, but I was a little embarrassed. Not because she was putting me down; it just seemed silly. Joey Forman was there and he gave me a shrug.

We talked about marriage. Debbie's mother, her friends, MGM, the press, were all for it. We weren't so sure. Things were moving too fast. I felt I was being backed into a corner. After my engagement at the Grove, I rented a house on Cold-water Canyon Drive, and when we could get away from the parties and the reporters, Debbie and I had wonderful times together. We did all the silly, impulsive, intimate things young people in love are supposed to do. Still, the idea of marriage frightened me. I didn't know what a happy marriage was. My father and mother were divorced; Debbie's father and mother seemed to live in separate worlds. Mike Todd was always in trouble with women; Max Jacobson and his wife were in constant battle; Milton Blackstone wasn't married at all. I wanted my marriage to be perfect. And how much did I know about love? I thought I loved Debbie and she said she loved me, but somehow there seemed to be a wall between us—things we couldn't talk about, things we didn't understand. I wasn't sure I knew who Debbie really was.

It was almost with a sense of relief that I went back to New York to begin the fall season of *Coke Time*. I needed time to think things over. As usual, Milton advised caution. "I don't think you're ready to be married, Eddie," he said. "Debbie's a nice girl, but maybe you should wait a little bit. Be sure." Unsought advice came from another quarter. Representatives from the Coca-Cola Company marched into my dressing room and told me bluntly that they thought it would *not* be a good idea to marry Debbie, or anyone else. Very happy with things just the way they were, they didn't want anything to interfere with my image as the Coca-Cola Kid. I said, "Thank you very much," but inside I was seething with anger.

If I thought separation would cool the public's interest in "Debbie and Eddie," I was wrong. The faucet had been turned on full blast and there was no way to shut it off. Whenever I went to Los Angeles to see Debbie or she came to New York to see me, usually chaperoned by her mother, the press had a field day. But a new note was beginning to creep into the questions fired at us by reporters. It was taken for granted that we were going to get married; now they wanted to know when. The press and the public were growing impatient. So was Maxine, who made it very clear that she thought we should set a date, and Debbie felt the same way.

I still wasn't sure. I searched Debbie's eyes, listened to the tone of her voice, for some reassurance that if we got married, it would be for us, because we really loved each other, not just to please the public. If she had any doubts, she didn't express them. She had already decided that marriage was what she wanted. And finally I decided I wanted it too. I was performing in Chicago the day our engagement was officially announced, and after hearing the news, Milton retreated to his hotel room, where he spent the next three days with cold towels on his head.

*   *   *

Eddie and Ida Cantor gave us an engagement party at the Beverly Hills Hotel in October of 1954. It had all the intimacy of a Hollywood premiere, with Debbie as the star of the show, smiling, waving, hugging people, showing everyone the fifty-thousand-dollar ring on her finger. Posing for pictures, she clung to my arm with adoring looks in a perfect performance of a bride-to-be. Is she acting, is she always acting, I can remember thinking; why can't she just be herself?

We set the wedding date for the following June because only then would our schedules permit any kind of honeymoon. Debbie stayed in Hollywood and I went back to New York, and our engagement, like our courtship, was conducted over long distance. When I asked if *Coke Time* could be broadcast from the NBC studios in Los Angeles, the answer was no. And Debbie, of course, couldn't leave Hollywood. So we saw each other only on weekends, under the watchful eyes of her mother and reporters who began to speculate that a two-career marriage could spell trouble. But Debbie was always pictured as a devoted, patient, long-suffering girl eager to settle down with the man she loved. As reporters saw it, her career wasn't the problem.

I don't know whose idea it was to have me record Irving Berlin's "A Man Chases a Girl" with Debbie singing the phrase "Until she catches him." That was exactly the way I was beginning to feel about our relationship. And it seemed to me that too many people were eager to capitalize on it. In March of 1955, I was scheduled for another appearance at the London Palladium and Debbie, who was between pictures, insisted on going with me, chaperoned, of course, by Maxine. I thought the whole arrangement was silly; we barely had a moment together except to give interviews to the press. But audiences at the Palladium loved it when Debbie sang her part of "A Man Chases a Girl" offstage and then came on to take a bow. "Debbie and Eddie" had become a vaudeville team.

I wasn't able to slip her into my act during a Royal Command Performance at Blackpool, and even though I begged them, she was not permitted to meet the Queen because she was not listed on the bill. So I was standing alone in the receiving line when Prince Philip shook my hand and said, "You're not really going to marry that girl, are you?" I couldn't believe that he knew—or cared—about "America's Sweethearts." But I stammered, "Yes, sir, I am."

In fact, I was having second thoughts. In public, Debbie was always very warm and loving; in private, there was an increasing coolness between us. Sex was much more important to me than it was to Debbie. Her response to me in both public and private sometimes seemed like an act. And the fuss she made over my mother. Was that real or an act? There must have been a lot of things about me and the way I led my life that Debbie disliked too—the frantic pace, the late hours, my dependence on Milton and Max, some of my friends. But none of that seemed to matter as long as we got married.

Both Lenny Gaines and Joey Forman were dead set against the marriage. It was obvious to them that I was being pressured into something I didn't want to do. "She's a dingbat, a phony," they said. Mike Todd was against the marriage too. "If you marry that Debbie Reynolds, you little Jew bastard," he told me, "I'll kill you." Milton continued to be evasive; "Well, you are both very young and you both have good careers." Everybody had an opinion, but there was no one I could sit down with to talk things through. Did I really want to marry Debbie? If I did, why wasn't I happy and excited? If I didn't, how the hell could I get out of it?

I decided to postpone the wedding. There were good reasons—I had commitments right up to the last minute—but I was stalling, still unable to make up my mind. Debbie was very unhappy. She and her mother had already begun to plan a big Hollywood wedding, but putting on her usual brave front for reporters, she announced she was going to Korea to entertain the troops. It was a calculated play for sympathy and it worked. Any sign of trouble between "America's Sweethearts" made good copy, and the public, bored with reading about what an ideal couple we were, ate it up. I was the heavy, naturally, and when Debbie got sick on her way back from Korea and was put in a hospital in Honolulu, I was made to look like an even bigger heel. Fans who had been angry at me for wanting to marry Debbie in the first place were now angry because I was "toying with her affections." And later, when she returned to Los Angeles, her mother called to tell me the same thing. The pressure was still on.

Debbie and I decided we had to meet and talk. To avoid reporters, we went to the house of her aunt and uncle in Desert

Hot Springs, a dusty, deserted little town with winds strong enough to take the paint off a car. And that weekend, I discovered that Debbie was still determined to get married, but to me it seemed her vision went no further than becoming a bride. If she foresaw any problems, she thought she could handle them. And the embarrassment of being rejected by a man would be far worse than a difficult marriage. I couldn't escape the suspicion that she wanted to get married just because that's what girls were supposed to do, and wanted to marry *me* because it would be good for her career. Or maybe she did love me; maybe she did think we could be happy together. Debbie was an enigma to me, a complete mystery. I couldn't figure her out. She was trying very hard to be everything she thought I wanted in a wife. And I wasn't sure what I really did want.

Meanwhile the press had become sardonic and even hostile. *TV Guide,* in an article titled "Eddie Fisher, Boy Corporation," blamed my organization, which included an entourage of "old friends, volunteer bodyguards, devoted fans and an occasional panhandler," for keeping Debbie and me apart. My old adversary, Jack O'Brien, was more specific. Citing Maxine as his source of information, he wrote that Milton Blackstone was responsible. We met in a car parked in front of the Essex Hotel and I told O'Brien angrily that Milton had nothing to do with my private life.

It was true. Milton did try to stay out of my private life—unless he thought I was hurting my career. And in his opinion, my indecision about marriage was destroying my image. After we announced the postponement and the publicity had turned sour, Milton stepped in and made his pronouncement. "This thing has gone too far, Eddie," he told me. "You've got to go through with it now."

Was he right? Had it gone too far? Wasn't there still time to admit that marriage would be a mistake and end our relationship gracefully? I could survive whatever bad publicity there was. Debbie, if anything, would benefit by it, and gradually the public would lose interest. But only my friends saw it that way. Everyone else—reporters, gossip columnists, fan magazines, the public—all were clamoring for a marriage. Even so, the decision was mine alone to make.

Debbie and I announced a new date, in September, for our wedding. Why, with all my doubts and conflicting emotions, did I make that decision? I was very weak, very timid, not very bright in the head. I wasn't able to resist the pressures from Debbie, the press, and a nice boy does not walk out on a nice girl. A performer cannot disappoint his fans. Everybody was supposed to love Eddie Fisher. That's what I had been taught, that's what I believed, and I sincerely thought I was doing the right thing.

Both Debbie and I were victims of our own publicity.

Grossinger's was my idea. I wanted nothing to do with a big Hollywood wedding and Debbie agreed, probably because she realized if we were going to get married at all, it had to be my way. Grossinger's had always been lucky for me. It was a sentimental choice, but it was also my territory. I called Jennie and she was delighted. The ceremony would be small and private, with just family and close friends in attendance, no reporters and photographers.

Then I discovered the day we had picked for our wedding was Yom Kippur. Debbie was with me in New York when I told her we were going to have to postpone it again, and suddenly she was in hysterics, crying and screaming that I was backing out. I thought she had gone insane. She calmed down finally after I explained that Jews couldn't get married on the holiest of our holidays; it only meant we would have to postpone the ceremony for one day.

We went to Grossinger's a couple of days before the wedding. We had adjoining rooms but we stayed together and talked. I made no secret of my feelings, and Debbie was unhappy too. Yet whenever there were people around, she was part blushing bride-to-be, part comedienne.

Lenny Gaines remembers the day before our wedding. "Every time it looked like you might change your mind and call it off," he said, "Debbie fainted. People rushing in and out of her room and her mother right there, every minute. You didn't want to get married. You were pacing back and forth, saying, 'I don't want to do this. I'm not going through with it.' And I said, 'Eddie, for God's sake, we've got a car downstairs. You can be out of here in fifteen minutes. Why throw your life away just because somebody else tells you to get married? You don't love her.' Then Milton came in and I told him the same thing. 'It's too late now,' he said. 'Besides, many people get married without love. Let's just let things happen here the way they're supposed to happen. It's too late to change now.'

"I couldn't believe Milton would say something like that. Marriage without love. So when he left I decided to give it one more shot. 'You dumb kumquat,' I said, 'forget Milton. Let's get out of here.' But you didn't move."

The ceremony was to take place at sundown on Monday, September 26, in a house that had just been built for Jennie's daughter, Elaine. Debbie and I moved to the Milton Berle cottage on the grounds and spent Sunday night in separate rooms. Our relationship had grown even more strained that day, and we were not on very good terms when we said good night and Debbie went into her room alone. The next morning I knocked on her door and there was no answer. I ran out and found Paul Grossinger, who came and broke into the room. There was a shattered water glass on the floor and Debbie was lying beside it, apparently unconscious.

Paul's brother-in-law, a doctor, was summoned to examine her. "She has the strongest pulse of anyone I've ever seen who just fainted," he said. And I left the room wondering what Debbie was trying to do. Was it another performance? Or maybe she didn't want to get married either, and that was the only way she had been able to express her real feelings.

There were reporters and photographers around the house that evening when Debbie and I appeared for the ceremony. The air was chilly and Elaine Grossinger permitted them to wait in the unfinished basement of the house. They would be allowed to take pictures at the reception but not at the wedding. Milton was my best man, Jeanette Johnson, Debbie's high school gym teacher and best friend from California, was her maid of honor, and Maxine was in her glory as Mother of the Bride. My mother was still on her way from Philadelphia and the ceremony was delayed until her arrival. She and my father stayed at opposite sides of the room, and I thought, Is that going to happen to us? Will Debbie and I end up hating each other? But as we finally stood before Judge Lawrence Cooke, we exchanged glances that said, We can try to make a go of this marriage. Jennie had filled the house with flowers, and Debbie was subdued and more beautiful than I had ever seen her. Her smile at the ceremony was radiant and real. We drank champagne and cut into a big cake that had been sent over from the hotel. There were toasts and laughter. Everyone was happy for us. And after posing for pictures, Debbie and I left in a shower of rice to spend our wedding night in a little farmhouse a few miles down the road.

There the mood changed. We were like strangers. The next morning, I got up early, dressed, and started to walk back to the hotel. Then for some reason I found myself running, running as fast as I could through the fields away from that house.

9

Debbie and I spent our honeymoon at a Coca-Cola bottlers' convention in Atlanta, Georgia. After *Coke Time* was broadcast from a local auditorium, I brought her on stage to introduce her to the audience, and we got a thunderous ovation. "America's Sweethearts" were married at last. Holding my hand, Debbie stepped up to the mike. "I don't drink Coke," she said, making a wry face. Startled, and afraid of what she might say next, I dug my fingernails into her palm to stop her. She ignored me. "It's bad for your teeth," she said, flashing the audience a big smile. "I drink milk." There was a moment of stunned silence and then a burst of laughter. I wanted to fall through the floor; for me Coca-Cola was like holy water. But all the bottlers and their wives thought Debbie was just being cute. They loved her.

For about a month after our marriage, we lived in my suite at the Essex House. Debbie was a fish out of water; she missed her mother and her friends in California, and didn't fit comfortably into my life in New York. When she had to return to Hollywood to start a new picture, I saw no reason why we shouldn't make our home there. The Coca-Cola Company and NBC no longer had any objections to broadcasting my show from the West Coast. I liked California and in the back of my mind there was the thought that if this marriage had any chance at all, Debbie and I would have to be together.

We rented a sprawling ranch house tucked into a hillside on a huge estate in Pacific Palisades. Once the home of Norma Shearer and Irving Thalberg, it was an architectural master-piece, built on several levels with steps up and down, angles everywhere, his and her bath and dressing rooms in the master and main bedrooms. Every room was beautifully, and com-fortably, furnished in the Early American style. There was even a playhouse on the grounds that was three times bigger than any house I had lived in as a kid. The only thing missing was a swimming pool, so we built one. A house wasn't a home to me without a piano and a swimming pool.

For Debbie, it was a long way from that bungalow in Bur-bank. She referred to herself, sometimes as a joke and some-times quite seriously, as "MGM's hottest property," and now she had the house and the income to prove it: Norma Shearer's house and my income. Because the money I earned was so much greater than what Debbie made, I suggested that she just put her salary in the bank. She got an allowance of $2,500 a week from me, more if she needed it, and I never kept track of how it was spent. We were married; what was mine was hers. That formula didn't necessarily work both ways, I soon discovered. Debbie spent my money but saved hers. She had always saved it. She saved everything. Living in Burbank, wearing homemade clothes—things I once thought rather touching and sweet about Debbie—I began to see in a different light. It was cheaper to live in her family's house; why buy clothes as long as her mother could make them, or she could borrow them from the studio? Even after we were married and Debbie's allowance from me was larger than her salary, Maxine *still* made her daughter's clothes.

Debbie economized on everything, including food. Once, she called the house to find out who was there, and when our cook told her it was Joey Forman, she said, "Well, I can't do anything about that. But don't feed him." Another time, I asked if Lenny Gaines could stay for dinner and she said, "Oh, I'd love to have him, Eddie, but we've only got two steaks in the house." "Here you were," Lenny recalled, "living on ninety-nine acres of the most expensive real estate in California, and the refrigerator was empty."

I didn't know why Debbie was so concerned about money.

She had never been poor growing up, never gone hungry as I had. Why did she squirrel away every dollar she could lay her hands on? Why, for that matter, couldn't I get rid of the dollars I made fast enough? Now I think the reason may have been the same for both of us: an emotional insecurity that was only symbolized by money. Somewhere there should have been a middle ground between my open hand and Debbie's tight fist, but we never found it. I was puzzled and annoyed by her attitude and she resented mine. Money was probably the source of our greatest conflict from the beginning of our marriage.

I adored Debbie's father. Ray Reynolds was often as bemused by his wife and daughter as I was. But he was a proud man, who pretended to be nothing more than he was and had somehow insulated himself from the insanities of show business. Even if Debbie was a star, he still kept his job on the railroad, and I admired that. We played chess together and he was very welcome in our house. As far as I was concerned, Maxine was not always so welcome. She would have moved in with us if I had let her. Debbie had been a mama's girl long enough; nobody's mother should be around too much—hers or mine. So I was very cool to Maxine and she retaliated by turning her sarcasm and snide remarks on me. Quick to take Debbie's side in any disagreement, outspoken in her resentment of me for coming between her and her daughter, she was the classic mother-in-law. She didn't like me—she never had. I couldn't forbid her to come to the house; she was there as often as Debbie wanted to see her. I just tried to stay out of her way.

With my mother, Debbie was a devoted daughter-in-law, but there again she tried to cut corners. Mom never complained. "These are things you're hearing for the first time in your life," she told me just recently. "I didn't have anything against Debbie. She was your wife and I loved her. But I sometimes got the feeling she resented the things you were doing for me. You were getting ready to be married and she wanted to buy silver and crystal, so we went shopping together in New York and she spent a lot of money. Believe me, I'm so happy when my sons do good for their wives. I was the happiest mother in the world that day, until we got back to the hotel and Debbie said to me, 'Mommala'—she always called me Mommala—'you know Eddie supports so many people, he has so many obligations, that if he continues that way, we'll have a piece of ground, but we won't have enough money to build a house.'

I knew what she meant; she was talking about the help you were giving me and your father and everybody else in the family. I said, 'Well, Debbie, I never asked Sonny Boy how much he makes or how much he spends. You know all about the money, I don't, so if he's doing wrong, as his wife you should see that he does different.' That's all I said, but when I got home I thought I would die. Why should she say something like that to me? What were you giving me that she couldn't build a house? Debbie was like that. You squeeze the pennies but you spend the thousands."

I invited my mother and stepfather Max to stay with us for a couple of weeks just after Debbie and I were married. "I remember that place you rented," my mother recalled. "A very big home. When Max and I went to bed at night, we had one whole side of the building all to ourselves. You showed us the town and it was beautiful. But what did I know about Hollywood? What did I know about movie stars? All I know is you were unhappy. Married two months, three months, and already you were unhappy. That's one thing about you, Sonny Boy. You never like to lie. I could tell you thought this marriage was a lie."

Lenny Gaines once said that my family had always been one of the biggest problems. When I became a celebrity, he said, they became celebrities too. I never learned how to handle the changes my success brought about in their lives, and they never learned how to handle me. According to Joey Forman, I was too generous in sending them money, buying them presents, giving them everything they wanted. Mike Todd once said, "Eddie, you can't take care of everybody. You have to make your own life first." But I used to think no one could survive without me. Not only my family, but everyone who worked for me, my friends, everyone I knew. I was somehow responsible for all the people in my world.

I was brought up to believe it was the duty of a son, if he became rich and successful, to support his mother and father, to relieve them of the burdens they had been under all their lives. As soon as I started making money, I had sent my parents part of it; I sent them money separately after their divorce, and now that both of them had remarried, I decided to give them enough to make them comfortable. "Mom, you can have everything you want," I told her proudly. "Daddy, you can retire."

They were pleased and grateful. My mother and Max said they wanted to buy and run a supermarket; Max knew the business and with my financial backing, they thought they could make a go of it. "It'll be something for the rest of the family too," Mom said. "That's a great idea," I said. "Maybe from one store you'll end up with a whole chain." I went to Philadelphia for the grand opening, but within a year the store folded. They had to sell everything at a loss, even the fixtures. It was more than Mom and Max, or anyone else in the family, could handle by themselves.

My father really did retire. From the age of fifty-three until he died at seventy-two, he never worked again at anything. His friends used to call him the Mayor of Horn & Hardart, the cafeteria in Philadelphia where he held court. He accepted the money I gave him and came back for more. Everyone seemed to want something. For my older brother Sol, it was a succession of jobs. For my younger brother Bunny, it was an operation. Someone told him his nose made him look more like Tony Bennett's brother than mine, so I paid for a nose job. Whether the problem was little or big, both Sol and Bunny came to me to solve it.

How does anyone cope with the kind of fame I brought my family? My sisters married, had children, and made good lives for themselves; my mother lived for all her children, not just me. But my father gave up his own life and made a career out of being "Eddie Fisher's father"; my brothers found it all but impossible to compete with my success. And how do people who have never had a dime cope when a son or a brother suddenly has all the money in the world? How did *I* cope? Whatever I spent, I thought there would always be more where that came from. Could I blame my family for feeling the same way? If I was naive enough to believe that money was all it would take to make them happy, could I blame them for believing that too?

To help my family was the right thing, but that was the wrong way to do it. I hadn't yet learned how to spend money— or even how to give it away. I wanted to be loved by everybody. All my family and friends had to do was ask and I gave them whatever I could, or felt guilty and ashamed if I didn't. I never resented their requests, but I would eventually come to feel that no matter what I did for them, it was not enough, never enough.

Coke Time was canceled in February 1956 after a run of nearly three years. The program was still very popular, but when many of the bottlers refused to handle the new family size, the company retaliated by stopping all its national advertising, including my show. My association with the company had been a perfect marriage. As the Coca-Cola Kid, I had become almost as familiar as the Coke bottle itself, part of the family, an institution.

I remember the night I was asked to sing the national anthem at a banquet where President Eisenhower would speak. I had just fifteen minutes to get from the NBC studios to the Astor Hotel, changing my shirt in the car along the way, and I didn't make it. The program had already begun by the time I got there, so I just sat down at the far end of the dais until someone came over and said the President wanted to see me. I went to the head of the dais and the President said, "I'm sorry you missed singing the national anthem, Eddie. Would you like to sing something else for us before I go on the air?" I sang Irving Berlin's "Count Your Blessings" from the movie *White Christmas,* a song I thought was appropriate for the occasion. So did the audience; they gave me a tremendous ovation. I went back to my seat and again someone came and told me the President wanted to speak to me. "Eddie," he said, "how would you like me to introduce you on television, singing that song?" His address was being broadcast nationwide, and about thirty seconds later the lights and cameras went on and the President stood up and said, "Fellow Americans, I heard a song a few moments ago and I liked it so well that I wanted Americans everywhere to hear it. Mr. Fisher, would you mind singing one more verse of that song?"

It was an extraordinary moment. As far as I knew, I was the only performer ever introduced on television by a President. And the song, which had laid an egg when I first recorded it, became an overnight hit for me and for Irving Berlin. It was his last hit. Years later, at another banquet at the Astor, given to honor then former President Eisenhower by Roger Blau, chairman of United States Steel, I was asked to say a few words and told the audience what had happened to "Count Your Blessings" after the President introduced me on television. President

Eisenhower, grinning broadly, nudged me with his elbow and said, "Pretty good press agent, huh, Eddie?"

Mrs. Eisenhower had her own favorite song. Over and over again, Mrs. Robert Woodruff, the wife of the president of the Coca-Cola Comapny, called up or wrote to ask me to sing "You'll Never Walk Alone" for her friend Mamie. Thanks to *Coke Time,* I had an audience in living rooms all across America, including the White House. Still, I wasn't sorry the show was canceled. I had been doing the same thing twice a week for three years: four songs, a few words and a duet with the guest star, good evening, good night, and that was it. More often than not, I sang my hit records: simple melodies, simple lyrics, bubble gum songs.

Al Jolson's songs had also become a popular part of my repertory. My identification with Jolson started as early as my nickname, Sonny Boy, and it was enhanced on *Coke Time* when Milton hired Harry Akst to be my accompanist. A talented and very funny man, Harry had been Jolson's best friend and accompanist for forty-five years, and working with him, it was impossible to escape Jolson's influence. My medley of Jolson songs always stopped the show and I would go on singing them for years. But they were only a small part of a broad range of songs, new and old, that I wanted to sing in my own style.

Seldom satisfied with my performances on *Coke Time,* I wanted to do better, to do more. And I was bored. The only excitement on the show came with the words I spoke just before my closing song, often written by Milton while the show was on the air. That was my only challenge. It was time to change, to grow, to mature professionally. At twenty-seven, I was getting too old to be the boy-next-door.

But no one dared try anything different or new; don't mess with success. For the people in charge of *Coke Time,* my voice, my grin, my "boyish charm," were enough. I was searching for those extra ingredients that transform a pop singer into an entertainer of distinction and depth. Crosby had found them, Sinatra, Dinah Shore. I knew what I was looking for: quality, originality, excitement, humor. There was no time for any of that on a fifteen-minute show like *Coke Time.* I was hemmed in by a format that was already going out of style, replaced by the hour-long variety show. That's where television was going and that's where I wanted to go.

For a time I thought the problem could be solved by hiring

better writers. I even asked Skipper Dawes to join my writing staff. I wanted to help the man who had done so much to help me, and because Skipper knew me better than almost anyone, I thought he could write for me again. It didn't work out. He was still writing for the *Magic Lady Supper Club,* and his drinking had become a serious problem. But I kept him on until he himself realized he had to go back home to Philadelphia.

Milton was the best writer I had. He could always come up with something original for *Coke Time* and often wrote the additional dialogue that was dubbed into the radio version of the show. If I had to speak a few words at a testimonial or a benefit, I went to Milton. But he was the man in the middle. To keep me happy, he passed on my complaints to sponsors and producers, hired and fired writers and directors, and took the flak when people started to say that Eddie Fisher was temperamental, tough to work for, impossible to please. Milton could understand why I wanted to get out of the rut I was in, but as always, he advised caution, patience—don't rock the boat. "We'll talk about it tomorrow."

As always, I followed his advice even if I did feel a little like a robot. Then, suddenly, the show was off the air and I rediscovered that beyond the cameras and the cue cards of a television studio, there were still real people out there, live audiences. I would go back to television; other sponsors wanted me and Milton and MCA were eager to sign me up for another show. And I was still turning out hit records—twenty-two in a row. But now I was free to perform more frequently in nightclubs, particularly the big clubs springing up in Las Vegas. That was one dimension that had been missing from *Coke Time:* the challenge of meeting head-on the big black giant, as Oscar Hammerstein once called the audience. I loved reaching out to touch people, and to give my best performances I needed their reactions, their love, in return.

I guess I always wanted to be in motion pictures. The remake of Al Jolson's *The Jazz Singer* would have been a wonderful opportunity, and I was heartbroken when Danny Thomas was picked for the part. The offers I did get were turned down because they were wrong for me, but then RKO put together a package for a musical remake of the old Ginger Rogers-David Niven film *Bachelor Mother,* and that seemed right. It was the story of a girl who finds a baby on her doorstep, which leads to all kinds of trouble at the department store where she works, particularly with the son of the owner, until they fall in love and everything ends happily. The new title was *Bundle of Joy;* I would play the son of the department store owner, and Debbie would be borrowed from MGM to play the girl. America's Sweethearts starring in their first film together: that kind of commercial exploitation of our relationship was probably inevitable. But I was struck by one sour note about the project from the very first: Debbie was pregnant. By the time the picture was released, we would have our own "bundle of joy," and I knew that coincidence would be exploited too.

Other sour notes followed in quick succession. *Bachelor Mother* had been sophisticated and funny; the script for *Bundle of Joy* was corny when it wasn't cute. The title gave it away and I went to William Dozier, the head of production at RKO, to ask if we could try to find a better one. "Sorry, Eddie," he said. "We've already spent $65,000 publicizing that title. We can't change it now." The man hired to direct the picture was Norman Taurog, whose chief claim to fame was his ability to work with singers who couldn't act, and that made me uneasy. It was like bringing in a doctor before anyone was sick. And there were too many musical numbers, probably on the assumption that all the clichés in the plot wouldn't matter if the characters just kept singing and dancing. The budget for the film was minimal, and when we finally started shooting, the sets, costumes, and everything else had the markings of a third-class production. It seemed that the whole project was being built around the "Debbie and Eddie" gimmick, and no one cared whether or not the picture was any good.

But what did I know about making movies? Even though I owned 65 percent of the film, that's what I was told whenever I voiced an objection or tried to make a suggestion. "Eddie, these men are professionals," Milton said. "They've been in the business a long time and I think you should go along with them." I did, but I didn't have any real faith in the picture, and my basic instincts told me that neither did anyone else.

Debbie was marvelous. A natural comedian, a natural singer and dancer, a natural actress, she was a complete professional whatever she may have thought of the movie. This was her world, her life, and in front of the cameras she forgot everything else, including her pregnancy. One day, with the temperature on the set about 120 degrees, we were doing a scene together and she stood under the hot lights in a mink coat during at least fifteen takes, just because the director wanted a few reaction shots. It was obvious that everyone was in a hurry to finish the picture before Debbie's pregnancy could no longer be covered up. I finally protested when I saw her being tossed around by male dancers in a rehearsal of one of the musical numbers. "My God, Debbie," I said, "we can cut that number. You're seven months pregnant." "Of course not," she said. "It's a wonderful number. Don't worry, everything will be fine." She was right. Our daughter, Carrie, a beautiful, healthy baby, was born just two months later.

I tried my best to do a good job. In fact, both Debbie and I worked so hard that we didn't even go home during the last few weeks of shooting. We stayed in a bungalow on the lot. Then I saw the final cut. As bad as I was, the picture was even worse, a bomb. I had to sit through the whole thing at the Hollywood premiere, but at the premiere in New York, at the Capitol Theater, I couldn't take it again and decided to wait in the lobby. There I met a steady stream of my friends, walking out. At the party after the show, everybody said, "Marvelous! Your voice never sounded better, Eddie. You never danced better, Debbie. Great acting, a great script, great direction, great title, great everything." Great bullshit.

Bundle of Joy laid a financial egg, the songs disappeared without a trace, and Debbie's was the only movie career that managed to survive. The next offer I got was the starring role, a big, red-bearded patriarch, in a biblical epic called *The King of the Jews*.

According to the fan magazines, Debbie and I had achieved the impossible: a blissful marriage in spite of the demands of our separate careers. Joey Forman remembers our marriage the way it really was. "It was always strained, Eddie. The two careers *were* a problem. Not only two careers but two stars, an actress and a singer. How could it be anything but strained? I think you were both trying—trying to be in love, trying to have a relationship—but all these other forces kept pulling you apart."

Our careers were important to both of us, and with the exception of the weeks we worked together on *Bundle of Joy*, they took us into different worlds. But it was our very different personalities that really pulled us apart. Opening day at Disneyland, I had ridden in the lead car of a motorcade with Walt Disney himself and later was mobbed by hundreds of youngsters as I passed out free Coke. But I wasn't the Coca-Cola Kid anymore, and I was outgrowing my image as the boy-next-door. Throwing caution to the winds at a Friars Club roast MC'd by Mike Todd, I sang a rather raunchy parody of Sammy Cahn's "All the Way" which he wrote for me that left Jack Benny, George Burns and a host of other show business veterans rolling in the aisles. Almost in spite of myself, I was acquiring some sophistication and moving on a faster track in Hollywood and Las Vegas. But Debbie clung to her image as the girl next door and remained relentlessly unsophisticated. In Las Vegas for the grand opening of the Tropicana Hotel, she attended my premiere performance as the star of the show, before an audience packed with celebrities, in a home-made dress, one of Maxine's creations. She seemed to be saying that here was one Hollywood actress who hadn't been spoiled by stardom, and many people loved her for her simplicity and lack of affectation. To me, it seemed like a pose.

Debbie *was* a star: actress, dancer, singer, mimic—and comedian. During my engagement at the Tropicana, she and I attended a seder on the first night of Passover. Seated around the table were some ten or twenty comedians, including Milton Berle, Jack E. Leonard, and Red Buttons. As the eldest, my friend Joe E. Lewis led us through the ceremony, others also took part, and as the youngest, I asked the Four Questions. Then Debbie, with her perfect timing, piped up and said, "Now I'd like to say a few words on behalf of Jesus Christ." Everybody rocked with laughter. Debbie, the only woman as well as the only non-Jew in the room, stole the show from some of the toughest comics in the business.

She was a clown, a very funny one, but clowns have to be in the spotlight. And Debbie, like any comic—or any singer, for that matter—sometimes didn't know when to get offstage. No matter where we were, no matter who we were with, she competed for attention, even with me. Just after we were married, I was elected to head a committee of people who organized charity shows for Cedars of Lebanon Hospital. I brought Debbie to one of the meetings, and the next thing I knew, *she* was head of the committee. I let it slide, like so many other things. I felt secure; there was no necessity for me to compete with

Debbie. Even if I had tried, she always got her own way in the end. The only person who stood up to her was our cook Olivia Smith. One night she told Debbie to get out of her kitchen, and when Debbie didn't move fast enough, Olivia chased her out, brandishing a butcher knife. I sympathized with Olivia, but after that incident I had to let her go.

I commissioned Gari, Eddie Cantor's son-in-law and a very skillful artist, to paint a portrait of Debbie. "Put me somewhere in the background," I said. And he did. Debbie, dressed as a clown, dominated the picture; I was a gray outline behind her. It was symbolic of our relationship. Debbie wanted to have everything in perfect order: me, our house, our lives. There seemed to be little we could work out together, little we could share. She had her friends, I had mine, and because they didn't mix, we seldom invited them to the house at the same time. Even the joy of having Carrie didn't bring us closer together. We both wanted children. In fact, the day Carrie was born, I was literally dizzy with the excitement of becoming a father, just as if I were drunk. Debbie went back to work almost immediately, but her love for the baby was deep and genuine. She made a wonderful mother. And I was a proud father—even a good one when I was around. But with my schedule of performances, I wasn't around that much. The nurse and Maxine took over, everything was done the way Debbie wanted it done, and I wasn't sure where I was supposed to fit in.

I felt left out in the bedroom too. It seemed to me that Debbie just wasn't interested, or at least not as interested as I was. Hurt by her rejections, I confided in Rory Calhoun, who, with his wife Lita Baron, were the only friends Debbie and I had in common. I was the godfather of their daughter Cindy. "Take it easy. Give it time," Rory advised me. And I tried. I had no thoughts of looking elsewhere. That was the way I was brought up. Very conscious of my responsibilities and my image, I couldn't fool around with other women. Debbie was my wife.

Both of us were unhappy. I wasn't what Debbie wanted me to be; she wasn't what I wanted her to be. But for Louella and Hedda, for the reporters and the photographers, everything was sweetness and light. During an appearance on Edward R. Murrow's *Person to Person*, Debbie made several suggestive remarks and gestures in the direction of the bedroom, as if we just couldn't wait for the program to end. "We're going to do everything in our power to stay together," we always told the fan magazines. "Nothing is going to keep us apart." We were married to the fan magazines, not to each other. We fed them the stories they wanted to hear and I found myself saying things I didn't mean, playing a role. For Debbie that may have come naturally, part of her job as an actress; I felt like a hypocrite, trying to live up to an image that was at variance with my real feelings. Maybe that was the name of the game, but did Debbie and I have to pretend to *ourselves* that our marriage was ideally happy?

In spite of the way I felt, somehow I couldn't talk to Debbie. We didn't argue; we seldom even had a serious conversation. Our first fight, when it finally occurred, was my last. My accountant advised us to file a joint income tax return, which would have saved many thousands of dollars, but Debbie refused. She said *her* accountants advised her to file separately to avoid any liability I might incur. Who was she married to, I asked, her accountants or me? Then I swore at her under my breath and she slapped me.

It was a trivial matter, something another married couple might have resolved easily. But to me it seemed that the gulf between us was too wide and I gave up trying to understand Debbie. There was no way I could reach her. It was as much my fault as hers. Seldom very good at finding the right words to express myself, I kept my emotions bottled up inside. And when I didn't know what to say in situations that caused me confusion and pain, I simply turned my back and walked away.

I turned my back and walked away from Debbie.

10

Milton Blackstone seemed able to function only in situations over which he had complete control. Things had to be done his way. He didn't like to make concessions or compromises. Polite, humble, he was a benevolent dictator. At Grossinger's, his authority remained unchallenged, but after my marriage to Debbie his hold over me began to loosen. The distance and the differences between New York and California were partly responsible. Milton's beat was Broadway. He thought Hollywood might be a place to live, but New York was the only place to work. And although there was no other man I respected more, I had come to recognize that his advice was not automatically the best advice. Our business association remained unchanged, but the father-son relationship was falling apart. It was tough for both of us, and we could both behave like kids. If I refused to do something he wanted me to do, he withdrew and let me flounder. If he didn't approve of something I wanted, I hurt him with cutting remarks or became moody and uncommunicative. We had been too close too long, yet we couldn't let go.

In California, the influence of Max Jacobson's powerful personality also began to recede, although I still thought injections were essential to my performances. Both Milton and

Max always flew out to attend a major opening or an important appearance. Then Max gave me an injection, and he and Milton would sit together in the audience like conspirators. But on the West Coast, in Max's absence, I became a patient of Dr. Hans Schiff, a far more conventional and less controversial medical man than Max. Although he was an adherent of Max's theories, Schiff didn't experiment with his patients, and the shots he gave me were always intramuscular—in the cheek of my ass. When Schiff died, I went to Max's son, Tommy, who had just moved to the West Coast to establish his medical practice.

With Milton and Max fading into the background of my life, a very different kind of man emerged to take their place— Mike Todd. Mike was in Hollywood now, and right in the middle of the two most flamboyant ventures of his entire career: his film *Around the World in 80 Days* and his romance with Elizabeth Taylor.

Mike and I had become best friends since our meeting in Florida. We had seen each other frequently over the years and Mike always made the time we spent together an adventure. Deeply involved in every aspect of show business, from the smallest technical details to the finished production, Mike was in love with the theater. In New York we went to plays that hadn't got very good reviews, laughing and applauding wildly to encourage the actors and stimulate the rest of the audience. Once, as we were speeding through Riverdale in the Bronx after turning off the West Side Highway to elude a carload of fans, he said, "Let's pay a call on Arturo." I said sure, thinking he meant a famous maître d' we both knew. Arturo turned out to be Arturo Toscanini and we walked into his house without an invitation. But Toscanini welcomed us warmly and he and Mike sat down to discuss Mike's latest inspiration: a film of the Maestro's life.

Mike was on top again. Both Cinerama and Todd-AO had become realities and big money-makers. Mike and I went to the opening of *Oklahoma!*, the first film in Todd-AO. There had been so many previews of the picture that the print was badly worn, and Mike begged George Skouras, of 20th Century-Fox, to postpone the premiere until they could get a new one. Skouras refused, and that night Mike and I sat together in the audience watching all the streaks and scratches on the screen. It was awful. The picture got good reviews, but a new print could have made a dramatic difference and Mike had every right to be furious. All he did was walk to the men's room, take a leak, and forget about it. He had the marvelous ability to let failure roll right off his back and move on.

Mike had produced *Around the World in 80 Days* himself and it was fourteen-carat Todd all the way, no expense spared to make it one of the most lavish productions in Hollywood history. Mike had spent more on a couple of scenes in his film than the entire budget of *Bundle of Joy,* even though he didn't always know where the money was coming from. Toward the end of the production, he called me at NBC. "Eddie," he said, "tell Mannie Sacks I need half a million from RCA by tomorrow."

I immediately spoke to Mannie, who told me he would have to talk to the board of directors. "Well, then," Mike said when I called back, "ask him for a quarter of a million."

Mannie said he still had to have a board meeting, so I phoned Mike again. "Look," I said, "I've got $365,000 in the bank. You can have that by tomorrow."

"I don't want your money, you little Jew bastard," he said. "I'll get it someplace else." And he did—from William Paley at CBS, who didn't have to call a meeting of the board. Paley eventually made at least ten million dollars on the film.

Mike wanted me to play one of the cameo roles in the picture. He had charmed a long list of stars into appearing for nothing—or next to nothing. Sinatra got a Thunderbird. I would have gladly paid Mike to be in it, but under my contract with RKO, my first movie appearance had to be *Bundle of Joy.* Then I heard the title song and asked Mike if I could have an exclusive to record it. That was impossible, he said. The top stars of all the major record companies were doing it; nobody had an exclusive. But impossible or not, Mike kept Victor Young and an eighty-two-piece symphony orchestra standing by one evening until I could get to the Goldwyn Studios to cut the record, and my version was the first to be released. Then we found out that RKO wouldn't even permit my voice on the sound track of the movie. We got our revenge. My recording of the title song was often played before and after a showing of the film, and I sang it so often it was almost embarrassing.

I idolized Mike. I wanted to be like him and he became the most important and influential man in my life. We were constant companions whenever we both had free time; one New

York columnist dubbed us "Damon and Pythias." With a lot of friends in common, there were usually other people around, yet our relationship seemed to be separate, unique, something very special. We found an escape in each other's company from all the pressures in our lives. Neither one of us drank, and once, I remember, we got bombed on one vodka gimlet in the Polo Lounge at the Beverly Hills Hotel and then drove to Palm Springs. Mike was behind the wheel and we laughed and horsed around like a couple of high school kids on a Saturday night spree. Mike didn't want to hear about my troubles with Debbie or Milton, and I could forget them when I was with him. He strongly disapproved of the injections, whether I got them from Jacobson or from anyone else. But that was my business, not his. He assumed I was smart enough to lead my own life.

There were things in his life we never talked about either— his early years of struggle, when he did almost anything, including barking at the Chicago World's Fair, to make a buck; his first marriage, which ended in tragedy; his second marriage, to Joan Blondell, who, his son Mike Todd, Jr., once told me, was the greatest love of his life. Past and future didn't seem to matter to Mike; he lived in the present, and he lived fast. His relationship with Evelyn Keyes had lasted for a number of years, but other women came and went. He asked me to give one of his girl friends a couple of weeks' work in *Bundle of Joy*, which I did, seeing her once or twice at the studio before she vanished. He was even briefly involved with Marlene Dietrich, who also appeared in a cameo role in *Around the World*. One night at a party Mike was giving for Edward R. Murrow, Marlene was at his house acting as hostess. "Mike," I said with surprise, "what are you doing with Marlene?" "Oh, she's just here to help with the party," he said. But I knew when Mike was lying and when he wasn't, so I looked in the closet in his bedroom and there were Marlene's clothes—not just a couple of dresses; an entire wardrobe. Mike knew of my romance with Marlene and was obviously a little embarrassed, but Marlene was as gracious as ever and I said nothing more about it.

I met Elizabeth Taylor again at a small party at Mike's house for just a few friends: Debbie and me, David Niven and his wife, Elizabeth and her husband Michael Wilding. Mike was with Evelyn, and the moment I arrived I sensed a peculiar tension in the air. Evelyn was too animated, Elizabeth too quiet, and Mike too busy at the outdoor grill by the pool, barbecuing steaks and roasting corn. Elizabeth was obviously the center of his attention as the evening wore on. Mike was always doing things for people he liked, but the way he catered to Elizabeth seemed a little excessive, even for him.

When Debbie and I left, Mike walked with us up the long flight of steps from the pool to the house. I thanked him for the evening and as I opened the door to the car, all of a sudden it hit me. Something was going on between Mike and Elizabeth. "Wait a minute," I said with a big grin. "You're in love."

"Get in the car," he said. "Scram. Get the hell out of here."

"Okay, okay," I said. "I'll talk to you tomorrow."

Debbie and I drove off, leaving Mike standing in the driveway with a smirk on his face. He was the worst actor in the world and that expression told me all I wanted to know.

I'm not sure how it happened, or when. Elizabeth's friend Hedda Hopper had talked her into attending a press party Mike gave aboard the boat used in *Around the World,* and knowing Mike, the sparks probably started flying the moment he looked at her. His long and tempestuous relationship with Evelyn didn't seem to present any problems. They had split up and reconciled many times, and I remember seeing beside Mike's bed a picture of Evelyn that had obviously been torn to shreds and then carefully pasted together and put back in the frame. I liked Evelyn. She was beautiful, intellectually stimulating, and in her own way, just as zany as Mike. I always thought they were perfect for each other, but I didn't question Mike when he admitted he was deeply in love with Elizabeth and wanted to marry her. I had never seen him more excited about anything in his life. "But for God's sake, don't tell anybody," he said. "I don't want the whole world to know."

The whole world soon found out, which was exactly what Mike had in mind. Elizabeth was in love too, and neither she nor Mike was noted for being inconspicuous. Elizabeth already had a husband, but in fact, her five-year marriage to Michael was really over, and I wondered if they had ever had much in common. Michael was aloof and detached. You could never tell what he was thinking, while Elizabeth usually made no secret of what was on her mind. After a string of costume epics, she had finally been given a chance to act in *Giant* and her career was booming. Michael, who had been heralded as another David Niven, wasn't quite making it in Hollywood. To add to their other problems, Michael drank too much. Debbie and I had met them a few months before when we were looking at property near their house, and it didn't look like a good relationship to us. They had two young sons, Michael and Christopher, who may have been the only reason they were still together.

The moment was right, the chemistry was right, and Mike and Elizabeth were drawn irresistibly toward each other. I could understand why Mike wanted to marry her: Elizabeth was beautiful, a famous Hollywood star, but as far as I was concerned she could also be a pain in the ass, a spoiled brat. Of course, Mike was sometimes pretty childish himself. I loved watching the way they behaved together, but their courtship, if that's what it could be called, was like free-play period in kindergarten.

One night I was already undressed and in bed when I got a call from Mike. Debbie and I had had a spat and I was staying at the Beverly Hills Hotel, but Mike tracked me down. "Look," he said, "I'm here at Harold Mirisch's house playing gin and Elizabeth is bored. Come on over and talk to her, will you? You know what to say."

I got dressed and went, even though it was the last thing I wanted to do. Elizabeth was sitting in the living room drinking champagne, and Mike was in another room with William Wyler, John Huston, and some of his other cardplaying cronies. I sat down and started talking to Elizabeth, telling her every tale I knew about Mike, what a wonderful man he was, a good friend, brilliant, funny, a genius. Elizabeth's eyes lit up with each new story. Mike came running in after every hand to give her a kiss, and finally said, "We're almost finished, Elizabeth. You should go home and get your clothes." They were driving down to Joe Schenck's house in Palm Springs.

"Mike," I said, shaking my head, "she shouldn't go by herself."

"Then why don't you take her and bring her right back?"

Elizabeth was separated from Michael, waiting for a divorce, still living in the house they had bought together. I drove her home and she said, "Pour me a brandy and tell me more about Mike." We sat down and I continued the Mike Todd saga until we suddenly realized it was three-thirty in the morning. "Oh, God," Elizabeth said. "Mike will be furious."

I didn't see why. "Just call and tell him we're on our way back," I said.

"No, *you* call him," Elizabeth said.

Finally she picked up the phone. Harold Mirisch answered and told her Mike had left over an hour before, mad as hell.

Elizabeth was very upset and I had to persuade her to call Mike at home. He started screaming at her over the phone. I could hear it. "You've walked over everybody you've ever been with," he said, "but you're not going to do that to me!" And he hung up.

By this time Elizabeth was in hysterics, so I called Mike. "Well," he said indifferently, "I hope you had a good time."

"Mike, you're crazy," I said. "We were talking about *you!* I'm bringing Elizabeth over."

"Don't do me any more favors. Stay out of this. Go home." And he hung up again.

"Come on, Elizabeth," I said. "Pack your clothes, fix your face, and I'll take you to Mike's."

"But he doesn't want me," she whimpered.

"He wants you," I said, and pushed her in the direction of the bedroom. I sat down and waited, wondering what the hell I was doing in a situation like this. Ten minutes, fifteen, twenty. "Elizabeth, come on. Hurry up," I yelled. There was no answer, so I walked into the bedroom and saw that the bathroom door was closed. God, I thought, she's committed suicide. I threw open the door, and there was Elizabeth staring at herself in the mirror, very slowly, very carefully making up her eyes.

Another fifteen minutes passed before she was ready to go, padding across the living room in her bare feet because she couldn't find her shoes. "Bring that bottle," she said.

I drove the car with one hand and held a glassful of brandy for her in the other. I spilled it, of course, and the smell was overpowering. What would happen if the police stopped us or we had an accident? I couldn't wait to get Elizabeth out of that car. But the night wasn't over yet. There was a policeman standing at the front door of Mike's house, and now I thought *he* had committed suicide. I left Elizabeth in the car and spoke to the cop, who told me a disturbance had been reported in the neighborhood. But he recognized me and I convinced him that Mr. Todd was all right; I had just spoken to him on the phone. The officer left and I went back to the car to get Elizabeth.

"Don't leave me," she said. She seemed terrified, as if it wasn't the first time something like this had happened.

"Don't worry," I said. "Everything's going to be okay. I won't leave you." I helped her out of the car and we stood together at the front door of the house.

I rang the bell and knocked loudly several times before Mike came to the door. He tried to pretend he had been asleep. His hair was mussed but his white silk pajamas didn't have a crease in them. "Mike," I said, "it's me."

"Well, what do you want?"

"Elizabeth is here."

"Oh," he said with a shrug. "Come on in."

I followed him into the living room, with Elizabeth clinging to my arm. Mike didn't even turn around; he just kept on walking toward the bedroom. "Mike," I called, "where are you going? Elizabeth is here."

"Okay," he said.

Elizabeth was pleading to me with her eyes not to leave her. Turning and heading for the door, I couldn't get out of there fast enough. Elizabeth started after me, but Mike grabbed her. And the last thing I saw was her bare feet in midair as he picked her up and carried her into the bedroom.

I wasn't attracted to Elizabeth. I sometimes found it hard even to like her, but I was drawn into her life because of the way we both felt about Mike. She loved to talk, especially when she was drinking champagne, and she would sit down with me in some quiet corner and tell me the most intimate details about herself. I don't know why and never asked; she probably felt she could confide in me because Mike and I were so close. As I got to know her better, I felt sorry for Elizabeth. Her beauty was a curse. She had grown up fighting off every man who came near her, fighting to prove she was an actress, not just a beautiful face, and it made her tough. She could drink with the best of them, she swore, she was the antithesis of her ethereal, ladylike screen image. Yet she was also timid, insecure, and vulnerable, a little girl trapped inside a woman's body. Thank God, it would be Mike's job, not mine, to live with all the contradictions in her character.

Around the World in 80 Days premiered in October of 1956 at the Rivoli Theater in New York. Mike, Elizabeth, Mike junior, and I met at Mike's Park Avenue apartment the night before the opening. Debbie was still pregnant and couldn't come. This was it—boom or bust for Mike Todd—but he was just as cocky and confident as ever. The phone rang. Otis Chandler of the Los Angeles *Times* was calling to offer Mike $25 million and 25 percent of the picture, or $15 million and 50 percent, granting Mike control. It was a tempting offer. The picture hadn't yet made a dollar and Mike was millions in the hole, but he said, "Just a minute, we'll take a vote." Holding his hand over the receiver, he explained the deal to us.

"Take the money, Dad," Mike junior said.

"Take it," I echoed.

"No," Elizabeth said. "Let's gamble."

Mike smiled. "You guys lose," he said to Mike and me. "Majority rules." And then into the phone, "Thank you very much, Mr. Chandler, but no dice."

The premiere was black tie, by invitation only. Mike and I sat in the back of the theater, working a little box that controlled the sound system, twirling the dials to raise or lower the volume at the dramatic moments, as if this were a Movieola, not a multimillion-dollar picture. Mike spotted a lady on the aisle who had fallen asleep. "What are you doing?" he said loudly. "Wake up!" The lady jumped and he glared at her furiously. The picture ended, the audience began to applaud and cheer, and Mike was beaming, until he saw Walter Winchell walking up the aisle. "Stop him, for God's sake," he said. "He hasn't seen the credits yet. That's the best part."

I intercepted Winchell and literally held him there as the credits flashed across the screen. He was scowling when he left the theater and I was certain he was going to give the picture a bad review.

Mike, Elizabeth, and I saw him later that evening at Lindy's, sitting all alone at his usual table, and because he and Mike were supposed to be having some kind of feud, we wanted to ignore him. But he waved us over. "I just thought you might like to see this," he said, reaching into his pocket and handing Mike a sheet of paper. It was the review he had already written—a rave. Other reviewers said the same thing; there just weren't enough superlatives to go around. *"Around the World in 80 Days,"* one headline proclaimed, "will run forever." Mike had come up winners on the biggest gamble of his career. *Around the World in 80 Days* was a smash and later went on to win the Academy Award as the best picture of the year.

Mike and Elizabeth were married in Acapulco in February 1957, a fairly modest production compared to the way Mike usually did things, because Elizabeth was still recovering from an operation on her spine. Remote and beautiful, Acapulco was not yet overrun with tourists. Mike and Elizabeth were staying in the seaside villa of a distinguished Mexican architect, one of four houses built along a private beach guarded by soldiers of the Mexican army. The lights would flicker and go out, the water sputtered in the faucets, and at the last minute Mike decided there weren't enough flowers for the ceremony. So he and I commandeered a whole truckload from the marketplace and raced around strewing them all over the house. Mike had two best men: Cantinflas, one of the stars of *Around the World,* and me. Debbie was the necessary choice as Elizabeth's matron of honor.

That night we all sat on the beach and watched the display of fireworks Mike had arranged. They were a perfect symbol of their relationship: noise, excitement, surprise. Every day was like the Fourth of July. Mike and Elizabeth fought constantly; for them that was as much fun as making up afterward. They played games with each other, teasing, taunting, just to see how far they could go, how much they could get away with. Both of them were quick-tempered, theatrical, but there was another side to their marriage, a quieter side. If Mike treated Elizabeth like a toy, an expensive plaything, he also treated her like a woman, perhaps the first man in her life to recognize that behind her beautiful face was a sharp and inquisitive mind. He introduced her to a world bigger than Hollywood; he took her, sometimes kicking and screaming, out of her preoccupation with herself.

I watched them together with utter fascination—and envy, not because I was in love with Elizabeth, but because there was so little love in my own marriage. Nothing had changed between Debbie and me. If anything, we were drifting even farther apart, both of us busy with our separate careers, our separate lives, still scared to admit that we had no life together. We had moved from the Thalberg estate, first renting the house on Mapleton Drive where Judy Garland had lived, then another house in Beverly Hills, an English Tudor mansion, which I bought. We talked about doing it over and Debbie picked out thousands of dollars' worth of antiques to furnish it. We were going through the motions of marriage, pretending we had a future together, and all the while I thought, We can't go on this way: it's too painful for both of us.

Dean Martin and his wife Jeannie lived across the street, other friends were nearby, and Debbie and I were invited to their houses as a couple for their big parties. When it was just neighbors and close friends, I usually went alone. Debbie and Elizabeth were oil and water. Both were Hollywood creations, but they might have come from two different planets. The contrast between them was almost comical: Elizabeth with her flashy dresses and even flashier jewelry, Debbie in clothes that made her look like everybody's high school sweetheart; Elizabeth with a cigarette in her mouth and a drink in her hand, Debbie giving us all prim lectures on the evils of smoking and drinking. She thought her virtue was her one superiority over Elizabeth, so she played her girl scout role to the hilt. Elizabeth simply accepted Debbie for what she was, although she and Mike did tease and laugh at her, trying to get her to loosen up, to be herself. Sometimes it worked. Mike was the catalyst; he brought out the best in all of us.

I wanted to end our marriage, but whenever I could get Debbie to talk about it, she always came up with some reason to stay just the way we were: Carrie's need for a father, the effect of bad publicity on our careers. Divorce wasn't part of the master plan she had devised for her life. In her latest picture, *Tammy and the Bachelor,* her cuteness and virtue had once again triumphed. Her recording of the title song, "Tammy," was an enormous hit. The reality of a failed marriage could not be allowed to interfere with her image, or mine.

I went along with her, thinking that in time we could find a way to end our marriage gracefully. I didn't want to hurt Debbie, didn't want to antagonize her fans or mine; I wanted to be a nice guy, a gentleman—the very same rationalizations that had led me to marry Debbie in the first place. I still hadn't learned to say no. But I did begin to see other women, one a show girl I met during my engagement at the Tropicana in Las Vegas—Pat Shean, who later married Bing Crosby's son Dennis. For a time I kept a small apartment in Los Angeles as a hideout, a place where I could retreat rather than face my troubles at home. And I began to gamble—in a small way at first, then for larger and larger stakes, until I was hooked.

Like many kids, my first experience with gambling was pitching pennies in the schoolyard. But later, if I was asked to join backstage poker or pinochle games, I usually found some excuse. I preferred chess; it was more intellectual. I wasted money in a lot of other ways, but I didn't like to lose it on the turn of a card. My real introduction to gambling came from Mike. He had a regular poker game at John Huston's bungalow at the Beverly Hills Hotel, with John, William Wyler, Kurt Frings, Carl Laemmle, Jr., and a couple of other guys. If I was around, they asked me to sit in. Why not? I had no business being in the game, but Mike always said, "Don't worry about it. If you lose, I'll win it back for you from Willie Wyler." I enjoyed the games, even if I was way out of my league, and Mike usually lost too. Gin was his game, so he would take Wyler into the bedroom, play a few hands, and give me back my money. Painless and fun.

Mike in Las Vegas was another matter. He usually played craps and never for anything less than the limit; as much as seven thousand dollars would be riding on each roll of the dice. Sometimes he won, but nobody wins for long and it upset me to see him sinking deeper and deeper in the hole. Once he ran out of money, or credit, and asked to cash a ten-thousand-dollar check. This was before *Around the World* had come out, and no one would touch it. He was angry and embarrassed, but determined to find some way to keep on playing, so I got the check cashed and he lost that too.

Mike was a terrible gambler. I sometimes thought he liked to be taken. Once, he lost a quarter of a million dollars to Darryl Zanuck in a gin game, and on another occasion, the Del Mar racetrack, which he owned. But win or lose, he didn't seem to care. Mike gambled the way he lived—for the risk and excitement of it. Elizabeth couldn't bear to watch him; they had their biggest fights over Mike's gambling. But I was fascinated, and when he pushed a few left-over chips in my direction, I'd bet with him or put them on a number of my own. The chips multiplied or disappeared—I had no idea what I was doing.

The bug really bit me when I was playing the Tropicana. Between shows there wasn't much else to do but gamble, so

I started hanging around the craps table, playing with silver dollars. One night I went partners with Debbie's mother; she put up two dollars and pulled out when we had won twelve. Then I went partners with her father, who pulled out when he had won forty dollars. So I kept on playing alone. And winning. It was incredible. The whole place was going wild. I wouldn't take hundred-dollar chips; I wanted the piles to look really big. When I finally quit and cashed in, I'd won $25,000.

After that, I began to play constantly—before shows, between shows, after shows. I still didn't know what I was doing, but I was smart enough to put all my winnings in a safe-deposit box, and when I lost, I owed the house. I went partners with everybody—show girls, the guys in the chorus, stagehands, friends—and eight weeks later, I owed the house $25,000. I went to count the money in the safe-deposit box: $25,000! I had broken even, something that was virtually impossible. I just stared at the money as if I had found it on the street.

That was the beginning. I had beaten the odds, and a gambler always remembers that even if he loses for the rest of his life. Gambling became a habit, a release from the tensions of performing, an escape from becoming too deeply involved in anything else. But I can't blame Mike for leading me up to the tables. And I can't blame Debbie because I sometimes stayed there for hours rather than be with her. I was running away from no one but myself.

Elizabeth was pregnant and, ignoring the warnings of her doctor that it would probably kill her, decided she wanted the child. Mike was delirious with joy. The incredible success of *Around the World in 80 Days,* marriage to Elizabeth, a baby—now he had everything. He and Elizabeth were traveling all over Europe, promoting the film, attracting enormous crowds wherever they went. Fitted with a special brace because of her back problem, a third Caesarean a certainty if she did not miscarry—Elizabeth got through it somehow. Watching over her like a mother hen, Mike rented a $20,000-a-month villa at Cap Ferrat, where they could rest and relax, and they asked me to join them.

I couldn't resist. I made arrangements to sing at the Palladium, timing the engagement to coincide with the London premiere of *Around the World.* Debbie came with me, and there was a noticeable difference in the way we were received by the British press and public. Before were were married, Debbie had shared my spotlight; now, with a popular movie and a hit record, she had a spotlight of her own and reporters wrote that our marriage was in trouble because I was jealous of her. It wasn't true. I was happy for Debbie. She was working hard and had earned her new success. Amusing, I thought, that the British press, so eager for our marriage two years before, now seemed equally eager to predict a divorce.

Reporters even fabricated a rift between Princess Margaret and me. According to their version of the story, she walked out of a party to pay me back for declining the original invitation, so I stood up and sang "Wish You Were Here." My secretary, Eileen Thomas, did decline originally, because she thought the caller was joking, but when she reported it to me, I told her the invitation was probably genuine. The princess didn't walk out, and I didn't sing anything at all that evening. I was just a guest. From a romance between "The Princess and the Pop Singer" to "Wish You Were Here"—a good story, I guess, but another indication of just how fickle the press can sometimes be.

The London premiere of *Around the World* was another triumph for Mike, and to cap it off, he rented the Battersea Amusement Park and threw a party for two thousand people, which lasted until dawn. After another spectacular opening in Paris, Mike and Elizabeth, Debbie and I, retreated to Cap Ferrat for a vacation which, for me, was highlighted by an appearance at a gala in Monaco for Princess Grace and Prince Rainier. I had first met Grace Kelly at a cocktail party at the Hampshire House in New York. We were both unattached and both Philadelphians—although her family lived in rather a better neighborhood than mine—and I asked her for a date. "I'd love to," she said with a warm smile, "but I'm sailing for Europe tomorrow." Her trip took her to Monaco and I never had a chance to ask her again.

While I was in London, Bob Hope had called to ask me to join him in North Africa, where he was entertaining American troops. I told him about the gala in Monaco; but he said there wouldn't be any problem: he'd send a plane. The afternoon I was supposed to fly out, Princess Grace and Prince Rainier invited me to the palace, and I found them both so interesting and their conversation so fascinating that I kept a planeload of generals and army brass waiting for three hours before I could tear myself away.

The trip to North Africa was brief; I flew back almost immediately to rejoin Mike, Elizabeth, and Debbie at Cap Ferrat. Awaiting their baby, Mike and Elizabeth were closer than ever before—not quite as many fights and temper tantrums. But even though he was gravely concerned about her condition, Mike couldn't sit still for long. Monte Carlo was not too many miles away and every once in a while he got the urge to gamble.

"Elizabeth," he said one evening after dinner, "Eddie and I are going to the casino."

"Oh, no you're not," she said.

"We just want to look around."

"You can't go."

"Please. We'll be back in twenty minutes. I promise."

Elizabeth gave in. "All right," she said. "Go ahead, but if you're not home in exactly twenty minutes, you can't come in the bedroom."

There was no way we could be back in twenty minutes. It took that long just to get to the casino. But we drove there like madmen and began to gamble. Nothing of importance; just a couple of guys out to have a good time. I kept looking at my watch, reminding Mike of Elizabeth's threat. "Don't worry," he said. "She never means it."

By the time we returned to the villa, it was pretty late. We tiptoed in and Mike turned the knob on their bedroom door. It was locked. He rapped gently. No response. He began pounding and yelling, "Elizabeth, let me in!" He spent the night sleeping on a hard little bench outside the bedroom door.

The next morning, they played their usual reconciliation scene. All was forgiven. Even Debbie and I had moments of intimacy while we were there. But for us it was not a reconciliation. After many long talks, we had finally decided to get a divorce. Done the way I wanted to do it, quietly, gracefully, it would be the right way to end a relationship that had become so difficult for both of us. We planned to go in different directions after we left Cap Ferrat. Debbie was spending the remainder of her vacation in Spain, with her friend Jeanette Johnson. I was going to Israel. When we got back to Los Angeles in a few weeks time, we could see a lawyer.

I had done a lot of work raising money for Israel bonds and

other Jewish causes, but this was the first time I had been to Israel and it was one of the most exciting countries I had ever seen. The spirit and dedication of the people were infectious. I felt like a new man, a free man, and even had a brief affair with a young Israeli woman, without the usual pangs of guilt about being unfaithful to my wife.

Not long after Debbie and I returned to Los Angeles, we went to see my lawyer, Mickey Rudin, and sat in his office for hours, discussing the divorce: separation, child support, community property, the custody of Carrie. Everything was very friendly, very agreeable, and Debbie was not always known to be agreeable. The process would begin with an immediate separation while Mickey drew up the necessary papers.

Debbie and I drove home together without saying a word. I went to the bedroom and started going through the drawers, getting a few things together. I planned to stay at the Beverly Hills Hotel until I could find a permanent place to live. Debbie followed me into the room, watched me for a few moments, and then turned to look out a window. "I'm with child," she said.

"You're with what?" I said.

"I'm pregnant."

I sat down on the corner of the bed, unable to conceal my exasperation. "Debbie, couldn't you have told me this *before* we went to see Mickey? I can't leave you now. Well, what do you want? What's the next step?"

It was a question with only one answer and I figured it out for myself. That night I moved into another bedroom.

11

Debbie later told me that she had planned this pregnancy. If nothing else, she wanted a companion for Carrie before our marriage ended. She may even have hoped her pregnancy would prevent, or at least postpone, a divorce. Her reasoning was as confusing as ever, but her timing was perfect.

Debbie was always throwing curves like that, always catching me off balance. What was I supposed to do? I could have gone ahead with the divorce, but I wanted the baby too, and I couldn't walk out on Debbie while she was pregnant. So I stayed and the fan magazines cooed that "America's Sweethearts" were happily expecting a new addition to their family. It was another round for Debbie, another lie obscuring the truth of our marriage.

Elizabeth and Mike had their baby in August 1957. Premature and thought to be stillborn, the little girl finally began to breathe and miraculously survived. Elizabeth, too, survived, in spite of all her doctor's predictions, but after three Caesareans, she agreed to have her tubes tied. It didn't matter. She and Mike had each other, they had Liza, and Elizabeth's other children, Michael and Christopher. They thought their life together would go on forever.

*　　*　　*

I was back on television in the fall of 1957 on *The Chesterfield Supper Club*, a weekly hour-long variety show on NBC. Because the sponsors, Chesterfield cigarettes, were looking for the same instant identification with their product that I had achieved as the Coca-Cola Kid, I was forbidden by contract to so much as mention Coke. And I had to do all the commercials, even though I didn't smoke. I had tried it only once, when I was about ten years old, puffing away under a blanket, and I nearly choked to death. Mike smoked cigars, and imitating him, I sometimes played around with one of those, but for the Chesterfield commercials—five in one hour—I had to look as if I were really smoking. I didn't even know how to hold a cigarette but I faked inhaling and for the year and a half I was on the show I didn't choke once—a major accomplishment on live television.

The show was put together by Sonny Werblin of MCA, the most powerful theatrical agency in the world, and Terence Clyne of the McCann-Erickson advertising agency, who bought more television time for sponsors like Chesterfield and the Coca-Cola Company than any other man in the business. "Eddie Fisher" was obviously an important commodity, and I soon discovered I had very little to say about how I was going to be sold. I was paired with George Gobel, another of MCA's clients. I liked George and enjoyed his brand of humor, but since both of us had the same kind of shy and low-key personality, I didn't think the combination would be strong enough to carry the show. I fought against it until Clyne told me, "Just do one thirteen-week segment, Eddie, and if you're not happy with it, you'll go it alone."

The first three or four shows were good, but in my opinion not good enough. They lacked excitement, the right chemistry, so I called Clyne and said, "Well, it doesn't work and you said I could go it alone if I wasn't happy."

"It's too late now," Clyne said.

Even though Clyne and I had been friends and close associates for years, there was nothing more I could do; the contracts were signed. And a fight with MCA, which, in theory at least, took a percentage of my earnings for representing my best interests, was always a losing battle. The agency had a stranglehold on television because it both produced shows and represented a long list of top entertainers, and I felt the pressure again when I objected to using Kate Smith and Charles Laughton on my show. Both were MCA clients who had recently made the rounds of the other variety shows the agency produced, and I wanted guest stars who hadn't been so overexposed. I was informed I had no choice; MCA controlled the sponsor, the show, the guest stars, and me. As usual, I thought I had to do as I was told: "Sit down, you're rocking the boat."

Sometime later, when my contract with MCA was due for renewal, I decided to terminate it. The agency was unhappy about that and asked to have a meeting. "Just come on over to the Beverly Hilton Hotel for a few minutes," I was asked. There I was button-holed in a suite by four of the agency's top executives, who told me, "If you leave MCA, we'll see to it that you never work again." I didn't laugh, but I smiled and said, "Well, then I guess I won't work again."

MCA's monopolistic practices eventually came under federal investigation. I was called in as a witness and shown a memo that had been circulated around the agency at the time I objected to using Charles Laughton and Kate Smith. It read: "Let's show this little bastard who the boss really is." Muscling me was a minor offense compared to some of the other things the investigation turned up, and MCA was ordered to relinquish either its production or its agency activities. It sold the agency.

In spite of a lot of behind-the-scenes problems, *The Chesterfield Supper Club* had its moments. The premiere celebrated the first anniversary of *Around the World in 80 Days*. Mike introduced the program and I took it from there, bringing on elephants and acrobats and everything else we could think of— all live. Jule Styne, who produced the show, asked me to sing very difficult material—an operatic aria from *Tosca,* the Soliloquy from *Carousel*—from memory. "No more cards or TelePrompTers," he said. I accepted that as a welcome challenge. Styne wanted spontaneity and I wanted a spectacular in the Mike Todd tradition. In that show we got both.

Sometimes there was more spontaneity than I bargained for. Don Rickles made his first appearance on the show and couldn't remember a line. He played a waiter in a skit, and even with his lines written all over a menu right in front of his eyes, he still screwed everything up. It was hilarious. He was a smash and I wanted to use him as a regular, but he upped his price from $1,000 to $7,500, and I couldn't afford that every week. Oscar Levant, who also began his television career on my show, stretched an eight-minute bit into sixteen, with ad libs and asides. At one point he turned to Debbie, who happened to be a guest on the show that week, and said, "Did anyone ever tell you, Debbie, that you dominate wistfully?" For one of the rare times in her life, Debbie didn't have a comeback.

The stars of the variety shows on NBC often played a television version of musical chairs: I would appear as a guest on Perry Como's, Dinah Shore's, or Bob Hope's show, and a few weeks later they would appear on mine. Dean Martin, my neighbor and very good friend, was about to begin his own show, so one day at his house, I said, "If you do my show, I'll do yours." Dean agreed, and I appeared on the premiere of his show for a token $7,500, which is what he would be paid for my show. But then his agent at MCA, Johnny Dugan, who was also *my* agent, came to me and said, "Dean would like to have a new kitchen instead of the money. Is that okay with you?"

I said fine. Whirlpool, another sponsor of my show, had just installed a new kitchen for Debbie and me, and Dean's wife Jeannie wanted one like it. The estimate came to over $11,000 and Dugan told me Dean didn't want to pay the difference. "Okay," I said. "He's a friend. And I love Jeannie. Give him the kitchen."

The next time I spoke to Dugan, about a week before Dean was scheduled to appear on my show, he told me, "Look, Eddie, Dean's just got an offer from Dinah for $25,000."

"That's great," I said, "but what's it got to do with me?"

"Well, that's Dean's price now. If you want him, you have to pay him $25,000."

I was furious. Here was MCA telling me I had to pay another one of its clients $25,000, after I thought we had already agreed on an exchange. I told Dugan that if the kitchen wasn't enough, I wasn't interested. The papers picked up the story with front-page headlines and a quote from Dean telling "Mr. Fisher" what he could do with his kitchen sink. I had lost my guest star, and a friend.

Jerry Lewis read the story and called me. "I'll do your show for $20,000," he said, "and you can do mine for the same amount." He also assured me that he would direct me personally, and although I had qualms about that, I agreed. Dean and Jerry had been on very cool terms ever since they split up their team, and I knew that was one reason he had made the offer. Whatever his motives, it saved the show and created a memorable moment on television. That night, right in the middle of a routine Jerry and I were doing together, Dean suddenly walked on stage—unexpected and, of course, unrehearsed. And with him was none other than the Groaner, Bing Crosby. Handshakes, jokes, a lot of horseplay, all on live television. Jerry was flabbergasted and I literally doubled up with laughter. The next day, the papers announced that Martin and Lewis had been reunited on the Eddie Fisher show, which was true, even though the reunion was brief. More important, as far as I was concerned, Dean and I made up and became friends again.

With the introduction of videotape, live television dramatic and variety shows were gradually becoming a thing of the past. While I was on the Chesterfield show, I took part in one of the earliest experiments with color videotape. For a test, Nanette Fabray and I were introduced by the head of RCA, David Sarnoff himself, and after we both sang a song, all three of us raced like excited kids up a circular staircase to watch a fuzzy playback. It was magic, even to General Sarnoff.

Just as television was growing up, I achieved a new maturity as an entertainer on the Chesterfield show. After almost ten years, the teenage idol image was finally beginning to fade. And a live, hour-long variety show demanded a lot of versatility. I was still no great shakes as an actor or a comedian, and never would be, but I could hold up my end of the stage with men like Bob Hope, Red Skelton, Milton Berle, and all the other seasoned pros who appeared on the show. Musically, my stature had grown too. I no longer sang only my own hit recordings or currently popular tunes. And interpreting both the music *and* the words, I performed selections from the standard repertory—Berlin, Gershwin, Porter, Rodgers and Hart, Rodgers and Hammerstein, Lerner and Loewe—with new assurance and sophistication. I also sang duets and medleys with incomparable performers like Ethel Merman and Ella Fitzgerald, Jimmy Durante, Perry Como, Gordon MacRae, and Nat "King" Cole. Week after week I had to stretch and prove what I could do, and as usual, I wasn't always satisfied. But the show was nominated for Emmy Awards and won a Golden Globe, and a two-hour special for the Ford Motor Company, called *I Hear America Singing,* on which I was the host, got the highest ratings of the year. The pop singer had become a personality.

As I was trying to expand my abilities and take a larger share of responsibility for my career, Milton Blackstone and I moved further apart. He respected my growth and knew things had to change, but, no longer in complete control, he didn't quite know how to respond. When I asked questions and sought advice in areas where hardly anyone had much experience, he couldn't provide the answers. Or if he came to the studio and I confronted him with a problem, he would say, "Hmm, we'll talk about that tomorrow," and then simply disappear. It was an unfamiliar and uncomfortable situation for Milton, and rather than face me directly, he often sent typewritten memos, page after page of rambling remarks, or he would ask about me through my friends: "How is Eddie today? Is he feeling all right? Is he getting enough sleep?" For the first time in my life, I was the one who had to deal with producers, directors, writers, agents, sponsors, and everyone else connected with my career. Without Milton's experience to guide me, I made some wrong decisions. And without Milton at my elbow telling me not to rock the boat, warning me about my "image," I made some enemies. I wasn't always the nice guy I had promised myself I would be. But I thought I was too big to worry about that now. I was a star.

When Debbie gave birth to our son in February 1958, I got dizzy all over again, just as I had when Carrie was born. I was overjoyed to have a son, but even though I loved both my children, that didn't change the way I felt about our marriage. I began planning for a separation, and after selling the Beverly Hills mansion, I bought a furnished house in Holmby Hills that would be perfect for Debbie and the children. I didn't know where I would go, or when. There was no other woman in my life. I only knew I couldn't go on living with Debbie.

We named our son Todd Emmanuel to honor two of my dearest friends, Mike Todd and Mannie Sacks. Tragically, before my little boy was a year old, both men would be dead.

Mike and Elizabeth had spent the last several months globe-trotting to promote *Around the World*. Mike never did anything small. To celebrate the first anniversary of the premiere in New York, he threw a party at Madison Square Garden for eighteen thousand of his "intimate" friends. Then he took Elizabeth to Russia, where that personification of freewheeling capitalism and his glamorous movie star wife must have created quite a stir. For his travels around this country, Mike used a twin-engine Lockheed, which he christened the *Lucky Liz*. Like a kid with a new toy he loved to show off, he was always urging his friends to use it. I flew on the *Lucky Liz* only once, when Mike and Elizabeth invited Debbie and me to join them on a flight to Las Vegas to celebrate New Year's Eve.

Three months later, in March 1958, Mike was selected to receive an award as "Showman of the Year" from the Friars Club at a testimonial dinner at the Waldorf-Astoria in New York. I was invited to attend and asked Sammy Cahn to write a parody of "Around the World in 80 Days," which I would sing at the dinner.

Mike called me up. "Let's take the *Lucky Liz* to New York together," he said.

"Mike, I'd love to but I can't. I've got to go to North Carolina to film a Chesterfield commercial. I'll be flying to New York from there."

"Take my plane to North Carolina," Mike said.

"That doesn't make any sense," I told him. "How will you get to New York?"

Mike didn't like to take no for an answer. He called again and again, urging me to take his plane, but still I refused. I flew east on a commercial flight, and later on the night of March 21, in a torrential rainstorm, Mike took off for New York from the Burbank airport in the *Lucky Liz*.

Elizabeth was not with him. A couple of days before, she had been sent home from the set of *Cat on a Hot Tin Roof* with a high temperature and a severe case of bronchitis. She begged Mike to let her come, but the doctors advised against it and for once Mike didn't give in to her. They said their goodbyes and Mike promised to call her from Albuquerque when the plane landed to refuel. He never made it. In the early hours of the morning on March 22, the *Lucky Liz* went down in the mountains of western New Mexico.

I was in New York at the Essex House when I heard the news. Jim Mahoney, my press agent, and a couple of other friends were waiting for me in the living room that morning. "Eddie," Jim said, "Mike's dead. His plane crashed in New Mexico."

I just stood there staring at them, too stunned to speak. Then I turned and started back into the bedroom. My friends tried to follow me but Jim stopped them. "No," he said. "Let him be by himself."

I shut the door behind me. This was my first experience with the death of someone very close to me and it didn't make any sense. It can't be true, I thought; it can't have happened, not to Mike. I put my hands over my eyes, sat down on the bed, and cried.

There were guards at both the front and the back doors of their house in Beverly Hills. Reporters, photographers, and curiosity seekers were milling around outside. Inside, friends and relatives had gathered to do what they could for Elizabeth. I had taken the first available flight to Los Angeles and went directly to the house. I spoke briefly with Dick Hanley, Mike's secretary; Elizabeth's friend Sydney Guilaroff, the hairdresser; Arthur Loew, Jr.; Rex Kennamer, Elizabeth's doctor. Everyone was very worried about her.

Then Elizabeth appeared, dressed in a nightgown and obviously heavily sedated, wandering down the steps from the bedroom in a daze. She didn't speak to me. She looked right at me without the slightest sign of recognition and walked into the living room. Suddenly she started screaming, and just as suddenly stopped. One moment she would be talking rationally, and the next crying hysterically. Everyone urged her to go back to bed.

She recognized me as she began to climb the stairs. "Eddie," she said, "come back tomorrow and we can sit and talk."

I was deeply concerned about Elizabeth, afraid she would try to commit suicide or lose her mind completely. But the next day, when Debbie and I came to the house for dinner, she seemed to be in control of herself. There was a kind of unreal serenity about her, as if all her emotions had been drained. She asked me to stay after dinner. There were thousands of letters and telegrams in boxes by her bed, and she wanted me to come upstairs and read them to her.

We sat there for hours that night, as I read the letters and Elizabeth listened. They had been written by the famous and the unknown, they came from friends and even enemies, and not one of them said an unkind word about Mike. Both Elizabeth and I cried. Each new letter reminded me of the friend I had lost. For Elizabeth they seemed to have the opposite effect: it was a comfort to her to know that so many other people had loved Mike. We would repeat this scene several times in the weeks ahead, me reading and trying to forget, Elizabeth listening to keep the memory of Mike alive.

Elizabeth asked me to come to the funeral. Howard Hughes put a DC-7 at her disposal for the flight to Chicago, where Mike was to be buried. Hughes had once asked Elizabeth to come see him in Palm Springs. He said he had a proposition he wanted to discuss with her. Very reluctantly, she went with Greg Bautzer, Hughes's lawyer and confidant, and when she arrived, Hughes proposed, offering her a million dollars if she would marry him. She laughed and told him to go to hell. Hughes had no ulterior motives in offering the DC-7. He must have realized that Elizabeth could not have traveled any other way, and the offer was made to me impersonally, through his longtime business associate Noah Dietrich.

There were a lot of people on the plane: a couple of newspaper reporters, but mostly friends of Mike's. I sat in the back and didn't speak to Elizabeth at all until just before the funeral. We were staying at the Ambassador and she came to my room, sat on the bed, and began to talk. Still under sedation, still barely able to cope with her own grief, she knew how I felt about Mike and was trying to comfort me.

The cemetery looked like a county fair. Hundreds of people were sitting on the tombstones, eating ice cream cones and drinking soda pop, littering the ground with bottles and bags. They began screaming and shoving to get a better look when the hearse and limousines arrived. Police barricades had been erected to keep them at a distance, and a tent covered the grave site, but all through the brief service, we could hear their shouts: "Come on out, Liz! Come out so we can get a look at you!" Elizabeth held her emotions in check, with the exception of a flash of anger when one of Mike's relatives made a fuss about the seating arrangements around the coffin. Nothing was left of Mike; as far as I knew, the coffin was empty. The only thing that had been recovered from the crash, I was told, was a small piece of a pair of platinum cuff links I had given him.

Reporters later wrote that Elizabeth hurled herself hysterically over Mike's grave. It wasn't true. After the service, she asked us all to leave the tent and then spent a few moments there alone. When she emerged, the crowd surged through the barricades, surrounding her, shouting and snatching at her clothes, just like the funeral scene in *A Star Is Born,* only this was hideously real. Rex Kennamer, Mike Todd, Jr., and I tried to protect her, and pushing our way through the crowd, finally made it to the limousine. We couldn't drive away. People swarmed all over the car, rocking it back and forth and pounding on the windows, while Elizabeth sat huddled between Rex and me in the back seat, numb with horror.

I saw Elizabeth quite often during the next several weeks, although not as often as many of her other friends, and never alone unless she asked me to read more of the letters. I had grown to admire her, but the strongest bond between us had always been Mike, and now he was gone. She went back to work and then left the house she had shared with Mike to stay with Arthur Loew, Jr., the heir to a large Hollywood fortune. Loew was a friend and I liked him; he was a humorous man, but he had the reputation of being something of a playboy, and even though it was none of my business, I wondered why Elizabeth was staying at his house. What I didn't realize at the time was that she could never be alone.

In June, three months after Mike's death, I was due to begin a six-week engagement at the Tropicana in Las Vegas, and Elizabeth called to ask if she could come to the opening. I was very happy that she wanted to be there, and also a little worried; it would be the first time she had appeared in public since the funeral, and everyone was still concerned about her. But when I introduced her at the end of my act and the spotlight swung around to pick her out of the audience, she looked radiant. She had come with Loew, Mike Todd, Jr., and other friends, and outwardly at least, she seemed to be recovering from Mike's death.

My dressing room was jammed with well-wishers after the show, including Elizabeth. Photographers took pictures of us, and it was later said that we were gazing at each other with love in our eyes. It wasn't so. At that moment there was nothing more than a warm friendship between us. Even though we had lost Mike, we wanted to keep that.

Later we were all sitting in the lounge and I heard Elizabeth complain that she wasn't able to sleep. Both Milton and Max were with us—Max had given me the usual injection before my performance—and after Elizabeth left, it occurred to me that he might have something to help her sleep. I called Elizabeth's room and she invited us both to come up. Max gave her a mild sedative and then left but I stayed a few minutes longer. We talked, and I realized then that Elizabeth was still deeply mourning Mike.

I didn't see her the next day; she went back to Los Angeles. But after my last show that night—it was about three in the morning—I got a call from Elizabeth. "When are you coming back?" she said. "I must see you."

There was both an urgency and a new intimacy in the tone of her voice, and I wondered why she wanted to see me. Was it just because of Mike, to keep his memory alive through me? Or did she want to tell me something she had been unable to say the night before? I was puzzled, but I intended to see her as soon as I got back. I wanted to stay close to Elizabeth, whatever else happened in our lives. It seemed like the most natural relationship in the world, a way to keep Mike's memory alive for me too.

I got back to Los Angeles just in time to celebrate my thirtieth birthday. Debbie gave a surprise party for me and about twenty-five of our friends at Romanoff's, and when we sat down at the table, the chair next to mine was empty— Elizabeth's. She hadn't shown up. I was hurt and disappointed, but thought to myself, Well, that's Elizabeth. She called right in the middle of the party: "Eddie, I'm so sorry. I've got my period and I feel terrible."

"Come on, Elizabeth," I joked. "The only thing you've got is a hangover."

She giggled. "Well, anyway, happy birthday. And can you come over and see me tomorrow? I want to give you something of Mike's."

I went to Loew's house the next day and found her dressed in a flesh-colored bathing suit, dangling her feet in the pool, with little Liza between her legs. Our eyes met and that was it. Not a word was spoken. I was in love with Elizabeth. And remembering the intimacy in her voice when she called me in Las Vegas, seeing the expression in her eyes now, I was certain she was in love with me.

She gave me little Liza to hold while she went into the house. She returned with a gold money clip that had belonged to Mike. I couldn't seem to catch my breath to thank her. My feelings were in such turmoil that I just wanted to get out of there. Cradling Liza in her arms, Elizabeth walked with me to the door. There, I turned to her and said. "Would you like to go for a drive tomorrow?"

She nodded yes.

I picked her up the following afternoon. She brought Liza and held her in one arm. I reached over and took her hand. We drove way out past Malibu, holding hands, again without saying a word. Finally, I said, "Elizabeth, I'm going to marry you."

She looked at me and said, "When?"

"I don't know. But I *am* going to marry you."

She smiled but didn't say anything, and we drove on until we found an isolated spot on the beach. We played with Liza on the sand for a while. Then we kissed. And at that moment we both knew we belonged to each other.

We began to see each other constantly. We went for long drives or had lunch together in some quiet, out-of-the-way restaurant, talking and holding hands under the table. We made up excuses to meet. Elizabeth would call the house, pretending she had some problem she wanted to talk to me about, and I would stop whatever I was doing and pick her up for another drive. One problem was real enough. Mike had left his affairs in a mess and Elizabeth was completely helpless about money. Like Debbie, she was under contract at MGM and had never earned more than a salary from her pictures. She wasn't poor, of course, but she and Mike had lived extravagantly, and with Mike's death the money just wasn't there anymore. She was even told by Herman Odell, one of the lawyers handling Mike's estate, that she would receive no further income from the share of *Around the World in 80 Days* that Mike had left her, now or in the foreseeable future. Elizabeth showed me the letter and we spread it out on the table in front of us in a restaurant, pretending to talk business when we were really talking about love.

I was hardly a financial wizard about handling my own affairs, and I was so overwhelmed by my feelings for Elizabeth that I wasn't sure I could make sense out of anything. But I did try to help her and spoke to Ed Weisl about the letter. He was chairman of the executive committee at Paramount; I had met him on a boat trip to Europe. He called back twenty-four hours later and said that Paramount would pay Elizabeth ten million dollars for her share of the picture. Perversely, Elizabeth said she didn't want to sell. So much for her financial problems. But we both knew there was no easy solution to the problems our love would create.

As Mike's best friend, it was quite natural for me to be seeing Elizabeth, and as time went on, we made no secret of our meetings. We spent many evenings with friends at La Scala or the Polo Lounge and more often than not Debbie was with us. We all went to a preview showing of *Cat on a Hot Tin Roof*. Our feelings for each other were the secret, and they were so intense, so necessary, that I was sure all who saw us, unless they were blind, saw love. I was afraid we couldn't hide it for long, afraid, too, of what people would say when they found out. But oddly, no one seemed to notice, not the usually sharp-eyed gossip columnists, not our friends, not even Debbie. At a party or a restaurant, the three of us would be sitting together and Elizabeth would reach for my hand under the table. When it was time for me to take Debbie home, she would beg me to stay. Elizabeth seldom bothered to conceal her feelings and she made it very difficult for me to conceal mine. But if Debbie suspected there was something going on between us, she didn't say a word.

We knew we would have to tell Debbie, but somehow I could never find the right moment. Is there ever a right moment to tell your wife you're in love with another woman? Elizabeth would have done anything I asked her to do, but neither of us was sure what was right and what was wrong. Was it too soon after Mike's death, were we doing a terrible thing to Debbie? Divorce, Elizabeth's children, mine—it all seemed hopelessly complicated. We were desperate, knowing the time had come when something had to be done. But what?

Finally Elizabeth decided to go to Europe. She had planned the trip as a vacation—and had spent a fortune on clothes—before we discovered how we felt about each other. I fabricated a meeting with my sponsors in New York to be with her for a few days before she sailed, and made reservations at the Essex House. Elizabeth had a suite at the Plaza. We met there when she arrived. The rooms were filled with flowers, and as soon as we were alone, Elizabeth said, "When are we going to make love?"

I stayed at the Plaza that night. It was the first time we had done anything more than kiss and hold hands. And the next day we walked to the zoo in Central Park and then took a ride in the horse-drawn hansom. Incredibly, nobody bothered us, nobody paid any attention, or if they did, we didn't notice. Our feelings for each other were even more intense than before, so fierce they were painful.

Back at the Plaza, Elizabeth got a call from Cary Grant and motioned to me to listen in on the extension. After a few moments of conversation, he asked her for a date. Giggling, she refused and my male ego soared. That night I stayed at the Plaza again and we sat up very late, talking about our future together. But before we could do anything else, we had to tell Debbie. I called California and when she was on the phone, I said, "Elizabeth and I are here together in New York and we're very much in love."

We were certain Debbie had already heard about us, but for a moment she seemed genuinely shocked. Then she said, "Well, we can't talk about it over the phone. We'll talk about it when you get home." She acted as if I had told her I had a toothache; nothing serious, nothing she had to worry about.

Elizabeth and I were puzzled by Debbie's reaction. Still it was a relief to us that she knew. We felt less guilty about our emotions, less anxious about being seen in public, and we began to go out together in New York. We saw a play and went to nightclubs and restaurants, always with friends so we wouldn't be alone. We wanted to avoid publicity, but people were beginning to notice, and once when a photographer tried to ambush us at the Blue Angel, I had to duck out the back door. The heat was on. We were being indiscreet.

Elizabeth canceled her trip to Europe; it was impossible for us to separate. But where could we go to be together? I took her to Grossinger's. We would be safe there; people would leave us alone. Jennie couldn't have been more wonderful. She liked Debbie, but she loved Elizabeth on sight and we stayed at her house. Jennie knew we were sleeping together, of course, but she never once criticized us or made us feel uncomfortable in any way. She didn't have that in her. And in her wisdom, she probably knew that these were the last peaceful moments that Elizabeth and I would have together for a very long time.

We told reporters that I had come to Grossinger's to cut the ribbon on the new indoor swimming pool. I even went through the ceremony, but at least one reporter wasn't fooled. Earl Wilson wrote about Elizabeth and me in his column and the hue and cry began. It was the Labor Day weekend. Exactly nine years earlier Eddie Cantor had "discovered" me at Grossinger's and my whole life changed. Now I had been discovered again at Grossinger's, this time in the company of Elizabeth Taylor, and my life would take a new and totally different direction.

12

Elizabeth and I took separate flights back to Los Angeles. Sailing through a pack of reporters who wanted to know if there was any truth to the story that we were having an affair, she said just one word: "Garbage!" I wouldn't have known what to say, and to avoid reporters I arrived late at night at the airport in Burbank. Joey Forman put me up in his apartment on Sunset Boulevard. And then I went to see Debbie.

The moment she met me in the front hall of our house, Debbie started to cry, and before I could say a word she sat down on the floor, sobbing uncontrollably. I tried to pick her up, but she twisted away from me, ran upstairs, and locked herself in the bathroom. She wouldn't come out or listen to anything I had to say. She knew now that what I had told her on the phone was true; if she didn't see it on my face, it was plastered on the front page of every newspaper in town. I was in love with Elizabeth. This was the end of our marriage. No more excuses, no more waiting for the right moment for a divorce. I left her there, and walking downstairs and out of the house, I smelled the overpowering odor of lima beans, my favorite food. Debbie was trying to save our marriage with lima beans.

The lawyers took over after that, but Debbie still tried to

postpone the inevitable. She called and asked me to go with her to see a marriage counselor. "Why, Debbie?" I said. "There's nothing more to say. We've had all our talks. We know where we stand."

"Please," she said. "Just do this one thing for me."

In the marriage counselor's office I expected a replay of the scene that had occurred a year or so before, when Debbie and I went to see a psychiatrist together, hoping he could help us iron out some of our problems. After listening to us talk, the psychiatrist asked Debbie why she was so concerned about money and owning property. He really put her through a wringer. But the marriage counselor hardly said a word; he just sat there gravely with his arms folded. Still, from all the things we told him, it was obvious to me there was no hope of our staying together. And as we got up to leave, I felt that Debbie herself, perhaps for the first time, realized that we had never had a real relationship, even from the very beginning.

Even so, she wasn't ready to give up our marriage. People I knew to be her friends told me how unhappy she was and tried to talk me out of a divorce. Howard Strickling, the head of publicity at MGM, called and said, "Why don't you go home, where you belong?" But Debbie's most powerful ally turned out to be Hedda Hopper. Hedda, who had been like a second mother to Elizabeth for years, asked her for an interview and then proceeded to misquote her or print her remarks out of context. Elizabeth and I, according to Hedda, were sinners, thinking only of ourselves, not of Debbie and the children, not of the memory of Mike Todd. It was the kind of hatchet job only Hedda could do.

The interview was the first rumble in a rock slide of unfavorable publicity. Elizabeth was cast as the vamp in this domestic drama, I was the villain, and Debbie was the innocent victim. If she wanted sympathy, she got it. Greeting reporters and photographers with her hair in pigtails and little Carrie slung over her shoulder, a diaper pin stuck in her blouse, she told them exactly what they wanted to hear. She still loved me, she said, and had never had the slightest indication that I didn't love her too. Elizabeth was the culprit, the femme fatale, the home wrecker; she had seduced me and I was too weak to resist. But Debbie was willing to forgive and forget to save our happy marriage.

The irony was that as far as the public knew, it *was* a happy marriage; we were still America's Sweethearts. If reporters were aware that our marriage had been unhappy from the very beginning and I had planned to divorce Debbie long before Elizabeth and I fell in love, that's not what they printed. The Debbie-Eddie-Liz triangle was the juiciest scandal to hit Hollywood in years, and it spread like a canyon brushfire, throughout the world.

Elizabeth and I expected a lot of criticism, but not hostility and moral outrage. Elizabeth said she didn't give a damn what anybody said, but I knew she was hurt, particularly by newspaper stories quoting remarks like the one from Maxine Reynolds, who called her "the biggest slut in town." I cared very much, because I loved Elizabeth and because she had done nothing more sinful than fall in love with a married man. If anyone, I was to blame, and was willing to accept that kind of criticism. But that's not where the stories ended. I was accused of taking advantage of a grieving and helpless widow or, just as absurd, of having had an affair with Elizabeth before Mike's death. It was even written that we had made love on the plane that took us to his funeral in Chicago. The charge that stung most deeply, however, was that I was betraying my friendship with Mike. Hedda Hopper said that Mike had loved me, but I had never loved him; I was incapable of loving anyone but myself. Reporters who wrote stories like that couldn't possibly know how I felt about Mike, how I would always feel about him. They couldn't know how Elizabeth felt about Mike either, or how we felt about each other. It didn't matter; whatever they wrote made great copy and the public swallowed it whole.

I could understand why Debbie said the things she did, even if they weren't true. The shock of such a public rejection must have been devastating for her. And her first impulse was to protect herself and her image as the girl next door, the perfect wife and mother. She may have thought that public opinion would bring us back together, just as it was one of the forces that led to our marriage in the first place. It didn't, and lawyers began to discuss the terms of our divorce.

I agreed to a million-dollar settlement: Debbie would get forty thousand dollars a year as long as she remained unmarried, the house, three cars, insurance policies—she got everything she wanted. But shortly after divorce proceedings began, she called me in the middle of a dress rehearsal for the Chesterfield show to say that her brother had cracked up one of the cars and asked for a white station wagon to replace it. "Oh, and by the way," she said, "is there any chance of getting back to-gether?"

I said yes to the station wagon, no to the reconciliation. I didn't care what the divorce cost; it was worth it. I was truly in love for the first time in my life; someone was very much in love with me. I didn't enjoy hurting Debbie. Nor did I regret what had happened, only the way it happened. Naturally it wasn't pleasant to see my "nice guy" image tarnished: the Coca-Cola Kid had become Peck's Bad Boy. But I thought all that would change as soon as people accepted the fact that I wasn't really the boy-next-door. I was a man, no better or worse than any other man. And the whole thing would blow over eventually. Reporters would find someone else to write about; the public would get bored. I was wrong. The press and public would never lose interest in Elizabeth Taylor. And if some people envied me, a lot more would never forget what they thought I did to Debbie Reynolds.

Years later, I found many thousands of letters stored in boxes—hate mail from all over the world, written about this time and separated from my regular fan mail so I wouldn't see it. The usual number of kooks and cranks were represented, but many others expressed feelings of shock and anger that were evidently sincere. Reading them, I realized for the first time how deeply I had offended many people, how profoundly I had violated the standards of conventional morality. One letter read: "Dear Eddie Fisher, You will never be allowed in our living room again. We will do everything in our power to tell all our friends not to buy your records or to go to see your movies. You have brought shame upon your name and your people, and you will never be forgiven."

And so our romantic idyll began. No more long drives in the car, no more lunches together in quiet restaurants, holding hands under the table. Elizabeth and I took refuge with her agent, Kurt Frings, and his wife, Ketti, at their house in Beverly Hills. Kurt was a funny, energetic, explosive man, and he could handle Elizabeth. It was his stock-in-trade. A German by birth, he had been a boxer, the lightweight champion of Europe under the name of Kurt Flick, before emigrating to Mexico. The story of his efforts to enter the United States and his marriage to Ketti were later made into the poignant film *Hold Back the Dawn,* with Charles Boyer and Olivia De-Havilland. Kurt had become one of the most powerful agents not only in Hollywood but around the world. Besides Elizabeth, he represented Audrey Hepburn, Olivia De Havilland, Maria Schell, Cary Grant, Joel McCrea, Edward G. Robinson. If anyone could stand up to the storm swirling around Elizabeth and me, it was Kurt. Reporters took up permanent residence on the grounds of his house. Elizabeth and I had to sneak in and out the back way, and if photographers spotted either of us, they gave chase, trying to get our pictures.

We were living in sin, which only added to the public's indignation and the curiosity of the press, and we finally decided to look for a house of our own that would provide a little more privacy. Elizabeth wanted to be with her children, I wanted to be free to see mine, and we both hoped we could be together without feeling constantly under siege. We found a Spanish villa with a beautiful courtyard on Copa de Oro in Bel Air, but for appearance' sake, I also rented an apartment in Hollywood. I moved in, gave a housewarming party for my friends, and then left before it was over, to go to my real home, which was with Elizabeth.

We never found the privacy we wanted, and somehow learned to live without it. There were no guards around the house and Elizabeth was terrified that a photographer would force his way in and take a picture that could be used against us. Weeks, months passed and still the press followed our every move. If we went to the houses of friends, reporters said we were flaunting our immorality; if we stayed home, they wrote that our friends had ostracized us and we were ashamed to show our faces in public. Either way we couldn't win, but we really didn't care. The more people criticized us, the more we needed each other and the closer we became. We preferred it that way: just the two of us against the world.

Nobody was as happy as we were. We loved nothing better than being by ourselves. There was so much to talk about, so much to learn about each other, and I began to spend every possible moment with Elizabeth, doing only what was essential to rehearse and perform on my television show. Nothing was more important than our love. Besides, I was worried about Elizabeth, afraid of what might happen to her if I wasn't there. Something was always the matter with her, and whenever she was sick, whatever illness she had, it was always an emergency and she thought she was going to die. Her problems were real enough—she was in continual pain from an injury to her back that had occurred during the filming of *Giant,* and she was very susceptible to respiratory conditions. But at the slightest sign of a cold or even if she felt a little faint or had a little fever, she would collapse in a panic. Once she got hiccups that lasted all night. We had to leave a private screening at Frank Sinatra's house, rush home, call every doctor in Los Angeles, and try every trick and home remedy until she was sedated and they went away. Everything was a crisis.

I sometimes thought Elizabeth had the power to bring on her various illnesses and used them to attract attention and sympathy, or just to get her own way. As tough as she tried to appear on the outside, inside she was a very insecure little girl. That I could understand, and it made me love her even more. I felt I had to protect her. The use of various tranquilizers and sedatives was not uncommon in show business, or anywhere else for that matter; they were readily available and frequently prescribed. Elizabeth took painkillers for her back and sedatives to help her sleep. After all, she was not in good health, her professional schedule was grueling, and she had suffered many personal tragedies. But I was concerned that she didn't always take her medications in the prescribed doses. And if she drank on top of that, the combination could be lethal.

Elizabeth's doctor, who prescribed most of the medication she took, shared my concern. Samuel Rexford Kennamer— Elizabeth and I called him "Sexy Rexy"—was a mild-mannered Southern gentleman in line to succeed to the celebrity practice of the famous Myron Prinzmetal. He made house calls, and Elizabeth, sipping a glass of champagne, loved to sit down and gossip with him. She adored Rex, but because she didn't always follow his advice, he suggested that I might be able to talk her into seeing a psychiatrist as a way of helping her cope with the stress and anxiety of her very demanding life. I agreed to give it a try and one night while we were still living at the Fringses', I said very casually, "You know, Elizabeth, don't you think it would be a good idea if you saw a psychiatrist?" It was late, we were in bed together, and Elizabeth reacted as if I had hit her. She leaped out of bed, ran from the room, down the stairs, and out of the house. I followed and saw her jump into a car and start to drive away. I didn't know where she thought she was going, and running alongside the car, I begged her to come back to the house. She stopped, but refused to get out until I apologized and said *I* was the one who needed a psychiatrist. That seemed to satisfy her and I took her back upstairs to bed.

I never tried that approach again. There had been enough doctors in Elizabeth's life anyway. But I did try to keep track of the pills she took and warn her if I thought she was drinking too much. I also begged her to stop smoking. She liked having someone worry about her, someone to tell her she was being a bad little girl, but it had little effect. Once, just to defy me, she lit a cigarette, took a pill, and had a drink. So I had to learn to live with Elizabeth the way she was and felt I had to be with her, always, to watch her, to hold her, to reassure her if she woke up in the middle of the night.

We were both a little eccentric about our teeth. Terrified of dentists, Elizabeth always found some excuse to postpone an appointment. I had never finished the job of having my front teeth capped, and thinking I could solve both problems, I flew my dentist, Dr. Meyer Pearlman, from New York to Los Angeles. He urged Elizabeth to have her teeth capped, and she agreed, but then backed out at the last minute. So Dr. Pearlman completed the capping of my teeth and flew back to New York. I got Elizabeth to another dentist, finally, but our teeth remained a mutual preoccupation. I was afraid my caps would break or fly out of my mouth during a performance—a justifiable fear, as it turned out—and Elizabeth always made a ritual of brushing. She would spend at least twenty minutes in front of the bathroom mirror every night, brushing; if she had been drinking, she lost all sense of time and took even longer. I didn't mind waiting for her. I had all the time in the world—for Elizabeth.

She thought she was dead broke. She wasn't, of course, but if she sometimes worried about money, it was not a problem in our relationship. With record royalties, my television show, and a long-term contract with the Las Vegas Tropicana, I was earning more than enough for both of us, and I wanted Elizabeth to be my responsibility. I wanted to take care of her financially, as well as every other way, so most of the money we spent was mine. But it really didn't matter to either of us whose it was. One day a very young lawyer from the firm that took care of Elizabeth's affairs appeared at the house and announced that he had some papers for her to sign.

"What are they?" Elizabeth asked.

"Prenuptial agreements," the lawyer said, handing her the papers.

Elizabeth looked at them as the lawyer explained that there would be two moneys: Elizabeth's money would not be mine and mine wouldn't be hers. "Get the fuck out of here," Elizabeth said, tossing the papers at him, "and never come back again."

I loved buying things for Elizabeth; she was always so delighted and surprised, no matter what it was. The most expensive presents were jewels: an emerald wedding ring, the first gift I ever gave her, a diamond bracelet, an evening bag with "Liz" spelled out in twenty-seven diamonds for her twenty-seventh birthday. I bought black pearls, rubies—whatever caught my eye—and little charms for a bracelet she had: the NBC peacock in gold and different-colored stones; a platinum Michelob bottle, her favorite beer; a Dom Perignon bottle of platinum and emeralds. Eventually that bracelet weighed about forty pounds; it was ridiculous, but she wore it.

I went on sprees to buy her clothes—sweaters, slacks, blouses, bathing suits—all from the most expensive shops in Beverly Hills. Elizabeth had a rather unusual figure, so whenever I found something that fit her, I bought out the whole line. A dozen pairs of matching silk pajamas were custom made for us by Yvel—Levy spelled backward—my own shirtmaker, and on one visit to the shop of the famous Juel Park, I bought at least $35,000 worth of handmade silk lingerie. Pedigreed puppies, cats, a monkey, toys for her children—I threw gifts at Elizabeth and she gave me things in return, some silly and sentimental, some expensive and beautiful: A Cartier watch inscribed "When time began," her first gift; a Piaget platinum watch inscribed "You ain't seen nothin' yet"; diamond-and-emerald cuff links for dress; heart-shaped cabochon emerald-and-gold cuff links inscribed "E & E" for ordinary wear. It was Christmas every day.

I wanted to be Santa Claus, Daddy Warbucks, Prince Charming, everyone and everything to Elizabeth, just as she was everyone and everything to me. We were drugged with love. Our sexual relationship was perfect, and a lot of our time together was spent in bed. We weren't always making love; we talked endlessly, listened to music. I went on a poetry binge and read Elizabeth every love poem I could find. I felt she needed me, desperately. I was a father, a brother, a friend, a lover. She was a baby I held and rocked in my arms, a girl, a woman—all the things *I* needed. And we were very selfish about our love. The rest of the world could go to hell, as long as we were together.

"You gave up everything," Lenny Gaines told me recently. "You went to bed with Elizabeth and read poetry. You hibernated and let everything else go right down the drain."

"I had to take care of her," I said, defending myself.

"So what's that?"

"That," I said, "turned out to be a full-time job."

The Chesterfield show was canceled in January 1959. Only rarely during its second season had the show risen above the mediocre, ratings had been slipping for months, and no one knew what to do about it. My dear friend Mannie Sacks had died tragically of leukemia and I found his successors at NBC very difficult to deal with. Shortly after Mannie's death, Terence Clyne came to me with a proposal for a program in his memory, to be called "Some of Mannie's Friends." Dinah Shore, Perry Como, Tony Martin, and many others were donating their time, and I was asked to do the same. I readily agreed; Mannie had been like a father to me ever since my early days in New York, when he got me jobs and gave me pocket money so I could eat. But as it happened, my contribution to the program was more than just a $20,000 or $25,000 performance fee. I donated my hour on television, which was worth about $100,000, and then Clyne replaced me as MC on the show with Perry Como.

NBC denied that my scandalous romance with Elizabeth had anything to do with canceling the Chesterfield show, which was probably true. If it had been a good show, people would have watched it no matter what was being said about me. But it wasn't, and both NBC and I were happy to bail out. The press saw it differently: the public outcry against my behavior had forced NBC to cancel the show. I was a sinner and had to be punished. The same was said when Elizabeth failed to win the Oscar for her role in *Cat on a Hot Tin Roof,* one of the best performances of her career.

There was another flurry of criticism, this time with an anti-Semitic tinge, when Elizabeth converted to Judaism. It was assumed that she wanted to become a Jew either in memory of Mike or because of me. Neither was true. She had first expressed an interest in converting while she and Mike were married, but he refused to let her do it. "Why? What difference will it make?" he asked her. I'm not sure what her religion was: Protestant, I suppose. She had been married to Nick Hilton in a Catholic ceremony, and now she wanted to become a Jew. It seemed a little unreal to me, but I didn't have Mike's power to deny Elizabeth what she wanted. And when she persisted, I was secretly pleased.

Along with love poetry, I started reading books on Judaism aloud to Elizabeth. She wanted to learn more, so I went to Rabbi Max Nussbaum of Temple Israel in Los Angeles, who gave me a pile of books, which I also read aloud. We talked about Judaism, discussed its beliefs and laws, and tried to analyze its difference from Christianity and other religions. Even though I had been brought up a Jew, it was an education for me; for Elizabeth, it was a revelation and she became even more determined to embrace Judaism.

She was converted to the Reform faith in a ceremony at Temple Israel by Rabbi Nussbaum, who was famous for his other celebrity conversions as well as for being quite a ladies' man. He let me stand in the back, although I wasn't supposed to be there. Elizabeth's mother and father were there too, in what appeared to be a state of shock. That was the general reaction; the Los Angeles papers carried the news in banner headlines and her conversion stirred up an avalanche of hate mail. It didn't bother Elizabeth. She sincerely believed in what she had done, and then forgot all about it. We didn't go to synagogue; we celebrated Yom Kippur only once. But she was incensed by a newspaper story claiming in banner headlines that she had converted because she had gone insane and was now confined in the Menninger Clinic. We were going to sue, but then decided just to go to dinner at Chasen's, where everyone in Hollywood would see us. The newspaper eventually printed an apology in headlines of the same size.

There was another story going around, to the effect that Elizabeth had not fallen in love with me at all, but with a carbon copy of Mike. Maybe I had adopted some of Mike's superficial characteristics, but I wasn't trying to step into his shoes by lavishing gifts on Elizabeth or in any other way. I was still me: quiet, a little shy, not the steamroller Mike had always been. Sometimes I wished I could be *more* like Mike, particularly when it came to handling Elizabeth. True, Mike had been the original bond between us, but a bond grew between Elizabeth and me that was unique and as strong or even stronger than our love for Mike. We could never forget him; we cherished his memory. But no matter what the newspapers and fan magazines claimed, he was not some kind of male Rebecca, haunting our relationship.

The cruelest thing written about us was that Elizabeth and I, in our reckless rush to climb into bed together, were abandoning our children. In Elizabeth's case, nothing could have been further from the truth. She adored her children and always wanted them with her. She was continually concerned about their physical safety because of all the bad publicity, and worried, too, about what psychological effect it might have. Loving Elizabeth, I naturally loved her children too, and we agreed that after we were married I would adopt Liza. Michael and Christopher Wilding already had a father, but I wanted to take care of them all.

The situation with my children was more complicated. Carrie was a little over two years old, Todd wasn't even one; I couldn't sit down with them and explain what had happened in their father's life. And I honestly believed that children, especially at that age, needed a mother more than a father. Carrie and Todd had a mother, a good one, and wouldn't they be better off in a house without a father than in a house where the father and mother were unhappy strangers? I wasn't abandoning my children. I was asking for visitation rights and planned to see them as often as I could. And the terms of the divorce settlement would leave them financially secure. Elizabeth did, however, come first in my thoughts. At that time, my love for her took precedence over everything; her needs were more important than my children's. But I wasn't the inhuman monster I was accused of being. I loved Carrie and Todd deeply and wanted to be a part of their lives. I had no way of knowing that my love for Elizabeth was only the first of a long series of steps that would take me further and further away from my children.

*　　*　　*

In spite of all the publicity—and the reporters who dogged us every time we went out of the house—Elizabeth and I lived together like any married couple during the first months of 1959. The trouble was we weren't married, and it was the one unhappy thing about our relationship. For the world's greatest sinners, we were oddly old-fashioned and hoped that once we were married, we would be left in peace. But marriage was impossible in California until my divorce became final at the end of the year. Nevada's laws were less restrictive. If I established residence there, I could get a divorce in six weeks. I had to have Debbie's consent, however, and she refused to give it. When it became apparent that she might appear the heavy if she stood in the way of our marriage, she changed her mind.

Elizabeth and I went to Las Vegas just before I was scheduled to begin a six-week engagement at the Tropicana. My "official" residence was the hotel, but I leased a ranch on the outskirts of town for Elizabeth and her children, and we lived there. On opening night, I was shocked to see pickets parading in front of the hotel carrying signs that read "Liz Go Home" and "Keep the Marriage Vows, Eddie." I was also shocked to read in the papers that Elizabeth had come to Las Vegas and sat in the audience during my performances to bolster my sagging popularity. More nonsense. Elizabeth was in Las Vegas because we wanted to be together. We had taken a solemn vow never to be separated. When I was performing, she would be with me; when she had to make a movie, I would be with her. That was our naive solution to the problem of a two-career marriage. Naturally I was concerned that all the bad publicity would hurt us both professionally, but I wasn't aware that my career was in any real trouble. Even if it was, I wouldn't have cared—not as long as I had Elizabeth.

I certainly spent money more extravagantly than ever: the ranch and all kinds of help for Elizabeth and me; hotel suites for my family and friends; a bracelet of fifty diamonds for Elizabeth as an engagement present; and for good measure, many thousands of dollars lost at the dice tables. With my divorce and our marriage just a few weeks away, Elizabeth and I felt less constrained about appearing together in public. I knew we would never be ignored, but I wasn't prepared for the intensity of the reaction, mostly to Elizabeth. The only word to describe it is pandemonium. Elizabeth created a commotion wherever she went. And whether or not she liked it in public, she seemed to thrive on it privately. In Las Vegas I got my first real taste of what it would be like to live with her. Children, pets, servants, minor problems transformed into major tragedies, confusion, chaos, everything at fever pitch.

And illness. Elizabeth's most frequent complaint was paroxysmal tachycardia—too rapid heartbeat—and it often signaled a more serious condition. In Las Vegas a chronic sore throat suddenly became seriously infected and I remember looking in her mouth and seeing large white abscesses. We rushed to Cedars of Lebanon Hospital in Los Angeles, where Elizabeth's jaw had to be unlocked in order to cauterize the infection. It was a serious operation, yet just a couple of hours later, we were eating chili from Chasen's and sipping chilled champagne. That was another thing I learned about Elizabeth. Living with her was like living with a hurricane; each storm built in intensity, then subsided into an eerie calm as the eye passed, only to begin all over again.

We were married the same day my divorce became final. It was a madhouse, crazy. I didn't have a dime in my pocket and Bernie Rich had to loan me the money for the divorce fee. The marriage ceremony was conducted at Temple Beth Shalom by Rabbi Bernard Cohen of Las Vegas and Rabbi Nussbaum, who came from Los Angeles. Elizabeth's sister-in-law was her matron of honor; Mike Todd, Jr., was my best man. Just family and close friends were invited; my mother and my stepfather, Max, my father and his second wife, flew out from Philadelphia. The press wasn't allowed at the ceremony; reporters and photographers were separated from us by a wall, and were admitted after it was over. Then we had to get through a mob of people outside on our way back to the ranch for the wedding party. Again just family and friends and only a few people from the press. I remember thinking how funny it was: Elizabeth Taylor, the most famous woman in Hollywood, and Eddi Fisher, the Philadelphia kid, at a Jewish wedding party on a ranch in Las Vegas. But the ceremony itself hadn't been funny. It was beautiful. Elizabeth and I were married at last.

Even though we had been living together for months, we felt like newlyweds and wanted to be alone. My engagement at the Tropicana was over and we were on our way to Europe for a honeymoon before Elizabeth began shooting her next picture, *Suddenly Last Summer*. But we made the mistake of taking the first jet flight from Las Vegas to New York, and there was no way we could get away from Jim Bacon and all the other reporters on the plane. There was even more fuss when we were greeted at the Waldorf-Astoria and taken to a suite in the Towers with twin beds. Elizabeth and I just shook our heads and people started scurrying around trying to figure out what to do. Finally the beds were pushed together and the mattresses turned sideways so we wouldn't fall through the crack. Then everybody cleared out and we were all by ourselves for the first time as man and wife.

A couple of days later we took off for Barcelona, where we boarded the *Olnico,* a converted minesweeper leased by Sam Spiegel, who was producing *Suddenly Last Summer*. For the next few weeks we cruised the French and Italian Rivieras, putting in at Saint Tropez, Cannes, Portofino. Whenever we went ashore, the press was there waiting, but we got used to it. Avoiding reporters and photographers became a game, and if they got to be too much of a nuisance, we could always duck back to the privacy of the yacht. Our eventual destination was Torremolinos, Spain, where Elizabeth would film the exterior scenes for *Suddenly Last Summer*. We stayed in a hotel there, Elizabeth's children Michael and Christopher joined us, and she started work.

There was still time to play, to have fun with the children, and one afternoon we went to the local bullring. The matadors were testing young bulls and invited spectators to enter the ring to make a few passes. I watched several local boys scamper around and it didn't look too dangerous. The bulls weren't very big, and so I said, "How would you like to see *me* fight a bull?"

"Over my dead body," Elizabeth said. But the children cried, "Yes, yes!" and I couldn't back down.

I left my seat and spoke to the matador, who said he would hold the cape while I just stood next to him. But I waved him aside and took the cape myself. The bull looked at me, pawing the dirt, and I looked at him, flapping the cape. And then, ignoring the cape, he came straight at me. I backed up, dropped the cape, and found myself pinned to the wall between the horns of the bull. The crowd roared with laughter.

The matador distracted the bull's attention and I escaped. I should have quit while I was ahead, but thinking I had to do something to prove I wasn't a complete fool, I picked up the cape and the bull came at me again. I made one fast pass, threw the cape in the air, and walked away with as much dignity as I could muster. The crowd cheered and applauded; the children were delighted by my bravery. I was a hero. But as I sank down in my seat, I felt like an idiot.

With little or nothing to do while Elizabeth was working, I was like a stage extra, just hanging around waiting for my next cue. But that was part of our bargain. Elizabeth had stayed with me in Las Vegas; now it was my turn to stay with her. And our life together began to fall into a pattern. I was there when Elizabeth needed me: to get her to work on time, to keep an eye on her health, to make love, to fight. I had seen Mike and Elizabeth fight and I didn't like it at all; I thought they were going to kill each other. But I discovered that fighting was part of living with Elizabeth. She screamed at me and I shouted back, until one of us gave in. Once, in Spain, she worked herself into a fury over something so trivial that I have forgotten what it was. "All right," I said. "You want to hit somebody, hit me." She began pounding me with her fists and I said, "Okay, that hurts. Now try this side." That angered her even more and she became hysterical. Finally I had to grab her and pin her down, sitting on her chest with my knees on her arms, until finally she burst out laughing. And then we made love. All our fights ended that way.

13

Most of the time, Elizabeth and I ignored all the absurd stories written about us, or laughed them off. But one article in a British magazine, published just after we arrived in London to continue filming *Suddenly Last Summer*, was so blatantly false that we decided to sue. We had an airtight case. The article, with long quotes from Elizabeth, was based on an interview that had never taken place. I went to the Queen's Counsel and eventually we won both a settlement and an apology. It meant absolutely nothing. Papers and magazines on both sides of the Atlantic continued to print anything they pleased.

Hoping to find some privacy by living outside London, we rented a fifteen-room house in Windsor, which the papers, with typical exaggeration, described as a "palace" with gold faucets. The faucets were *painted* gold. It was the big house next door, Windsor Castle, that had the real gold. For some reason, we were never invited over. And after discovering that not even barbed wire and ground glass prevented reporters from climbing over our walls, we moved back to London.

The Oliver Messel suite at the Dorchester was the only suite in town big enough to hold us, the kids, their nanny, two white kittens, two Yorkies, and a Dandie Dinmont terrier. Looking for another surprise for Elizabeth, I went to a London cat show, where I spotted a huge gray Persian with gold eyes. The two little old ladies who owned it didn't want to sell until I offered them one hundred pounds, and when I went back to pick up the cat I learned it had just won the best of show over thousands of other entries. I added another fifty pounds to the sale price and the two ladies reluctantly gave me the cat. Elizabeth and I named it Buddha and tried to love it, but Buddha was bad-tempered, unsociable, and chose to do it in one or another of the tubs in the nine bathrooms of the suite. Without much else to occupy my time, I walked around filling all the tubs with water. Finally one night I tripped over him and that was the end. We called the two ladies and asked them to take back their cat. They spoke to reporters and the press had another story. Headlines in one of the London papers accused Elizabeth and me of that cardinal English sin, cruelty to animals.

Elizabeth had been looking forward to making *Suddenly Last Summer,* her first venture as an independent and a project she had chosen herself. The Tennessee Williams story had been adapted for the screen by Gore Vidal, Sam Spiegel was the producer, Joel Mankiewicz the director, and Katharine Hepburn and Montgomery Clift her co-stars. I wasn't sure how audiences would react to homosexuality, insanity, and cannibalism, all in the same picture, but Elizabeth saw it as an opportunity to "chew up the scenery," as she said, and work with people she admired.

Hepburn did not return her admiration. There were no fights or arguments, but Hepburn was very cool and distant; she and Elizabeth hardly spoke to each other on the set, and we never met her socially. Elizabeth remembered that Hepburn had snubbed her years earlier in the MGM commissary when she got the lead in *National Velvet,* a property that had originally been acquired for Hepburn years before. The picture made Elizabeth a star. Perhaps Hepburn was still jealous of Elizabeth, who was young and newly married, while she was growing older. She often spoke of Spencer Tracy. "Spence is coming over next weekend," she would tell us, or the week following, or the week after that. He never came. But Hepburn did not let jealousy or anything else stand in the way of her work. She was totally professional, punctual to the minute—a vivid contrast to Elizabeth, who was almost never on time. Also unlike Elizabeth, Hepburn didn't give a damn how she looked off the set and usually wore the same pair of baggy old gabardine pants. But on the set, every detail of her costume and appearance was important, and she always walked out in front of the cameras breathing fire. She was brilliant.

How Joe Mankiewicz handled both Hepburn and Taylor on the same set was a mystery to me. He was marvelous. If Hepburn demanded professionalism, Elizabeth demanded just the opposite, and Joe had to tease and haggle with her until he got what he wanted. He knew he couldn't be too strict with Elizabeth. No one, no matter who it was, could order her to do anything, because she would then do just the opposite. But as different as his leading ladies were, Elizabeth, too, was an actress. Not even Hepburn could overpower her performance in the film and I think she came to respect that. Sometime later Hepburn called me to ask if I didn't think it would be a good idea to star Elizabeth with Spencer Tracy in a film version of Thornton Wilder's *The Skin of Our Teeth*, which she and I would coproduce. I regret now that I turned down her proposal.

Sadly, Monty Clift was the real problem during the filming of *Suddenly Last Summer*. He was a remarkable actor, a remarkable man, and I was shocked when I saw him on the set. He was either drunk, or drugged, or both—completely out of it. But Elizabeth had insisted that he be in the picture, and somehow he got through it. Elizabeth had fallen in love with Monty years before when they worked together in *A Place in the Sun*. There were rumors of an affair, but whatever their relationship then, they became more than close friends, completely devoted to each other. They worked together again in *Raintree County*, and the car accident that so badly disfigured Monty's face and nearly took his life occurred as he was leaving a party at Elizabeth's. She rushed from the house and held his mangled and bleeding body in her arms until the ambulance arrived, an experience she would never forget. Since then, Monty's problems with alcohol and drugs had become steadily worse. A lonely and tormented man, he would come to our suite at the Dorchester and sit for hours, balanced precariously on the railing of the balcony with a drink in his hand, just staring into space. I felt very sorry for him, but Elizabeth didn't seem to pay too much attention to the way he was. She accepted it, and maybe even understood there was nothing she or anyone else could do to prevent him from destroying himself.

I saw some of the filming, but not an awful lot, just an

Gloria V. Luchenbill

Eddie in photos

America's number-one "Teenage Idol" surrounded by his fans in 1954.

The "stars" of The Magic Lady Supper Club (*left to right,* me, Joey Forman, Fred Bonaparte, Bernie Rich) pose with Eddie Cantor. Skipper Dawes, the man who first discovered the little kid with the big voice, stands behind us.

Entertaining troops in Korea in 1952, my most memorable army experience. *Inset,* Harry Truman called me his favorite Pfc.

Frankie and Eddie at the Friars Club with Jack Benny,
Georgie Jessel and George Raft.

Debbie meets my family. *Left to right,* my sisters: Shani,
Eileen, Nettie and Miriam; *front,* my stepfather, Max Stupp,
and my mother.

Above, "America's Sweethearts" on the cover of *Look* magazine. *Below*, Our wedding at Grossinger's, Judge Lawrence H. Cooke officiating. Milton Blackstone was my best man, Jeanette Johnson was Debbie's maid of honor.

UPI

The Todds and the Fishers at Epsom Downs.

Elizabeth made her first public appearance after Mike's death at my opening at the Tropicana.

Wide World, Gloria V. Luchenbill

Above, Elizabeth and I after our wedding ceremony. *Right,* Elizabeth as Cleopatra.

Wide World

Richard Burton arrives on the scene.

Trying to put on a brave front for photographers in New York after leaving Elizabeth in Rome.

Above, Tony Curtis and Frank Sinatra. *Below,* Princess Grace
and Prince Rainier.

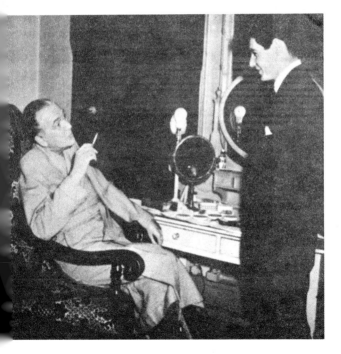

Above left, Irving Berlin; *above right,* Perry Como. *Below,* Noel Coward.

Top,
with Judy Garland.

Above, At El Morocco
with Ann-Margret. *Left,*
Terry Richard.

UPI

Above, Connie and I performed on opposite sides of the Las Vegas Strip. *Below,* Connie Stevens.

Top, my son Todd. *Below,* Debbie and I as the father and mother of the groom at Todd's wedding.

My daughter Carrie.

Lyn Davis.

occasional trip to the studio to make sure everything was all right. It was. Sam Spiegel was one of the most brilliant and creative of producers. When asked why he didn't come to the set more often, he said, "With a Tennessee Williams story, a Gore Vidal script, Joe Mankiewicz, and a cast like that, what am I going to contribute? I'd only be in the way." He had already done his work. Everyone had advised Elizabeth not to make the film: it was too weird, too special. So she went ahead and did it anyway, of course, and the picture became both an artistic and a commercial success. First *Giant,* then *Cat on a Hot Tin Roof,* and now *Suddenly Last Summer;* there seemed to be no stopping Elizabeth, and she was nominated for her third successive Academy Award.

Elizabeth had an offscreen image as a wicked woman and a reputation for being a very difficult actress to handle, but with a track record like hers, she was in enormous demand. There weren't enough hours in the day to read all the scripts and film projects submitted to her. While we were still in California, Walter Wanger had sent her the script for *Cleopatra,* which he was producing for 20th Century-Fox, and she hadn't even bothered to look at it. I don't know why I brought that script, among hundreds of others, to London with us; I don't know why I picked it up one day and read it. But I did, and it was terrible. Still, something about it hit me: Elizabeth Taylor as Cleopatra. She was in the bathroom, brushing her teeth as usual, and I called in to her, "Elizabeth, I think you ought to do it."

She laughed and kept on brushing.

"No, really," I said. "You ought to do it for a million dollars."

No reaction.

The phone rang about an hour later. I answered and handed it to Elizabeth. "It's Walter Wanger," I said.

She took the receiver. "Walter, I'll do it for a million dollars," she said with a laugh, and a moment later hung up.

"What did he say?" I asked incredulously.

"He'll get back to me."

An hour later, Wanger called again and said she had a deal.

Both Elizabeth and I were a little surprised, but I thought because the project had been submitted to Elizabeth, it would be a big-budget picture with the best director, the best cast, and above all, a better script. In fact, 20th Century-Fox had been planning for nothing more than a low-budget, back-lot pageant picture, with Joan Collins playing the part of Cleopatra. But Wanger knew exactly what he was doing when he sent the script to Elizabeth; it was the idea that had intrigued him, just as it had intrigued me. Elizabeth was more intrigued by the money. It would take several months to complete the negotiations, and more than a year before she could begin work on the picture, but her impulsive, only half-serious reaction to Wanger's call lit the fuse of the biggest bomb in Hollywood history. When it exploded, no one connected with *Cleopatra* would be left unscarred.

We came back to Hollywood in the fall of 1959, and unable to find a house to suit us, we moved into the Beverly Hills Hotel: Bungalow 8 for Elizabeth and me, Bungalow 12 for her children. It was enormously expensive, but it was comfortable, and oddly enough, living right in the middle of everything provided a certain amount of privacy. We stayed there for more than a year, whenever we were in Los Angeles.

Elizabeth's future employer, 20th Century-Fox, played host to Nikita Khrushchev in Hollywood shortly after our return. Like any tourist, the Russian premier wanted to see Disneyland and an American movie studio, and of the two, the movie studio must have seemed the more unreal. A gaudy dance number from the movie *Can-Can,* which was in production on the lot, was staged for Khrushchev's benefit, and then at a luncheon in his honor, Spyros Skouras, the chief executive of 20th Century-Fox, declared in a pompous and windy speech, "I am a coal miner's son and I grew up to become the head of this great motion picture studio." The remark was translated for Khrushchev, who smiled and replied, "I, too, was a coal miner's son and I grew up to become the head of the greatest country in the world." Elizabeth was only one of several Hollywood stars, including Marilyn Monroe and Debbie Reynolds, who were invited to attend the luncheon, and at one point things became so chaotic that Elizabeth kicked off her shoes and stood on the table to get a better view of Khrushchev. He took it all in stride, but it was not one of Hollywood's most dignified moments.

I opened at the Desert Inn in Las Vegas a few weeks later. With the exception of a special for the BBC while we were in London, it was the first time I had performed in several months, and Elizabeth came with me, of course. She didn't attend every performance, but when she did come, I couldn't ignore her. The audience wouldn't let me—nor would she. I often sang a romantic ballad directly to her. One night she dressed up in a waitress's uniform, put on a blond wig, and appeared in the middle of my act staggering under a huge tray of dishes, which she dropped with a loud crash right in front of me at the foot of the stage. I loved it and the audience screamed with laughter.

If I was becoming known as Mr. Elizabeth Taylor, or if audiences at the Desert Inn didn't think they were getting their money's worth unless they caught sight of "Liz," I didn't really care. I was enormously proud of Elizabeth, proud of the way audiences reacted both to her and to me. That was something else I could give her. But there were times when I found I would rather be with her than on stage, sing just for her rather than to an audience. We never ran out of things to do together or ways to express how much we cared. That kind of relationship was completely new to me. It consumed all my emotions, all my energy, and her need for me overshadowed my own needs as a performer.

We didn't dwell on comparisons, but Elizabeth told me that I was her greatest lover; she loved me more than she had ever loved anyone before, even more than she loved her children. Of course, I understood she didn't mean that, but I didn't yet understand that for Elizabeth every moment of a relationship had to be more intense than the last or there was no relationship. In time I came to realize that the man she loved at the moment she loved more intensely than anyone else. Her latest lover was always the best.

Mike Todd had negotiated Elizabeth's release from her long-term contract with MGM. After *Cat on a Hot Tin Roof,* she was obligated to do one more picture at her regular salary of $125,000, and MGM presented her with *Butterfield 8*. We tried desperately to get her out of it, but MGM must have thought the image was perfect—Elizabeth Taylor as a whore and home-wrecker—and refused to let her work on *Cleopatra* or anything else until she made the picture. It was going to be filmed in New York and we looked for a place to live in the suburbs. But when the owners of the house we wanted—a magnificent design by Frank Lloyd Wright—refused to sell, we settled for a suite at the Park Lane. Then just after I began an engagement in the Empire Room at the Waldorf, Elizabeth got sick. It would be my last job for a year and a half.

The diagnosis was double pneumonia, and Elizabeth had been so heavily medicated that she was out cold in the ambulance that rushed her to the Harkness Pavilion. Lights were flashing and sirens screaming as we turned in to the hospital. And at that moment Elizabeth sat up on the stretcher, took a compact out of her bag, and started fixing her face. "Get me my lip gloss," she said, handing me the bag. I found it and she made up her lips before she was wheeled into the emergency room.

As usual, she thought she was going to die. So did I, and for the next two weeks I was driven back and forth from the Waldorf, before, between, and after shows, just to be with her. I ate nothing but hamburgers, Cokes, and pickles, and one night on stage I looked down, saw my chin on my chest, and realized my dinner jacket was very tight. I had put on ten pounds. Elizabeth didn't die; in fact, her recovery was surprisingly rapid for double pneumonia, and before she left the hospital we consulted her doctor about another matter—untying her tubes, or reconnecting them, so we could have a child. He laughed and said, "If you want it that badly, Elizabeth, I'm sure it can be done." It never was.

MGM was willing to do almost anything to keep Elizabeth happy and get her to make *Butterfield 8,* including giving me a part in the picture. Monty Clift offered to help me with it. One morning he came to our suite at the Park Lane and I gave him my script to read while I finished dressing. When I came out, the script was burning in his lap. Monty had fallen asleep and set it afire with a cigarette. That was the end of my acting lessons.

My part in the picture was small, and I did my best, but almost anyone could have done it better. Elizabeth, whether she liked the picture or not, was perfect. Laurence Harvey, her co-star, was not. I don't know whose idea it was to cast that rather effete Englishmen as an Ivy League American, but he was all wrong. I liked him and thought he was extremely witty in spite of all his affectations. "Darling, we *must* go have lunch together," he would say every time we met. "We *must* get together." We never did. Elizabeth was put off by him at first, but as they worked together they became good friends. Friendship was impossible with Pandro S. Berman, the producer, and Daniel Mann, the director. She had trouble with both of them, and she hated the script. We called the picture "Butterball 4."

Elizabeth asked her friends Tennessee Williams, Joe Mankiewicz, Paddy Chayefsky, and Daniel Taradash to make suggestions and changes, which she then had to pass off as her own ideas because there was a strike of the Screen Writers' Guild. Mann filmed some of the revisions, which included rather explicit love scenes between Elizabeth and me, but Berman cut everything out later because he said they were amateurish and no actors were going to mess around with "his" script. As a director, Mann was pure Actors Studio, a dictator, but that didn't work with Elizabeth. One day as they were about to shoot a bathtub scene, he came over to her and said, "Make believe you're fucking the faucet. That's the expression I want." He thought he was relating to Elizabeth, teaching her how to act. Elizabeth gave him a well-known Italian sign of contempt and walked off the set. Finally she didn't care anymore. The picture was trash and she wanted to get the whole thing over with so it wouldn't interfere with our lives.

After the film had been shot and we were back in Hollywood, MGM arranged a private screening of the rough cut. Elizabeth and I had dinner at Trader Vic's that evening, and expecting the worst, took a couple of large containers of Scorpions, a powerful house drink, to the studio with us. We sat through the whole film, with Elizabeth growing angrier and more disgusted every minute, until at the end we both stood up and threw our drinks at the screen. Storming out of the screening room, Elizabeth led me to the office of Sol Siegel, MGM's head of production, and on the door in lipstick she scrawled her review of the picture: "No Sale!"

She wasn't always the best judge of her own work. In spite of her loathing for the film, Elizabeth gave a performance in *Butterfield 8*. My performance was slightly less than adequate, even though Elizabeth had presented me with a huge gold statuette of Saint Genesius, the patron saint of actors, inscribed on the back: "If you win the Academy Award before I do, I'll break your neck." There wasn't much chance of that, but I was voted the Worst Actor of the Year by the Harvard *Lampoon*. My real role in the picture, as I saw it, was behind the scenes, taking care of Elizabeth, getting her to work, keeping her out of trouble. It was my duty, and I was so involved with her, so obsessed by her, that I had time for nothing else.

If Milton or any of my other friends thought that was a little odd, they didn't say so. They were all in awe of Elizabeth, and Milton, especially, kept his distance. Leery of actresses, he was so polite and deferential it was almost embarrassing. Even Max Jacobson was abnormally subdued in Elizabeth's presence. Only Lenny Gaines told me what he really thought. "Maybe I should have kept my mouth shut," he said recently, "but I saw things happening to you I didn't like. I remember when the whole thing started; you were at the Essex House and Elizabeth was at the Plaza, and I said, 'Eddie, you don't need this now. You're getting yourself in too deep.' Then I met Elizabeth. By that time you were married and living at the Park Lane, getting ready to do *Butterfield 8,* and Joey Forman told Elizabeth the one guy who could help her out with her part was Lenny Gaines, because he knew all there was to know about the New York scene. I came up to your suite, sat down with Elizabeth, and we talked about New York. You were still in bed. In the middle of the afternoon, for God's sake. The next day the same thing, and the day after that. Beds, hospitals, and jewelry stores. That was your marriage to Elizabeth."

No one, including Lenny, could resist Elizabeth if she made an effort. She could be the bitch of all time or the sweetest creature in the world, and when she wanted to get along with someone, there was no one who could do it better. She won my mother over completely, called her Momma, teased her, sent her little gifts. "You know the bracelet I have with a charm for each of my grandchildren," my mother recalled. "Well, Elizabeth saw that and said, 'Momma, would you like a charm of my children?' And I said yes, I'd love it. So while you were on your honeymoon in Europe, she had one specially made— a four-leaf clover with pictures of her children on three leaves, and on the fourth it said, 'To Momma from her grandchildren.'"

I asked my mother what else she remembered about Elizabeth, and she smiled and said, "She was always very thoughtful of me, Sonny Boy. If I called you on the phone, I used to hear her in the background: 'Eddie, is that Momma? Tell her I love her.' And it was very nice of her to come visit me in the hospital. You had just finished making that picture and I had a little heart attack and you both came all the way to

Philadelphia. That was the time she slipped and fell on the ice. She scraped her knee or something. That was all. But oh, my God, it was like the whole world was coming to an end."

"I thought you loved Elizabeth, Mom," I said. "I used to get the biggest thrill when I saw the way you two got along together."

"What can I say, Sonny Boy? I didn't have much to do with Elizabeth. You were always in Hollywood or Europe. All I knew was what I read in the papers. But she always paid me the greatest respect. The only thing I have against Elizabeth is what she did to you."

Yes, I thought, that's what any mother would say. Or did I do it to myself?

The fall was not serious. Elizabeth sprained her ankle and had to use crutches for a while. She loved that. We both needed a vacation, and a friend of mine suggested the Marrakesh Hotel at Ocho Rios in Jamaica. The hotel was new and hadn't opened yet, so we had the whole place to ourselves. But the Jamaican government insisted on giving us police protection, and the hotel was surrounded by a platoon of guards, with a captain who had the specific assignment of protecting Elizabeth's jewels. I don't know why she bothered to bring them. We didn't even put on shoes for the three weeks we were there. One of the few places we went to was the local movie house, to see a Tarzan picture. We were the only tourists in an audience of at least a thousand Jamaicans, all of whom thought the picture was ridiculous, particularly the way Tarzan spoke English.

Elizabeth and I fell in love with Jamaica. The people were warm and wonderful to us, and hearing of some property for sale, we decided to buy it. It was a beautiful point of land overlooking Mammee Bay, and that name, pronounced exactly like the Jolson song "Mammy," clinched the deal as far as I was concerned. We sent for George MacLain, the architect who had built a house in Beverly Hills for Elizabeth and Michael Wilding; he flew in from Sun Valley, we looked at the property together, and he immediately began to make plans for a house. It was going to be our retreat, a place where Elizabeth and I could always come to get away from the rest of the world.

We left Jamaica and returned to the Beverly Hills Hotel. Elizabeth was now free to begin work on *Cleopatra*, not for the original million-dollar offer, but for $750,000 against 10 percent of the gross. We were told, however, that with delays in production and overtime, Elizabeth would be paid much more than a million. I was on the payroll too. I forget what my title was, but I was supposed to act as some kind of production assistant, for a salary of $150,000. Although I knew I was being paid to keep Elizabeth happy—and would have been given anything I asked to do it—I was genuinely interested in production and hoped I could make some creative contribution to the film. But the one real job I was assigned, a trip to Egypt with a second unit to film the exteriors, was canceled because as a Jew I wouldn't be allowed to enter the country.

Problems like that seemed to arise from the very beginning of the project. Even with my limited experience, I could tell that no one connected with the film really knew what he was doing. Stuck with Elizabeth, 20th Century-Fox had to justify the expense of hiring her, and everything else doubled and tripled in size, including the budget, which suddenly ballooned to fifteen million dollars. Neither Walter Wanger, the producer, nor Rouben Mamoulian, the director, knew how to spend that kind of money, or where. When plans were made to shoot the film in England, no one stopped to think that the sun just doesn't shine there very often. Or that the elaborate sets, both exterior and interior, could never be used again and would have to be scrapped. Peter Finch had been cast as Julius Caesar and Stephen Boyd as Mark Antony, both excellent actors, but they and Elizabeth would still be working with the original B-movie script. And to complicate matters even further, the film would either make or break 20th Century-Fox and Spyros Skouras, who was already under heavy fire for the way he was managing the company.

In August 1960, Elizabeth and I sailed to Europe with her children on the maiden voyage of the *Leonardo da Vinci*. We arrived in Rome in time to attend the opening ceremony of the Olympic Games. Naturally Elizabeth was late, and when she entered the stadium, every head turned in her direction and the huge crowd went completely crazy. I had never heard such a roar, and it crossed my mind that in an odd way, the moment was the modern equivalent of Cleopatra's entry into Rome. Elizabeth *was* Cleopatra.

She didn't think so. In London, once we had settled again into the Oliver Messel suite of the Dorchester, she began to wonder how the hell she was going to get through this picture. Bad weather and union troubles were fouling up the filming schedules and there was nothing for her to do but just sit around. And when she sat around, she became anxious and self-indulgent. She developed a low-grade fever which persisted without any apparent cause, and once again I found myself playing nursemaid. Bored with that role for the first time in the year and a half we had been married, I began to have second thoughts about never being apart from Elizabeth. Maybe that vow was a little foolish after all. It wasn't good to spend so much time with her, to be so involved in her problems. I had to assert my individuality, start doing something for myself. And with that extra sense that women are supposed to have, Elizabeth understood. We didn't have to discuss it; it showed on my face or in the way I was behaving.

I decided to go back to Los Angeles. Elizabeth and I had formed a new company, MCL Productions—a name that I took from the initials of her three children, Michael, Christopher, and Liza—and the purpose of my trip was to open negotiations with studios for future projects, which I would produce and in which Elizabeth would star. It was all part of our long-range plan for staying together. I certainly wouldn't have left Elizabeth if she had been seriously ill, or if I foresaw any major problems with *Cleopatra*—those would come later. And I relished the idea of trying my hand as a producer. Mike Todd was my inspiration, even though I knew I didn't have his experience or chutzpah. What I didn't know was that movie deals were just as complex, and could be just as venal, as anything I had ever encountered in the record business or television.

Joining forces with Kurt Frings, Elizabeth's agent, I went first to Mike's old friend Harold Mirisch at United Artists, who wanted Elizabeth to star with Paul Newman in a movie version of William Gibson's play *Two for the Seesaw*. Mirisch's original offer was one million dollars against 10 percent of the gross, but soon after we sat down to discuss it, I discovered he had already made an offer to Newman that took 2.5 percent away from Elizabeth. Kurt and I protested, but not too loudly, because Mirisch had had a series of heart attacks and I was warned that any excitement might kill him. So we talked and played interminable games of gin rummy until finally Mirisch took me aside in a bathroom with an offer to pay Elizabeth

$950,000 and give me $50,000 to go along with the deal. Elizabeth and I were on the phone at least three times daily, night and day, and when I told her what had happened, we both agreed that Mirisch could go to hell.

Elizabeth was also interested in doing *Irma La Douce,* but that project went down the drain too, after I discovered that no one was willing to make a straightforward, aboveboard contract. Expensive cars and other "considerations" always seemed to be part of the deal—the movie business's equivalent of payola in the record business. Everyone was expected to play footsie with everyone else; I was willing to play footsie with no one but Elizabeth. Obviously I had a lot to learn about being a producer.

Kurt Frings and I next went to Jack Warner at Warner Brothers with a proposal for four pictures—two with Elizabeth and two without—and among the ideas considered were a remake of *Anna Karenina* and the life story of Isadora Duncan. Warner set me up with a huge suite of offices at the studio while discussions were under way. Offers and counteroffers flew back and forth across the table until my head began to swim, and I soon got the feeling that all the executives and lawyers doing the negotiating were not too artistically inclined. They were talking about bucks and budgets and I wanted to talk about writers, directors, and scripts. Warner Brothers was willing to pay Elizabeth's price, not because she was a fine actress, but because she would be "bankable" no matter what she did. That made me uncomfortable, and when Elizabeth, whose instincts about her career were very sharp, agreed, I withdrew from the negotiations. Warner Brothers later presented me with a bill for over sixty thousand dollars for the office and other studio facilities they had invited me to use.

I saw my children in Los Angeles. A month or so before, Debbie had married Harry Karl, a shoe millionaire and a man much older than she was. Elizabeth and I had heard about it in Rome and spent an hour composing a congratulatory telegram. Amused by the possibility that Debbie had married Harry for his money, we wired: "Wishing you all the happiness you so richly deserve."

Time had not mellowed Debbie's feelings about me, I'm sorry to say. Even though two years had passed since we separated and divorced, she had never stopped reminding press and public that she and her children had been abandoned. My son Todd had to have an operation for a double hernia while I was vacationing with Elizabeth in Jamaica. Debbie called Louella Parsons to find out where I was and I was accused of sporting on a Caribbean island while my son was lying at death's door. There were items in the press about Debbie and Glenn Ford. And later Harry Karl. But her image as the girl next door was still intact.

Even her marriage to Harry became a publicity plus. As an older man, he would comfort Debbie and be a stable and secure influence on her children. Harry had been married twice before, first to the actress Marie McDonald, who was known as "The Body," and then, for a brief three weeks, to Joan Cohn, the very rich widow of Harry Cohn, head of Columbia Pictures. At a party at Joan's house one night, she took me aside and said, "Eddie, wait until Debbie finds out what Harry is all about." I pressed her for an explanation, but that was all she said.

Debbie and Harry had a house in Malibu, where I went to see Carrie and Todd. Carrie at four was pert and pretty, very much like her mother; Todd at two and a half was small and shy, like me. I noticed that they called Harry "Daddy Harry" and they began to call me "Daddy Eddie," but I said, "No, call me Daddy." And they did. I felt guilty because I hadn't seen them as often as I wanted to, and Debbie, who was conspicuously absent during most of my visit, finally made an appearance, and told me the presents I brought the children were too expensive. She said she had no intention of letting me spoil them.

During our divorce proceedings, Debbie had promised to bring up Todd as a Jew. It was a nice gesture, the one thing she had offered to give me in return for all the things I was giving her, and I was very pleased. Toward the end of my visit, I reminded her of her promise. Harry was Jewish and I thought there wouldn't be any problem. "What about Todd's religion?" I said. "Are you still going to bring him up as a Jew?"

"I've changed my mind," Debbie said.

"Debbie," I said, "I didn't ask you to do it. You brought the subject up yourself. It was your idea and you made a promise."

"Well," she said, "I was in love with you then. I'm not in love with you now."

"We have nothing against the Jews," Harry added. "But we

go to a very nice Methodist church with a very fine minister. If he had ever said anything against the Jews, would I have given him $7,500?"

I left their house full of anger and resentment. What could I do? What right did I have to do anything?

14

While I was in Hollywood, a photographer climbed over our balcony at the Dorchester and snapped a picture of Elizabeth in the company of three men. The picture, taken through curtains, was fuzzy, and the caption, when it appeared on the front page of the papers, proclaimed that in my absence "Liz" was playing around with other men. If it hadn't been such a gross invasion of privacy—and an outright lie—the whole thing would have been laughable. The men in question were Dick Hanley, who had been Mike's private secretary and was now indispensable to both Elizabeth and me; Bob Abrams, a man I met during my tour of duty with the army band, who had become a friend and associate; and Hank Moonjean, also a friend and associate of ours since the days when he was working as an assistant director on *Suddenly Last Summer*. The only "playing around" they were doing was a game of gin rummy.

I returned to London to find that Elizabeth didn't have much else to do. We saw friends and went to parties, and at least on one occasion I had a night out with the boys. Gary Cooper was in London and when I heard that he was dying of cancer, Bob, Hank, and I took him on the town. We went to a string of nightclubs and restaurants, and Coop, who was usually so conservative and shy, seemed to enjoy every minute of it, even

183

the adulation of the many people who recognized him and asked for his autograph. I wondered if he knew what we knew. Perhaps he did, and wanted to savor the little time he had left.

Cleopatra was slowly sinking of its own weight. Rouben Mamoulian, who was a great stage and screen director, simply couldn't handle the script, that cast, and a production that was being filmed outside in the dead of an English winter. After about three months work and expenses of at least ten million dollars, he had just six minutes on film, and in one sequence I remember seeing vapor coming from the nostrils of horses that were supposed to be in Rome. Stephen Boyd complained that he was freezing his ass off, and Peter Finch, who had appeared with Elizabeth in *Elephant Walk* a few years before, would come to our suite with his wife after work and in total exasperation just drink until he passed out. In spite of that, we hit it off from the moment we met and became great friends.

Elizabeth was in bad shape and getting worse, terrified that she was trapped in the biggest turkey of her career. Her reputation as an actress was very important to Elizabeth, more important, I sometimes thought, than her health, or even her life. With the picture at a virtual standstill while studio executives tried to figure out what to do next, she spent endless hours in bed or just sitting in a chair, playing cards, eating junk food, and gaining weight. And I became more concerned than ever by her drinking in combination with the many pills her various doctors prescribed, including Demerol, a potent pain-killer and sedative. A well-meaning doctor or two had tried to give her substitutes, but Elizabeth could always tell the difference. Nothing but Demerol seemed to offer her any relief.

No matter what her doctors prescribed, the low-grade fever Elizabeth had had for months persisted and she began to get headaches. Baffled, her doctors decided something was the matter with her teeth, so one day she was knocked out with gas on the floor of our suite while a dentist extracted a tooth. The headaches continued, and so did her need for Demerol. She was in such agony, and I had to summon one or another of her doctors to give her pills or shots so often, that finally I offered to inject Elizabeth myself if they showed me how. They argued against it at first, but when Elizabeth refused to have a nurse, they agreed.

It was very simple. The first time Elizabeth woke up and needed Demerol, I gave her an injection in the buttocks and she went back to sleep immediately. The following night the same thing happened. But on the third night, one injection wasn't enough, she asked for another and I refused to give it to her. Although I felt sorry for her and wanted desperately to help her, I didn't dare give her more than her doctors prescribed. They took over again after that, no matter what hour I had to call them.

Was Elizabeth deliberately making herself sick; was she manufacturing a crisis just because she couldn't face *Cleopatra?* Or if she really was sick, were the drugs making it worse? I didn't know what to think. I couldn't know what was going on inside Elizabeth's head, but I did remember that the last time she was happy and well was during the filming of *Suddenly Last Summer.* And the man responsible for that was Joe Mankiewicz.

At lunch one day with Walter Wanger, I mentioned Joe's name. I admired Wanger; he was a fine producer and a fine man. But like Mamoulian, he was overwhelmed by the sheer size of *Cleopatra* and had become the whipping boy for studio executives, who blamed him for everything, including the bad weather and Elizabeth's health. "You know," I said to him, "the three biggest problems you've got with this picture are the script, the director, and Elizabeth. The *only* way you're going to get it made is to bring in Joe Mankiewicz. He's a great writer, he's a great director—and he can handle Elizabeth."

I was not trying to play Mike Todd. To me the idea was nothing more than common sense. To Wanger it came as a divine revelation and he asked me to call Spyros Skouras and tell him the same thing. I did and Skouras reacted with enthusiasm. "God bless you, Eddie," he said. "I'll never forget you for this. Anything you want in this world is yours." Unknown to Elizabeth, 20th Century-Fox then proceeded to fire Mamoulian and hire Mankiewicz, in a complex series of negotiations that made him a multimillionaire overnight.

Elizabeth was outraged when she found out. She would not stand by and see her friend Rouben Mamoulian cast aside. "Joe Mankiewicz is *not* going to direct this picture," she cried. "I will *not* bow down to that man." It was all childish talk, of course, Elizabeth's usual act. But she kept it up even after

Mankiewicz arrived in London. "I don't know what you think you're doing here," she said with haughty indignation.

Mankiewicz got down on his knees and said, "I'm here to do whatever you want, Elizabeth."

She melted and Mankiewicz went to work.

Elizabeth loved and respected Joe Mankiewicz, and in truth, welcomed his arrival even more than I did. But her health did not improve. All work on *Cleopatra* stopped while Mankiewicz was rewriting the script, and Elizabeth was still worried and miserable. Night and day she was really happy only when, together, we were able to blot out the rest of the world, no matter what else was going on. But she had started taking a new kind of pill, a cute little white ball that one of her doctors had prescribed. I didn't know what it was, another painkiller probably, and I noticed that whenever Elizabeth took them, she drifted off into a daze. One Sunday as she and I were lying around in bed, I decided to check them out. From Elizabeth's reaction, I assumed they were more powerful than her other pills, but I didn't know how much more powerful. I went into the bathroom, took a pill, and then got back into bed. I was reading when it hit me. Suddenly everything began swimming in front of my eyes. My head seemed to be floating in space; I couldn't coordinate my arms and legs. I wanted to get up but I couldn't move. I had to lie back and just ride it out in bed.

Early the next morning I went to Elizabeth's doctor in Harley Street. "What the hell is this?" I demanded, showing him the bottle of little white pills. "Why are you giving my wife these?"

The doctor examined the bottle coolly. "Oh, is she still using this prescription?" he said. "I'm sorry, Eddie. I should have taken her off these pills."

I glared at him in a fury, and knowing Elizabeth certainly didn't need that prescription, I started stealing the pills, flushing them down the toilet and getting rid of the bottles. Then we would play a little game. Elizabeth and I would go on a house hunt, looking for her pills. She didn't understand how so many of them could simply disappear, or who could be stealing them. I felt like an idiot and quickly realized that what I was doing was both foolish and useless. Even if I threw away the little white pills, I couldn't prevent her from refilling the prescription.

But they continued to worry me, and once, while Elizabeth

and I were spending a weekend in Paris with Kurt Frings, I drew him aside and said, "Kurt, we've got to do something about these pills. I took one, I know the effect. I'm afraid they might kill her."

"Don't worry about it," Kurt said.

"Look, just try this one before you go to bed tonight. You'll see what I'm talking about."

Kurt picked the pill out of the palm of my hand and popped it in his mouth.

"What are you doing?" I said. "You're crazy."

"Forget it," Kurt said. "Come on, let's get back to the party."

Several people were gathered in our big, old-fashioned suite at the Lancaster. Kurt sat down on a sofa, lit a cigarette, and started talking to one of the guests. He was leaning over to put out the cigarette when it happened. I saw a startled expression in his eyes and then he passed out. Everyone laughed, thinking he had just had too much to drink. Elizabeth and I had to drag him to his suite and put him to bed. Elizabeth, too, thought he was drunk, and prying open his mouth, she forced him to take two Miltown, a tranquilizer sometimes used to kill a hangover. Kurt kept them under his tongue, screaming and shaking his head in panic. And when Elizabeth made him swallow them, he started yelling, "Come back, come back!" He was yelling at the pills to come back, terrified that the combination of Miltown and Elizabeth's pill would kill him. Finally he lapsed into a stupor and Elizabeth and I left him there to sleep it off. I later learned that those cute little white balls were a potent painkiller.

If I had made my point to Kurt, it was lost on Elizabeth. I didn't know what to do next. And on top of my concern for her, her illness was beginning to affect the children. Elizabeth always made a great display of love for her children, and the time she spent with them was very intense. Liza was still just a baby, but I could see that Michael and Christopher, even though they loved their mother and were probably used to her moods and illnesses, were puzzled and worried. Their father, Michael Wilding, who was in London, saw them from time to time, but he had his own problems. I tried to be a friend to the boys, spent time with them every day, took them out and bought them clothes, saw about their schools. I even sang to them, but they didn't like that very much. They were marvelous boys and when they started calling me Daddy, it sounded funny, but I must say I liked it.

No matter what I did for Elizabeth, it obviously wasn't enough, and I turned to Rex Kennamer. He flew to London from Los Angeles and after a long talk with Elizabeth, said to me, "Eddie, you're going to have to tell her to stop drinking while she's on so much medication."

"All right," I said. "But you're the doctor. Why should I tell her?"

"Because I don't want her to lose confidence in me," he said.

His logic escaped me. Was it more important, I wondered, for Elizabeth to have confidence in her husband or her doctor? But I went into our bedroom and said, "Elizabeth, you've got to stop drinking while you're taking all these pills. If you don't, I'm leaving you."

"No you won't," she said. That was all, and I walked out with my tail between my legs.

"Well," Kennamer said, patting me on the back. "Good try."

Elizabeth was right, of course; I would never leave her. That was part of the problem: she was dead sure of me. It was ironic. I had given up my own career to watch my wife suffer through hers; I had given up my own children to take care of children she had had by other men; I was giving up my life for the pleasure of standing by helplessly while the woman I loved seemed to care so little for her own.

In February 1961, we took the Orient Express from Paris to Munich for a few days of vacation, and stayed in the same hotel suite Benito Mussolini had used when he visited his friend Adolf Hitler. We went to a couple of parties. Elizabeth refused to cut down on her drinking and finally one night I was fed up. She was in the bathroom, brushing her teeth. "Elizabeth, come to bed," I called. "You've been brushing your goddamned teeth long enough."

"I'll be right in," she said.

Several more minutes passed and still she didn't come. Mad as hell, I went into the bathroom, pulled her away from the mirror, picked her up, carried her into the bedroom, and threw her on the bed. I got in beside her and turned my back. "This is the end, Elizabeth," I said, my heart pounding. "I can't take any more. I'm leaving in the morning."

"You're leaving in the morning?" she said. "Well, I'm leaving now." She reached for a bottle of Seconal on the bedside table, opened it, and began pouring pills in her mouth.

Horrified, I grabbed the bottle and put my hand in her mouth, trying to prevent her from swallowing the pills. She bit my hand, leaped from the bed, and ran into the bathroom, where she found a bottle of Miltown and started swallowing those. I struggled with her, scattering the pills all over the bathroom floor. Pulling away from me, she went back into the bedroom, sat down at the dressing table, and started brushing her hair.

"My God, Elizabeth," I said, "what have you done? What about the children?"

"You'll take care of the children," she said. She dropped the hairbrush and stood up. Her eyes were glazed and foam was coming from the corners of her mouth. Then she crumpled into my arms. I stumbled backward and she fell to the floor.

If there was ever a moment to keep my head, this was it. But I panicked. I didn't know whether to call a doctor or the police. Kurt Frings was asleep in another bedroom of the suite, and I rushed in, yelling, "Kurt! Kurt!"

He jumped up in terror. All he could see was my body outlined by the light from the living room; he thought he was having a nightmare.

I was hysterical. "What are we going to do?" I cried. "She's dying. Elizabeth took a whole bottle of pills and she's dying!"

Fully awake now, Kurt said, "Calm down, Eddie. Take it easy. We've got six hours. I've had experience with this before."

With whom, I wondered. How many of his long list of famous female clients had done something like this? He picked up the phone and I ran back to Elizabeth.

We were walking her around the bedroom when the doctor arrived. She was unconscious, dead weight. The doctor signaled us to lay her down on the bed and then opened his bag and began to prepare an injection. He was an old man, ancient, and I thought he would probably kill her. After examining Elizabeth briefly, he found a vein in her arm and gave her the injection. He reminded me of Max Jacobson, Dr. Needles, and I prayed to God he knew what he was doing.

Kurt had simply disappeared. The doctor straightened up and began to speak in German, telling me that Elizabeth would be all right; let her sleep. I put a thousand dollars in marks in an envelope and gave it to him. Speaking in a combination of high school German and Yiddish, I begged him to say nothing about this. He nodded and left.

I lay down beside Elizabeth on the bed. She was in a deep, deep sleep. Was the doctor telling me the truth? Would she be all right? I was crying. If Elizabeth died, I wanted to die too.

I stayed beside her for eighteen hours, until she finally woke up. We had a scene; I said I was sorry, she said she was sorry. We loved each other, things would be different from now on. But I had done a lot of thinking during those eighteen hours and decided I had to get away from Elizabeth, at least for a while. I had even come up with a plan. My friend Bob Abrams was with us in Munich, and after telling him what had happened, I asked him to make arrangements to get me into a hospital as soon as we returned to London.

"What's supposed to be wrong with you?" he said.

"I don't know. I'll think of something."

Once Elizabeth was back on her feet, I ordered food sent up to the room, but she wasn't hungry. I was, so I ate hers as well as mine—a double order of wiener schnitzel—and developed a case of heartburn. Not a very good reason to check into a hospital, but it would have to do.

On the way to the Munich airport, Elizabeth was drinking beer, laughing, looking as beautiful as ever, just as if nothing had happened. I was furious. It was my turn to be sick, damn it, and I magnified a slight case of heartburn into a major medical emergency. It may have been the best acting of my career. Elizabeth's doctor met us at the Dorchester and quickly summoned a surgeon. After they poked and prodded and asked me questions, the considered diagnosis of these medical experts was appendicitis. I was giving them all kinds of signals, trying to tell them there was nothing really wrong with me. The pain I did have was in my chest, nowhere near my appendix. But things had gone too far. I went to the hospital that same day and lost a perfectly healthy appendix. Well, I thought, after the operation, at least I won't have to worry about appendicitis anymore.

Elizabeth appeared at my bedside at nine o'clock the following morning. I was already up and walking around, but I complained of being uncomfortable and Elizabeth said, "There's no reason for any one in this day and age to be in pain." She called a nurse and demanded that the doctor give me a shot of something. I protested but got the shot anyway, and suddenly I really did feel sick. My head was swimming, I got the dry heaves and was terrified that my incision was going to burst wide open, a recurring dream I had had all my life. Elizabeth couldn't have been more sympathetic.

After she was gone, I remembered her words: "There's no reason for anyone in this day and age to be in pain." Did that mean there was a shot or a pill for everything? I couldn't face it. "I know I'm supposed to go home in a day or so," I told her doctor, "but I really don't want to, not right away. Can't we come up with some other disease to keep me here? How about heart trouble?"

He agreed and informed Elizabeth that he wanted me to stay in the hospital for tests and observation; he was very concerned about my heart. Alarmed, Elizabeth called Rex Kennamer in Los Angeles and then said to me, "Darling, I've just spoken to Rex and he says it's utterly impossible for you to have heart trouble."

"How the hell does he know?" I protested. But Elizabeth refused to listen to any argument. "You've been in this hospital long enough," she said. "I miss you, the children miss you, and it's time you came home."

The real crisis began when Elizabeth started to have trouble breathing and no one seemed to know why. Her doctors wanted to take her to a hospital, but she made such a fuss that they gave in to her, as usual. An oxygen tent was set up over her side of our bed and she just lay there, heavily sedated, gasping for air.

Some instinct told me that this was the calamity Elizabeth had been heading toward ever since we came to London. There was no question of my getting away from her now, even for an hour. Nurses were hired to watch her around the clock, but she refused to have them in the room, so I sat with her during the day and slept by her side at night. Or tried to sleep. On the third night, certain she really wouldn't know whether I was there or not, I decided to go to another, smaller bedroom. I put on a vicuña robe, picked up the book I had been reading, and started for the door.

"Where did you get that robe?" It was Elizabeth, her voice little more than a whisper.

"You know where I got it. You gave it to me," I said.

She smiled. We were teasing each other. She was going to be all right.

I told the nurse to take over for me and went to the other bedroom. I couldn't sleep there either. I tried to read, but all I could see before my eyes was Elizabeth lying under that oxygen tent. She had looked so beautiful, so peaceful. She couldn't die.

I heard a knock on the door. "Mr. Fisher, come quickly. Your wife is in a coma." It was the nurse. I leaped out of bed and rushed back to our bedroom. Elizabeth was lying just as I had left her. "How do you know?" I asked the nurse. "How can you tell?"

"By her breathing," she said, and I thought, My God, if I had been here instead of the nurse, she might have died and I would never have known.

That was the first stroke of luck that saved Elizabeth's life. The second was the prompt arrival of an anesthesiologist and resuscitationist sent by one of Elizabeth's doctors in response to my frantic calls. He realized immediately that Elizabeth's lungs were so congested she was slowly suffocating, and he began giving her mouth-to-mouth resuscitation. She was strapped to a stretcher, and carried down the back stairs of the hotel to a waiting ambulance, with the doctor working to help her breathe all the way to the London Clinic. Reporters and photographers were already there, waiting for us. It had all happened so fast; who told them, how did they know? They crowded around the stretcher, flashbulbs popping; one photographer pushed his camera right into Elizabeth's face. "Let her alone!" I screamed at them. "Let her alone!" Then she was gone and I was taken to a small, dimly lit waiting room, not knowing if my wife was alive or dead.

Joe Mankiewicz found me there. Neither one of us knew what was happening until a couple of doctors came in and said they would like my permission to perform a tracheotomy. They handed me a paper to sign. "What's a tracheotomy?" I asked.

One of the doctors explained that it was a surgical incision made at the base of the throat into the trachea, which would permit Elizabeth to breathe. "It will leave a scar," the doctor said pointedly.

I looked at Joe and he said, "Sign it, Eddie." I signed.

I don't know how long the operation took. Minutes seemed like hours. Joe sat with me in the waiting room, trying to reassure me. "Don't worry," he said. "It's a very common operation. These doctors know what they're doing."

When the doctors appeared again, I was certain they had come to tell me Elizabeth was dead. I was wrong. The operation had been performed, it was a success, and my wife wanted to see me. I was taken directly into the operating room. Elizabeth was lying on a table surrounded by doctors and nurses all dressed in green. The walls, the floor, even the sheet that covered her—everything was green. I looked down at her face, and then at the incision in her throat.

She was conscious and could see me in a mirror held by one of the nurses, but she couldn't talk. Another nurse gave her a pencil and a pad of paper and she scribbled a note to me: "Am I going to die because I feel like I am?"

I shook my head. "No," I said. "You're not going to die. Everything's going to be fine."

She started scribbling again: "When can I go home? Take me home. I love love you."

Her handwriting was barely legible and she was so drugged she was repeating words. But she was alive.

The initial crisis had passed. Elizabeth was able to breathe, but her life still hung in the balance as doctors struggled to clear the congestion in her lungs and restore normal respiration. The hospital issued frequent bulletins about her condition; she dominated the headlines of newspapers all over the world. From the window of the small room I was given to use, I could see the street in front of the hospital. Hundreds of people kept vigil there day and night while Elizabeth fought for her life; they weren't just morbid curiosity-seekers, but ordinary people, young and old. She received so many flowers and gifts that they had to be sent to other hospitals and churches. Thousands of letters, cards, and telephone calls poured in, almost all of them from strangers, but many from friends, including Merle Oberon, who called from Rome to express her concern and ask if there was anything she could do. The outpouring of sympathy, both private and public, was overwhelming. Two years before, Elizabeth had been the "biggest slut in Hollywood," the evil woman who had lured me away from my wife and innocent babies. Now all was forgiven. No matter what she had done, people everywhere loved her and were praying for her recovery.

In spite of a few fanciful stories, the press wasn't exaggerating the seriousness of Elizabeth's condition. For several days after the operation, she was perilously close to death. But no one outside the hospital seemed to know why. The press and public were told that she was again suffering from double pneumonia. That was the official medical diagnosis. But one of her doctors took me aside and suggested that in his medical opinion, a major cause of her illness, which later developed into double pneumonia, was respiratory failure induced by depressant drugs.

I knew Elizabeth's doctors were doing whatever was necessary to save her life, and I understood the reports they released to the press about the difficulty of curing the particular type of pneumonia she had contracted. But I couldn't help wondering why they continued to give her the same drugs that may have been responsible for her condition in the first place. I was all too familiar with the way Elizabeth could plead with her doctors to get what she wanted. Even when she was barely conscious, and so heavily sedated that she still repeated words, she had scribbled a note to me: "Tell tell doctor to give me shot shot not like like before much stronger." And as far as I knew, she got it.

Why? This wasn't a question of humoring a temperamental patient; this was a matter of life and death. And I couldn't get rid of the thought that saving Elizabeth's life had to be more important than giving in to her. But I wasn't a doctor. She had ten of them, including lung specialists. There were probably valid medical reasons for the way her case was being handled, and what right did I have to criticize doctors who were among the best in the world? Still I was frantic, not only because I thought Elizabeth might die, but also because other doctors had made mistakes in treating her. I couldn't sleep, I couldn't eat. I was so worried about Elizabeth that I was unaware of what I was doing to myself until her doctors became concerned about my health and insisted I get a B_{12} shot every morning.

After that, I realized I had been acting a little crazy. But hoping I could be of some help, I became a "checker." Elizabeth's room was filled with every kind of new machinery— new ways of taking her temperature and blood pressure, a machine to aspirate the congestion in her lungs, a machine to help her breathe. Almost every opening in her body was attached to something. Six nurses were assigned to watch her, but I was the one who sat by her bedside hour after hour, checking all the machines. I was there when Elizabeth gagged and began clutching her throat, and the doctor I called discovered that the breathing machine was backfiring into her lungs. But where were her doctors the night Elizabeth's temperature rose suddenly and her nurses told me the aspirin they needed was locked up in a cabinet and they didn't have the key? I said, "Break it open, for God's sake!" But they said no, they couldn't do that; it was against hospital rules. So they wound up bathing her with ice water and using a fan.

When I wasn't at Elizabeth's bedside, I sat on the bed in my own little room, making telephone calls. I must have spoken to a hundred doctors all over the world—anyone I had ever heard of or anyone friends recommended who might help Elizabeth, including doctors in iron curtain countries. They all had suggestions, remedies, magic potions; even if they didn't know what was wrong with her, they had a cure for it. Someone told me about a drug being tested in America, and I called Milton Blackstone. He went to a pharmaceutical lab in New Jersey to get a bottle of whatever this stuff was, flew to London, left the bottle at the airport for me, then boarded another plane and flew right back to New York. It was a typical Blackstone gesture; he was willing to do anything for me, but was just as frightened as ever of getting too close, too involved.

Milton suggested that I call Max Jacobson. He had remained Max's friend and patient over the years and thought he was the one doctor who might have a cure for Elizabeth. I rejected the idea; a man like Max Jacobson would never be admitted to the London Clinic. But finally, in desperation, I did call. There was something familiar and comforting about this gruff, guttural voice. And the first thing he said was, "Did they check her gamma globulin?"

At that very moment, one of Elizabeth's doctors walked into the room and said, "Eddie, we've just given your wife gamma globulin." They had injected I don't know how many millions of units in both her thighs, and that was the turnaround. A few days later, Elizabeth began to recover from the double pneumonia that was so difficult to cure. Max's mention of gamma globulin at the same moment the doctor mentioned it aroused my concern for her all over again. But it may have been nothing more than an eerie coincidence and at that point I really didn't care. Her doctors had saved Elizabeth's life: she was going to get well. That was all that mattered.

In the early stages of her recovery, yet another prominent physician was summoned to the clinic and proposed his own form of treatment for Elizabeth. After studying her medical records, he came to me and said, "Mr. Fisher, I would like to take your wife to my sanitarium for at least three or four months. Now I would like to speak to her alone."

I nodded my permission, but I was laughing to myself. This doctor was so confident that he was going to get Elizabeth into a sanitarium. He was in her room exactly one minute before he emerged with an angry scowl on his face. I never saw him again.

The one doctor who had any real influence over Elizabeth was Rex Kennamer. I asked him to come to London again and together we planned our strategy. As soon as Elizabeth had been able to eat and drink, she asked for champagne and, incredibly, got it. It was tough, but we convinced her champagne wasn't good for her. She was still on sedatives, chiefly Seconal, perhaps more than she really needed. Rex, in consultation with her English doctors, told her that she had to convince us she was well enough to do without so much medication, and that she couldn't leave the hospital until she stopped most Seconal during the day. Elizabeth agreed to that as long as she could get what she needed to sleep at night. It was a beginning.

Now the problem was to keep her amused until she was strong enough to leave the hospital. I was on the phone again, calling everyone we knew, telling them the crisis had passed and Elizabeth could see visitors. Truman Capote and Tennessee Williams, who were among the first to appear, were the best possible medicine. Williams had a marvelous sense of humor and quickly gave Elizabeth the giggles; Capote sat cross-legged at the foot of her bed and filled her in on all the latest gossip. I heard that John Wayne would be passing through London on his way home from location in Africa. I met him at the airport, rode with him to his hotel and waited while he shaved and changed his suit, then brought him to the hospital. He entered Elizabeth's room, eager to help. That tough, marvelous man would have ridden in on a white horse if that would have done any good. I stood there beaming as she and Wayne chatted. Elizabeth wore a big English threepence to cover the incision in her throat, which was still used to clear the congestion from her lungs. Without it, she couldn't talk. She coughed, the coin flew across the room, and Wayne was sprayed with mucus and blood. He laughed it off, said it was nothing. But when we left the room, he fell against the wall in the hallway, completely shaken. Yul Brynner came with a tiny camera and asked me to take his picture with Elizabeth. He posed with his arm around the bed, not Elizabeth.

An avalanche of letters, cards, and flowers kept coming. The hospital switchboard flashed night and day like a pinball machine. I spoke to the people I knew and took messages from the others. I also spoke to reporters and answered a lot of silly questions, trying to keep Elizabeth's illness in some kind of perspective. It had been a close call, but she hadn't risen from the dead. The press and people all over the world who had discovered they loved her after all thought otherwise. Elizabeth Taylor, Hollywood's most famous and glamorous star, a woman of unequaled talent and beauty, had been given back to them. It was nothing short of a miracle.

15

We flew back to America as soon as Elizabeth was strong enough to leave the hospital. Every vein in her body had been punctured by some kind of needle and her legs were so swollen that she was on crutches and had to be lifted on and off the plane in a wheelchair. The police formed a wedge to get us through the crowd at the London airport; crowds were waiting for us when we landed in New York and again in Los Angeles. Elizabeth was welcomed back to Hollywood with all the fanfare of a coronation.

She had received her fourth successive Academy Award nomination for *Butterfield 8* and was determined to go to the ceremony even though she was certain she would lose again. She won. When her name was announced, she looked at me in disbelief. I nodded and she shrieked and covered her face with her hands. I helped her to her feet, adjusted her crutches, and we began that long walk down the aisle. I'll never forget it. We were so close, both of us holding on to each other every step of the way. Elizabeth was terrified of live audiences and begged me to walk out on stage with her. I refused. "This is your moment," I said. "You take it from here, kid."

Now it was official; Elizabeth had been crowned queen and she held court in our bungalow at the Beverly Hills Hotel until dawn. Hundreds of people filed in and out to pay homage. There was no doubt that she had been voted the Oscar partly because previous, and much better, performances had been passed over, and partly because she had almost died. Still, it was a night of triumph for Elizabeth; she was an actress, not just a movie star, and everyone in Hollywood was there, hat in hand, to tell her so. Sinatra literally knelt at her feet and John Wayne was the last to leave.

For Elizabeth, it was sweet revenge. For me, whether she had won or lost, it was a victory. She was alive and I was so proud of her. But I couldn't help wondering what the hell I was doing there. While Elizabeth was in the hospital, just after the crisis passed and she knew she was going to live, she had whispered to me, "I saw God, Eddie. I touched His hand. And I talked to Mike and he told me to love you, love you." How much longer was Elizabeth going to need my love?

Several doctors and nurses continued to care for Elizabeth. Rex Kennamer came to our bungalow at least twice a day, and she gave him and everyone else a hard time. Forgotten were all her promises to take better care of herself, and Kennamer, after a stormy session trying to get her to undergo treatments she needed for her legs, said, "Eddie, how do you stand it? You should get out before it's too late."

Both Kennamer and I felt ridiculous trying to help Elizabeth when she would do so little to help herself. There was no way to prevent her from doing exactly what she wanted to do; no way to win an argument with her. Unable, as always, to find the right words to express my anger and frustration, I adopted a new strategy. I shut up. I refused to argue; sometimes I even refused to talk to her. It didn't faze Elizabeth in the least. She merely turned to others, including Max Lerner, the political journalist, who had no trouble with words.

We had met Lerner in London, and reappearing in our lives in California, he began to spend a great deal of time with Elizabeth and me. "Eddie," he said, "you've really got to pay more attention to her. She needs someone to be with her."

That came as no news to me, so when Lerner asked if he could go for a ride to the beach with Elizabeth, I said with a shrug, "Sure, go ahead. That's fine with me."

Lerner fell in love with Elizabeth. But it was a brief infatuation and he soon faded away, a little wiser, I hope, for the experience. Elizabeth could make almost anyone fall in love with her, but often she was looking for something more than just adoration. She felt very insecure about both her abilities as an actress and her intelligence. Her new Oscar was proof enough, for the time being, that she could act; the attention of a man like Lerner, a renowned intellectual, was proof that she had a brain. Elizabeth liked to collect trophies.

Cleopatra was floundering. Elizabeth's illness had shut down production completely, and both Stephen Boyd and Peter Finch left the cast. Millions of dollars in the hole and near bankruptcy, 20th Century-Fox had nothing to show for it but a contract with Elizabeth, which would have to be honored whether the film was made or not. Fox executives had to choose between abandoning the project or spending millions more to try to save it. Spyros Skouras decided to save it, even though the insurance companies demanded that he use *any* actress other than Elizabeth. It was a gamble, but Elizabeth's battle with death and now the Oscar had raised her to the pinnacle of superstardom, and Skouras was counting on that to make *Cleopatra* the biggest box office attraction of all time. At one point, he even talked of making the film in two parts and charging two hundred dollars a ticket.

I urged the Fox executives to shoot the picture in Hollywood. Elizabeth was still far from well and she would be home, close to doctors we could trust. They decided instead to resume production in Rome because it would be cheaper—another minor miscalculation. Everything had to be moved from London to Cinecittà, new sets built, new actors hired, including the two leading men, all of which would take months. Again Elizabeth was idle, and because I knew from past experience how dangerous that could be, I tried to cook up diversions for her.

Parties became a way of life. We were a respectable married couple now, and people who had crossed us off their lists a year or so ago were eager to attend our parties and invite us to theirs. Among our best friends and companions were Natalie Wood and Bob Wagner, Kirk and Ann Douglas, Desi Arnaz and Lucille Ball, Cary Grant and Dyan Cannon, Dean and Jeannie Martin. Most of our get-togethers were small and private, but we gave a big party for the renowned Russian Moiseyev Dance Company when it came to Los Angeles, at an unknown little nightclub called P.J.'s; the club became famous overnight. After the party, we all went to Joan Cohn's Beverly Hills mansion, a legacy from her husband, and the Russians were wide-eyed with wonder at Harry Cohn's incredible collection of French Impressionists. I was equally astonished. Mike Todd's collection, which he had bought from Aly Khan and which Elizabeth kept in storage, was meager by comparison. Cohn's library and wine cellar were almost as fine as his paintings, and I was surprised that a man who had been famous for his vulgarity had a sensitive and cultured side to his personality.

In spite of the language barrier and their apprehensions, the Russians had a marvelous time. Without the usual restraints of diplomacy and protocol—just performers meeting performers—we all did, even Elizabeth. At big parties, she usually preferred to sit quietly in a corner talking to one or two friends. But for some reason, she felt comfortable with the Russians, and after a few drinks, she kicked off her shoes and danced around the room with the troupe to *"Hava Nagila."* Maestro Moiseyev was so impressed by the spirit of the evening that he said he wanted to choreograph the song for his company. As far as I know, he never did; an Israeli song would be an unlikely choice for a Soviet dance troupe.

I asked the Russians what American films they would like to see. *Viva Zapata!*, with Marlon Brando, was their unanimous choice, and anything with Gene Kelly. So I arranged a special showing at 20th Century-Fox, complete with popcorn and soda, of the Brando film in its entirety along with selections from three or four other films, including a Gene Kelly dance number. After the ludicrous way Premier Khrushchev had been treated, Elizabeth and I wanted to show the company another side of Hollywood, and the public reaction to our gestures of hospitality was generally favorable. Hedda Hopper was the exception. Never one to forgive and forget, she blasted us for being Communist sympathizers. In retaliation we gave another party, this time in the Escoffier Room at the Beverly Hilton, attended by the entire Hollywood establishment. Entertainment was provided by such "Communist sympathizers" as Frank Sinatra, Sammy Davis, Jr., and Dean Martin. Hedda wasn't invited.

Elizabeth avoided making public appearances if she could. For me they came naturally, particularly charities and benefits, and again for a diversion, I persuaded her to be the guest of honor at a benefit for Cedars of Lebanon–Mount Sinai Hospital. Who better to symbolize the miracle of modern medicine? She even gave a little speech describing her recent illness, and we pledged $100,000 to the hospital. Bobby Kennedy, then the U.S. attorney general, was sitting next to us on the dais, and I remember slipping him several Scotches under the table because he didn't want to be seen ordering them himself.

If Elizabeth was content to play her role as the new queen of Hollywood, I was not entirely happy as her consort and went back to work at my old stamping grounds, the Desert Inn. Mel Ferrer offered to help me prepare my act. We had met because his wife, Audrey Hepburn, was a client of Kurt Frings. Mel and I were the husbands of two of Hollywood's biggest stars, which can be a problem in itself. But I sensed that Mel's relationship with Audrey was difficult not because she was demanding and unpredictable, like Elizabeth. Just the reverse: Audrey was always so gracious and perfect in every way that Mel must have found that almost impossible to live up to.

When we started working together, Mel insisted on one thing I had almost forgotten in the months I hadn't been working—discipline. We got up at six in the morning to play tennis, ate breakfast at seven, and then went to a huge, empty sound stage on the Fox lot to rehearse. Once the music and arrangements had been chosen, Mel wanted to leave nothing to chance. He made me work on my voice, my gestures, my movements. For someone like me, who had always preferred spontaneity, it was tough but rewarding training. Mel made me look at myself as a performer, not just some guy who happened to have a good voice. I called him "the bishop."

It paid off in Las Vegas, where I gave some of the most polished performances of my career. There was a point in my act when I would turn to Elizabeth, if she was in the audience, and sing the little-known but beautiful song "That Face." We rehearsed that too, although it came as such a complete surprise to Elizabeth on opening night that she began to cry. It felt good to be back on stage again, giving performances I could be proud of. Offstage, I was not so disciplined. Elizabeth and I stayed up all night long and usually slept from nine in the morning until six in the evening. But the people who accused me of pandering to Elizabeth, of capitalizing on her fame, were mistaken. It was Elizabeth who insisted on coming to as many of my performances as she could, Elizabeth who demanded that I never be too far from her side.

One evening we went to a seventh-anniversary party for Kirk and Ann Douglas at the Sands Hotel, where I sang a specially written parody of a Sammy Cahn hit, retitled for the occasion "Love Is Wonderful the Seventh Time Around." Frank Sinatra was performing at the hotel and Elizabeth and I sat in the audience with Dean and Jeannie Martin and Marilyn Monroe, who was having an affair with Sinatra, to watch his act. But all eyes were on Marilyn as she swayed back and forth to the music and pounded her hands on the stage, her breasts falling out of her low-cut dress. She was so beautiful—and so drunk. She came to the party later that evening, but Sinatra made no secret of his displeasure at her behavior and she vanished almost immediately.

Every time Elizabeth appeared in public, it was a performance. She loved parties, but only with friends, or in small groups where everybody was having a good time, would she really let herself go, singing, dancing, laughing, yelling—no one had more fun than she did. There were exceptions. One night she walked into the casino at the Desert Inn and began dealing blackjack. Everybody won and she kept calling for more chips. The patrons loved it. I wanted Elizabeth to enjoy herself, but I could never stop worrying about her. Once, when she had been drinking, she simply passed out, right in the middle of a sentence. And once I caught her just as she fell over her luggage, preventing what might have been a serious accident. I grew watchful and tried to anticipate trouble; there was nothing more I could do.

How could we still be so happy, still so very much in love? We would lie in bed for hours, talking about our dreams and all the crazy things we wanted to do. Someday we were going to live on a boat and build a house in every beautiful place we had ever seen. We talked about having a child of our own and because that would be physically impossible for Elizabeth, we began to consider adoption. We had been through a lot together, Elizabeth and I, and being with her, loving her, taking care of her, gave me a kind of strength I had never had before.

In July 1961, Elizabeth and I went to Russia as part of the official American delegation to the Moscow Film Festival.

Elizabeth's face, if not her work as an actress, was well known in Russia; she was the epitome of the Hollywood movie star and did nothing to change that image. Her retinue included Rex Kennamer, Kurt and Ketti Frings, and her hairdresser, Alexandre de Paris, who followed her all over Moscow with a comb in his hand. I had suggested the trip to the State Department, seeking another diversion for Elizabeth, and the Russians welcomed the idea not only because we had been hospitable to the Moiseyev dancers but also because they were eager to attract as many foreign celebrities as they could. Elizabeth was obviously the main attraction, but I was quite sure that I would be asked to sing.

I *was* asked, at the huge reception that opened the festival. Hundreds of Communist dignitaries were there, along with actors, actresses, producers, directors, and writers from all over the world, and after performances by the best Russian musicians, singers, and dancers, the minister of culture, who was sitting right in front of me, turned around and asked if *I* would like to do something. "All right," I said. "I just happen to have my accompanist with me." With Eddie Samuels backing me up on the piano, I sang my medley of Jolson songs. It was a weird and funny feeling to be singing "Mammy" in that huge room with white marble walls and crystal chandeliers—one of the most beautiful rooms I had ever seen—and one of the greatest thrills of my life to hear that audience cheer and applaud. The next day, the international edition of the *Herald Tribune* headlined "Eddie Fisher Rocks the Kremlin." I was the first American since Paul Robeson to sing there.

Elizabeth wore a Dior dress to the reception, one of the ten or so Diors she brought to Russia. I had bought her almost the entire collection. We walked into the great hall together and there, at the far end of the room, was Gina Lollobrigida. She was wearing blue with sapphires and Elizabeth was in red with rubies, but their dresses were identical. The odds against an American movie queen and an Italian movie queen attending a party in Moscow in the same Dior "original" must have been at least a billion to one, but it happened and Elizabeth was infuriated. The incident made headlines around the world, and in Paris, on our way back to America, she asked me to go to Yves Saint Laurent at Dior and find out why he had sold that dress to Lollobrigida. He told me that Lollobrigida sent her dressmaker to see his collections and she had probably copied the design. Unfortunately there was nothing he could do about it, but by way of an apology, he invited me to pick out another dress for Elizabeth, as his gift. I chose the most beautiful and expensive gown in his collection. Elizabeth was delighted.

As a courtesy to Elizabeth, the Russians wanted to show one of her films at the festival. I suggested *Giant* or *Cat on a Hot Tin Roof,* but Elizabeth chose *Butterfield 8* because she knew it would give me very little pleasure to watch my award-winning performance. We sent to Hollywood for a print and it was shown to an audience of cultural and political VIPs, who sat through it in dead and uncomprehending silence. The translator, speaking through a mike, was several lines behind, and that didn't help. The Russians wanted to like it; above all they wanted to be polite, but their only reaction to the picture came at the end, when the little red car went off the highway, killing Elizabeth. Then they burst into spontaneous cheers and applause. Deeply embarrassed, Elizabeth and I wanted to do something to apologize. And the only way I knew was to get up on stage and sing.

Relations were just beginning to thaw between Russia and America at the time Elizabeth and I were in Moscow, and the people we met there were wonderful—curious, polite, eager to know more about America. Two young Russians, a boy and a girl, stayed by our side wherever we went, acting as guides and interpreters, and Elizabeth and I decided to try to Americanize them. She had Alexandre do the girl's hair and I told the boy stories of the wonders of democracy, but we couldn't shake their belief in the Communist system. They had an answer for everything. We were taken to see Lenin's tomb; Stalin was lying next to him, and to tease our interpreters, I asked, "What ever happened to Trotsky?"

"It is well known," the boy replied, without batting an eye, "that they had a party at the Kremlin and everybody got very, very tipsy, and someone accidentally hit Trotsky over the head with a bottle and killed him."

I knew, of course, that Trotsky had been murdered in Mexico by Soviet agents, but reporters overheard my question and the story hit wire services all over the world.

As the festival drew to a close, Elizabeth and I had a private meeting with Premier Khrushchev and Yekaterina Furtseva, the Minister of Culture, who was rumored to be his mistress. Through an interpreter, Khrushchev urged Elizabeth and me to stay in the Soviet Union a while longer, but Elizabeth said she had to return to California for an operation to remove the tracheotomy scar on her throat. "There is no need to go to America," Khrushchev insisted. "We have the best plastic surgeons in the world right here in Russia."

Not everyone we met was quite so enthusiastic about the homeland. Several times, as Elizabeth and I were returning to our hotel, two men drew me aside and, whispering in Yiddish, begged me to help them get out of Russia. I knew that Jews were discriminated against, even persecuted, because of their religion, and I wanted to help them. But how could I get anybody out of Russia? It was a minor miracle that Elizabeth and I were allowed in.

We went back to Los Angeles only long enough for me to appear at the Cocoanut Grove. How times had changed! Seven years earlier, in 1954, I sang there for an audience of adoring teenage fans, and Debbie Reynolds was my date for the opening. Now Elizabeth Taylor was my wife; opening night was a benefit for one of Eddie Cantor's favorite charities, and the audience was overflowing with show business celebrities. Frank Sinatra, Dean Martin, Sammy Davis, Jr., and Joey Bishop, known collectively as the Clan, were right down in front. They had called to say they wanted to present me with a box of one hundred fine silk handkerchiefs, and I wasn't sure what to expect. I knew they would heckle me; it had happened a couple of times in Las Vegas, in the spirit of fun, and everybody enjoyed it. But that night, before I had a chance to sing a single note, the Clan walked on stage and took over completely, while I sat on the sidelines, watching them horse around. Then they presented me with the silk handkerchiefs. The box was full of rags. I loved it, but the people in that audience had witnessed the antics of the Clan once too often and were impatient for me to get on with the show. They began to hiss and boo until the Clan left the stage and I could begin my act. Elizabeth was very upset; I loved the whole thing, and it turned out to be a great opening night. These men were my friends.

We headed back to Europe after taking care of a couple of pieces of unfinished business in Los Angeles. A plastic surgeon removed the tracheotomy scar on Elizabeth's throat, and I legally adopted little Liza. It was Elizabeth's wish, and nothing could have made me happier. I adored Liza. But for some reason, children were very much on Elizabeth's mind. She wanted to be a mother again; wanted us to have a child of our own, even if it was adopted.

We were en route to Rome, where *Cleopatra* was scheduled to resume shooting in September. But first we cruised the Greek Islands in a yacht rented from Spyros Skouras, Jr., who was in the shipping business. It had a crew of twenty, a captain who looked like Nikita Khrushchev, and it cost a thousand dollars a day, not counting food and drink—all for Elizabeth, me, and Rex Kennamer, whom I had asked along to take care of Elizabeth. It was our second honeymoon, the most peaceful and perfect time Elizabeth and I had spent together since our first. We sunned ourselves on deck and I dove for beautiful colored stones in the shallow sea, which we used as chips in our games of gin rummy. I'll never forget the day we put into the tiny harbor of Lindos on the island of Rhodes. The ruins of an acropolis high above the town could be reached only by donkey or on foot, and Elizabeth couldn't go because of her back. I walked up alone and stood on the edge of a cliff that plunged straight down to the Aegean. It was the most spectacular spot on earth. Forgotten were my fears for Elizabeth's health and any apprehensions I had about what might happen when we got to Rome. I loved my wife, I loved every minute of our life together. Running around the ruins like a madman, I had never been happier.

We were told that it was easy to adopt children in Greece, and back in Athens, Elizabeth and I visited several orphanages. Elizabeth fell in love at first sight with one little boy and she was ecstatic when the nuns told us we could have him. "Come back tomorrow to sign the papers," they said, "and you can take the baby with you."

That night we picked out a name for our new son—Alexander—and the next morning we returned to the orphanage. The mother superior greeted us and began to ask questions. "Have either of you been divorced?" she said.

I nodded. "Yes, we've both been divorced."

"What is your faith?"

"We're Jewish," I said, and I knew at that moment the whole thing was over.

"I'm sorry," the mother superior said, "but it will be impossible to let you adopt the child."

Elizabeth didn't understand. "But they said we could have him. They said he was ours," she cried over and over again, and then broke down completely.

I tried to console her, but at the same time I thought it was ridiculous to cry about not getting another baby when we already had so many beautiful children, ridiculous to want another child when we couldn't give the ones we had all the time and care they needed. Still, if that's what Elizabeth wanted, I was hell-bent on finding some way to get it for her.

The opportunity came several weeks later, after we had settled in Rome and Elizabeth was back at work on *Cleopatra*. Maria Schell, another client of Kurt Frings, knew of our interest and sent us pictures of three German children who were available for adoption. We immediately chose a baby girl. We didn't know who her parents were or where she came from, nor did we care. That was the baby we wanted. Maria made all the necessary arrangements and we went to her home just outside Munich to pick up the baby. We both loved her the moment we saw her, and we named her Maria in honor of our benefactress. Maria Schell was marvelous to us. Pregnant herself at the time but separated from her husband, she loved our love for the new baby. We spent a week with her, carrying the baby around all day in a wicker basket and taking her to bed with us at night in a small sixteenth-century church that Maria had converted into a guesthouse. We were so proud and happy. Now we had a baby of our own.

Back in Rome, we soon realized that something was wrong with Maria. Kennamer had come with us to Germany to examine the baby before we brought her home, and he had pronounced her perfect. Doctors in Rome discovered a malformation of her pelvis. Her condition was serious, but it could be corrected in time. Elizabeth lavished all her affection and attention on the baby for a while, but gradually Maria became another member of a household already crowded with children, their nurses and nannies, their toys and pets.

* * *

Traveling with Elizabeth was an exasperating, and expensive, business. Getting her children, the animals, and all the people who worked for us to the same airport at the same time was a logistical nightmare. And there was always a mountain of luggage, most of it full of Elizabeth's clothes, which cost a couple of thousand dollars in overweight charges every time we boarded a plane. Reporters and photographers added to the chaos, shoving, shouting questions, snapping pictures. I often thought it would be a lot easier and cheaper to charter a private plane.

There was even more chaos than usual when Elizabeth and I arrived in Rome. The paparazzi picked up our scent the moment we landed and followed us around like yapping dogs wherever we went. Sometimes we played little games with them, but the paparazzi could be so unpleasant and persistent that more often than not we simply stayed at home.

One night Audrey Hepburn and Mel Ferrer invited us to dinner at their house in Rome. I adored Audrey and hoped that she and Elizabeth would become friends because Elizabeth didn't have many women friends. That night Audrey was bubbling with excitement; she had just been given the role of Eliza Doolittle in the movie version of *My Fair Lady*. Elizabeth seemed to share her excitement, but later that night, when we were in bed and had just turned out the light, she said without any warning, "Get me *My Fair Lady*."

I was stunned. "Elizabeth," I said. "Audrey has the part. You saw how excited she was about it."

"Get me *My Fair Lady*," Elizabeth repeated in a tone of voice I had never heard before.

"You know I can't do that," I protested.

"Get me *My Fair Lady*," Elizabeth said for the third time.

I didn't bother to argue with her. I had always given Elizabeth everything she wanted, done everything I could for her, but that was one thing I would *not* do.

I liked nothing better than spending a quiet evening alone with Elizabeth, although our rented villa was seldom quiet and was a far cry from my idea of home. There were at least seven servants in addition to our own household, including a majordomo who later sold an "exposé" of our life in the villa to the Italian newspapers. Rats scuttled across the cold, bare floors, the sewer backed up periodically and flooded the kitchen, and for that we paid three thousand dollars a month rent. Its sole advantage, as far as I could see, was its location about midway between Rome and the film studios at Cinecittà.

Because we tried to maintain at least a semblance of a private life, the Italian papers had to print fantasy rather than fact. One reported that Elizabeth kept a pair of lion cubs at the villa. We did have a Siamese cat and a Saint Bernard puppy named Rocky Marciano, which Elizabeth had given me for my birthday, but no lions. It was also reported that Elizabeth required constant medical care, which was not entirely false. Kannamer temporarily gave up his Beverly Hills practice and 20th Century-Fox paid him a $25,000 retainer plus expenses to look after her in Rome. My needs were tended to by Bill Jones, a valet I hired in England, who lived with us and eventually ended up as the custodian of Elizabeth's hats. Her secretary, Dick Hanley, rented an apartment in Rome with a friend.

For my birthday, Elizabeth surprised me with an olive-green convertible Rolls-Royce, custom built in England and delivered to me in Rome. The most beautiful car I had ever owned, it gave me a kind of freedom Elizabeth didn't have. She said she felt like a prisoner in the hired limousines that carried her around; she wanted a car of her own. Even though I knew she was a terrible driver, I bought her a gold Maserati, and it was parked in front of our villa wrapped in cellophane with a big red bow, waiting for her to get up on Christmas morning. She shrieked with delight when she saw it, we tore off the cellophane, and she jumped in and drove it around the corner. She returned a few minutes later, got out of the car, and said, "I hate it." I sold it to Tony Quinn.

I hadn't given much thought to what I was going to do in Rome while Elizabeth was making *Cleopatra*. We lived in two separate worlds professionally and I didn't have much in common with the movie crowd—makeup artists, hairdressers, costume designers—that hovered around her like flies. And wherever we were—Hollywood, New York, London—Roddy McDowall seemed to be there too. Now he had a part in *Cleopatra* and was living in Rome with his friend John Valva. Roddy and Elizabeth had appeared together in *Lassie Come Home* when they were children, and had been great friends ever since. A camera buff, Roddy would come to the villa and follow Elizabeth around, snapping pictures of every move she made. I thought him harmless enough—until he proved otherwise.

I guess I imported my own friends as a kind of protection. Bernie Rich and Bob Abrams came to Rome to work with me on various business projects; Hank Moonjean advised me in my fledgling career as a producer, and Eddie Samuels, my musical mentor, began work composing love themes for an album I was going to conduct. I had the time and money to do almost anything, and a lot of new ideas. Under the circumstances, perhaps I should have concentrated on the one thing I knew how to do best—sing. I did record a couple of songs from *Milk and Honey,* but other than that I let my career as a performer slide. I still thought my primary responsibility was taking care of Elizabeth.

Our production company had acquired the film rights to a book called *The Gouffé Case,* which was supposedly based on the true story of a beautiful and seemingly angelic woman who committed a series of horrible murders. There was one scene I remember where she kills Gouffé with the help of another man, they stuff his body in a trunk, and then make love on top of it. Elizabeth was going to play the murderess, of course, and I wanted Charlie Chaplin to play the police inspector who solves the case. I wrote him and he invited me to come to Switzerland to discuss the project. His home in Vevey looked like a miniature White House and he told me he liked to look at the mountains but didn't like to live in them. His children were running around all over the place and he whispered to me, "Oona's pregnant again, but don't tell anyone." He was intrigued by the idea of appearing in a movie with Elizabeth, and although no actual figures were discussed, every time money was mentioned he rubbed his hands together and gave me that crooked little Charlie Chaplin smile. He told me his whole financial empire was run by one old lady in a tiny office in Paris.

From Vevey I went on to Gstaad. For tax reasons Elizabeth and I had decided to establish residence in Switzerland and I was looking for a house. Shown an incredibly beautiful chalet on the side of a mountain—skiers could ski right underneath it—I was told that the owner, a Texas millionaire, had been building it for his wife, a ballerina, until they had a fight and construction stopped. Now it was for sale, unfinished, but a

steal at $285,000. I didn't bother to look any further. I called
Elizabeth in Rome, said I had found the perfect house, and
urged her to come to Switzerland to see it. "Why bother?" she
said. "If you say that's it, buy it. You have the greatest taste."
I bought it.

By the time we got to Rome, the roles of Julius Caesar and
Mark Antony had been recast. Passing through New York on
our way to Russia, Elizabeth and I had gone to a play called
The Fighting Cock to see her friend Roddy. The star was Rex
Harrison, and midway through the first act I whispered in
Elizabeth's ear, "There's Caesar." We went backstage after the
show and I asked Harrison if he would be interested in playing
the part. He was, but Spyros Skouras wasn't interested in hiring
him. We came to his suite at the Sherry Netherland and he
produced a financial report showing that almost every picture
Rex Harrison had made lost money. But it was no use arguing
with Elizabeth; that just strengthened her determination to get
what she wanted. Harrison was hired.

That left Mark Antony. Another time in New York, I was
thumbing through the theater section of the paper and saw a
name in one of the ads. "How about Richard Burton?" I said
to Elizabeth. "He'd make a good Mark Antony."

"Who?" Elizabeth said.

"Richard Burton. The guy who was in *The Robe*."

Burton had made several movies, but he was better known
as a stage actor, a Shakespearean actor at that, and Elizabeth
was intrigued by the thought of working with him. We didn't
know much more about him, or even where he was, until we
started making phone calls and finally found him at his house
in Switzerland. He consented to play the part.

I don't think 20th Century-Fox cared who played Julius
Caesar or Mark Antony; it was just a matter of hiring someone
so production could get under way. Elizabeth was the star;
everything revolved around keeping her happy, healthy, and
at work. And that's where I thought I came in. I saw to it that
she got up in the morning, sent her off to the studio, and then
waited impatiently for her to come home at night. It cost 20th
Century-Fox $100,000 a day if she failed to show up.

As soon as shooting began, Elizabeth and Joe Mankiewicz
started playing the same old games. Joe asking her, please, to
be there on time, knowing she would be at least an hour late,

and Elizabeth arriving even later than that, just to prove she was the boss. I used reverse psychology. I never told her to get up; I would get up myself and start moving around, talking to her, fussing with things and making it impossible for her to sleep. Then I'd point to the clock and say, "You've got about ten minutes if you're going in today. You want some breakfast?"

"No. I'm going to stay in bed. I feel terrible."

"I'm sorry. I'll call the studio and tell them you can't make it."

"Don't you think I should go?"

"Of course not. Not if you don't feel well."

"Well, maybe I'd better. Just give me a few more minutes."

I had a huge suite of offices adjoining Elizabeth's dressing rooms at the studio, but I had little or nothing to do there except talk with some of the people connected with the production, or just sit around doodling or staring at the wall. I was frankly embarrassed by my position. When Elizabeth and I first married, my career had been at least as important as hers and I earned much more than she did. Now the roles were reversed. My career was at a standstill, Elizabeth was earning most of the money, and I was just the husband of a star. But I didn't spend a lot of time worrying about my career or my male ego. Elizabeth and I were together; that was enough for me.

In fact, I didn't spend a lot of time worrying about Elizabeth either. She was healthier than she had been in months. She was working now, and that made a difference. It was hard for either of us to take *Cleopatra* seriously; everything about it was so big, so vulgar, so absurd. But then everything about Elizabeth herself was larger than life.

I remember the very first day she started work. She was scared and nervous as she was getting ready in her dressing room, and I sat with her awhile, trying to reassure her, until she began to make up her eyes. She never allowed anyone else to do that, and knowing how long it usually took, I left. I was standing near one of the elaborate sets that had been built for the picture, when she finally made her entrance. Her makeup and hair were perfect; she was dressed in the heavy gold costume that later became so famous. The stagehands, the camera crews, everyone stopped dead in their tracks to watch her. It was only a test, but she was incredible, regal; she didn't falter, didn't bat an eye. I was stunned, actually shocked to see her radiating such strength and self-confidence. The transformation from only a few months before, when she was sick and dying, was so complete, so miraculous, that tears came to my eyes.

And then I heaved an enormous sigh of relief. We're here, I thought to myself; she's made it this far and the rest is going to be easy. She's got Joe Mankiewicz, she's got Harrison and Burton, she's got me. She'll get through this ridiculous picture; she's an actress. And when it's finished, we'll go to our new house in Switzerland, and maybe start on the house in Jamaica. We'll spend more time with her children—*our* children. Liza and Maria were mine too. And I'll be able to see Carrie and Todd more often. Elizabeth and I will work together, live together, love together. There was so much to look forward to.

16

I met Richard Burton for the first time riding up in an elevator at the studio. We recognized each other and nodded; he said hello, the doors opened, and he walked out. I was surprised. On the screen, his voice and manner were very theatrical; in person, he seemed quite ordinary, not much taller than I was and not particularly handsome. But he did impress me as being masculine, virile, attractive. So that's Elizabeth's new leading man, I said to myself: a fine actor and a gentleman. Perfect.

Those impressions changed. Shortly after that first meeting, we were driving somewhere together and I noticed that his shirt was frayed and soiled; his suit looked as if he had slept in it. Elizabeth and I laughed about him. He reminded us of Arthur Freed, the brilliant Hollywood producer, who, it was said, could grow orchids under his fingernails. At a Christmas party, Elizabeth, who loved to blurt out our little private jokes in public to embarrass me, cried, "Eddie, come look. Richard doesn't really have orchids growing under his fingernails."

I knew nothing of Burton's reputation until long after he arrived in Rome and stories began to circulate about the affairs he had with his leading ladies. His drinking was also legendary, and apparently his wife, Sybil, tolerated both. I heard, too, that he had another girl, a so-called Copa cutie he had brought to Rome with the promise of a part in *Cleopatra*. Charming he was, when he wanted to be, but a gentleman he was not, and whatever his reputation, I couldn't consider him a rival.

Elizabeth's initial reactions were the same as mine. She would come home from the studio shrieking with laughter about some ridiculous thing Burton had done or said on the set that day. And I didn't think she was attracted to him physically. If anything, Elizabeth was even more fastidious than I was. She might scatter her clothes all over the bedroom and make a mess of her dressing table, but she would sometimes bathe three times a day. We spent hours in the bathroom together. She was fascinated by the way Burton behaved, however. He played the fool, a buffoon, the professional Welshman. She couldn't figure him out, but he certainly could act. He had all the right credentials, he spoke the King's English, and Elizabeth may have felt that with men like Burton and Harrison supporting her, this picture might even live up to Spyros Skouras's expectations.

There was another attraction. Burton loved parties and people; he could stay up all night drinking, arrive on the set the following morning with a tremendous hangover, and still get through the day's shooting. Elizabeth wished she could do the same, and at some point after she started working with Burton, I think she began to see me as a jailer. I was spoiling her fun. She didn't need me to monitor her medication and drinks and put her to bed at night. I wasn't comfortable in that role either, and thinking that Elizabeth was strong enough now to take care of herself, I stopped playing nursemaid. I went to the studio often, but seldom visited the sets or watched the shooting. That wasn't my business, and I ignored a lot of little signals that were telling me that maybe it should have been.

Elizabeth asked me to be on the set the day they were shooting a nude scene. I got there on time and she arrived three hours later, surrounded by the usual crowd of people fooling with her costume and hair. The makeup lady brought her a bottle of Coke and, thirsty, I took a sip. It was brandy. I said, "What the hell is this?" but the makeup lady just turned away.

I sat down in a director's chair next to Joe Mankiewicz, who was puffing on his pipe, the most patient man in the world. "Joe," I said, "what's going on here?"

He turned to me and said, "Eddie, she hasn't the faintest idea what she's doing."

She wasn't the only one. When I saw some of the early rushes, it was obvious to me that neither she nor Burton was performing well. And with his big, sonorous voice and her little, squeaky one, their scenes together were ludicrous. Rex Harrison was the only one giving a performance, and it would later earn him an Academy Award nomination.

Did anyone care? Could anything be done about it even if someone did? Walter Wanger had his hands full with all the details of that ponderous production, and Spyros Skouras, who came to Rome to see the rushes, fell asleep. We were looking at some of the most important scenes in the movie and suddenly the projection room was filled with the sounds of snoring. Skouras was still asleep when the lights came back on, then woke up with a start and began to applaud. "Wonderful," he said. "Wonderful."

Reporters were having a field day with *Cleopatra*, and the movie crowd that hung out on the Via Veneto could talk about nothing else. That wasn't my scene, and I laughed at rumors that Elizabeth was having an affair with Rex Harrison, and even Joe Mankiewicz. The first gossip I heard about a romance between her and Burton I put down to the imaginative Italian press and studio publicity. Consider the source. Even rumors that some of her friends, like Roddy McDowall and Irene Sharaff, the costume designer on the film, might actually be encouraging such a romance didn't trouble me. Petty intrigues were a part of that world, and I knew that Roddy and Richard lived in the same house in Rome and had become friends. But I was furious at Rex Kennamer when I heard he was hanging around with the gossips who were bad-mouthing Elizabeth. I considered him *my* friend as well as Elizabeth's doctor, and that was too much. After I chewed him out over the phone, he was so contrite that he sent me a handwritten letter of apology.

When did gossip become truth and Elizabeth's attraction to Burton become more than merely professional? The husband is always the last to know. I don't think I was smug or complacent about our relationship. There was plenty of proof of her love. If she came home a few minutes late from the studio and said she had been discussing a scene with Richard or visiting Roddy, I didn't question her. We had dinner and went upstairs to bed together, as usual. It was at a New Year's Eve party, at least in recollection, that I first noticed something different. Elizabeth and Burton were sitting together and there was a tremendous amount of giggling going on between them. It reminded me of the days when Elizabeth and I were falling in love and we sat together at parties, holding hands under the table, whispering, laughing. Their closeness troubled me for a moment, but it never occurred to me that Elizabeth and Burton were falling in love. And when it was time to take Elizabeth home and she knew she had to go but started behaving rather arrogantly, even sadistically, toward me, I blamed the champagne she had been drinking, not her.

I never once considered the possibility that there was something physical between them. I couldn't have made love to Elizabeth if I believed that. I was a puritan, or naive. Again, I thought back to the early days of our love, when we had been able to control our emotions. And so I blocked out every suspicion until the night Bob Abrams called. Elizabeth and I were in bed, running over the lines of a scene she had to play the following day, and the phone rang just as we turned out the lights. "Eddie," Bob said, "I think there's something you ought to know. There's a lot of talk going around about Elizabeth and Richard Burton."

"What kind of talk?" I asked. After listening to what he had to say, I hung up and lay there in the dark a moment, aware that Elizabeth was wide awake beside me. Then I turned to her and said, "Is it true that something is going on between you and Burton?"

She hesitated before answering softly, "Yes."

I put on the lights, called Bob back, and asked him to come to the villa in half an hour and pick me up. Elizabeth lay in bed watching me as I packed a bag. I could tell she was disturbed, but she didn't say a word. No taunts or threats, no hysterical scenes, and that, even more than her whispered "Yes," convinced me that what Bob had told me was true. I couldn't deny it any longer, nor could she. We were not play-acting. This was the real thing: a crisis in our marriage.

Bob, Bernie, and Eddie Samuels shared an apartment in Rome. I spent the night there and went to the studio the next day to talk to Joe Mankiewicz. A kind of light shock had set in, a numbness, as if I had been hit, but had not yet felt the pain of the blow. I didn't know what to do, whom to turn to, whom to trust. Joe smiled his wonderful smile and denied that he knew of any intimacy between Elizabeth and Burton, but later that day he called me at the apartment in Rome and told me to get the hell back to the villa before I was charged with desertion. It was the only honest advice I got from anyone at the studio. An affair between the two stars of *Cleopatra* was the best kind of publicity the film could have.

I followed Joe's advice and went back to the villa, hoping, wanting to believe that this was just a flirtation, not an affair. If Elizabeth was attracted to Burton, it was his fault, not hers. All we had to do was finish this picture and get away from him. But Elizabeth offered no apologies or explanations. On the contrary, she seemed to take pleasure in teasing me, trying to make me jealous. A little tipsy one night when she got back from the studio, just to get a reaction from me she said, "Guess what I did. I had a fitting with Irene—and then I had a drink with Richard."

I was usually a little tipsy myself, sipping vodka waiting for her to come home. "What else did you do, Elizabeth?" I asked. But nothing more was said. We had dinner, talking about trivial things, then went to bed. And there, for the first time in our marriage, I felt that something was coming between us, something we couldn't discuss or laugh about, something we were both afraid to put into words.

My friends urged me to do something, anything. "Get it out in the open, Eddie. Tell that bastard Burton to take a walk." One of them gave me a gun and told me to use it, a ridiculous suggestion, but I put it in the glove compartment of the green Rolls. One day at the studio I happened to mention to Walter Wanger that I had a gun. His face turned white. I had told the wrong man. Many years before, Wanger had followed his wife, Joan Bennett, and her agent at MCA to an apartment in Los Angeles the agency kept for "business purposes." When the couple emerged, he shot the agent in the groin and was sent to jail for the crime. Wanger must have feared that I might try something equally rash, because the next thing I knew, he and other executives were suggesting tactfully that I leave Rome, take a vacation, get away for a little while. I don't know whether they thought I was going to shoot Elizabeth or Burton. Either way, it would be bad for their investment.

I told Elizabeth I wanted to spend a few days at our new house in Gstaad and she said, "Yes, darling, I think that's a wonderful idea." But she changed her mind almost immediately and asked me to stay. She told me she was having lunch with

Burton, and when I asked why, she said, "Trust me. I have to figure out a way to continue working with this man." To me, that implied their romance, or whatever it was, was over. But I still intended to go to Gstaad, until she said to me, late one night, "Don't leave me, Eddie. You must stay and help me get rid of this cancer."

The desperate tone of Elizabeth's voice reminded me of the night I brought her to Mike's house and she begged me not to leave her. Then I had fled; this time I would stay. In my opinion, her attraction to Burton *was* a disease. Now it was out in the open and we could talk about it; now we could fight it together. But a day or so later, cancer again came up in our conversation. Elizabeth arrived home very late. She had been with Burton and told me that "something terrible" had happened. Burton's brother, she said, had hit him on the back with a chair and he thought he had cancer.

Her story made no sense at all but I was not about to ask how anyone can get cancer from being hit by a chair. So I just said, "I'm sorry. Is there anything I can do?"

"No. He's talking with doctors and he's going to call."

When we finally sat down at the table, Burton still hadn't called and I could tell Elizabeth was upset. "Why don't you call him?" I said. "Don't wait. You call." What else was I supposed to say?

She went to the phone, and sitting alone in the dining room, I heard her say, "Oh, darling, I'm so glad. I'm so happy for you." Her words—the way she said "darling"—tore me apart.

A day or so later, she brought Burton to the villa. I don't know where they had been or what they had been doing other than drinking, but Burton immediately went into some kind of act. He turned to Elizabeth and growled, "Who do you love? *Who do you love?*"

Terrified, Elizabeth looked at me and then at him and said, "You."

"That's the right answer," Burton said, "but it wasn't quick enough."

It was such a bizarre scene that I was speechless. Maybe I should have busted Burton in the mouth and thrown him out of the house. But the one beating I got as a kid from my father had turned me against any kind of violence. I walked away from them, down a long hallway that led to the living room.

They followed me and Burton started in again. He spotted

a silver-framed picture of Mike Todd, Elizabeth, and Liza that I kept with us wherever we went. "He didn't know how to use her," Burton shouted, pointing at the picture. "You don't know how to use her either," he said to me, "and what's that fucking picture here for?"

That was too much for Elizabeth. Weeping hysterically, she ran out of the room and left the villa. I had no idea where she was going; at that moment I don't think I cared. She had brought this on herself and in a way I was glad.

Burton and I were left alone. He collapsed in a chair and said, "What have you got to drink around here?"

I brought a bottle of brandy and glasses, and for the next several hours I sipped and he drank. I remember changing bottles more than twice. As much as I disliked Burton, I welcomed this chance to talk to him. I thought maybe I could reach him, find out what was going on inside his head.

It was a one-sided conversation. Burton did most of the talking, flattering me, insulting me, laying little traps, charming and apologetic one moment, crude and abusive the next. Even though he was so drunk I could have pushed him over with my finger, I sat there and took it, listening to him damn himself with every word he spoke. And when I finally said, "Richard, leave my wife alone," it was then he told me, "You don't need her. You're a star already. I'm not. She's going to make me a star. I'm going to use her, that no-talent Hollywood nothing."

At some point during our conversation, the phone rang. "If that's her," Burton muttered, "tell her I don't want to talk." The major-domo came in and said, "It's Mrs. Fisher on the phone," and I was very happy to deliver Burton's message to her. But Elizabeth said, "I've got to talk to him, Eddie. Please, go and ask him again—and don't hurt him."

I laughed. It had never entered my mind that I could, or would, hurt him. I went back to the living room and Burton still refused to talk to her, but finally he staggered to the phone and grabbed it out of my hand. "God, how can you do this to this man?" he said. "He loves you so much. If you're not careful, I'm going to take him upstairs and fuck him myself."

I could hear Elizabeth screaming on the other end of the phone, trying to block out his words. The man is crazy, I thought.

Burton finally left and I was more puzzled than before. Was he playing some kind of game with Elizabeth? How could she have anything but contempt for a man who behaved the way he did? And how much longer would she put up with it? I told Dick Hanley what Burton had said about her, he told Elizabeth, and she was devastated, refusing to see or speak to Burton until he found her at Hanley's apartment and literally battered down the door. Far from denying what he had called her, he added even more insults. After that, she began calling him on the telephone time and time again, pretending she had to talk about a scene they were playing together, only to have him hang up on her, or to be told by someone else never to call him again.

In a strange way, I enjoyed the craziness. It was a sideshow, a soap opera. No writer could get away with a script as absurd as this one. But I didn't want any part in it. I had to get out of that house, out of Rome, even if it was no farther than Gstaad. I wasn't planning to leave Elizabeth, just disappear for a while until she came to her senses and we could all think rationally again.

I decided to see Sybil Burton before I left. I don't know why. Maybe I wanted to find out how she was handling the situation; maybe I thought she could help me decide what to do. I liked Sybil, I think she liked me, and when we met, I discovered she had known about her husband and Elizabeth for weeks. In fact, Rex Harrison and his wife, Rachel Roberts, had come to see her and Rachel asked, "Is it true that Richard is in love with Elizabeth?" "Yes," Sybil answered. "Is it true that Elizabeth is in love with Richard?" Rachel said. "Yes, I think so," Sybil replied, and Rachel turned to Rex and said, "You ridiculous bastard, why couldn't something like that happen to you?"

I asked Sybil how she was coping with all this and she said, "Ever since Richard and I have been married, Eddie, he's had these affairs. But he always comes back to me. The thing with Elizabeth is over."

"It isn't over, Sybil," I said. "They're seeing each other constantly."

"It's not true," she said.

"Believe me, Sybil, it's true."

I admired Sybil's tolerance and powers of denial, but they were beyond me. With Hank, Bernie, Bob, and Eddie as companions, I headed north for Gstaad. Hank was at the wheel of the Rolls, driving a hundred miles an hour on the autostrada, while I sat beside him holding the gun in my lap. I later learned that Sybil was not as tolerant as I thought. She went to the studio after our meeting and created such a scene that production had to be shut down for the day. That cost the studio $100,000, and because I had spoken to Sybil, it was my fault.

We got as far as Florence, where we decided to spend the night. I was worried about Elizabeth and called Rome. She wasn't at the villa, and phoning Dick Hanley to find out where she was, I discovered she was with him. She came to the phone and began calling me every foul name she knew for going to see Sybil. My friends could hear what she was saying and the blood drained from their faces. Then Burton got on the phone. He and Elizabeth were at Hanley's together. "You nothing, you spleen," he said. "I'm going to come up there and kill you."

"Don't bother," I said. "I'm coming down there." Then I hung up.

The next day we drove as far as Lake Como and again spent the night. I had time to think and realized that going to Gstaad wouldn't solve anything. I would just be wasting my time there. If Elizabeth wanted Burton, she could have him. I wanted to go home—not to Gstaad, not back to Rome—home to America.

We drove to Milan and I got a ticket on the first available flight to New York. Then I called Milton Blackstone to ask him to meet me. Sensing my anxiety, he made another suggestion. My flight had an overnight stopover in Lisbon and he would meet me there. My friends took me to the airport, where we discovered that my bags were locked in the trunk of the Rolls and we couldn't open it. All my pent-up fury finally escaped. "Just leave the goddamned car," I shouted. "Leave *everything!*" We abandoned the Rolls in a parking lot and I boarded the plane. It was the last time I saw that car.

In Lisbon I checked into a double suite at the Ritz for the night. I couldn't sleep. Distraught, I paced back and forth from room to room, ordered vodka, and asked for the hotel masseur. Then I decided I had to call the villa and speak to Elizabeth. Bill Jones answered and said she wasn't there. I called Dick Hanley, but he wasn't home either. In desperation, I even called Roddy McDowall at the studio. He was shooting a scene but called me back, and I said, "Where's Elizabeth? What's going on?"

"I don't want to discuss it," Roddy replied. And then, referring to the visit I had paid Sybil, he said, "You didn't behave like a man."

The remark infuriated me, and I slammed down the phone. Now I really went crazy. I drank more vodka. I had another massage. I didn't know what the hell I was doing.

Finally I called the villa again, and again Bill Jones answered. "Eddie, something's happened here, but don't worry. It's nothing serious."

"For God's sake, Bill, tell me what's happened!"

Suddenly Dick Hanley was on the phone. "Where are you?" he asked.

"In Lisbon," I said. "What's going on there? Is something wrong with Elizabeth?"

"She's in the hospital, Eddie, but it's nothing serious."

"I'm coming back."

"Really, don't bother."

"Damn it, Dick, don't tell me not to bother. I'm coming back."

More phone calls, canceling my flight to New York, getting a seat on the next plane to Rome. Milton had arrived and a look of surprise crossed his face when I told him I was going back to Elizabeth. He took me to the airport. It was six or seven in the morning, I hadn't slept, I hadn't shaved. I looked like death, and the first person we saw was Francis Cardinal Spellman, who greeted us with the remark, "Well, it's nice to see you two together again." Milton left us, and Cardinal Spellman and I sat side by side on the flight to Rome. We chatted for a while and then he opened a copy of *Life* or *Look* and we laughed to discover there were articles about both of us in the same magazine.

My friendship with Cardinal Spellman dated back several years. I was singing on *Coke Time* in New York and Milton Blackstone arranged an introduction, probably for the same reason he arranged everything else in my life in those days: it would be good for my image. A young Jewish pop singer and the most distinguished and powerful Roman Catholic churchman in the country were an unlikely combination, but Cardinal Spellman encouraged our friendship. He invited me often to his residence behind Saint Patrick's Cathedral for lunch or dinner, and I was always welcome to bring my friends. Once I asked Rocky Marciano to come with me and I was startled to see a man who was a killer in the ring fall to the floor and kiss the cardinal's feet. There were other surprises. Cardinal Spellman confessed that he was a songwriter, or rather he had written several poems which a young priest had set to music. I sang some of them for him, with the young priest at the organ in the residence, and I chose one entitled "To My Mother on My Birthday" to sing on *Coke Time*.

Cardinal Spellman went to Korea every Christmas during the years we were at war there, and one evening when Milton and I were dining at the residence, he asked me to come with him on his next Christmas tour. I was very excited by the idea. I had made other appearances with him at various benefits around New York, but this would be a chance to go back to Korea, a Catholic and a Jew together, and to me that would have been a wonderful thing. I said I would be honored to go, but in my enthusiasm for the idea, I forgot about my television show and couldn't go after all.

Cardinal Spellman and I had seen each other only once or twice in the intervening years, and here we were sitting together on a plane en route to Rome. He was as warm and genial as ever. He knew nothing of what was going on between my wife and Richard Burton; he knew nothing of what was going on inside my head, although I was certain that fear and anxiety were written all over my face. He praised Elizabeth and me for overcoming so many obstacles in our marriage; he congratulated us for adopting little Maria. And all the while I was thinking, Yes, we have so much together. Please, God, don't let it be over. I was very grateful to the cardinal; his words, his presence, made that flight back to Rome a little easier for me.

With no idea what I would find when I got there, I went directly from the airport to the hospital, where her doctor told me Elizabeth had taken too many sleeping pills. The press was told she was suffering from an intestinal complaint. The doctor asked me not to stay too long. I entered Elizabeth's room and saw her reclining on the bed, playing Cleopatra. "Why," she asked imperiously, "did you go to see Sybil?"

"Elizabeth," I said, "I love you and would do anything to keep you."

She just looked at me and I could tell she was satisfied with my answer.

I didn't want to go back to the villa. I went to the apartment my friends shared in Rome, wondering what I was supposed to do now. Was it all over; was this the end of our marriage? I was ready to believe the worst until the telephone rang. It was Elizabeth. "Eddie, come and pick me up at the hospital tomorrow morning at ten."

That was all she said. That was all she had to say. It was a reconciliation. Elizabeth wanted me back, and God knows I wanted her. She called again a few moments later. "Come at nine instead of ten," she said, "and bring a change of clothes, a pair of sunglasses, and some beer."

It was Sunday and Bob Abrams had to scout all over Rome for sunglasses and beer. I went to the villa to get her clothes. Then I had to force my way through a crowd of reporters waiting outside the hospital, and knew it would be even worse when Elizabeth and I left. She greeted me as if nothing had happened. In her usual tempo, she got dressed, drank some beer, donned the sunglasses, and we were ready to go. It was just like old times; we were holding hands, laughing, playing games with the paparazzi, who got so excited they climbed all over our car. Sitting in the back seat, leaning close to Elizabeth, I whispered, "Smile," under my breath, but the expression on my face looked like a grimace, as if I were muttering a threat, and that was the picture that hit all the front pages.

The paparazzi followed our car all the way to the villa and clamored to take pictures of us standing together at the front door. I was so happy to be back with Elizabeth, I wanted to believe that nothing had changed between us. But somehow I felt that pictures like that would be hypocritical, a lie. Things *had* changed and I knew they would never be the same. I said "No" to the photographers and ducked inside the door, leaving Elizabeth to face them alone.

I wasn't sure what was going to happen next. I saw that Elizabeth had formed a new relationship, a new bond; she needed something from Burton that I couldn't give her. Still, she wasn't yet willing to break the bond between us. In an emotional turmoil, she wrote me a note saying that it was possible to be torn between two men, but she still loved me and begged me to stand by her to ride out this storm. Obviously, Burton needed something from her, too, and both he and Elizabeth were playing a very dangerous game, hoping they could hold on to what was solid and secure in their marriages and still have each other.

I knew the way Elizabeth's mind worked. The unknown factor in this crazy equation was Burton, and who could figure out the way his mind worked? Now I realize he knew exactly what he was doing, and even enjoyed it. He scorned Elizabeth's abilities as an actress, but she had the one thing that had always eluded him—superstardom. By becoming involved with her, he probably thought he could achieve that, as if it were contagious and he could catch it from Elizabeth. All he wanted was a little fun and a lot of publicity. But Elizabeth was demanding much more. She was nobody's fool, and what he had begun as the usual affair with his leading lady, she was taking seriously. The pursuer had become the pursued, and by humiliating her—humiliating me in front of her—he was trying to keep her in her place. To Elizabeth that meant only one thing—rejection. No one could treat her that way. *She* had to be the one who did the rejecting. Now she had to have Burton, she had to bring him to heel. This wasn't a love affair; it was warfare.

I wasn't smart enough to understand all that then. I didn't realize that the more Burton insulted Elizabeth, the greater grew her determination to beat him at his own game. I thought if I could be patient, swallow my pride, ride out the storm as Elizabeth had asked me to do, our marriage would survive. But I had forgotten the fights and loving reconciliations that had been so much a part of her marriage to Mike. Elizabeth thrived on them, and now she could play even more passionate scenes with Burton. I had forgotten, too, that she also thrived on pursuit; it was she, after all, who had come to me for the love and security she needed after Mike's death. I had offered no resistance then, or since, and in Burton she saw a new challenge. I saw a new victim. And I had forgotten that Elizabeth never did anything halfway. Her commitments were total. If she saw something she wanted, she went after it until it was hers for keeps. Marriage, I knew, had no part in Burton's original calculations; for Elizabeth romance and marriage were inseparable. Once she had decided she wanted Burton, our marriage didn't have a chance.

It was agony for me, waiting to see which of us Elizabeth would choose. But I was still so deeply in love with her that there was nothing else I could do. I had no strategy, no plans; I simply couldn't picture the future without Elizabeth. I just tried to hang on, telling myself this was a bad dream, a nightmare that would be over soon. Then I did an impulsive thing. I gave Elizabeth a ten-thousand-dollar yellow-diamond ring for her thirtieth birthday. And as if that wasn't extravagant enough, I presented her with a folding mirror of gold and emeralds I had ordered from Bulgari's; "I will always love you. Eddie," was etched in my handwriting on the glass. I was trying to buy back Elizabeth's love. The diamond was a bauble, but the folding mirror was so expensive, so beautiful, that I thought Elizabeth would always keep it and always be reminded of me.

Consciously, I was still playing the role of the devoted husband; subconsciously, I must have known the end was near. Over Elizabeth's objections, I invited her parents to come to Rome to celebrate her birthday. This was a tough situation for Elizabeth to handle; she needed people who loved her to help her through it and somehow I felt I wasn't going to be one of them. Oddly, all my thoughts were of her and the hell Burton was putting her through. I wasn't really aware of what they were doing to me until one night Bill Jones found me sitting alone in the villa, drinking straight vodka from a glass, waiting for Elizabeth to come home. "Eddie, my lad," he said, "you know I love you."

"Yes, Bill," I said. "I know."

"Then why don't you do yourself a favor? Go home."

He saw what I refused to see: that the situation could only get worse, and if I had lost Elizabeth, I had to save myself. But I thought there was still time. Nothing had appeared in the papers yet. And whatever Elizabeth did with Burton during the day, she still came home to me at night. Then we seemed as close as ever and not even Elizabeth was that good an actress. Or was I kidding myself? Were our feelings for each other as strong as ever, or did they seem so intense because I was afraid that every moment we spent together would be the last?

One night she didn't come home. After waiting for her until two or three in the morning, I finally went upstairs to bed. But I couldn't sleep and I heard her when she got in. It was five o'clock. She didn't come upstairs to bed. She went to sleep on a couch in the living room. That was the end. Even I could see it now.

She did come up about six. I was wide awake, lying on the

bed. Her hair was uncombed, her clothes disheveled. She looked ugly. I don't know what my feelings for her were at that moment: anger, jealousy. I guess I could have hated her. "Elizabeth," I said, "I'm leaving."

She whirled around with a look on her face as if she wanted to kill me. "If you leave," she said, "you'll never see me again."

Did she honestly believe I would always be there, waiting for her to come home? Did she think she could have *both* Burton and me? "That's a very familiar line, Elizabeth," I said. "I'm sorry, but I have no choice. I want to live."

Realizing I meant what I said, she began to scream, then ran downstairs and out of the house. I was unmoved. Numb. But Elizabeth always looked as if she were about to topple over when she ran. And I remember thinking that this time I wouldn't be there to catch her if she fell.

I didn't see Elizabeth again until 1964, two years later. Burton was playing Hamlet on Broadway and every night thousands of people jammed Times Square just to catch a glimpse of that famous couple as they left the theater. They were staying at the Regency and I arrived in the middle of an argument. Her makeup smeared, her voice loud and shrill, Elizabeth was furious about something and I thought, I was married to that woman, that wild thing. Burton was trying to soothe her, and as I watched him walk around their suite, apologizing, straightening up, retrieving things she had dropped, I saw myself.

"Where did you get those cigars you used to smoke?" he asked me.

"The Connaught Hotel," I said. "Mike used to smoke them too."

He called London and ordered cigars. He was doing the same things I had done, the same things Mike had done. The battle was over and they both got what they wanted. Burton was a superstar. And Elizabeth had someone else to pick up after her.

17

Where to begin picking up the shattered pieces of my life? I turned to Milton Blackstone and Max Jacobson for help. With Milton, it was as if I had never married Debbie or Elizabeth, as if we had never disagreed in the past. He was more than pleased to have me back. I was still the kid from Philadelphia and Milton was in complete control again, making plans, arranging bookings, talking about my image, even worrying about when I got to bed at night—just like old times. He told me exactly what I wanted to hear. "Nobody thought your marriage was going to come to an end this way, Eddie. But look at Sinatra. He was down when his marriage to Ava broke up, and now he's back on top. No matter what else you've lost, you can't lose confidence in yourself. It's a special magic, the way you mesmerize an audience. People still love you; they still want to hear you sing. That hasn't changed. You've got a future and it's going to be even bigger and better than your past."

My immediate future was planned with the care and precision typical of Milton. First the Cocoanut Grove in Los Angeles, a showplace to let the Hollywood crowd know I was back, then the Desert Inn to refresh the memories of Las Vegas audiences, Grossinger's, of course, for the Labor Day weekend, and a sentimental reunion with Eddie Cantor, and then the Latin Casino in my hometown of Philadelphia—Eddie Fisher retracing the steps that had led to stardom. Milton mapped it all out as if it were a political campaign; he spoke of momentum and constituencies. And once I had captured the voters' confidence in these key locales, I would be swept back into power at the Winter Garden, Broadway's largest legitimate theater, in the show business equivalent of a political convention at Madison Square Garden.

Obviously there was no difficulty finding me work: everybody wanted to get a look at Eddie Fisher. I was a curiosity and I would have to learn to live with that. But my personal and professional lives had always been inseparable in the minds of my audiences. The problem now would be to achieve some kind of balance, to make that work for instead of against me. If people came to see me because of what had happened in Rome, fine; *I* was up on that stage to sing.

The problem arose almost immediately, with a recording of "Arrivederci, Roma" and "After You've Gone." They may not have been the best choice; to me they seemed like a crass commercialization of my personal life, which is exactly what a lot of critics said. But they were good songs, and in a funny way I felt good about recording them. It was a kind of catharsis, and singing was always the way I got things out of my system.

I really didn't want to go back to work, not right away. I was physically and emotionally exhausted. And that's where Max came in. During the years Elizabeth and I were together, I had scarcely seen him at all. Now he gave me three or four injections every day even though I wasn't performing, and prescribed Librium to put me to sleep at night. I started hanging around his office, talking to his other patients, his celebrity-in-residence. Jumpy and nervous after every injection, depressed as its effects began to wear off, I was a great advertisement for his treatments. My left arm was numb with some kind of paralysis which seemed to get worse every time I saw a man and a woman holding hands or kissing on the street. I couldn't watch love scenes on television. Whether it was a side effect of Max's injections or just something going on inside my head, that same dull ache persisted for months.

Max had no sympathy for any of my complaints. His injections were always accompanied by a string of obscene commands to stop feeling sorry for myself, get off my ass, and go back to work. But he was so concerned about my condition that he didn't want me out of his sight for more than a few hours. He genuinely cared about me, and that, more than his magic elixir, helped me conquer my self-pity and kept me on my feet.

One morning I arrived at his East Seventy-second Street office, to find everything in turmoil. Max was pulling chemicals and syringes from cabinets and shouting orders at his nurses, who were packing them in two small black medical bags. "Come," he said as soon as he saw me. "We go to Washington."

I laughed in disbelief. I knew what Max's usual medical bag looked like—a jumble of dirty, unmarked bottles and nameless chemical concoctions which he would just dump out on a table when he began to mix up an injection. These medical bags were brand-new, everything was carefully labeled and arranged. Max had to assume at least the appearance of a conventional doctor for the President of the United States.

The next thing I knew, I was sitting outside Evelyn Lincoln's office in the White House while Max was in the Oval Office, injecting Jack Kennedy with a special formula he prepared on the spot. It was the first of several times I went to Washington with him. I heard that Mark Shaw, a patient of Max's and a photographer close to the Kennedy family, had recommended him to Jackie Kennedy, who then recommended him to her husband. Kennedy became a patient, over the vehement objections of his regular doctors, his brother Bobby, and his press secretary, Pierre Salinger, who was at least successful in keeping any mention of the association out of the press, even when Max and his wife accompanied President and Mrs. Kennedy on their trip to Vienna to meet Khrushchev.

I saw the President once or twice in Washington. He always wanted to know if I was there, and when he had the time he would come out, shake hands, and ask how I was. He loved show business, and of course events in Rome were still making front-page headlines. His interest and concern gave me a big lift. I didn't notice any particular change in him after an injection; he was always full of energy. But once I heard him say, "I don't care if there's panther piss in there, as long as it makes me feel good." Max never told anyone exactly what was in his formulas. If asked, he would say with exasperation, "If I tell you, are you going to know?" You weren't supposed to question God. He even refused to let White House doctors analyze the injections he gave the President. Max had guts.

I was worried about the impression he created on the President. Max just didn't *look* like a doctor, particularly his fingernails, stained black with chemicals. At the Statler in Washington, one night before he was scheduled to see Kennedy, I tried to scrub them clean while Max was sound asleep in the bathtub. It was useless. But in spite of his appearance, and his usual gruff manner, Max had a wonderful sense of humor and could behave with great dignity. He would fall asleep every time he sat down, in the bathtub or anyplace else, and once, waiting for the President outside Evelyn Lincoln's office, he dozed off in a chair. Kennedy came out, and as he crossed in front of Max his shadow woke him. Max looked up and said, "I guess if this were wartime, Mr. President, I'd be shot for sleeping while on duty." I saw Kennedy offer him a five-hundred-dollar bill after one of his treatments, but Max shook his head and said, "If I cannot serve the President of the country I live in, then I'm not worth anything."

On my last trip to Washington with Max, I didn't see the President. My limousine was stopped at the gate by a guard who told me that Evelyn Lincoln wanted to talk to me. I got out of the car and spoke to her over the phone at the guard post. "Eddie," she said, "the Shah of Iran and his wife have just arrived and the press is all around the President. I think you'd better not come in." I was a little hurt, but I understood. I did see Kennedy again, however, not in Washington but in New York. I was sitting in Max's office when the door opened and there he was. He had come from the Carlyle, leaving secret service guards trailing in his wake. They caught up with him a few minutes later and waited outside the office while Kennedy got a shot.

In my eyes, Kennedy was more than just a skillful politician; he was a very charismatic man. And a very romantic one. I later got to know several of the young women he was involved with, including Judy Campbell, and they all adored him. His many liaisons were no secret to his wife, but like his association with Max Jacobson, they were carefully concealed from the press and the public.

In May 1963, I helped Alan Jay Lerner, who was also a patient of Max's, stage a show for Kennedy's forty-sixth birthday party, a thousand-dollar-a-plate political fund-raiser which was held in the lobby of the Waldorf-Astoria and spilled over into the Empire and Sert rooms. I persuaded Louis Nizer and

Ed Sullivan to dance in a chorus line, and also got Sugar Ray Robinson, Tony Randall, and Robert Preston to perform. Audrey Hepburn sang "Happy Birthday" to the President, and the party was a huge success.

There was an enthusiasm, a warmth and candor about Kennedy that inspired everyone. He created an atmosphere, an aura, wherever he was, no matter how many people were in the room, and even if you didn't see him leave, you knew he was gone. That evening I was standing in line next to Audrey, waiting to greet the President, and after speaking to her for a moment, he passed right by me without a sign of recognition. But suddenly he did a double take and grasped my hand. "Well," he said, with a big grin, "how are you feeling *now?*"

It was the last time I saw Jack Kennedy.

Just after my return from Rome, I was sitting in front of a television set in my suite at the Pierre, still feeling very sorry for myself. I hadn't even dated another woman since I left Elizabeth; the idea of becoming involved with anyone else was abhorrent to me. I would never fall in love again. Lenny Gaines was with me, and as we watched the Academy Awards show, my thoughts drifted back. One year earlier, I had helped Elizabeth down the aisle when she won the Oscar. Would I ever be able to forget her? I was paying very little attention to the show until I saw someone called Ann-Margret do a musical number. Then something happened to me; something I thought had died was coming back to life. I had never seen Ann-Margret before; this was her television debut and she was fresh and natural, her dancing really quite dynamic. "She's marvelous," I said to Lenny. "I've got to meet that girl."

"Oh, God," Lenny said. "Here we go again."

Getting Elizabeth out of my head and heart, however, would not be as easy as just finding someone else to love. Her rejection tortured me, and in moments of deep depression I blamed myself, not Elizabeth, not Burton, for what had happened in Rome. I wanted to turn back the clock and start all over again with Elizabeth. No one else could ever make me as happy. I had lost so much—not only Elizabeth. My ego had suffered a severe blow. I had lost my own sense of worth. Obviously I was still in love with her, and I couldn't read all the stories pouring out of Rome about her affair, and her fights with Burton without feeling physically ill.

One newspaper story in particular alarmed me. Burton, according to the story, was beating Elizabeth until a bodyguard stepped in to protect her. I called Maria Schell in Germany and begged her to go to Rome. I thought Elizabeth needed a friend, a woman to talk to, at least one sane person in that crazy situation.

"Of course I'll go," Maria said. "I'll do everything in my power to help the two of you."

"No, Maria," I replied. "This is not for me and Elizabeth. That's over. There's nothing anyone can do about that. It's for Elizabeth. She needs your help."

Maria want to Rome, even though she was eight months pregnant, spent a few days with Elizabeth and Burton, who were now living together, and then called me. "Eddie," she said, "I stayed there as long as I could, but it was just impossible." When she told me that she had barely been able to talk to either Elizabeth or Burton because both of them were in such a terrible state, my heart sank. Even after what had happened, I couldn't get the habit of taking care of Elizabeth out of my system.

It would be as difficult to disentangle myself from Elizabeth legally as it was emotionally. I went to Louis Nizer, who had represented us both on several other legal matters, including libel suits against fan magazines—which at one point numbered at least fourteen—and asked him to arrange a divorce. But my ties to Elizabeth were complex; a lot of money was involved, not to mention questions of custody of my adopted children, Liza and Maria. And what I hoped would be a quick and painless termination of our marriage would turn into a long and lingering death.

Between visits to Max's office, I spent a lot of time at the Commodore steam baths, as if I could sweat Elizabeth out of my system. One afternoon I spotted a man at the opposite side of the huge dry-steam room. "Do you know who that is?" I asked Kurt Frings, who was sitting with me. "Frank Costello."

"How do you know?" Kurt said.

"I used to see him years ago at the Copacabana."

"Introduce me," Kurt said.

"Not on your life. I've got enough problems."

I dragged Kurt out of the steam room, we showered, and were dressing hurriedly when an attendant tapped me on the shoulder. "Mr. Fisher," he said, "Mr. Costello would like to see you."

He took us to a small room where Costello was lying on a table getting a massage. I introduced Kurt, who said, "Nice to know you, Mr. Costello. How was your trip?"

Costello had just returned from serving a brief sentence in a Southern prison for tax evasion. I cringed at Kurt's remark, but Costello ignored it. "How are you feeling?" he said to me in the gravelly voice that Marlon Brando later imitated in *The Godfather*. "You look good. If you ever need anything, you can always get in touch with me at the Waldorf barbershop. I'm there every morning at ten o'clock. Remember. Anything you want, because I like you. And you got talent."

"I didn't know you had such good connections," Kurt remarked as we left the Commodore. Events in Rome were complicating his already difficult relationship with Elizabeth and he foresaw more trouble ahead with Burton. "Why don't you take Mr. Costello up on his offer?" he said. "Get him to break Burton's legs."

I looked at him with surprise.

"One leg?" Kurt said, and we both burst out laughing.

I headed for Los Angeles a few days later. There was no point hanging around New York like a whipped dog. I had lived so long in Los Angeles that I considered it my home, and I was beginning to feel a little better about myself and my future, ready to go back to work at the Cocoanut Grove. Maybe it was false courage. I still got three or four shots from Max every day and used Librium to sleep at night. Before he would let me go, Max insisted I stop taking the Librium, and for one solid week I lay wide awake all night long, staring at the ceiling. I couldn't even read. I called Max at all hours: "For God's sake, why are you putting me through this? I'm in pain. You've got to give me something." But Max was adamant, and finally one night I picked up a copy of the *Reader's Digest*, read two articles, and fell asleep. I woke up at six in the morning and called Max. "I did it," I said jubilantly. "I fell asleep."

"*Ja*," he said. "Good."

Max made no attempt to take me off his own magic elixir. On the contrary, he presented me with a generous supply of syringes and his special formula premixed in little bottles, and after I again practiced giving myself intramuscular injections under his supervision, he sent me on my way to California with a "Now get the hell out of here."

I was deeply embarrassed about injecting myself. I always did it in private, stabbing the needle in my buttocks just as I had in the bathroom at the Waldorf-Astoria the night of the Friars Club dinner for Joe E. Lewis. But I thought I couldn't perform or even survive without a shot to get me going in the morning, a shot to keep me going at night.

They weren't very powerful, they didn't last very long, and their effects were probably as much psychological as physical. How could they be wrong? After all, I was only doing as my doctor ordered, and I followed his instructions to the letter. It was medication, and I needed it as a diabetic needs insulin.

If I had any apprehensions about how audiences would react to me after my Roman holiday, my reception at the Cocoanut Grove reassured me. Their response to my performances there was more enthusiastic than ever. No matter what had happened to my ego, my voice hadn't changed, and I thought that with another hit record or two, I would be right back on top again, just where I was before I married Elizabeth. Look at me, kid. I can live without you. Mr. Elizabeth Taylor will survive.

Ann-Margret was in the audience opening night at the Cocoanut Grove. I couldn't believe it, and when she came to my dressing room after the show, it happened—boom—just like that. Why did I think I would never fall in love again? Ann-Margret was making the movie version of *Bye Bye Birdie,* and her career was just beginning to soar. Young and passionate about everything, she did more than take my mind off Elizabeth.

Jack Kennedy admired Ann-Margret too. He wanted to meet her and asked her to come to the Carlyle the evening of his birthday party at the Waldorf-Astoria, where Ann-Margret was scheduled to perform. "If you go, we're through," I told her, then realized she couldn't refuse to see the President. But I insisted on taking her to the hotel in my limousine and waiting for her to come out. Their meeting lasted only a very few minutes.

Ann-Margret and I spent as much time together as we could for about a year, but neither of us wanted to be tied down. We never lived together. I wasn't ready to make even that kind of commitment, let alone marriage. Not another *actress.* That would be crazy. I had learned at least that much from being married to Debbie and Elizabeth. But no matter who the girl might be, marriage was the farthest thing from my mind. It had brought me the greatest happiness I had ever known—and the greatest pain. That's why when Ann-Margret began to talk about marriage, I said, "Your career has got to come first. You're on the right track, Ann-Margaret Olsson. Don't ruin it by getting married." That remark was the end of our relationship. We met once or twice after that, and I haven't seen or spoken to her since.

There were other women in my life, even while I was going with Ann-Margret. And parties almost every night. I rented a house on Gloaming Way in Coldwater Canyon and filled it with people; my old friends, new friends, the more the merrier, everybody was welcome. It was a happy house, but I wasn't always happy in it. I can remember floating alone at one end of the pool watching people paddle and splash around at the other. And sometimes, when I felt depressed, I would just get up and go to bed right in the middle of a party, falling asleep to the sounds of talk and laughter that filtered through the walls. I had my work, I had my friends, I was seeing interesting and beautiful women. But it still hurt whenever I thought of Elizabeth.

Juliet Prowse came to see me at the Cocoanut Grove. I was attracted to her immediately, but I knew she had been going with Frank Sinatra and I thought it wise to check with him first. I called him in London, where he was appearing after a tour of performances that had taken him around the world. He gave me his gracious permission to date Juliet and then invited me to come to London when my engagement at the Cocoanut Grove was over. A lot of his buddies were there and he was forming some new kind of rat pack. Why not? I thought. Frank and I had had fun together in the past. Why the hell not?

I had known Frank for years, and had admired him even longer than that, ever since I was a kid in Philadelphia, dreaming of following in his footsteps. There could never be another Sinatra—I soon learned that. He was unique, an original, but our lives and careers did have curious parallels. He was the teenage idol of the 1940s, I was the teenage idol of the '50s, and both of us were indebted to Mannie Sacks for the success of our recording careers. When I was going with Joanie Wynne in New York, Frank was going with Joanie's roommate, Betty Carson, who was also in the chorus line at the Copa. And

Frank had divorced his wife to marry the incredible Ava Gardner, just as I had married Elizabeth after my divorce. He, too, had been badly burned, and maybe because he could identify with what I was going through, he called me soon after I returned from Rome to offer the use of his house in Palm Springs. "Anything you want, kid," he said. "Just name it and it's yours."

In my opinion, Sinatra was the greatest interpreter of a popular song there ever was or will be. No one had more integrity as a performer, but as a person he sometimes confused and even shocked me. One moment he could be extremely generous and kind; the next, aloof and insensitive.

Friendship with Frank had to be on his terms, and he was just as demanding of his audiences. Once at Bill Miller's Riviera, the packed house began to cheer and whistle and shout, "Hey, Frankie," the minute he walked out on stage. He stood there waiting for all the commotion to die down so he could begin his performance, and when it didn't, he called out, "Waiter, menu." He looked at the menu, ordered a steak, rare, a salad, and a baked potato, said good night, and walked off. The audience was stunned into silence and waited politely for him to return. Somebody else would have come back, but not Frank.

I had seen him give only one bad performance, years ago when I was singing eight shows a day at the Steel Pier in Atlantic City and he was at the 500 Club. He was having more than his usual problems with Ava, his career was at a low point, and the audience was aware that he wasn't really there. Yet not much later, his opening at the Riviera was one of the greatest performances I've ever seen. Same songs, but this time he couldn't sing a wrong note, couldn't make a wrong move. It was electrifying. Monte Proser was sitting with me in the audience. Sinatra had often said he would sing at the Copa and never had, but that night Proser remarked with awe and admiration, "I forgive him for everything."

There was only one empty seat on that opening night—the one reserved for Ava. But she did come the following night, and sat with me while Frank gave another great performance. Ava didn't seem to care. Her head was lowered, her hair fell over her face, and she never bothered to look up from her glass.

Frank wore his emotions on his sleeve and I always thought

his cocky, tough-guy attitude was probably just a way of protecting himself from being hurt. He seemed to prefer respect to love and when he thought he had been insulted he was like a wild man. I saw his quick temper flare while we were together in London. All his friends used to hang out in his suite at Claridge's, and one morning I walked in and saw a young woman with a scarf around her head. I had no idea who she was and I said to Frank, "Good morning, your highness." *She* was the highness, Princess Alexandra, and we all sat around and had a nice chat. But somehow the newspapers found out about her visit and Frank blew his stack. He swore he was going to get the guy who told reporters, and one by one, he buttonholed his friends, including me, demanding to know who had betrayed him.

The night before he was due to leave London, we all wound up at his suite again for drinks and a healthy dose of Sinatra tapes, a usual feature at his parties. "I've narrowed it down to two people," Frank announced, still playing detective, "the assistant manager of the hotel and the elevator operator, and I want everybody here tomorrow morning at ten."

"Frank," I said, "these things happen. Forget it. You've just come off this marvelous world tour. Don't blow it now." *I* was worried about Sinatra's image.

"Who the fuck asked you?" he snarled.

I don't know what Frank thought he was going to do, but he left London the next morning without doing anything. Typical, I thought: a lot of energy and anger wasted.

The papers reported that I had asked Sinatra to act as some kind of intermediary in a reconciliation with Elizabeth. Utterly ridiculous. I wasn't interested in a reconciliation, and even if I had been, Elizabeth would hardly listen to anything Frank had to say. But if I had asked him, Frank probably would have given it a try. That was exactly the kind of favor he liked to do for his friends. He always stepped in at critical moments with offers of help. He *was* a very generous man.

Back from London and appearing at the Desert Inn in Las Vegas, the second step on the campaign trail Milton had charted for me, I ran into Edie Adams again. I had known Edie ever since she appeared on *Coke Time* in New York and saw her often in Los Angeles while she was married to Ernie Kovacs. After her husband's sudden and tragic death, Edie had returned to show business and was now on the bill with Liberace at the Riviera. As musical as she was, and even with all her experience, Edie felt insecure and was having personal problems adjusting to her husband's death. She was virtually paralyzed by stage fright before every performance, and at first our relationship was professional as I did what I could to help her overcome it. But soon we were having a romance, and a very nice one—nothing that either of us took too seriously. Edie was a marvelous woman, but our relationship ended abruptly the day Ann-Margret came to town. We were in my dressing room in a very intimate embrace when Edie, wearing her full-length chinchilla coat, walked in, took one look at what we were doing, and ran out, crying, "I'll be at the bar." I found her there later; we both apologized and remained friends.

My affairs didn't always end on such a friendly basis. I went a little crazy after I got back from Rome, completely out of character, obsessed by trying to live down Elizabeth's rejection and prove to the world—and myself—that I was still a man. Headwaiters always seated beautiful women down front during my performances, thinking that would please me, and among them there were at least two or three Elizabeth Taylor look-alikes hoping to attract my attention. Friends were eager to fix me up too, and one of them told me there was a show girl at the Tropicana who was a dead ringer for Elizabeth. Not exactly what I had in mind, but when I saw her on stage it was true. She *was* Elizabeth. Then we met and I discovered that the lights, her makeup and costume—and my imagination— had been playing tricks on me.

I was not interested in finding another Elizabeth. Nor was I interested in one-night stands. But whatever I was looking for, I couldn't seem to find it. I was too busy; I didn't want to get too involved; I thought nothing could match what Elizabeth and I had had together. Even though I needed a relationship with a woman, there always seemed to be some reason to break it up. It was never easy to do. I didn't want to hurt anyone, but didn't want to be hurt either. Unwilling to risk another rejection, I made enemies of both lovers and friends because I had to do the rejecting first.

Milton, as usual, stayed out of my personal life, even though people were probably beginning to think my brains were in my cock. His job was to keep me working, and so far everything was right on schedule. My appearances at both the Cocoanut

Grove and the Desert Inn had been very successful, and Grossinger's welcomed me home like a prodigal son. Audiences had always rooted for me, but now there was another sort of feeling in the air. I was singing well and that meant I had survived, I was overcoming. At the Latin Casino in Philadelphia, it didn't matter how well I sang. People started screaming and crying the minute I walked out on stage; nobody heard a note, just like the old days at the Paramount after I got out of the army. It was funny: people who had loved me because I was a sweet, unspoiled kid still loved me even though I wasn't sweet and unspoiled anymore. My image, to speak in Milton's terms, was taking on a whole new dimension. I was the guy who had "deserted" his wife and kids to become Mr. Elizabeth Taylor—my audiences couldn't forget that—and while they were happy I had lived through that, they couldn't help wondering what I would do next to screw up my life.

The business agreement Milton and I had signed years before, providing for a very loose partnership, was still in effect and I saw no reason to change it. The money I earned went into the till and was there for both of us, whatever we needed, no questions asked. That till was probably pretty close to empty when I got back from Rome, but it began to fill up again quickly as soon as I started working. I made top dollar in Las Vegas, $40,000 a week, and the Latin Casino paid me $60,000 a week plus for my engagement there. Lee Solomon at the William Morris Agency, which now represented me, was prepared to accept an original offer of $20,000 a week, but I was so sure I could do better than that in my old hometown that I held out until the offer was tripled. I packed the 2,300-seat club twice a night for three weeks.

If I was getting a little smarter about making money, I was no smarter about how I spent it. Hotel suites, cars, clothes, women and the gifts I bought for them—it was probably going out almost as fast as it was coming in, and old friends and even passing acquaintances climbed aboard for the free ride. That kind of extravagance wasn't new, nor was it Elizabeth's fault. If anything, I should have learned my lesson. But like the many women in my life, spending money was an enjoyable distraction. My gambling wasn't new either, but the *way* I started gambling was. "You were never a high roller until you left Elizabeth," Lenny Gaines remembered. "When you came back from Rome, you went bananas. And you didn't gamble with a brain. You didn't even gamble with half a brain."

At the end of my four-week engagement at the Desert Inn, I stayed over for another day to see Bobby Darin and Pat Boone. Waiting for a friend beside one of the dice tables in the casino, I said to the croupier, "Let me have two thou." It was a little game we played; whenever I made that request, he handed me two hundred dollars' worth of chips, not two thousand. My friend arrived and said, "Come on, let's go." And I said, "Let me roll the dice just once." I won.

And kept winning. People crowded around the table as the chips began to pile up. A blackjack dealer who was a friend of mine eyed the pile and said, "Quit, you son of a bitch. You've got $125,000 there." I didn't quit. I missed Darin and Boone. When I was paged over the loudspeaker, I ignored it. The limit, seven thousand dollars, was riding on every roll of the dice, and Milton, who was standing at my elbow, begged me to be careful. "Take Lloyd's of London insurance," he said. "Cover the seven." I ignored him too. Bells were ringing in the casino. Everyone was buzzing with disbelief. The owners of the Desert Inn, summoned from their offices to the casino, stood at a discreet distance to watch the action.

Nothing like this had ever happened to me before. I just couldn't lose. The piles of chips grew larger and I was going crazy with excitement. Nineteen hours later, exhausted, I finally quit and cashed in my chips. I had won $165,000. I stuffed $35,000 in hundred-dollar bills in my pockets, put the rest in the hotel safe, and patting the bulges in my suit as I left the casino, I said, "This is easier than singing."

A few weeks later, eager to try my luck again, I couldn't wait to get back to the tables at the Desert Inn. And this time I didn't start with a mere two hundred dollars. I bet the limit on every roll—and within minutes lost $25,000. I walked away from the table with a shrug, and leaving the Desert Inn along with my friend Edie Adams, tried my luck at another casino. And then another. It was the same wherever I went. In less than an hour and a half, at five different casinos, I lost $125,000.

I often saw other performers lose even more than that, sometimes their entire salaries before they opened. Some worked solely to pay off their gambling debts, which was not uncommon in Las Vegas. If I was a high roller, at least I was smart enough to know that nobody comes out ahead in the long run. In the years that followed, I would lose more than half a million dollars at the dice tables, but like all my other extravagances, I thought I could afford it. I didn't gamble to win; I gambled to forget, to shut out the rest of the world—or because there wasn't much else to do in Las Vegas. Gambling was a good recreation for me, or so I thought, an addiction no more dangerous than my dependence on Max Jacobson's drugs.

Back on the East Coast for my appearances at Grossinger's and the Latin Casino, I fell again under his personal care. I was still having trouble with paralysis in my left arm and Max cursed me out for being so weak as he mixed up batches of different formulas, tried them on himself and then on me—all to no effect. One day he took me to his grimy little laboratory out on Long Island and experimented with some new concoctions. Still no effect. We spent the rest of the day at Max's place on the ocean, and I just sat there sulking and feeling sorry for myself while everybody else was swimming and having a good time. I glared at Max accusingly and he gave me dirty looks in return; neither one of us was going to give in.

That night we went back to his office in the city. The place was crowded with people waiting to see him and for the first time I became one of the waiters. It was two o'clock in the morning and I was mad as hell before he deigned to see me. He made me sit down on the table and roll up my sleeve. Having already mixed up a bottle of whatever he was going to use, he drew it up in a syringe and came at me. I extended my arm, but suddenly, the syringe clenched between his teeth, Max grabbed my arm with one hand and whacked it under the elbow with the other. My arm flew up in the air and I uttered a cry of pain. Cursing him, I began to rub my elbow, and then I was aware that it was gone—the paralysis had disappeared! It would never come back. I couldn't understand what Max had done or why. It didn't matter; he was a miracle worker. But I did begin to wonder why he used needles and drugs if he could do something like that without one.

Even if the paralysis was gone, I was still in pretty bad shape, partly because of the grueling schedule Milton insisted I keep, and partly because of the way I was living—late nights, bad food, no exercise. I might have been able to get away with that when I was a kid; now it began to take its toll. Opening night at the Latin Casino, Max was there to give me a shot, and judging from the audience's reaction, no one was disappointed in my performance. But I was scared. I knew what I had to face: the excitement of coming back to my hometown, my family, singing with such intensity that I could sometimes lose as much as five pounds during two hour-and-a-half-long performances. Max had to be there *every* night. He agreed. "Have a limousine in front of my office at six o'clock," he said. "That'll give me time to get there."

Sometimes it did, sometimes it didn't, depending on the traffic. Totie Fields, the comedienne, who was on the bill as the opening act, ad-libbed to cover for me if Jacobson was a few minutes late. One night, fifteen minutes, half an hour, an hour passed, and still he hadn't arrived. Totie told every joke she knew and finally walked off. The huge orchestra, more than thirty musicians, filed on stage and just sat there waiting for me to appear. The audience began to whistle and applaud in rhythm.

The owner of the club was frantic. Screaming and waving his arms, he pleaded with me to begin my act. "Not until my doctor gets here," I said, convinced I couldn't sing a note without my usual shot. There was a telephone in Max's limousine and Lenny Gaines kept in touch with him as he sped down the Jersey Turnpike toward Philadelphia. "He's at Exit 7," Lenny said, sticking his head through the doorway of my dressing room. Five minutes later he was at the next exit, then the next. He arrived two hours late, and by that time the audience was booing and hissing, while the owner offered to pay me more money—anything to get me on stage. Lenny cleared everybody out of my dressing room as Max marched in, carrying his big black bag. Bang—he gave me a shot and I was ready to go. I sang the opening notes of my first song from the wings and walked on stage, expecting the usual cheers and applause. Instead I was greeted by hisses and boos, a new—and terrifying—experience. I had never faced a hostile audience before. There was nothing I could do but keep on singing; I couldn't leave that stage until I won them back. I sang for more than two hours that night and then collapsed completely in my dressing room, my clothes drenched with sweat.

I don't know how I got through the rest of the engagement. Everybody I had ever known in Philadelphia came to the Latin Casino and I introduced them all from the audience: Elkie, the cop on the corner, Moxie, the man who used to chase me out of his poolroom, Ruby, the barber, who had a picture of me in his shop so big that it filled the whole front window. Every night my dressing room was crowded with people, hugging and kissing me, talking about old times. I wanted to be friendly, but I had to have some peace and quiet. I had to rest my voice before each performance, and above all, I had to have complete privacy when Max gave me a shot. My brother Bunny came to my rescue. He acted as a traffic cop, screening visitors, telling people politely that I couldn't see them now. They took it from him. Everyone knew and liked Bunny; he was family and did the job so well that I asked him to become my road manager. He had been sort of drifting ever since he got out of the army, and accepted gratefully.

All my sisters and brothers came to see me, of course, along with their husbands and wives. My mother and father were in the audience every night, through both performances, at front-row tables at opposite sides of the room, sitting at an angle so they wouldn't have to look at each other. "Mom, you're going to get a stiff neck sitting that way," I said. But she never changed her position, and never took her eyes off me. My father, after several performances, got restless and one night, right in the middle of a song, he stood up and started walking out. I stopped singing and called, "Daddy, where are you going?" "Don't worry, Sonny Boy," he said. "I'll be back." He got a tremendous laugh from the audience.

Whatever the Latin Casino took out of me physically, it was an enormous psychological boost. I was working hard again and loving every minute of it. There was no time to feel sorry for myself, less time to think about Elizabeth. Then late one night at the Barclay, where I was staying, the phone at my bedside rang and I picked up the receiver. "What?" I said.

"Eddie?"

"Who is this?" I said.

"Elizabeth."

Suddenly I couldn't breathe. My heart was pounding.

"Eddie," she said. "I want to come back to you. I want you to take me back."

I didn't know what to say.

"Are you still there?" Elizabeth said.

"I'm still here," I said. "I'm just a little surprised to hear your voice."

"Eddie, I've made a mistake and I want us to be together again."

"Why?"

"Because you're kind and gentle and you love the children and they love you. I love you too. Richard is a selfish bastard. I can fly to New York the day after tomorrow and I want you to meet me there."

I couldn't believe it. My head was spinning with excitement, but all I could say was, "I can't meet you in New York, Elizabeth. I'm working in Philadelphia."

"Eddie, please."

"Okay," I said. "I'll send a car to pick you up at the airport and bring you here."

She was calling from Switzerland and told me what plane she was going to take and the time it would arrive in New York. This wasn't an impulse; she had it all planned.

We talked for about an hour, and I can't remember all that we said. I felt flushed and feverish after we finally hung up, as if I had just been jolted by one of Max's shots. Had I been dreaming? Six months had passed since I left Rome, I was suing Elizabeth for divorce, and now we were talking on the phone as if none of that had happened. Time and time again, I had imagined just such a scene. Elizabeth calling to say she was sorry and asking to come back. It was a fantasy come true. I wanted to shout. I wanted to sing at the top of my lungs. Elizabeth loved me and wanted to come back.

And then all of a sudden it hit me. Did I really *want* her back? I still loved her, but how could I live with her after what she had done? How long would it last this time—a week, a month, a year? And when it ended, could I go through that agony all over again? Yes, she was worth it. No, I had a life of my own now; I couldn't live in Elizabeth's shadow again. I argued with myself until I grew dizzy. The joy, the pain. The beauty, the ugliness. Yes. No. Yes.

No. That morning I called Dick Hanley in Switzerland. "I know you love Elizabeth, Dick," I said. "And I know you love me. She called me last night and wants to come back, but it won't work. It can't work. I want you to think of some reason. Talk to her, make up some excuse. You know what to say. Tell her she really shouldn't come at this time."

Dick said he understood completely and would do what he could.

The next day I got another call from Elizabeth. "Eddie, I can't come after all."

"Oh," I said, trying to sound surprised. And then I began to tease her. "Why can't you come, Elizabeth?"

"I just can't. Something awful has happened."

"What's happened?"

"Something awful," she said. "I can't talk about it now. But I know we'll get back together soon."

And that was the end of that. I wondered what Dick Hanley had told her. Had he made up some story to avoid hurting her feelings? Or had he just told her the truth: that I really didn't want her back. Either way, my ego couldn't have asked for anything more. *I* had rejected Elizabeth Taylor. Not for revenge. I just knew we could never live together again—now, "soon," or ever. But if I knew that, why did I feel so sad and empty?

18

Immediately after three killing weeks in Philadelphia, I was booked for four more in New York at the Winter Garden. I begged Milton to postpone the opening. My voice was tired and physically I was in even worse shape. "Just a couple of days," I said. "What difference can that make?"

He refused. I would lose my "momentum." We had leased the theater in a four-wall deal, a thirty-three-piece orchestra, complete with a full string section and French horns, was already in rehearsal, and the sets had been created by Broadway's leading designer. Dick Gregory and Juliet Prowse would perform on the first half of the bill; I would fill the second. For Milton, it was the climax of his carefully laid plans for my triumphant return to stardom. Eddie Fisher wasn't just a night-club singer; this was Broadway and the Winter Garden, the "House That Jolson Built," and now it was my turn.

With Max backing all of Milton's arguments and reassuring me that he would be there every night with his magic needles, I was overruled. What did these two men want from me? As in the past, I began to bridle under Milton's domination, but I did as I was told and gave the most ambitious performances of my career. The show was a success, four weeks were extended to five, and on the double album *Eddie Fisher at the*

Winter Garden, I sounded better than I had in years, even though it was recorded live on the last day of the engagement and I went on stage with a temperature of 102 degrees. Dorothy Kilgallen panned me, which was to be expected, but favorable mention came from another quarter. A movie critic reviewing *Cleopatra,* which had just opened at the Criterion on Broadway, wrote that there was a much better show across the street at the Winter Garden. In fact, he said, it was the best show in town.

Max was backstage almost every night with his big black bag, and probably had to give me stronger and stronger injections to achieve the desired effect. Once, he did an incredible thing. Plunging the needle into his own arm, he drew up some blood, filled another syringe with it, and injected me in the buttocks. That night I gave the greatest performance of my life, and back in my dressing room, I cried, "Max, give me *all* your blood!" He never did anything like that again; on the contrary, he seemed deeply ashamed of himself, which was not characteristic of a man who usually played God.

To me he *was* a god. I never questioned what he did, and in the months that followed, I closed my eyes to a lot of evidence that his injections were not the magic elixirs I thought they were. Kurt Frings got sick from the first and only injection he received from Max. Later, he had another kind of reaction. I was on my way to London to join Sinatra and asked Kurt to come with me. He said no, he had just returned from London and was too tired. So I gave him a shot myself of the fairly mild formula Max had made up for me to take to California, and suddenly Kurt was raring to go. We boarded the plane together and he couldn't stop talking or even sit still during the entire flight. He told me later that he wasn't able to sleep for the next forty-eight hours.

Max's injections had vastly different effects on different people. Once he got an emergency call from Zero Mostel, who was playing in *A Funny Thing Happened on the Way to the Forum*—the line I used to open my act at the Winter Garden, which always brought down the house. Mostel had injected himself, presumably with something Max had given him, and after racing to the theater, we found him hyperventilating and shaking so severely that I had to hold his hand while Max prepared another shot. That seemed to calm him, and a few moments later Mostel was able to go back on stage.

One day in Max's office, I ran into Anthony Quinn, who announced he was going to make his debut as a singer on *The Ed Sullivan Show*. "Tony," I said, "you can't sing a note." "Maybe not," he replied, "but I'm a great actor and that's all it takes." Just by accident, I happened to see the show. Quinn sang "Summertime," and his singing was as bad as my acting. Max told me the rest of the story. He had given Quinn a shot before the show and, justifiably upset by his performance, he came to Max's office in a rage and said he was never going to take another one of his lousy injections. Max's reaction was typical. He offered Quinn some bottles of his formula and said, "Either use this for the rest of your life or get yourself another doctor." It was an absurd thing to say, but that was the tyranny, the arrogance of the man.

Alan Jay Lerner, who, next to me, may have been Max's most devoted disciple, sometimes fell asleep after an injection. Or he got dizzy, and Max would apply a blue plastic cold pack to the back of his neck. He had a refrigerator full of them, just in case. Milton never seemed to have an adverse reaction, no matter how many shots he took. But a very dynamic and popular singer whom I will call Jimmy Cunningham, had a disastrous experience.

In December 1962, I brought Max to Puerto Rico while I was performing at the El San Juan. Victor Borge did the dinner show and I came on at midnight. At the end of his act, Borge used to say, "Now don't go away, ladies and gentlemen, because later on a young man with a glorious voice, Eddie Fisher, is going to come out here and sing a medley of everything." Under the influence of Max's methamphetamine, I probably came pretty close to doing just that. Jimmy Cunningham was performing in San Juan at the time, and he and Max were among several friends waiting for me in my suite after my last performance on closing night. Max passed out his usual favors, almost everybody was on meth, and it was quite a party. But gradually people began to drift out, and Max, Cunningham, and I were the only ones left.

We sat down to talk. I had known Cunningham ever since his early career days in New York. Merv Griffin, Dean Martin and Jerry Lewis, Cunningham and I used to hang around together and had some wonderful times. Max and Cunningham seemed to know each other, and that night Max volunteered to treat him. Cunningham had almost no sight in one eye, and

Max, always eager to work medical miracles for his friends, said he could fix it.

"It can't be fixed, Max," Cunningham said. "I've been to every doctor in the world and there's nothing anyone can do."

That didn't stop Max. Not just any doctor, he insisted he would succeed where all others had failed.

"Max," Cunningham said, getting angry, "I love you for trying to help, but forget it. The eye is shot! *Nothing* can be done about it."

Max wouldn't give up. He kept after Cunningham until six o'clock in the morning. "Okay, Max. All right," Cunningham said finally. "Do whatever you want to do."

With a triumphant smile, Max dumped his medical bag out on a table and began to mix something up. He injected Cunningham, then stood back and said. "Well?"

I think he honestly believed Cunningham was suddenly going to cry, "I can see! I can see!" But he just shrugged and said, "Sorry, Max."

"Wait, wait," Max said. "I'll try something else." He went back to the table and mixed up a different formula, while Cunningham and I continued talking. When it was ready, he gave Cunningham another shot and again stood back, waiting for the miracle.

Nothing. "It didn't work that time either," Cunningham said with a laugh. "But thanks anyway, Max."

"Okay," Max said, undaunted. "I'll tell you what I'll do. I'll treat you for your show. I'll take care of you and you'll do a great performance."

I went to see Cunningham's show. Max gave him the promised injection just before the show and then came out front to sit with me. I loved watching Cunningham; he was a marvelous performer. But the minute he walked out I could tell something was wrong. He was sweating even before he began to sing. His timing was off and I recognized the twitches and uncontrolled movements of someone who had taken too much meth.

"How was he?" Max asked after the show was over and Cunningham had left the stage.

"Terrible," I said. "I've never seen him give a bad performance before."

"Oops," Max said. "I guess I missed that time."

I hurried up to Cunningham's suite without Max. I had

never heard Cunningham so much as raise his voice in anger. That night, he was in a rage, frantically trying to get Bobby Kennedy on the phone. "I'm going to have that bastard prosecuted," he screamed at me and everyone else in the room. "I'm going to have his license taken away!"

I went back down to Max. "How is Jimmy?" he asked. "Does he want to see me?"

"Max," I said, "I don't think you ought to come up right away. As a matter of fact, I don't think you ought to come up at all."

I said "Sure" when Frank Sinatra asked me to appear at Cal-Neva Lodge in Lake Tahoe, Nevada, a hotel and casino in which he had an interest. Skinny D'Amato, the owner of the 500 Club in Atlantic City and a very close friend of Sinatra's, was running Cal-Neva. He was also a good friend of mine. I loved Skinny. He treated me like royalty whenever I played his club. I couldn't refuse Frank or Skinny anything.

Milton was very annoyed. Cal-Neva wasn't part of his master plan. He was extremely proud of the half-million-dollar deal he was putting together with Harrah's, also in Lake Tahoe, which could go right out the window. And there was no comparison between Cal-Neva and the elegant, well-run Harrah's, the most prestigious and profitable casino-hotel in the world. I was unhappy about being paid a lot less than half of what I could get at Harrah's, but I was doing a favor for friends.

Frank was a genial host. I brought Ann-Margret and her parents up for the opening, which was around the time of my thirty-fourth birthday, and "The Voice" himself wheeled a big cake with candles right out on stage. I must have been good for business, because the same day I left, I got a call from Frank. Somehow he tracked me down at La Scala in Los Angeles, where I was just about to have dinner, and told me in a hoarse whisper that he had lost his voice. Would I do him another favor and come back to Cal-Neva? I went.

Frank put me up in the bungalow next to his. Every day I looked over the fence to find out if he wanted me to sing that night, and every day he nodded his head and pointed to his throat. By Saturday night, however, Frank's voice had recovered, but he asked me to come to the first show anyway and sit with his mother. At the last minute, I changed my mind.

I felt tired and called Frank's valet, George Jacobs, to say I wouldn't come to the first show, but would be there for the second. I was just climbing into bed when there was an enormous explosion on the roof—then another, just outside the door. Frank was throwing cherry bombs at the bungalow. It was a little prank, a charming way to tell me he wanted me to be at the first show. I got the message and went.

A few months later, while I was singing at the Latin Casino, I got another call from Frank. It was the day Marilyn Monroe was found dead and he was very upset. Then he again asked for a favor: he was tied up making a movie and wanted me to open for him at a club called the Villa Venice, outside Chicago. "Frank, I can't do it," I said. "I've been working too hard. I'm too tired to go to Chicago." That wasn't good enough for Sinatra. He persisted until I said, "All right. But I'm supposed to go back to the Desert Inn after I close at the Winter Garden. If you can get me out of that, I'll come to Chicago."

"Okay," Frank said.

I thought I had the perfect excuse. Among his other business ventures, Sinatra owned a piece of the Sands Hotel in Las Vegas, one of the Desert Inn's chief competitors, and I was certain there was no way the Desert Inn would let me go. But somehow Frank arranged it, and now I had to go to Chicago.

The Villa Venice had a checkered history. In the thirties and forties, it had been called Papa Bouchet's and featured gambling and prostitution among its attractions. In the fifties, it became a restaurant and a favored hangout for Chicago hoods because of its remote location. And in the sixties, it was sold and turned into a nightclub. The place was still being redecorated, and the kitchen wasn't even finished, the night Joey Forman and I opened there. But a couple of blocks away, an illegal gambling operation, housed in a Quonset hut, was ready for business.

Joey began the show with his comedy act, including a routine about the Mafia, based on the television series *The Untouchables*. The many men in the audience wearing sharkskin suits were not amused, and Johnny Roselli, who was sitting next to Joey's wife, Janine, leaned over and whispered in her ear, "I think you should tell Joey to cut out that bit." With the exception of that small lapse of taste, the opening was a great success, which seemed to please one man in particular. He had been introduced to me as Dr. Goldberg, and after he appointed a guy called "Big Joe" to be my chef and "Big John" to be my bodyguard, I realized he was a very important part of the operation.

I was staying at the Ambassador East with Bunny, who was acting as my road manager and real bodyguard. No one was allowed to disturb me in the morning, so one day when a caller asked to see me at nine o'clock, Bunny put him off until three. Then at about five minutes to three, he walked into my bedroom and woke me. "Somebody's coming to see you," he said.

"Who?" I said.

"The FBI."

Suddenly I was wide awake. "What does the FBI want to see me about? I haven't done anything."

"I don't know," Bunny replied. "He didn't say."

I just had time to put on a robe and slippers before *three* FBI agents entered my suite, dressed in business suits, white shirts, and felt hats. I was fascinated by them, and curious to know why they wanted to talk to me. My only previous contact with the FBI had occurred at a dinner for President Eisenhower, where their boss, J. Edgar Hoover, had called me over to his table and told me what a fine young American I was. Maybe he had changed his mind.

The three agents removed their hats and started asking me questions. "Do you know Momo Giancana?" one of them said.

"No."

"Do you know Sam Giancana?" another one asked.

"No."

"Do you know Sam Mooney?" the third one said.

"Never heard of him."

"Do you know Dr. Goldberg?"

That was a name I recognized. "Sure," I said.

"How well do you know him?"

"Just from the club where I'm working, the Villa Venice. I've had dinner with him and his friends. That's all I know about him, except I gather he's the boss."

"He's the boss, all right," one of the agents said. "Dr. Goldberg is Sam Giancana, Mr. Fisher, a very notorious underworld figure. Haven't you been reading the articles about him in the Chicago paper?"

"No, I really haven't had the time," I said.

"I can recommend these articles. And when you read them, you'll understand why we're interested to know what you're doing at the Villa Venice."

"I can tell you that," I said. "I'm there because a friend asked me to do him a favor."

"And you know nothing about Sam Giancana and his business activities?"

"If I could help you, I would. But I really don't."

The agents picked up their hats and started to leave. "You know, Eddie," one of them said, "we don't want to get on a soap box, but there may come a time in your life when you'll need us."

It wasn't a threat. I think they knew I was telling the truth. They thanked me for my time and left, and that night, at the Villa Venice, I told Big Joe that the FBI had paid me a visit. He didn't say anything. Neither did "Dr. Goldberg," but after that I started calling him Sam.

Giancana and I became friends. He was a small man who was known to have a vicious temper and a foul mouth, but I never saw that side of his character. Warm, generous, funny, he seemed more concerned about my reputation than his. When I asked him to take me to the Quonset hut to do a little gambling, he said, "Forget about it. Stay away. You don't need it." And he trusted me. He was then involved briefly with Judy Campbell, a very beautiful woman, and if Giancana was busy, Judy and I sometimes went out together, accompanied by the usual bodyguard, but he wasn't there to protect her from me.

One night I took Judy to a party at Hugh Hefner's Playboy mansion. It was an incredible place, a male fantasy that Heff had made real for himself and his friends. His parties could only be described as "bashes" and I was invited to the mansion as his special guest whenever I was in Chicago. We became good friends. But the night I went with Judy, I felt I couldn't partake of all the pleasures that were provided. I learned later that Judy had been one of Jack Kennedy's girlfriends, a relationship that was terminated abruptly the moment he was told of her association with Giancana. Judy and I became more than just friends after she and Giancana broke up. She was quite a wonderful woman.

Sammy, Dean, and Frank himself followed me into the Villa Venice, all within a few weeks. Debbie and Dinah were also scheduled to appear, but they didn't make it. The Quonset and the club suddenly closed. I never found out why. I was paid next to nothing and even got stuck with a huge hotel bill at the Ambassador East. Doing favors for friends could be very expensive.

I grew up with Judy Garland, just like every other kid who went to her movies in the late thirties and forties. I always wanted to sing the way she sang—from the heart. Judy gave everything she had to her audiences and they loved her for it. I loved her too, but we never met until early in 1954, when Debbie and I were engaged and trying to find our way to a party at Louella Parsons' house. Somehow we ended up on Mapleton Drive in Holmby Hills instead of Maple Drive in Beverly Hills, and the first house we went to belonged to Humphrey Bogart and Lauren Bacall. They invited us in and we made a phone call, but then we got lost again and wound up at Judy's. Her husband, Sid Luft, met us at the door. He and Judy were invited to the same party and we all decided to go together, as soon as she was ready. Waiting for Judy Garland to get dressed was an experience I'll never forget. It took forever, and after she finally appeared, we just sat down and talked. We didn't get to Louella's until well after midnight. Judy had been nominated for the Oscar for *A Star is Born,* but she was convinced that Grace Kelly, who had been nominated for *The Country Girl,* would win the award. I felt sure she was wrong and told her so. As it turned out, Judy was right. She lost.

Judy's name was often mentioned as a possible guest star on *The Chesterfield Supper Club* but there were always objections. She was too unpredictable, too self-indulgent. So we never had a chance to sing together, and the next time I saw Judy was in New York, where she was performing at the old Metropolitan Opera House. Elizabeth and I had just been married and were on our way to Europe for our honeymoon. We sat in the first row, right behind Gordon Jenkins, who was conducting in the huge orchestra pit, racing back and forth, waving his arms, trying desperately to draw a performance out of Judy. I don't know whether she had been drinking or had some other problem, but she just wasn't herself. The audience didn't seem to mind. In those days, Judy's fans still loved her no matter what she did.

We met again in Lake Tahoe in 1962, after Elizabeth and

I had parted company and I was appearing at Cal-Neva. Judy, who had just finished an engagement at Harrah's, came to see my act and got up on stage with me. I was singing with Judy Garland at last, and it was magic. Judy's career was going well at that point: she was about to start her television series and I knew she wanted me to appear on the show. But I had been avoiding her. There were so many stories about Judy and her troubles, and the moment I heard the word suicide mentioned in connection with anyone, I refused to get involved. It was a rule I had made. But that night Judy was in great shape and we hit it off as if we had always been friends.

A couple of nights later, we had a date. I picked Judy up at Harrah's and brought her back to Cal-Neva for a little gambling. She was just drinking wine and when she went to the ladies' room, I thought nothing more about it until someone tapped me on the shoulder and said, "Come quick. Judy's passed out in the john." Obviously she had started drinking long before I picked her up, but she came to and I took her to Sinatra's bungalow, which wasn't being used at the time. As I was putting her to bed, she asked for Seconal—three grains—and I looked at her in surprise. Half that amount was the usual strength and would have been enough to knock me out for eight solid hours.

I had no idea where to find a three-grain Seconal at that late hour. I asked the security guard and everyone else I met back at the lodge, until finally Arturo, the maître d', located one. I gave it to Judy, and as soon as she swallowed it, she became a different person. She didn't fall asleep; she woke up and suddenly she was all together again, sweet and bright and funny—the Judy Garland I had secretly been in love with for years. We spent the night together in the bungalow.

Back in Los Angeles, we began to see quite a lot of each other. Judy was such fun to be with. She told marvelous stories and her imitations of people we both knew were devastating. She had so much love to give, so many people loved her in return, but for Judy that was never enough. I thought of our affair as just a beautiful friendship; Judy wanted much more than that and became very demanding and possessive. We talked for hours over the phone, and when she started screaming at me, I didn't know what to do. I loved her and didn't want to hurt her, but there was no way I could be everything and everyone she asked me to be.

We drifted apart gradually and didn't meet again until I was playing at the Villa Venice in Chicago and Judy was in town to give a concert. She lost her voice in rehearsal but went on anyway and it was a disaster. Then later that same evening, she came to see my second show and again got up on stage with me. Even though she had been drinking and could barely sing above a whisper, she was someone very special to me—and everyone else. The audience cheered. She was Judy Garland.

We were both staying at the Ambassador East and I took her up in the elevator to her floor. "Aren't you going to come in and listen to some music?" Judy asked.

"I'd love to," I said, "but I'm really tired and I've got two shows tomorrow."

I kissed her good night, went down to my suite, and was climbing into bed when the phone rang. It was Judy, again asking me to come up, and again I said no. After two more calls, I finally said, "Judy, why don't we have lunch tomorrow? That way we can both get a good night's sleep."

"Okay," she said. "What time?"

"How about twelve o'clock?"

The phone woke me the next day. Bunny answered it and I heard Judy's voice, clear as a bell, cursing me out: "Who the hell does he think he is? How dare he stand me up for lunch?" I looked at my watch. It was after one. I tiptoed out of my bedroom to listen. Bunny was trying to explain that I hadn't left him a message to wake me up, which was true, and I was still asleep, which wasn't. But he couldn't get a word in edgewise, and Judy's vocabulary made him blush. I didn't dare talk to her, and a few minutes after she had slammed down the receiver, room service wheeled in a table with lobster and wine, everything specially prepared by the hotel chef. There was a note: "Thanks for lunch." Even when she had been rejected, Judy had style.

We saw each other off and on after that, just as friends. She came to parties at my house in Beverly Hills, full of jokes and fun, and once she invited me for an evening of poker with some of her other friends. Mia Farrow came with me to the little house in Brentwood where Judy was living all by herself. For Judy, that house was quite a comedown, and at one point she went upstairs and returned waving a hundred-dollar bill. "This is all I've got left in the world," she said. We never got around to poker at all. Judy played recordings of songs by new, young composers she had discovered in England and wanted to sing herself. No matter what shape she was in, her whole life was her music.

Occasionally I saw Judy in New York too, where she was trying to cut down on her drinking and sipped liebfraumilch from a bottle wrapped in a brown paper bag. And when I gave my house in Beverly Hills to Tony Bennett for three weeks, I heard that she was up there almost every night, singing with Tony and all the other musicians who gathered there. We met for the last time at a party at my house. Judy was on her way to Mexico City the next day for an engagement and begged me to come with her. She thought it would be a wonderful idea if we appeared together. No rehearsals; we would just get up on stage and sing. "Sure, Judy," I said. "I'll be there." I knew, of course, that all she really wanted was someone to go with her. She didn't want to be alone.

Judy's death in London in 1969 came as no real surprise to me. She had always been a "cliffhanger." But I was terribly sad and deeply shocked by the way English audiences treated her toward the end. They had always loved Judy more than any other American star, yet they threw tomatoes at her during some of her final performances. Then a few years after her death, I saw a beautiful young woman sitting by the pool at the Beverly Hills Hotel. I just stared; there was something so hauntingly familiar about her, but I had no idea who she was until the pool boy brought me a note: "Dear Eddie. My name is Lorna Luft and I remember the Teddy bear you gave me and the long conversations you had with my mother." Judy's other daughter, Liza Minnelli, told me the same thing one night at Arthur, the disco in New York. "I always listened in on the extension," she said to tease me, and I laughed. I had all but forgotten those telephone calls, but I could not, and will not, ever forget Judy.

Esquire magazine, in its first issue of 1963, elected me "Bachelor of the Year," which was about as appropriate as the "Father of the Year" award I won when Debbie and I had Carrie. After months of separation, Elizabeth and I were still married, and while an equitable financial settlement was part of the problem, the chief obstacle to our divorce was Elizabeth's adamant refusal to let me have anything to do with Liza and

Maria, whom I had legally adopted. This wasn't my first experience with a custody case; Debbie had made it very difficult for me to see Carrie and Todd, and I was determined not to let Elizabeth cut Liza and Maria out of my life. I had done nothing to deserve that and told my attorneys I would fight for my rights as their father.

Elizabeth wouldn't budge an inch and neither would I. Then one day, out of the blue, I got a call from Frank Sinatra, who told me to stop "harassing" Elizabeth and forget about Liza and Maria. Livid with anger, I couldn't believe that Elizabeth would ask Sinatra to make that call, although I found out later that she had. I was furious at him for getting involved.

A few weeks later, in April 1963, Frank was the MC of the Academy Awards telecast. I had been asked to sing and worked for four solid weeks with Colin Romoff, preparing an eight-minute medley of Oscar-winning songs. It was a smash. I got a standing ovation, and Sinatra, who kept shouting "Wow" into the microphone, couldn't stop the applause. Finally, I went over and kissed him, and after that night he started calling me "Singer." From Sinatra that was high praise, and I had to forgive him.

At the party after the show at the Beverly Hilton, Hedda Hopper came up with tears in her eyes and said, "Oh, Eddie, when I heard you sing 'The Last Time I Saw Paris,' I could tell you were thinking of Elizabeth. Now I know how much you loved her and I forgive you for everything."

As a matter of fact, I wasn't thinking of Elizabeth at all. And forgive me for what? I wondered. If anything, Hedda should have asked me to forgive her, for the many vicious lies she had written about Elizabeth and me.

Some time later, she invited me to her house for a drink. I didn't want to go, but I was curious to know what Hedda Hopper was up to now. She opened a bottle of champagne and became very chummy. And then she got down to business. In her recent book, she had written that Michael Wilding was homosexual, and he was suing her for libel. Because I had been married to Elizabeth, Hedda thought I would know all about Wilding and would testify against him to support her claim. She was wrong on both counts. Wilding won his suit.

A lot of people were eager to capitalize on my relationship with Elizabeth. I was offered a million dollars to write a book about our marriage, which I declined. And a lot of people seemed to think I needed sympathy for becoming involved with a woman like Elizabeth in the first place. "Marrying her," Ralph Pearl wrote, "is like trying to flag down the 20th Century Limited with a Zippo lighter." Even Debbie offered me some advice. I tried to see Carrie and Todd as often as I could, and usually Debbie made a point of avoiding me. But one day she was there and we began to talk, first about the children, and then the conversation drifted into the things that had happened in our own lives. We spoke of Elizabeth, of course, and Debbie said, "Why did you have to marry her, Eddie? Why didn't you just have an affair? I would have waited for you."

She still didn't understand. "Debbie," I said, "I was in love with Elizabeth."

19

I was a pursuer. Once attracted to a woman, I went after her, turning on the charm, singing songs to her, showering her with presents. I was still a nice guy, always the gentleman, but I could be very persistent. Sometimes, of course, nothing worked; sometimes I was just lucky—so lucky that there were many women I had never even met who claimed they had been to bed with me. Because I was a Hollywood bachelor, rich, a "star," a lot of women pursued me. Some thought it would be a mark of distinction to become involved with the man who had once been married to Elizabeth Taylor. But I was a one-woman man, one at a time at least. I preferred to do my own pursuing, and when I was in love, I was king. For me, there was only one thing comparable to the love of an audience: the love of a woman. And I had to have both. In fact, I began to think I performed well only if I was in love. The exhilaration, the sadness, the self-confidence, the uncertainty I felt—the emotional highs and lows of love—somehow made my songs more meaningful. Love was a drug, like Max Jacobson's shots, that I was growing to depend upon. But still wary of the kind of love that implied commitment, I settled for *being* in love. And if something went wrong and those special feelings faded, I was soon looking around for another fix.

Bob Evans and I had been friends ever since the days when we were both not much more than eighteen and I was just getting started in New York. Stiff and formal, always very conservatively dressed, and apt to come up with phrases like "How do you do, gentlemen," he struck me as funny and a bit affected. But I liked him, and with the possible exception of money, which he already had, he admired all the things that came with my success. It wasn't long before he figured out how to get them for himself. He was in the family clothing business for a while, and once, just after Elizabeth and I were married, he sent her more than a hundred pairs of slacks. Then he left New York for Hollywood, and through his relationship with Norma Shearer began to get acting parts in the movies, including a role as Irving Thalberg, Norma Shearer's late husband. He was on his way.

Kurt Frings was Evans's agent and one day we were invited to lunch at his brownstone in New York. "You're going to meet a girl there today," Kurt announced, "and you're going to fall in love with her because she's the most beautiful girl I've ever seen." That didn't surprise me. Evans went out with a lot of pretty girls. Kurt and I had once talked him into marrying one. She was beautiful, very talented—and very young. "The perfect girl for you," we told him. We were kidding, of course, but he took us seriously and their marriage lasted about three weeks.

Usually Kurt was a great exaggerator; this time he spoke the truth. One look at the girl at Evans's house and my jaw dropped. She was more beautiful than Elizabeth. Blond, about twenty-three, although she looked much older, she was a German model who had become famous for posing with a black cat in a series of ads for Smirnoff vodka. Her name was Renata Boeck and I was hooked. The trouble was she hardly spoke English and all I had a chance to say to her was hello and goodbye.

I saw her again in Miami Beach in May of 1963. I was playing at the Eden Roc, she came to my opening with Evans, and a while later a whole crowd of us went out together on a chartered yacht. There the pursuit began. I found Renata alone, sat down beside her, and started to talk. She was very shy, apart from her difficulty with the language, and when I told her I wanted to go out with her, she said simply, "But why?"

Hoping I wasn't making a complete fool of myself, I tried to answer that question. My persistence paid off and she finally agreed to have some sort of date with me after she returned from a modeling job in Nassau.

Then I got a call from Evans. "What are you doing?" he said. "Renata's with me."

"I know that," I said. "All I did was ask her for a date sometime later on."

"You're wasting your time," Evans said.

"Maybe," I replied.

"All right, then, let's have a duel."

"A duel," I said. "You've got to be kidding."

"Well, may the best man win," he said, and hung up.

I just laughed. A remark like that was typical of Evans, old-fashioned and slightly stuffy.

It wasn't my usual practice to move in on the girl friends of friends. On the contrary, my friends often came to me with their love problems and if there was anything I could do to help them stay together with their wives or girl friends—or smooth out a separation—I did it. But Renata was special and we had our date in New York when, a few weeks later, I was playing at the Americana. I forget where we went or what we did, but by the time the evening was over, lightning struck and we both fell head over heels in love. She told Evans, and the next thing I knew, he came looking for me at the Americana. Fortunately I wasn't there. An irate rival was a new experience for me, and the best way to handle it, I decided, was to call Evans and have a talk. "Look, I'm sorry," I said, "but these things happen. We're in love."

"How could you do this to me?" Evans cried. *"I'm* in love with her."

"Well," I replied, "you said, 'May the best man win,' whatever that means."

There matters stood until a day or so later, when Renata was supposed to meet me at the Americana and didn't show up. Evans had taken her to an apartment somewhere in New York, along with her two dogs and a blind cat.

I called him again. "This is getting pretty silly," I said. "What have you done with Renata?"

"Never mind," he said. "She doesn't love you and you'll never see her again."

"Don't you think she should be the one to decide that?"

"All right," he said. "Let's talk. I'll meet you on Fifth Avenue and we'll discuss it."

Was he again going to suggest a duel? I could just see the headlines: "Singer Slain on Fifth Avenue." That's not the way I wanted to go, so I brought along a second—Willard Higgins, who was working for me again as my valet. "Don't let me out of your sight," I told him.

Evans and I met right in the middle of the sidewalk somewhere in the sixties at about three in the morning, after my last show. Willard was half a block behind me, trying to look inconspicuous. The whole thing was so absurd that I was tempted to laugh, but Evans was serious. "Look, Bob," I said. "You're a smart guy. You just can't hide Renata."

"I'll tell you what let's do," he said. "We'll let a jury decide. Whatever a jury says, we'll abide by."

"Who's going to be on the jury?" I asked, still refusing to take him seriously. Evans suggested a few prominent Hollywood lawyers and gin players, and I said, "That's okay with me, just as long as you let her go."

"No, I've got a better idea," he said. "Let's send her to Europe, and you're not to talk to her on the telephone, because I know how you are on the telephone."

I thought he was completely crazy, but by that time I was ready to agree to anything. "Okay," I said, "we'll send her to Europe."

Renata took matters into her own hands. She managed to leave New York and no one knew where she was until she called me, a couple of days later. She had fled to Los Angeles with her pets and was staying with Evans's lawyer. "I just had to get away from all that craziness," she told me, but she wanted to see me again.

My next engagement was at the Desert Inn in Las Vegas, and Renata said she would call me as soon as I got there. I arrived three days before my opening in order to have time to rehearse, but I couldn't keep my mind on business until I heard from her. Two days went by; still no word. Finally, she called. "You must come to Los Angeles," she said.

"Renata, I open tomorrow night," I said. How could she ask me to do that? She just didn't understand what an opening meant. New things were going into the act. I couldn't leave now. But I did. Renata met me at the airport, we spent the rest of that day and night together at my house on Gloaming Way, and flew back to Las Vegas the next day. That night I went on stage without an hour of real rehearsal. What difference did it make? I never sounded better. I was in love.

I had one of Howard Hughes's penthouses at the Desert Inn, with Wilbur Clark, a most respected citizen of Las Vegas and a man who had helped put the town on the map, right next door in the other. But I rented a bungalow at The Tally Ho with a private pool, right next to the golf course, at a hundred dollars a day, for Renata, her two dogs, and the blind cat. I adored watching her romp with her pets around the golf course, but when they started climbing all over me, I rented the bungalow next door, at another hundred dollars a day, just for them. A few days later we moved back to the penthouse apartments at the Desert Inn, pets and all. And the night Renata asked if she could bring them down to my dressing room, I said, "Sure, why not?" I was so much in love I didn't care if she brought them on stage. I forgot that animals shed, and right in the middle of my act that night, I looked down at my suit. It was covered with hair.

I taught Renata how to play craps. She was a fast learner, betting at first with the vigorish—five, ten, twenty-five dollars at a time—while I bet the limit, which was over $7,000 every roll of the dice. I was a high roller and she was my partner. If I won $10,000, she won $5,000; if I lost $10,000, she lost nothing. The perfect partnership. We gambled every night and every night Renata brought the money she had won up to the penthouse and counted it—many, many thousands of dollars stacked in neat little piles. I didn't care how much she won, or how much I lost; I was enraptured by her. Nothing else mattered, not even her pets, until the night she said to me, "Darling, could I have ten dollars for the vigorish?" It was as if somebody had stuck a knife in my stomach. By that time, Renata had stashed away a small fortune, and asking for that ten dollars was the end. Love flew out the window. Our affair was over. She went back to Los Angeles with her winnings and later used at least some of the money to build her mother a house in Hamburg.

We met again about a year later at the Democratic National Convention in Atlantic City. Renata was there with Jim Aubrey, the head of CBS Television, and she slipped a note under my hotel room door, asking me to meet her on the roof. I ignored it. Bob Evans had forgotten about her long before. I imagine that Sidney Korshak, who was a friend of Evans and of mine, had acted as an intermediary in our feud. Evans found other women, just as I did. He moved from his career as an actor into the production end of films, and our paths would cross again at Paramount years later when he was finally in a good position to have the last laugh.

Stephanie Powers, whom I met at the Daisy, a disco in Beverly Hills, replaced Renata in my affections. Not just a pretty girl, she was a very bright and talented actress. We respected each other, and my relationship with Stephanie was more mature than some of the others. She used to come to see me in Las Vegas, chaperoned by her mother, and when Mrs. Powers excused herself to go to bed, she would smile and say to me, "Now take care of my little girl." Like most of the mothers of the girls I went out with, Mrs. Powers was genuinely fond of me. I always courted them as well as their daughters, which was probably not the way they were usually treated.

Stephanie was very serious about her career, so serious that she was literally starving herself to achieve the thin, hollow-cheeked look that Hollywood seemed to favor. Her figure was perfect as far as I was concerned, and I protested when she began to waste away before my eyes. But she wouldn't listen to me, and as her flesh disappeared, so did my affection. I admired both her and her ambition, even if I couldn't compete with it, and after our romance cooled we became good friends.

I often found myself in that peculiar male bind, particularly with the young actresses I knew. If they were more interested in their careers than in me, that bothered me. But if a girl said she was willing to give up everything just to be with me, that bothered me too. Pamela Turnure wasn't an actress, nor was she a girl. An attractive, intelligent, and poised young woman, she was about twenty-seven when we met at various Kennedy parties and fund-raisers, and she had a career, a very important one, as Jacqueline Kennedy's press secretary. We started going around together; I took her to theaters and nightclubs in New York and we saw each other frequently at her house in George-town. Pam was different from any woman I had ever known, and with her I broke all my usual patterns. I wasn't smitten at first sight; there was no mad romantic pursuit. I don't know how it happened, really. We just fell in love.

Somewhere in the back of my head, I had a picture of the woman I thought I wanted to marry, and Pam came very close to that ideal. Everyone I knew thought I should marry her too, including Jacqueline Kennedy's brother-in-law, Prince Radziwill, whom I had met because he was a patient of Max Jacobson's. Jennie Grossinger adored her. I took Pam to Miami Beach when I was singing at the Eden Roc and we went to see Jennie at her home there. Jennie, who knew more than my own mother about the kind of women I usually went out with, and married, this time really approved of my choice.

Pam even got a nod of approval from Sam Giancana. We were sitting in the balcony at the Copacabana one night, watching Sammy Davis, Jr., when a stranger tapped me on the shoulder and said that Dr. Goldberg wanted to see me. I got up and followed him out to a limousine, which took me to a nearby Italian restaurant. There was Sam and we talked for a few minutes about Judy Campbell, who was having financial troubles. I was concerned, but Sam said, "Don't worry, I'm taking care of it."

I had to get back to the Copa and asked Sam to come with me. "I want you to meet someone."

"Who?"

"Pamela Turnure. Do you know who she is?"

He didn't, so I explained and asked him, please, not to come on too strong.

We returned to the Copa and I introduced Sam as Dr. Goldberg. He sat down next to Pam, and ignoring everything I had said, started teasing her. "You know," he remarked, "there are bad guys and good guys in this world, and a nice young lady like you should be very careful about the company she keeps."

I nearly choked, but Pam laughed. Even if she had known who Dr. Goldberg was, she probably thought he meant me. Then, as Sam got up to leave, he whispered in my ear, "That dame has got a lot of class."

I agreed. Pam and I had wonderful times together. Always so cool and dignified on her job, she felt she could be just herself with me. "Please don't make me go home," she said once while we were in California.

"But you'll lose your job."

"No, I won't. I just want to be with you. I won't bother you."

I was flattered, of course, but embarrassed. And at the same time I had that nagging feeling that maybe I was getting too involved. What the hell was the matter with me? Here I was in love with a marvelous woman, she was in love with me, and still I was wary.

I didn't make her go home. Pam came with me to New York, where I was recording my *Tonight* album, a collection of show tunes, and we went everywhere together. She even came to the recording studio and sat there taking notes on how things were being done. Then it happened. I brought both Pam and Prince Radziwill to the studio one evening for a final session, and it was late and we were all very tired even before we left to meet some friends at Shepheard's. The prince had been drinking at the studio and drank even more at the restaurant. Everyone was drinking a lot, including Pam, who started saying things she would not have said otherwise. I was really jolted when she remarked, "if we don't stay together, Eddie, I think I'm going to die."

I didn't know what prompted Pam to say that; I didn't know whether she was kidding or meant it seriously. And I didn't call her the next day, or the day after that, to find out. Pam didn't call me either, and within the next few weeks she returned every gift I had ever given her—a unique experience in my relationships with women.

I could have been more careful about the women I pursued, and where. In Innsbruck, as entertainment director for the 1964 United States Winter Olympic Team, I presented a show at the Olympic Village, which was taped as a television special, and Kurt Frings introduced me to a beautiful young woman I had seen at some of the rehearsals. She was an actress—Eva—and Kurt told me he was thinking of taking her to Hollywood and making her a star. The moment I met Eva, I had other thoughts in mind, which I had to express in Yiddish because she understood very little English. Eva was returning to Munich for the end of carnival season and I wanted to come with her, but she said no. She had to go back with the friends who had brought her, or it wouldn't look right. Then I said I would come anyway and Eva agreed to meet me at the masked ball at the Vier Jahreszeiten Hotel.

It was all so ridiculously romantic—the snow that blanketed Munich when Kurt and I arrived, the parades and street dancers of the carnival, the prospect of meeting a beautiful woman at a masked ball. Kurt and I wore dinner jackets that night, but everyone else was in costume and I looked in vain for Eva. Then someone announced that I was there, I was asked to sing, and after a rousing rendition of "Oh! My Pa-Pa," a group of young Germans carried me around the ballroom on their shoulders. Eva couldn't miss that, and we finally found each other.

Kurt and I invited her and several other people up to our suite for a party. It was very late when Eva said she had to go home, and I offered to go with her. I forgot that I had taken off my shoes, and with Eva on my arm, I walked out in the snow, wearing only socks and a pair of bedroom slippers. We took a cab to her apartment and Eva asked in German if I would like to come up for a cup of coffee. *"Ja,"* I said, hoping I didn't sound too eager.

We couldn't have been in the apartment for more than three or four minutes, just time enough for me to take off my coat and dinner jacket, when I heard a key turn in the lock. And there standing in the doorway was the biggest man I've ever seen, a giant. Both Eva and I jumped up as he entered the room. But he didn't even look at me. He strode over to Eva, snarling, *"Nicht in mein Haus,"* and hit her brutally in the eye. She fell to the floor, struck her head on the edge of a coffee table, and began to bleed profusely. He picked her up, yelled, *"Hier ist dein Hollywood!"* and smashed his fist into her other eye. Her face was unrecognizable as she again crumpled to the floor, screaming, "Eddie, Eddie!"

I just stood there, petrified, waiting my turn. I remember thinking that it was lucky I had brought along my extra set of caps, because this monster was going to knock out every tooth in my head. Then I realized I had to get help. But where? I grabbed my dinner jacket and coat, raced out of the apartment, and ran through the snow all the way back to the hotel in my bedroom slippers.

Kurt was sound asleep in our suite. "We've got to do something," I cried, shaking him awake. "Call the police. I just saw a man kill Eva!"

He didn't believe me, but I refused to let him go back to sleep, so he got up and found the number of Eva's apartment in his address book. "Call her," he said, "and you'll see she's all right."

I called but there was no answer, and now I was convinced that Eva was dead. Kurt took the phone and called someone

else; apparently he knew quite a lot about Eva's private life.
Whoever it was called back a few moments later and said Eva
was fine. She had gone to the country to visit her father.

That sounded pretty phony to me. If Eva wasn't dead, she
was certainly in a hospital, and I told Kurt I couldn't leave
Munich until I knew she was all right. For two days I called
her apartment again and again, and there was still no answer.
Finally I had to leave for Paris and called one last time from
the airport. Eva answered the phone. She sounded very weak,
and even though I couldn't understand what she said, at least
she was alive. Kurt didn't bring her to Hollywood and I never
saw her again.

My affair with Maria Schell had a much happier ending.
She was appearing in a play in Paris and I went backstage to
congratulate her on her performance. Although I had spoken
to Maria many times on the phone after I left Rome, we had
not seen each other since Elizabeth and I went to her home
outside Munich to adopt little Maria. We had so much to talk
about. Maria showed me pictures of her own beautiful baby,
but she had just divorced her husband and seemed rather sad
and lonely. We went to a Russian restaurant Elizabeth and I
used to frequent, violinists were playing in the background,
and I told Maria I could stay in Paris only a very few days.
We decided to spend them together.

Eva and Munich had been a shattering experience. No more
foreign actresses in foreign cities for me. But Maria and Paris
were a romantic combination impossible to resist. Even though
we both knew our affair had to end, love was worth it, however
long it lasted. When it was time for me to go, Maria gave me
a beautiful icon as a parting gift and drove me to the airport
for a tender farewell. We didn't meet again until more than
ten years later, at a party at Kurt's house in Beverly Hills.
"Oh, Eddie," Maria cried the moment she saw me. We kissed
and then she announced to everyone in the room, "We had the
most wonderful, the most marvelous love affair!"

I thanked her for that. Maria was one of the very few women
who had something nice to say about me after our romance
was over.

The women I was attracted to had to be beautiful; it was
necessary for my ego, I suppose. In many ways, I was still a

kid—eager but shy and a little unsure of myself. No matter how smooth and amusing I tried to be, I was vulnerable, very much in awe of women, and devastated if a relationship didn't work out. With all my experience, I had never become jaded. There was always some new surprise.

Nathalie Delon, the wife of France's leading romantic actor, Alain Delon, caught me completely by surprise. I had known Alain for many years; we met in Europe and I gave him a party when he first came to Hollywood. Later I spoke to him and his manager about playing opposite Elizabeth in *The Gouffé Case*. Now he was back in Hollywood to make a Western with Dean Martin and I gave him another party. He walked in with Nathalie on his arm. She reminded me of Julie Christie, and the moment I saw them, I thought they were the perfect couple. They were *both* beautiful.

We became friends and went as a threesome to the Daisy and private clubs and parties all over town. Nathalie was a marvelous woman; her charm, her style, her French accent, her sense of humor—everything about her was enchanting. We teased each other and played little games, but I didn't think of her romantically in any way. How could I? As Alain's wife, she was untouchable. I tried to play by the rules. She and a girl friend often came to my house after horseback riding and scampered up the ladder that led to the sauna I had built in the attic. Max Lerner, who had remained a friend of mine in spite of his romantic notions about Elizabeth, was my houseguest at the time, and he could hardly speak when he saw them. "Forget it," I said. "They're both married."

Nathalie and Alain seemed happy to me. They argued and fought a lot, just like any man and wife, but as far as I knew, their relationship was a very good one, although Alain once told me, "I can't be married, Eddie. I must have at least six different women in my life." I wondered how Nathalie handled that, but thought no more about it until Kurt Frings called me one day and said she wanted to talk to me alone. I said, "Fine. Have her come up to the house." She was already there, standing by the pool, when I got back from wherever I had gone. We kissed, as friends do, and then she said, "Thank you for letting me come. I am in love with you, Eddie."

I was shocked. A breathtakingly beautiful woman had just told me she loved me: what was I supposed to say? I didn't dare ask her why. And if I thought it would be very easy for me to fall in love with her too, I didn't dare do that either. She was married to my friend.

All three of us kept going out together. If Alain wandered away to flirt with another woman, Nathalie and I would sit by ourselves, our eyes would meet, and my heart would start to pound, but nothing more was said about how she felt—and how I was beginning to feel. Then one night, as we were all playing pool at Dean Martin's house, Nathalie asked me to take her to see Alain's picture *Purple Noon,* which was playing at some small theater. Sitting there in the dark, watching her husband up on the screen, we didn't even hold hands. It was unbelievable. Married twice, and involved in more affairs than I could remember, I was still behaving like a teenager.

I planned to go to Las Vegas to see Buddy Hackett at the Sahara, and Nathalie asked Alain if she could go with me. He didn't mind at all, but apprehensive about what people might think if we went alone, I booked four suites at the Sahara, one for Joey Forman and his wife, Janine, who was also French, one for me, one for Nathalie, and one for another girl I brought along as my date; I can't even remember her name. We watched Buddy's show and then went over to the Sands to see Frank Sinatra and Dean Martin. Afterward all three of us got up on stage in the lounge to give an impromptu show, and I was in my glory, singing as I sang only when I was in love. Martin made a very corny pitch for Nathalie that night and I had to smile. Couldn't everyone tell that she and I were mad about each other, even if there was nothing we could do about it?

We went back to the Sahara and parted to go to our separate suites. My phone rang. "Eddie, will you come down now?" Nathalie asked.

Something like a charge of electricity went all through my body, but I said, "Nathalie, we can't do that. It wouldn't be right."

That night I didn't sleep a wink. Pacing back and forth in my room, I don't know how many times I reached for the phone and put it down again. I was a wreck when we met a few hours later to go back to Los Angeles. Nathalie was smiling. "Thank you," she said. "Of course it would have been wrong." We were so pure, so virtuous. But I wasn't sure how much longer that would last.

Nathalie suggested to Alain that they both come to my

opening at the Fontainebleau in Miami Beach. He thought it was a wonderful idea. So did I. What could happen if he was with us? We checked into the Frank Sinatra Suite at the Fontainebleau, Nathalie and Alain in a bedroom on one side and I on the other, and they came to the opening. Then, after my second show that night, Alain suddenly announced that he had to go back to Los Angeles for an interview. He was sorry, but it would only take a day and he would come right back.

Nathalie was just as surprised as I was. Or at least I think so. We had not expected to be alone and both of us tried to convince Alain to stay. We all knew he could have postponed the interview, but he insisted on going—and never returned. All our resistance crumbled and Nathalie and I had nine wonderful days and nights together. I still felt very guilty about committing a terrible sin but all my doubts dissolved in a romantic haze.

Alain met us at the airport on our return to Los Angeles— no explanations or apologies from anyone—and we started going around together again. Nathalie and I could never be alone, but whenever she came up to my house with Alain, she would scribble little notes in French—"I love you," "I want you"—in books and on album covers and napkins, anyplace where she knew I would find them. Alain picked up a book in which she had just written something, read it and gave her a very dirty look, but he didn't say a word. And that ridiculous situation lasted for a few more weeks, until Alain finished his picture and had to go back to France. All three of us were crying at the airport. Yet in a way, I was glad the whole thing was over.

It wasn't. Nathalie began calling me on the telephone, every night, every day, from Paris or Saint-Tropez or wherever she was. And she sent me love letters in English, so beautiful that I was sure she hadn't written them all by herself. She begged me to come to France and I begged her to come back to America, neither of which was possible. Then I went to New York for an engagement at the Plaza, and the afternoon before the opening, as I was rehearsing in the Persian Room, someone walked in. All I could see was a white leather suit. I couldn't tell who was wearing it until I moved out of the lights. It was Nathalie. I stopped right in the middle of a song, and we were in each other's arms.

She wore a backless dress to my opening, and just to tease

me, sat facing away from me. I played the whole show to her beautiful back. I put a lot of extra feeling into my songs that night, and during the days that followed we walked around town together, holding hands, stopping to kiss on street corners. We didn't care who saw us. It was too good to last. Alain called from France and said, "Nathalie's got to come back to me, Eddie. Put her on a plane."

"I can't do that."

"Didn't you once say you were my friend and would do anything to help me?"

"Of course I would. But I can't make Nathalie come back if she doesn't want to. She has to come back on her own."

"Then let me speak to her. Is she there?"

"No. She's down the hall."

She wasn't, but I had to say that to avoid hurting Alain's feelings even more. Quickly I took Nathalie down the hall to another suite and asked the operator to transfer the call. They spoke for over an hour and I could hear Nathalie yelling and screaming at her husband. Alain insisted that she come back, she told me tearfully after finishing the call, but she wanted to stay. I told her she had to return. There was an urgent and important reason for her to go back. She had lost custody of a child when she left her first husband to marry Alain, and she would certainly lose custody of the son she'd had with Alain if she left him. Nathalie reluctantly agreed. We spent one last night together, promising each other to find some way to meet again, and I took her to the airport the next day for another tearful farewell.

On the way back to town, I wondered why these things always happened to me. Lovers, husbands, women who cared too much, or didn't care enough—wasn't I ever going to fall in love without so many complications? Falling *out* of love was just as complicated, and almost always painful. Was I too romantic, too old-fashioned? Were my expectations for a lasting relationship totally unrealistic? Or was there something about me, a need I wasn't able to fulfill or even express? Maybe I should settle for an affair, no strings, no complications. Somewhere there had to be a woman who wanted the same thing. And then, by sheer coincidence, I found her. Walking through the lobby of the Plaza, I bumped into Connie Stevens, whom I had met in Hollywood. I knew she had just been divorced from Jim Stacy and the first thing she said to me was, "I'm never going to get married again, Eddie. I'm just going to have a relationship with a man for three months at the most. Come on, let's go have a drink."

I couldn't believe my ears. Here she was. This was the girl for me.

20

For years, many of Max Jacobson's friends, including Milton and me, had tried everything to make him respectable. But Max was his own worst enemy. He kept few if any medical records; his office and laboratory procedures were haphazard; his diagnoses and treatments bore little resemblance to standard practice. In many cases, he was a miracle worker, but a doctor like that, who numbered among his patients the President of the United States, could not escape the attention of medical authorities and the Food and Drug Administration. He was under surveillance, and whenever I heard that the FDA was about to visit his office, I made it a point to be there, as if my mere presence could lend him credibility. Milton and I attempted to get him together with the City of Hope, to give him at least one legitimate connection, and I staged a benefit evening at the Winter Garden to raise money for the Constructive Research Foundation, which supported his experiments in rejuvenation.

Who the members of that foundation were, and how the $65,000 raised that night was spent, I didn't ask. But after more than ten years as Max's patient, a few questions about his practice of medicine, and about Max himself, began to worry me. I was very pleased when he hired a woman as a medical technician. Efficient and well-trained, she was a welcome sight in that chaotic office. I was less pleased when, in Max's absence, she was left in complete charge of treating his patients. And I was horrified to discover that she mixed up her own formulas and injected herself. One day, just after giving me a shot, she got a phone call from Max, and as she spoke to him, I watched her prepare another syringe and tie a tourniquet around her arm. Then she wanted me to inject her intravenously. I couldn't do it. I had injected myself and others many times, but always in the muscles of the arms or buttocks. Never intravenously, which was a whole different ball game. More than just dangerous, that was the way junkies did it— for kicks, not for any legitimate medical purpose. She laughed at my squeamishness, finished the call, and gave herself the shot. She laughed, too, whenever I tried to warn her about getting hooked. "I can handle it," she said. She was wrong. About a year after she had vanished without a trace from Max's office, she wrote me from the hospital where she was under treatment for an addiction to drugs. Another memento from Max, a pregnancy, had been terminated by an abortion.

Max was insatiable. There were many women in his life. Once, as my guest and attending physician in San Juan while I was performing there, he said it would be nice if he could find a little "entertainment." I was in his suite at the El San Juan when three hookers arrived. He was on the telephone to his office in New York, talking to one of his nurses, specifying the ingredients of the injection he wanted her to give a patient. "No, no, you idiot," he said. "One and a half cc of dextromethamphetamine and one-half cc of procaine." He looked up at the girls. "Take off your clothes and lie down," he said with a wave of his hand. "I'll take care of you in a minute." Then he went back to his phone call.

My "god" was all too human. And not everyone thought he was a medical magician. He was sued by the family of a patient who lapsed into a coma and died in his office. I just happened to be there, and for ten or twelve hours I watched Max try to revive the man. His whole body from head to toe was covered with injection marks. The family claimed that Max was responsible for the stroke or heart attack, or whatever it was that killed him, and the inner circle of his friends, including Milton and me, Alan Jay Lerner, Mark Shaw, and others, rallied around Max to provide him with the best legal help money could buy. The case was eventually thrown out of court.

Whatever happened to some of Max's other patients, I still thought his injections were beneficial for me, even though little things started to go wrong with my performances. Immediately after a shot, I would stride on stage, charged with energy, singing in top form, the audience in the palm of my hand. There was nothing I couldn't do. But what I did wasn't always predictable. Sometimes I sang too many songs, told jokes without punch lines, got involved in long stories and floundered around trying to find my way out. "Don't talk, Eddie," people would shout. "Sing!" It didn't bother me. I welcomed the challenge of winning back a restless audience and bantering with hecklers, because I was bored doing the same thing night after night. But after a performance, as the effects of the shot began to wear off, I found I was short-tempered and rude to friends in my dressing room, critical of the audience, the lights, the conductor, the orchestra—and above all, myself. Up and then down. Wasn't that the way it had always been? Only the ups were getting harder to achieve and control, and the downs seemed deeper and longer lasting.

I could put two and two together. No matter what else was in Max's injections, I knew that methamphetamine was the ingredient responsible for both the ups and the downs. And I had to take a few elementary precautions. Max gave me Cordex-Forte in pill form to prevent an adverse reaction, antibiotics to combat infection from impurities in his formulas, and sedatives to help me sleep. I was concerned about the downs, but willing to live with them because the ups were worth it, on stage and off. On one of Max's shots, while it lasted, I had all the self-confidence and enthusiasm in the world. Everything was speeded up—my movements, my thoughts, my speech, even my ability to read. I discovered books and began to devour them as a way of channeling my excess energy. Kant, Nietzsche, Tocqueville, Freud, Maslow, Koestler, Kierkegaard—works of philosophy, psychology, and science came as revelations to me, filling my head with new ideas and insights. I would flip rapidly through the pages of a book, reading with what I thought was perfect comprehension, and then corner my friends to enlighten them. No one could challenge my interpretations; no one else had read the book. And if they couldn't understand what I was talking about, that wasn't my fault. It made perfect sense to me. For a kid with barely a high school education, I was brilliant.

Nowhere was I more brilliant than in Max's office, just after a shot. "I'm reading Albert Einstein," I told him one day. "Max, he's a genius. I don't mean just as a physicist. As a philosopher. He says that—"

"Ja, ja," Max said, cutting me short. "I haven't got time to listen to all that. People are waiting. Roll down your sleeve and get the hell out of here."

Alan Jay Lerner and I met occasionally in Max's office. *Both* of us were brilliant. I wanted to record an album of his songs, and he suggested making a musical of *Mr. Smith Goes to Washington* for me. The ideas flew back and forth at a furious pace. But there was one thing Lerner refused to discuss. I wanted to know if he had ever had bad reactions from Max's treatments. Did he lose his appetite or did his hands shake? What other medications did he take, and did he have trouble getting to sleep at night? Lerner either stared right through me or changed the subject.

There were warnings from others. At a party at my house one night, Sonja Henie advised me to leave Max. Even Max's wife gently suggested that perhaps I should look for another doctor. But it was Max himself who finally drove a wedge between us. He was growing more erratic and tyrannical than ever. His patients, including me, were treated like laboratory rats. Scores of them were kept waiting for hours in his outer office; others sat in little cubicles until he could get around to them. The place was a nut house and it was gradually dawning on me that Max was a little crazy too. He had a dual personality; one moment he could be funny and charming, the next abrupt and cruel. If I told him I felt sick, he would fly into a rage. That was not permitted. As his patient, you might not feel well, but once he had treated you, there was no reason for complaint. You were cured. For years I had put up with his weird ways, his vulgarity, his god complex, because I loved him. I needed him. Now I was beginning to wonder.

The bond that tied us together snapped early in 1964. And like the end of so many of my previous relationships, the break was sudden and irrevocable. I was singing at the Diplomat in Miami Beach and asked Max to come down to give me my usual send-off on opening night. He arrived early, with his familiar black bag, and prepared to inject me immediately. "Pull up your shirt," he commanded.

"My shirt," I said. "Why?"

"Don't ask," he replied as he filled a syringe. "Just do as I say."

"Max, I'm asking, whether you like it or not. The arm, yes. Even my ass. But why do I have to pull up my shirt?"

He glared at me angrily. "Because, you fucking idiot, I'm going to give you a shot right there." He jabbed his finger in the middle of my chest.

I looked at him with contempt. I had seen Max inject other patients in the solar plexus, but he wasn't going to do it to me. "No," I said. "That's not for me."

"What do *you* know?" Max said scornfully. "Who's the doctor?"

"I don't care who the doctor is. Nobody, not even you, is going to stick a needle in me that close to my heart."

Without saying another word, Max began repacking his medical bag. I had defied him. I was unworthy to be a patient of the great Max Jacobson. He stormed out of the room and returned to New York.

I felt as if an enormous burden had been lifted off my shoulders. He *was* crazy. The man was a monster and I was well rid of him. Then I panicked. Max had left me no little bottles or syringes. What was I going to do now? Where could I find another doctor? I called Max's son Tommy in Los Angeles, and understanding the situation instantly, he agreed to fly to Miami in time for my opening.

Tommy Jacobson bore little resemblance to his father. Young—he was three years my junior but we were born just two days apart—soft-spoken, only mildly eccentric, he fit the conventional medical mold. I often went to him for treatment in California. And we were friends. He had stayed at my house with his wife and three children just after they moved to the West Coast and he worked at the Veterans Administration. Although he might have lived comfortably on just what I paid him, he had built a very profitable practice, which included a number of people I sent to him for injections. And in that department, Tommy was much more conservative than his father in the use of methamphetamine. He wasn't eager—and he wasn't an exhibitionist. Max would inject anyone anywhere—at parties, in dressing rooms, cars, airplanes, bars. For Tommy, it was a private thing. He felt the same way about giving an injection as I felt about getting one. This was a legitimate medical procedure, not a sideshow.

I grew to depend on Tommy. I went to his office in Los Angeles; he came in person to my openings or wherever I was when I needed an injection. Unlike his father, he listened to me, and explained what he was doing and why. We both agreed that Max was a very difficult man to deal with. Tommy, who could have inherited his father's lucrative practice in New York, had chosen instead to put a continent between them. And I preferred to keep my distance too, until the summer of 1964, when I was singing at the 500 Club in Atlantic City and would appear at the Democratic National Convention. Just as I was getting ready to do a show, Max called from the airport. He had flown down from New York, but couldn't get into town because the roads were blocked and asked if I could help. I made a couple of calls, and minutes before I had to go on, he strode into my dressing room carrying not one but two black medical bags. I wondered whom he had come to Atlantic City to treat. To my surprise and embarrassment, he emptied his bags on a table and starting mixing up a shot for me. Oh, God, I thought, here we go again—the usual performance with the usual props. I had lost my complete trust in Max, but he was just as domineering and persuasive as ever, and I let him inject me. What was one more shot?

On stage that night, I was awful. I don't know whether Max had tried something new that didn't work, or whether his success in the past had stemmed as much from the power of his personality as from his medications. Now I no longer believed in the magician or his magic, and I never let him treat me again.

If I could get along without Max, I still needed Tommy. But somehow his injections didn't have quite the same effect as his father's and because they were much less powerful and I got them less frequently, I began to go through periods of mild depression. I didn't call them that. I just felt low. And I wasn't singing well either. The old energy and enthusiasm weren't there. Unaware that I was suffering symptoms of withdrawal, I thought I had some medical problem and ought to consult another doctor. Then I met a man whom I will call Clyde.

Introduced to me at a party in Los Angeles, Clyde came on like a snake oil salesman—big smile, hearty handshake, broad accent, ridiculous clothes. He told me he was in the air-conditioning business and dropped the names of a few men he claimed were interested in a gimmick he was promoting. I assumed he was looking for another investor. And in a way, he was.

Not many weeks later, I was playing at the Frontier and one afternoon Clyde just popped into my suite. What a coincidence that we were both in Las Vegas at the same time. He was obviously a character—a middle-aged man who talked and dressed like a dude—but he was very open and friendly, and very eager to please. We had a long conversation and when I remarked that I wasn't entirely happy with the medication I was taking, Clyde smiled and nodded. What was the trouble, he wanted to know. I wasn't really sure, I said; I just wasn't feeling up to par. "Well, sir," Clyde said, with another ingratiating smile, "maybe I can help."

He reached down beside his chair and retrieved the briefcase he had been carrying when he walked in. He put it on the coffee table and I saw that it wasn't a briefcase at all, but rather a small suitcase. Then he clicked it open and revealed its contents. It was all there—the little bottles, the ampules of calcium, the disposable syringes and needles in plastic envelopes.

"Help yourself," Clyde said. "Whatever you need. Absolutely free of charge."

Sitting in the steam room of the solarium at the Desert Inn in January 1964, I was served notice that Elizabeth had been granted a divorce from me on the grounds of abandonment. The papers were in Spanish and came from Mexico, where Elizabeth and Burton were staying while he filmed *The Night of the Iguana*. I took them to my attorneys. They consulted an expert in Mexican law, who questioned the validity of the divorce. Two months later, Elizabeth and Burton were married in Montreal.

After two years of separation, Elizabeth and I were still married, at least as far as I was concerned, and I challenged the Mexican divorce. During that time, Elizabeth's image had undergone another transformation, as remarkable as the one that had occurred after her near-death in London. From the wanton woman denounced by the Vatican for flouting the laws of marriage, she had become a noble and long-suffering heroine who wanted nothing more than to spend the rest of her life with the one man she truly loved. And since Sybil Burton had finally obtained her divorce, only I, her greedy and vengeful husband, stood in the way of her great happiness. Once again, just as in my divorce from Debbie, I was cast as the heavy.

My attorneys, on the other hand, told me I was being much too easy on Elizabeth. I asked for no division of property, to which I would have been entitled. Elizabeth could keep the jewelry I had given her, the house in Switzerland, and everything else. Burton, I had heard, was driving my green Rolls around Rome immediately after I left, and that, although he didn't know it, was his wedding present from me. There were other moneys, other corporations, but my lawyers, on my instructions, were asking for a million-dollar share of MCL, the production company Elizabeth and I had formed to develop film properties. And even there I was being generous. The newspapers headlined my demand as if I were trying to rob widows and orphans, when in fact a million dollars was less than a third of the estimated worth of the corporation. Knowing that, I wanted stock; and Elizabeth would settle only for cash. That little difference of opinion had kept lawyers on both sides busy for two years, and I was willing to negotiate. But my rights as Liza's and Maria's legal father remained non-negotiable.

Although the newspapers made our divorce sound like the battle of the century, Elizabeth and I were actually on speaking terms, at least over the long-distance telephone. She and Burton were using the house in Gstaad, and once Elizabeth called to complain that the master bedroom didn't even have a bathtub. "Of course not," I said. "I told you the place wasn't finished. How do you like it otherwise?"

"I love it," she said. "It's perfect. Except I don't know what to do with that huge ballet studio."

"I was going to convert it to a projection room."

"Oh, what a wonderful idea."

Quite by accident, I had also spoken to Sybil Burton. After attending the Broadway opening of a new play by Ketti Frings, I went to El Morocco with Dick Hanley, Montgomery Clift, and a few other friends to wait for the reviews. Sybil walked in with Roddy McDowall, who had somehow managed to remain friends with both Elizabeth and Burton and with Sybil.

On impulse, I got up to speak to her. She had been through an even more difficult time than I and I just wanted to say there was no reason for either of us to go on being unhappy. Her reaction was one of shock as I sat down at her table. "You can't do that," she said.

"Why not?" I asked.

"It just isn't done."

For the next several minutes, Sybil and I talked about why we shouldn't be talking, but finally she smiled and we both wished each other well.

My brief meeting with Sybil gave me courage to call Elizabeth and ask if we couldn't have a talk. That just wasn't "done" either, but I thought we might be able to settle our differences face to face. To hell with all the lawyers. Elizabeth agreed. She and Burton were in New York while he was playing Hamlet. We met in their suite at the Regency, and I was astonished by the way they both had changed: Elizabeth the more strident and demanding, Burton humble and domesticated. But I had changed too. We were all very different from the way we had been in Rome.

Our conversation was civilized, and Elizabeth and I quickly came to a satisfactory financial settlement. Our children were another matter. There was no question about Maria; Elizabeth and I had adopted her together. But she still refused to allow me to share custody of Liza. To my surprise, Burton began to argue on my side. Elizabeth didn't like to be crossed and I wondered why he was doing it. Maybe because he was a father too, and knew how I felt, or maybe he just wanted to be the good guy in this situation. After all, he had everything else he wanted. He was a very shrewd talker, a manipulator, and finally Elizabeth gave in.

Burton had to get to the theater. "Would you mind if I took Eddie with me?" he said to Elizabeth as he was preparing to leave.

"Get the fuck out of here," she said.

Did he honestly think I wanted to see him play Hamlet, or was he concerned about leaving Elizabeth and me alone together? He didn't have to worry. We just talked awhile longer, and the last thing I remember saying to her was, "Don't screw this one up, Elizabeth."

"Oh, I won't, Eddie," she said. "I won't. Don't worry."

I left with a good feeling. Everything was settled at last,

and I had seen Elizabeth without wanting to kiss—or kill—her. Then, just as I walked out of the Regency, incredibly I bumped into Louis Nizer, the attorney who had been representing me for two years. I told him what I had done and assumed the divorce would soon be final. But my talk with Elizabeth accomplished nothing.

Greg Bautzer, tall, handsome, a number one ladies' man, and Hollywood's most powerful attorney as well as a great friend, took over the case. Aaron Frosch, who had been Burton's attorney, was now representing Elizabeth, and when she changed her mind about Liza, we were back where we started. Only after I began legal proceedings to obtain visitation rights did Elizabeth reluctantly agree to let me see her. Dick Hanley met me at the door of Elizabeth's house in Beverly Hills. Liza was in the garden. A beautiful little girl with dark hair and eyes, she reminded me of both Elizabeth and Mike. I knelt beside her and we talked. She remembered me, but very shy and probably frightened, she wouldn't play. Unsure of how I was supposed to behave, I was frightened too.

Why fight it, I thought sadly, after my visit. I loved Liza. I had adopted her and she was the daughter of the two people, other than my own children, I had loved most dearly in my life. I wanted her to love me too, but I realized it would probably be better for her if I just disappeared. I surrendered my rights, but still negotiations between Elizabeth's lawyers and my lawyers dragged on until I just wanted to end it. Perhaps sensing that, Elizabeth became stronger and stronger in her stand on money matters as well as custody of both Liza and Maria. And I became weaker and weaker in mine. I finally gave in and settled for $500,000. It was over.

Not long after the divorce, Elizabeth called to ask a rather odd question. At one point in our marriage, we were giving each other so many ridiculously expensive gifts that we decided anything else we bought would be for the house in Gstaad. We didn't abide by that decision, of course, but in a few months' time I managed to acquire four complete sets of silverware, one of them a Danish modern design with knives, forks, and spoons that seemed to weigh a pound apiece. Elizabeth wanted to know if she could "borrow" one of the sets.

I laughed. "Of course you can. They're all yours." And then I began to tease her. The date was May 10, and I thought it was our anniversary. "You know, Elizabeth," I said, "I'm really very upset that you've forgotten our anniversary. Whatever else has happened between us, we should remember some things."

We talked awhile longer and after hanging up, I thought Elizabeth had probably called for some reason besides silverware. Then I got a wire: "Eddie. I didn't forget. Happy anniversary. Love, Elizabeth." The wire arrived on May 13, but she had sent it on the twelfth, the day of our wedding. *I* was the one who had forgotten.

I saw her again one night at the Daisy. I was leaving, Elizabeth and Burton were just coming in, and our eyes met for an instant. We didn't stop to speak or even smile at each other, but there was that split second of something in my eyes that is always there when you look at someone you love, or once loved. And I thought I saw it in Elizabeth's eyes too. Had I really gotten her out of my system, I asked myself as I drove home that night. The answer was yes, even though at unexpected moments like that your head and your heart can play a lot of tricks. Whatever I still felt for Elizabeth, I hoped she was happy with Burton. And if any bitterness remained, it was because Liza Todd Fisher was now being called Liza Todd, and Maria Fisher had become Maria Burton. My name, friends told me, was scarcely mentioned at all in a book Elizabeth had written about her life and her idyllic new marriage. I wondered why. I had no wish or reason, to blot her out of my memory.

At the age of fifty-eight, Milton Blackstone got married one late afternoon at Temple Emanu-el in New York. There was no previous announcement and I wasn't invited to the ceremony.

Ruby Blackstone, a widow in her mid-fifties with a teenage daughter, was an attractive woman, but I was prepared to resent her. As a bachelor, Milton's primary concern had been my career; now he would have to spend more time with his wife, or so I thought. I even suspected that Ruby was after Milton's money. As it turned out, she had plenty of her own. He and Ruby had first met thirty years earlier, before her first marriage, when she was a dancer in show business. She was the one love of his life, and as soon as I saw that Milton, for the first time in all the years I had known him, was acting like a man in love, I put all my reservations aside. I wanted him to be happy.

The marriage was over almost before it began. Milton's idea

of an evening out was standing at the bar in one of his favorite haunts until four in the morning. He usually came home late and sometimes disappeared completely, only to show up again in the strangest places. He showered Ruby with gifts. They had two apartments in New York—one a lavish corner suite at the Plaza—and an apartment in Florida. "Milton," I said, "you remind me of me." Although he tried to please Ruby, he just wasn't cut out to be a husband.

He knew his marriage wasn't working and came to me for help. "Talk to her, Eddie," he said.

"Me? I know I'm an expert on marriage," I protested, "but what am I supposed to say?"

I did talk to Ruby. She just couldn't understand Milton, and I couldn't explain his behavior. "Ruby," I said, "Milton has always been a little eccentric. You're just going to have to live with it. He'll never change."

Ruby couldn't live with it. They separated and Milton, married at fifty-eight, was divorced at fifty-nine. And about the same time, Milton and I began an undeclared, silent war. He *had* changed, whether I realized it or not. Friends and business associates were the first to point it out, coming to me with stories about something Milton had said or done that was even odder than usual. His mind wandered and his conversations rambled; he couldn't make decisions. Yet he still permitted no one to question his authority; he talked and you listened. There were flashes of his old brilliance, but I often came away from our meetings baffled and angered by his behavior. Finally, even I had to admit that Milton was not the same man I had always loved and trusted. He was drinking too much, he was still getting injections from Max Jacobson, and both drugs and alcohol were taking their toll. I could see it in his hands and face, the way he spoke and the way he walked. Sadly, I knew I had to end our relationship.

How could I do that, after all Milton had done for me? I couldn't face it, hoping we could patch up our differences as we had in the past. But if Milton had changed, so had I. No longer a compliant kid, I was determined to have things my way, not Milton's. And because I had broken with Max Jacobson, he could no longer rely on Max to reinforce his authority, and became even more indecisive and evasive. I needed Milton, I depended upon him, but he just wasn't there. The gulf between us widened and our silent war boiled over into angry battles. I saw it happening and still didn't want to believe it. Raising my voice to Milton was like shouting at my own father. But I wasn't his son; he wasn't my father. He was my manager and he could no longer handle the job.

Milton's world was crumbling. On top of his divorce, his mother died at the age of eighty-six, and he was alone. His two brothers, Daniel Blackstone and Leo Schwartzstein, alarmed by his physical condition and erratic behavior, begged him to leave Max Jacobson. Milton refused and they began a bitter feud that set brother against brother. There were also problems at Grossinger's. Jennie Grossinger was seriously ill and the management of the hotel had passed into the hands of her son Paul. Under Jennie, Milton's word had been law. Everything was done the way he wanted it done. Jennie had always followed his advice. Now Paul was beginning to establish his own authority. For Milton, it was a near-fatal blow.

Paul and I found ourselves in exactly similar situations. Without Milton Blackstone, there would have been no Grossinger's, no Eddie Fisher, but we could no longer depend upon his judgment. Looking for an easy way out, Paul proposed that he and I pay Milton thirty thousand dollars a year as an adviser—with the proviso that he wouldn't get angry if we didn't follow his advice. I thought it was a ludicrous idea. There was no way to put a price on what Milton had done for Grossinger's and for me, and to offer him such a small amount, in light of what Grossinger's and I earned every year, was an insult. Even more insulting was our intention to ignore Milton's advice, whatever price we paid for it. We were stripping him of his power, which had always been more important to him than money. I was right on all counts. At the meeting where Paul and I made our offer, Milton reacted with indignation. "I'm not looking for charity," he said, and walked out.

That was the end of his forty-year association with Grossinger's; he never went back. Paul's problem with Milton had been solved, but I was still tied to him in a variety of ways—the Fisher-Blackstone Corporation, Ramrod Productions, contracts, investments, royalty payments—and Milton controlled it all. I couldn't even write a check without his approval. For years, I had left everything in his hands because it was convenient, and because I never paid much attention to money as long as there was plenty of it. I thought, too, that Milton was a brilliant businessman. He was not. I discovered that opportunities had been missed, and several important matters had been ignored, postponed, or simply forgotten. Even if I hated to criticize Milton, it was an intolerable situation.

I offered to buy him out, but Milton could not, or would not, name a figure. In meeting after meeting with lawyers and accountants, he would agree to one proposal or another and then change his mind. Unable to concentrate, he launched into long and almost incoherent stories about things he had done years before. Watching him and remembering the charm, the intelligence, the wisdom he had once had, I couldn't believe this was the same Milton Blackstone. He was a very sick and frightened man. My heart was full of love and pity; I wanted to help him, not add to his already overwhelming problems. But he not only refused help, he refused to admit he needed it. There was no alternative; I had to proceed.

I went to Senator Jacob Javits, whose firm set up a Delaware corporation so that I could work outside my contractual obligations to Milton while our negotiations continued. Javits also attempted to settle the personal differences between us, and Milton latched on to him, even finding out when Javits took the air shuttle to Washington and following him on the plane. I asked Javits if he wanted me to speak to Milton and he said no, he could handle it. He was one of the most powerful men in the Senate, but Milton became so irrational and persistent that Javits finally called me from Washington and said, "Eddie, please speak to Milton." Morris Uchitel, a New York businessman and the brother of the owner of the Voisin restaurant, was at last able to negotiate the terms on which Milton and I agreed to sever our relationship. I thought we could still be friends, but angry and bitter, Milton told everyone he had been tricked into signing the agreement.

Unfortunately the years ahead would grow even darker for Milton. In spite of the efforts of his family, he remained a patient of Max Jacobson, and his physical and mental decline continued. Max, too, grew increasingly erratic and irresponsible in his behavior. My two Svengalis. Without them, my life would have been quite different, and I would always remember that. But I chose to ignore another legacy. If I cared about what the long-term use of methamphetamine might do to me, I had to look no further than Milton and Max, the men who had been my closest associates. Now both of them were gone. There was no one to tell me what to do, or provide the drugs that gave me the self-confidence to do it. I was in charge of my own life. Whatever mistakes I made in the future would be solely my own.

21

I had another hit. "Games That Lovers Play" was a single recorded in 1966 for RCA Victor, the company I had left a few years before, and it did so well I was offered a new long-term contract. Recordings made with Dot and my own company, Ramrod, were some of the best I had ever done, but without any exposure or exploitation, they died early deaths. So I was happy to see my name back on the charts, and happy to rejoin RCA, even though an audit revealed that the company owed me royalties of well over a quarter of a million dollars for the sale of seven million records under my previous contract. All that was straightened out under the new contract, however, and "Games That Lovers Play" was expanded into the biggest-selling album I had ever made. I was back in the recording business.

I sold the hell out of that record, traveling cross-country to talk to every record librarian and program manager, and appear with every disc jockey and television talk show host who would have me. To Johnny Carson's surprise, I turned up on his show every night for a week. RCA Victor hired ten publicists, I hired ten more. A classic campaign, it was the subject of an article in *Time* magazine titled "How to Make a Hit Record." But it was my last hit. Teenagers were screaming for Elvis Presley and the Beatles now; the big voice and my kind of romantic music were becoming a happy memory. I did have one more successful single, "People Like You," which also became an album. But I ran into trouble on my next recording, an album called *You Ain't Heard Nothin' Yet*. I originally intended to sing contemporary songs the way Al Jolson might have done them, but that idea was abandoned because no one could find the right songs, and I ended up recording all the old Jolson favorites. I had to call his widow, Earle, to ask her permission to use Jolson's photograph on the album jacket. She had been badly hurt by a very unflattering television documentary of her husband's life and had since refused to allow any likeness of him to be reproduced. But knowing how I had felt about Jolson, and that I intended the album as a loving tribute, she let me use his picture. It was a good album and later became a collector's item, but its original sales were disappointing. It was the last of my records to be released and I severed my relationship with RCA Victor—an unwise decision. Without realizing it, I was giving up the part of my career that had brought me fame in the first place, and might have prolonged my popularity.

In 1965–66 I also joined forces with Buddy Hackett, the former Leonard Hacker, an upholsterer turned comedian, for a seventeen-week cross-country tour that concluded with six weeks at the Palace Theater in New York. The collaboration was Hackett's idea, and I welcomed it as an opportunity to break the monotony of doing the same act night after night on my own. Hackett was a headliner, but he saw it as an opportunity to reach a new and larger audience and advance his career. That was fine with me. I agreed to equal billing and everything else he asked for. The tour wasn't well planned; we did record business in some cities and bombed in others, but the chemistry between us on stage was generally very good. Offstage, I couldn't really warm up to Hackett. There was a hostile streak in his humor. "You know," he told me a few years later, just before we worked together in Las Vegas for the first time, "I didn't really need you on that tour." Soon after that, working together again in Las Vegas, I decided I didn't need him.

Even if musical styles were changing rapidly, my career continued to go well—almost too well. I worked steadily and made very good money without really trying. One attempt to do something different proved disastrous. For an engagement at Howard Hughes's Frontier Hotel in 1967, I worked with Jule Styne to put together a whole new act. But I wasn't happy with it, and almost as if I wanted to sabotage the act—and myself—I clowned around instead of rehearsing seriously. Then at the last minute, I was petrified I would forget everything and fall flat on my face. Styne came up with the brilliant idea of using sheet music propped on a stand. Sinatra had done it once, he said; that was enough to convince me. But opening night, the sheet music wasn't the only innovation. I wore a black velvet suit with a black turtleneck, not the usual and much more comfortable tuxedo. A forty-carat blue sapphire surrounded by square-cut baguette diamonds dangled on a pendant from my neck. Sinatra was wearing a ruby; it was the "in" thing. I hated being in costume; I hated that kind of jewelry; and my custom-made Italian shoes threw me slightly backward, off balance. Even worse, as soon as I walked on stage I realized I would have to wear my glasses to read the music. I fumbled for them in my pocket and put them on, but the lights blinded me and I still couldn't see. Somehow, by moving the stand around and glancing at the music sideways, I sang for about twenty-five minutes and limped off. There were so many complaints the audience was given its money back.

For the second show that night, we all decided to do my old act, easy enough if there hadn't been one more fiasco. The music had gotten mixed up with Peggy Lee's and sent back to Los Angeles in her station wagon. I had to sing the few songs from my old act that had been included in the new, still in costume with that same silly pendant around my neck. Stumbling and ad-libbing through the second show, I had never been more terrified in my life, and the audience was again given its money back. The ax fell the following day. After a meeting of the hotel brass, Robert Maheu, Hughes's chief deputy, called me in person and said, "Eddie, you know we're both in the same business of giving people what they want. Now you go out there and do what you're supposed to do best. And apologize to the audience for what happened last night." Apologies were unnecessary; I sang the songs I was expected to sing and the audience got more than its money's worth. The stage manager handed me a phone as I walked offstage. It was Maheu. "That's the Eddie Fisher we all know and love," he said.

But giving that kind of performance wasn't the challenge

it used to be. Singing was becoming just a job, the way I made my living, which was something very new in my attitude toward my work. With the exception of the years I was married to Elizabeth, my career had always been more important to me than anything else. Now the emphasis began to shift as I looked elsewhere for excitement. Still dreaming of becoming a motion picture producer, I had acquired an option to Harold Robbins's best-seller *The Carpetbaggers,* for $25,000, but dropped it after Louella Parsons scolded me for proposing to make a movie out of "that filthy book." It was later produced by Joseph E. Levine, a terrible movie, which became the biggest moneymaker of 1964. I also optioned Irving Wallace's *The Man,* a novel about the first black President of the United States. Sidney Poitier, who held the option with Stirling Silliphant before I bought it and originally intended to play the part, told me why he had dropped it: the main character was always walking on eggshells. "If you make the film, Eddie," he said with a laugh, "I'm sure you'll give the guy some balls." With that advice in mind, my choice for the role was Rafer Johnson. I literally kidnapped him from Hickory Hill, where the Kennedy clan was playing touch football with him, and we flew to New York to meet my backers. They took one look at Johnson, their faces fell, and their checkbooks snapped shut. Johnson, in a very heartfelt note, later thanked me for seeing him as something more than just a black athlete. I gave up the project, finally, because my agents, Freddie Fields and David Begelman, told me no one would touch such a controversial subject. It was eventually made into a television film, and not a very good one.

I still held the option on *The Gouffé Case,* which Elizabeth and I had acquired, and worked with several writers to develop a script. But the project that truly captured my imagination was a movie version of Alan Jay Lerner's *Paint Your Wagon.* I loved the score; at one time or another I sang almost all the songs from the show in my act, particularly "Cariño Mio" and "Another Autumn," which were my favorites. Lerner, of course, was a good friend, and although he had no interest in producing the film himself, he encouraged me to buy the rights from the estate of Louis B. Mayer. Then one night I met Charles Bluhdorn, chief of Gulf & Western Industries, at Greg Bautzer's house. In Hollywood to look over the movie business, he asked, "Tell me, what is this *Paint Your Wagon?*" I told him at length, and even drove him back to the Beverly Hills

Hotel after dinner. Sometime later, Gulf & Western acquired Paramount, and the very first day Bluhdorn took over, we shook hands in his office on a deal. I was in the movie business at last.

Troubles soon began. My old friend Bob Evans, who had just been made Paramount's vice-president in charge of production, blew up because he had not been consulted. But once the project got under way, he was all sweetness and light, assuring me of his full cooperation. "Anything you want, Eddie, anything you need, just ask," he said. "My door is always open to you." I was then assigned two tiny rooms in a remote corner of the Paramount lot for an office and never saw him again—his subtle revenge for the Renata Boeck incident.

Paddy Chayefsky was commissioned to write the screenplay for *Paint Your Wagon* and I was very happy with the results. Lerner, who said it read like a Sears, Roebuck catalog, was not. Envious of all the publicity I was getting as the producer of the film, he suddenly decided to take a more active interest, including writing the screenplay himself, and we couldn't agree on anything. I had approached Gene Kelly to direct; Lerner wanted Josh Logan, who I thought had done a terrible job with the screen versions of both *South Pacific* and *Camelot*. Logan was hired. I had better luck with the leading man. When my first choice, James Cagney, who was in retirement, ruled himself out with the remark, quoted in Hedda Hopper's column, "I ain't paintin' anybody's wagon," my second choice, Lee Marvin, got the part. But my suggestion to consider Kim Novak for the leading female role was greeted with a cry of outrage from Logan: "My God, she's the worst actress in the world!" Lerner told me that Jean Seberg was going to play the part, and taking him at his word, I mentioned it to Dorothy Manners. After she ran an item in her column under the headline "Seberg Set for Eddie Fisher's 'Paint Your Wagon'"—no mention of Lerner—I got an angry note from him, accusing me of the highest form of unprofessional behavior he had ever encountered in his life. Although Seberg did play the part, she had not yet been signed, and he said, "You have ruined this girl's career."

As our differences grew, Lerner took over as producer and I was kicked upstairs to become "executive producer," a job I accepted because I thought Lerner and Logan, two veterans, knew what they were doing. But Lerner and I still couldn't get along—even though he often referred to me as *"the* friend of his middle years"—and realizing that either I was going to kill him or he would kill me, I decided to bow out. There was no other solution. At a meeting attended by my agents Fields and Begelman, Bluhdorn, and a number of other Paramount executives, with the exception of Bob Evans, I made my announcement. "I shook hands with Mr. Bluhdorn on a deal," I said, "and I don't want to do anything to disrupt it or stand in the way of a project of this magnitude. I'll step aside and go on to something else."

That was all they wanted to hear. Paramount bought me out and I negotiated a new agreement to develop and produce *The Gouffé Case*. In a way, I was lucky. *Paint Your Wagon* was a box office bomb, the biggest disaster in Paramount's history, and I may have been the only one who made money on it. My great friendship with Lerner didn't survive, and after working for months and spending thousands of dollars of my own money to record an album of his songs, I couldn't release it, but not because I bore him any personal grudge. I loved his songs and thought my performance didn't do them justice. Eventually I gave up *The Gouffé Case* too, when it proved impossible to find a suitable screenwriter or cast for such a bizarre story. Thus ended my career as a producer.

That left me with plenty of time and money, but no real idea of what to do with either. And approaching forty, without any responsibilities or plans for the future, I discovered a new diversion. Parties. I had moved from Gloaming Way to a spectacular new house on Beverly Estate Drive designed by George MacLain, a disciple of Frank Lloyd Wright and the architect for the house Elizabeth and I had wanted to build in Jamaica. Tucked into a hillside, with the city of Los Angeles as a backdrop, it was constructed of wood, stone, and glass, and looked as if it were growing out of the ground. The natural rock pool was fed by a waterfall, another waterfall tumbled over rocks in the dining room, and there was a third behind the bar in the living room. Inside and outside blended as one. MacLain's former wife designed the interior furnishings—elegant, comfortable, simple—and I equipped the house with the best electronic recording and sound equipment available. What better place to entertain my friends?

Willard was still with me and I rehired Olivia Smith, the cook I'd had to fire for chasing Debbie out of the kitchen with a butcher knife. I found her working for Greg Bautzer, and one night at dinner there, she whispered in my ear that she wanted to come back to me. With Olivia's help, I gave so many parties at my new house that one columnist headlined me as the "Perle Mesta of Hollywood." Everybody came: Rex Harrison, Georgie Jessel, Rock Hudson, Claudia Cardinale, Richard Harris. The Gordian Knot, the band at the Factory, played by the pool. There were indoor and outdoor bars, indoor and outdoor buffets. Even Bob Evans, who had avoided me at Paramount, came one night to see what these parties were all about.

Steve Brandt did most of the organizing and invited the guests. I just played host and paid the enormous bills. Stephanie Powers had introduced Brandt to me one night at the Daisy. "Be nice to him," she said. "He's very homely and doesn't have many friends." Both of which were true, but as a fan magazine writer, he knew everybody in town, especially the young starlets. I liked Brandt; he was obviously a troubled young man, but he was very amusing and often outrageous. Although his own interest in girls didn't go beyond dancing with them, he became a sort of unpaid press agent for the ones he liked. And to show off his power, he introduced them to me. I met Peggy Lipton, Sue Lyon, Sandy Grant, Michelle Phillips, Barbara Parkins, and Sally Kellerman. During one three-week engagement at the Cocoanut Grove, he brought a different girl to my show every night and then to my dressing room—eighteen of them. I thanked God for Monday nights off.

Brandt populated my parties with a mixture of celebrities and unknowns, including a generous dash of the hippie types, rich and poor, who were beginning to hang out in Hollywood. He knew Jay Sebring, and of all the actresses in his stable, Sharon Tate was his favorite. Three and sometimes four hundred people wandered in and out of my house during these parties, not all of them in show business: Don Drysdale and Sandy Koufax from the sports world, Pierre Salinger from the worlds of politics and journalism—and everybody got along just fine. A lot of good food and booze was consumed, but as far as I knew, nobody was on drugs. That wasn't my scene— not in public.

Brandt confided to me that he had taken a couple of LSD trips, one good and one disastrous. And I knew he used sleeping pills. Once, at my house, he said, "I think I'll go home now," and then popped a three-grain Tuinal into his mouth. "Why did you do that?" I asked. "Why not wait until you get home?" "Oh, the cab will be here in a couple of minutes." It didn't come for at least fifteen minutes, and by that time Brandt was sound asleep, snoring, on the floor.

People warned me to stay away from Brandt, that he was a pain in the ass or would slit my throat, and he could be difficult. Still, I liked him, and he developed a kind of hero worship for me. I may have been the only one who talked to him straight, as a friend. "Who cares what anybody says about you?" I told him once. "Live your own life." He seemed to value my advice and confided everything in me. "You know, I tried to kill myself once," he said.

"Come on, you've got to be crazy," I replied. But he showed me a scar that crossed his scalp and the back of his neck. He had taken pills in his apartment, then fallen down in the shower; the tub overflowed with blood and water, and his landlady discovered him.

"I'm going to do it someday," he said, laughing. "I just want you to know."

If I had made the same rule about suicide for men as I had for women, that would have ended our relationship right there. But I didn't believe him, and I valued our friendship. He valued mine too, even if he often abused it. Once he walked unannounced into my dressing room at the Cocoanut Grove just before I went on stage. "Hi," he said. "You weren't here earlier, so I stopped off at the coffee shop, had a cup of coffee, and signed your name."

I wasn't in the best frame of mind at that moment and I exploded. "You did *what?*"

"It was just a cup of coffee," he said meekly.

"I don't care what it was. *Nobody* signs another man's name! And while we're on the subject, how about knocking before you come barging in here? And I'd appreciate a 'please' and a 'may I?' once in a while too."

I overreacted. Brandt's offense was trivial—something like fifty cents. But other friends had been doing the same thing for years, for much larger sums of money, and I was fed up with it.

Brandt looked as if I had struck him, and was so upset he threw up in my dressing room the whole time I was on stage.

I decided not to see him for a while, and after I refused to take his calls for a couple of days, he dropped off a cigarette lighter, inscribed "Your brother Steve," at my house as a peace offering, then committed himself to the UCLA hospital.

As soon as I heard where he was, I said to myself, "Oh, God, I did it. It's my fault." It wasn't, of course. Brandt was very screwed up, and no one ever knew what he might do next. We resumed our friendship after he got out of the hospital, and I could see that he was going downhill rapidly. Once, and perhaps twice, I may have saved his life. In Las Vegas, I got worried when I realized I hadn't seen him hanging around my dressing room at the Frontier for a couple of days, and I went to his room to find out if he was all right. The door was locked, so I called a security guard to open it and then told him to go away, because I wasn't sure what I might find. The curtains were drawn and there were three room service carts in the darkened room. Brandt, who had taken too much of something, was on the bed out cold. I was able to revive him, and the first thing he said was, "Don't tell anyone."

The second time, the phone rang in my suite at Caesar's Palace at about four in the morning. It was my secretary, calling from the lobby. "I just spoke to Steve Brandt in Los Angeles," she said, close to hysterics. "He called to say goodbye to you. He's going to commit suicide." I told her to notify the Los Angeles police and then tried to reach Brandt. There was no answer on his private line and a very tough lady picked up on his service. She was used to handling people with crazy reasons for wanting to talk to Brandt and she wouldn't believe me. "I don't care what you believe," I yelled at her. "Just keep ringing his phone! The police are on the way." Crying, she rang until the police got there. Brandt was still alive.

I spoke to him about a week later. "Look, Steve, you are not going to do anything like that again."

"Oh, no, no," he said. "I'm on my way to New York. I'll call you when I get back. Bye."

I should have suspected something by the way he said "Bye." It was a final farewell and I didn't know it. Everyone had heard that he had tried to kill himself, and he was deeply embarrassed. But it may have been his distress over the brutal murder of his friends Sharon Tate and Jay Sebring by the Manson gang that finally pushed him over the edge. He took an overdose of sleeping pills at the Chelsea Hotel in New York and never woke up.

I was standing at a crossroads the afternoon that Clyde just happened to drop into my suite at the Frontier. When he opened his suitcase to reveal all the paraphernalia so familiar from my days with Max Jacobson, I should have kicked him out. But I took the wrong turn. He stayed, and I let him give me an intravenous injection in the arm. With a running line of patter, he explained what he was doing every step of the way. First the formula, which was an almost exact duplication of Max Jacobson's magic elixir; Clyde and Max, it so happened, were very good friends. Premixed in little glass bottles, the formula consisted of a small amount of dextromethamphetamine, riboflavin or vitamin B_2, B_{12}, Celestone, testosterone, procaine, silicone, placenta, a trace of an antibiotic, and purified water. Calcium, which acted as a buffer, had to be added at the last minute from a tiny glass vial or it would crystallize into a white powder on exposure to air. Once that was done, the formula was drawn up into a syringe. Then an elastic tourniquet was tied around the arm to make the vein bulge, and a spot was chosen for the injection and dabbed with alcohol. The needle was inserted into the vein and a small amount of blood drawn back into the syringe to make sure it was in properly. Otherwise the injeciton would infiltrate muscle and flesh and cause a very painful hematoma. The injection itself was a gentle push of the thumb which pumped the formula into the vein.

So simple. And the reaction was instantaneous. The methamphetamine in an intramuscular injection usually took about twenty minutes to work. An intravenous injection, which went directly into the bloodstream, acted in seconds. There was only one drawback. If that was the effect I wanted, I would have to learn how to inject myself. An intramuscular shot was like playing darts; you just grabbed the right muscle somewhere and stuck a needle in it. I had often done that, but I had always depended on Max for intravenous injections. Because they were more complicated, and much more dangerous, I was scared to death of them. Clyde reassured me. "Nothing to it," he said, "once you get the hang of it." Even though the whole idea repelled me, I was more than willing to learn.

I realize now that Clyde's appearance that day was not an

accident. He knew of my long dependence on meth and of my break with Max. And it was hardly an accident that he had in his suitcase just the right number of bottles of his formula, needless and syringes to last the length of my engagement at the Frontier. I was a sitting duck. A grateful one. I stuffed five one-hundred-dollar bills in his pocket. "Well, sir, that's very kind of you," he said. "Good luck, and be sure to look me up when you get back to L.A."

I followed Clyde's instructions to the letter and once I got over my aversion to intravenous injections, I became very adept at them. For a kid who had passed out in a doctor's office when someone stuck a needle in his arm to take a blood sample, I had come a long way. Injecting myself soon became a daily routine. When I was performing, I usually woke up about one or two in the afternoon, ordered breakfast—I always had to have breakfast—and then went into the bathroom to give myself the first shot of the day. That would last until just before my first performance that evening, when I gave myself another shot, and then another, my third, just before my second show that night. No matter how exhausting my performances were, by that time I had so much meth in my system that I couldn't go to bed. I stayed up, gambling, hanging around with friends, sometimes until six or eight in the morning, and still I needed a sedative to get to sleep. A one-and-a-half-grain Seconal would knock me out for six or seven hours, and then I woke up, groggy from the sleeping pill, ordered breakfast, and started the procedure all over again.

Gone were the days as Max's patient when getting a shot was like a parlor game everybody played. This was a very personal thing, a secret. I kept all my gear in a case with a double combination lock and always injected myself in complete privacy. If my friends knew what I was doing in the bathroom just before every performance, they let it pass, or I evaded their questions. And gone were the days when I was proud to be associated with the man who gave me this miraculous medication. Clyde wasn't a doctor; he was a pusher, and I was ashamed to admit I knew him. I did look him up, of course, back in Los Angeles. He had everything I needed, including, among his many friends, a most reputable doctor who gave me prescriptions for Seconal. I later discovered that I could buy syringes and needles, and many of the ingredients in the formula, just by asking for them at some drugstores. But for the time being, Clyde was my source of supply, and he was a very generous man.

I could only guess where he got all his supplies, or the extent of his own involvement with meth. But Clyde looked like a "speed freak" to me, a man constantly in motion, walking, talking on the phone, typing, driving around town in his white Cadillac, a new one every year. He was busy twenty-four hours a day, and struck most of the people who met him as a real jerk. Everything about him was a little strange, including the nicknames he made up for all his clients. For some reason he called me "Jungle Boy." The less I was seen with him the better, as far as I was concerned. But that was not the way he operated. He was a celebrity hound, eager to capitalize on his connection with me. That was one of his forms of payment. Even though I often gave him cash, thousands in big bills, he expected other expensive favors. I made all the arrangements and picked up the tab for hotel suites, airplane tickets, nightclub reservations, meals; nothing was too good for my pusher and his friends, wherever they wanted to go. If I was performing, he was often there, at a front-row table. And after the show, in my dressing room or suite, he was there too, with enough of his "joy juice," as he called it, for an army. I cringed every time I saw him, but I wanted him there. As much as I disliked the man, I *needed* him.

He asked me to introduce him to Barbra Streisand. I didn't say no. I thought Streisand would take one look and tell him to get lost. I had been her number one press agent ever since the first time I saw her perform, and when she opened at the Cocoanut Grove I brought Danny Kaye, Alan Jay Lerner, everyone I knew, to see the show. In my opinion she was the greatest singing phenomenon of our time, and backstage in her dressing room on opening night, after everyone else had cleared out and only she and I were left, I said, "Good night, greatest." And she replied, "Good night, next to greatest." Then I got an early look at *Funny Girl,* her first film. She was known to be impossible to work with, but her performance was better than anything I had seen in years. I picked up the phone and called her. "Barbra," I said, "forget about singing. You're Garbo." "Yeah, yeah," she said. "Tell me more about that part."

Now she was making *Hello, Dolly!* and I took Clyde to the set to meet her. To my surprise, she actually spoke to him for a few minutes and Clyde was jubilant, eager to add her name to his celebrity list. I begged him not to bother her, but a couple of days later, ignorning me, he wrote her a long letter. Clyde was famous for his letters, pages and pages of pure craziness typed at one hundred words a minute when he was high on meth. He sent me a copy and it was even crazier than usual. "That's it," I told him. "You'll never hear from her again."

"Oh, yes I will," he said. "You wait—you'll see." He waited a week, which must have seemed like a lifetime to him, and then came back to me. "Hey, Jungle Boy," he said, "why don't you give her a call?"

That request I refused. Streisand was just a little too smart for Clyde and he never heard from her.

Most of Clyde's friends were as strange as he was. His address book, stained and smelling of the chemicals in his formula, had the names and numbers of women all over the country. He would call them up at three or four in the morning and say, "Oh, I'm sorry, honey, did I wake you?" Several women hung around his house, willing to do whatever he asked, for the same reason I was. But they weren't his only interest, although no one was supposed to know that. "If I ever switch, Jungle Boy," he once told me, "you're going to be the first." And I replied, "If *I* ever switch, you'd be the last."

Sometime later I heard a tape of a sadomasochistic session between Clyde and a young boy. I was sickened by it. Compared to this man, Max Jacobson was a saint. But he had a very powerful hold over me—meth. At first I was very cautious about the amounts of meth he gave me. Then I seemed to need larger and larger amounts to keep me going during waking hours, and stronger and stronger Seconal—two, three, and finally four grains—to put me to sleep at night. There were times when I felt this wasn't me. I was living in someone else's body, watching myself on a merry-go-round, spinning faster and faster. It was a hell of a ride, until more than five years had passed almost without my knowing it and I suddenly realized there was no way to hang on without killing myself, no easy way to get off.

Sam Giancana had gone into exile in Mexico since our last meeting in New York. Dethroned as a don of the Chicago Mafia and hounded by the FBI, he had committed the cardinal sin of the underworld: people knew who he was. He couldn't resist hanging around show business celebrities, and as a result of his well-publicized relationship with Phyllis McGuire, one of the three popular singing McGuire sisters, he became a celebrity himself. Sam was not the shy, retiring type; he waged a fierce battle with the reporters and government agents who dogged his every move, even in church. But it was a battle he couldn't win, and he finally "retired" to Mexico, where, it was thought, he was in charge of investing mob money in ventures outside the United States.

Even with a penthouse in Mexico City and a two-and-a-half million-dollar home in Cuernavaca, Sam was a lonesome man. Many of the people he once thought of as his friends could no longer afford his company. He wasn't even sure I'd be happy to see him when I arrived at the María Isabel Hotel in Mexico City just before opening at the Forum. I got a phone call: "Eddie, this is Sam. Can I come over?"

"Of course you can come over."

"Well, you never know," he said.

Later that day, I came out of the bedroom and saw Willard talking to a stranger on the balcony. As I was wondering who the man was, he turned around. It was Sam. He had grown a beard and was wearing a toupee. We greeted each other like brothers.

Sam was an actor—a bad one. I was staying in the Presidential Suite of the hotel, and after going through an elaborate routine to inspect the layout, he said, "If the phone rings, don't answer it. And don't answer the door. I'll take care of everything. Where can you put me up?" He chose a small servant's room off the suite, then left to pick up a shaving kit from his own luxurious penthouse, came back, and stayed with me for the next three weeks.

We played gin and talked; he used to wait up for me sometimes until five or six in the morning. "Where are all the tomatahs?" he asked me one night, disappointed that a man with my reputation didn't have a steady stream of girls in and out of the suite. But when three or four did stop by, he said, "Eddie, I think you better take it easy. You're going to kill yourself." He insisted on cooking for me, and he was truly a great cook. One night he prepared an elaborate and delicious meal for my entire entourage and served it just before I had to go on stage, a time when I am never hungry. But just to please him, I picked, while he hovered over me like a Jewish mother, saying, "Eat, eat."

On my days off, Sam took me to his house in Cuernavaca, about an hour away from Mexico City, honking the horn as he drove through the gates and looking around very carefully. I saw four or five men fixing the house, painting, working in the garden. They were always there. But if Sam was worried that someone might take a shot at him, I never saw it. He used to stop his car in the streets of Cuernavaca and give coins to crowds of Mexican kids. I don't know why he loved me, but he did. Once he sat in his car outside the Forum with the engine running for more than an hour while I signed autographs. And when my engagement at the Forum ended and he took me to the airport, there were tears in his eyes as we embraced and said goodbye.

I loved him too. Blocking out anything I heard about his ruthless underworld reputation, I saw him only as I wanted to see him, as a kind and loyal friend. We got together whenever I came to Mexico and I often stayed in his penthouse or the house in Cuernavaca. "My home is your home," he said. He was always doing little things for me and never asked anything in return. I knew nothing about his business activities. I never asked him what he did or why he traveled all over the world. If he called up to tell me where he was, I didn't want to know. The one place he couldn't go was back to the United States, but somehow he managed to cross the border from time to time. A "Dr. Goldberg" would call and ask to see me in San Francisco. "Dr. Morris" phoned me in New York. He always surprised me. Once, after I had married Connie Stevens and we were in Mexico City, I wanted her to meet Sam. It was very late at night and I brought him to our bedroom, where they chatted for just a few minutes and then Sam left. "You know," Connie said, "that's the nicest man I've ever seen you with." Later he heard I was divorcing Connie and I got another call. "Are you sure you know what you're doing?" Sam said, trying to talk me out of it. "Divorce you think about a little more."

The last time I saw him, we were having dinner with another McGuire sister, Dorothy, Guy Marks, and other friends at the Chianti restaurant in Hollywood. There was a big window behind our backs and I said, "Sam, we shouldn't be sitting here." He shrugged. The Mexican government had kicked him out, and he was back in the States. Sick and growing old, he had returned to Chicago. Less than a year later, he was found dead in the basement kitchen of his home. Seven shots had been pumped into his mouth by someone he thought was a friend.

I often saw Merle Oberon when I was playing Mexico City. Retired from the screen and married to millionaire Bruno Pagliai, with beautiful homes in Beverly Hills, Mexico City, and Acapulco, she was the queen of jet set society. Elizabeth and I had been invited to many of her parties in Beverly Hills. One memorable night, her guests, including David Niven, Jack Benny, Danny Kaye, Elizabeth, and I, waited about an hour for the Duke and Duchess of Windsor to arrive. They finally appeared, and as they made their entrance, the Duke tripped over a rug and fell flat on his face. Everyone gasped, with the exception of Elizabeth, who giggled. The Duke wasn't hurt; he got to his feet with as much dignity as possible and the party continued as if nothing unusual had happened.

Merle was as gracious and thoughtful as she was beautiful. She was among the first of Elizabeth's friends to offer help when Elizabeth was near death in London. And after we separated, Merle was one of the few people who remained a friend of both hers and mine. She once did me an enormous favor. I just happened to mention that the last time I worked in Mexico, I hadn't been paid, and she immediately offered to contact her friend Senator Jacob Javits. That was how I got to know Javits, whose firm, working through a lawyer in Mexico, eventually got the money due me—some fifty thousand dollars. Later he came to my aid again in my legal conflict with Milton Blackstone.

Merle was in the audience my opening night at El Patio in Mexico City. I hadn't expected her, but I was very happy to renew our friendship. She invited me to several dinner parties at her house, where I met Dolores Del Rio and all of Merle's society friends. Merle gave a lot of parties; I suppose she had very little else to do. And she was lonely. I was again staying at the Presidential Suite at the María Isabel and one afternoon she came to see me. We walked out on the balcony together, and as we stood side by side, gazing out over the city, Merle began to talk as if we had been in the middle of a conversation and had spoken of this before. "I have all the money in the world," she said softly. "I can have anything I want, but I don't

have love. I've chosen the wrong friends. . . ." And her voice
trailed off.

Sometime later, she invited me to the Acapulco Film Festival, a favorite project of hers. Merle's husband owned, among
other things, a small airline and we flew down together from
Los Angeles on a private plane. Her house in Acapulco had
not yet been completed and she had made reservations for both
of us at the Ritz. Late one afternoon she came to my room and
asked if I wanted to go swimming at former president Miguel
Alemán's house. It was on the beach, just two doors away from
the house where Elizabeth and Mike Todd had been married.
We went into separate dressing rooms and all of a sudden I
heard a scream. Rushing in, I found Merle naked, cowering
from a big spider crawling across the floor. I killed it and I
was a hero.

It was twilight, the sun was setting over the bay, and we
swam together in the nude. I agreed to come to her room that
night at a certain time, up the back stairs, and I was a little
embarrassed when I got there. Merle had made all the advances
and ordinarily I preferred to do the pursuing myself. Still, I
was flattered. She could have had anyone she wanted, and she
had chosen me. Even if she was well over fifty, she was one
of the most beautiful women in the world. Exquisitely dressed
and made up, with every hair in place, she made our night
together a ceremony, as if we were performing a sacred ritual.

Later I thought of the other legendary beauties I had known.
My brief affair with Marlene Dietrich remained one of the most
vivid of my memories. And I remembered that during dinner
at her house in Hollywood, Joan Crawford had made a pass
at me and I got out in a hurry. The night I spent with Merle
Oberon left me with a feeling of sadness. I wasn't all that
inexperienced, not anymore. I knew that many older women
pursued, and often paid, younger men. Acapulco was famous
for its beach boys; the same sort of thing happened even at a
place like Grossinger's. But it was different for men as they
grew older, wasn't it? Why, then, did Merle's words seem to
haunt me: "I can have anything I want, but I don't have love.
I've chosen the wrong friends . . ."?

22

Steve Brandt had encouraged me to meet Connie Stevens. "Call her," he said. "She's a wonderful girl." I did, but she was on her way to Tokyo and we didn't connect until the afternoon I ran into her at the Plaza. We had that drink and a long talk. Connie wasn't very happy about her life at that moment and neither was I. She had just divorced her husband, I had just put Nathalie Delon on the plane to Paris. We both needed company and a little consolation, but that's as far as we went until the night I took her to a party at Buddy Hackett's house in Fort Lee, New Jersey. There, she came out of her shell a little and all the men were buzzing around her like flies. I broke up one conversation she was having with a man. "You came to this party with me," I said. I was jealous of her even before I fell in love.

Back in Los Angeles, we started seeing quite a lot of each other, and I came to realize what a really nice girl Connie was. Everybody liked her. She didn't have an enemy in the world, which is rare in Hollywood. Half Irish, half Sicilian, Connie had a fiery temper and a fierce determination to succeed, which isn't rare in Hollywood, but she was willing to work harder at it than anyone I had ever known. Ordinarily that kind of ambition turned me off. With Connie, for some reason, it turned me on. Not only jealous of her, I was jealous of her dedication to her career.

We flirted for months with the idea of a more committed relationship. Marriage was out of the question for me; my legal hassles with Elizabeth were still going on. But when Connie announced that she didn't intend to marry anyone, *especially* me, it sounded like a rejection and that became a challenge. Two big and very fragile egos were at work here, both trying to prove a point. I stepped up my pursuit and became very possessive of her, but we stopped short of living together.

In early 1967, Connie was asked to do *Star-Spangled Girl* with Tony Perkins, and no one could pass up the opportunity to star in a Neil Simon comedy on Broadway. It meant, of course, that we would be separated, and if I didn't want to live with her, I didn't want to live without her. We compromised. I rented a penthouse in New York and flew back and forth from the Coast whenever I was free. I remember the first time I stayed there with her. She was awake and out of bed very early in the morning and said, "Okay, let's go. Up and at 'em."

"Connie," I protested. "I have just flown three thousand miles to be with you. We've been up all night. It's only seven o'clock. I want to sleep."

Connie always had something to do, and whatever it was, she never quit. *Star-Spangled Girl* was not Neil Simon's best play and the critics killed it. I urged her to leave the show, but even though she was miserable the whole time, she stuck it out. Remembering how important success had been to me, how hard I had worked, I could understand why. That kind of persistence came with the territory. God, I thought of myself, I must be totally out of my mind to get involved with another actress.

We were both wrapped up in our careers, but I had another preoccupation—drugs. Connie never knew the extent of my addiction, or if she knew, we never discussed it. What I didn't know was how profoundly drugs were affecting my behavior and my feelings for her. It was almost as if I were two people: one who rejected the whole idea of marriage, the other filled with old-fashioned notions of true love and fidelity. If Connie seemed to be moving away from me, I tightened my grip and pulled her back. If she got too close, I pushed her away. It was like a tug-of-war, only I was pulling against myself and Connie was caught in the middle. Friends told me that she really did want to get married. I refused to believe it. We did talk about houses; clothes, jewelry, and every single kind of fur coat were more than welcome. But she seemed willing to play the game any way I wanted to play it, and that deepened my indecision. I wasn't thinking straight. Drugs were blowing both the positive and the negative sides of our relationship way out of proportion, and the only decision I could make was to make no decision—until Connie told me she was pregnant.

She wanted to have the baby. I wanted her to have it too. But I could foresee serious, unresolvable problems if we got married. I loved Connie and didn't want to hurt her. But wouldn't a bad marriage hurt us both? It was a dilemma and again we compromised: the baby yes, a wedding no.

Other men have faced the same dilemma, but not in public. Connie's pregnancy was impossible to hide for long and comment from the columnists was inevitable. This was worse— far worse—than what I was supposed to have done to Debbie and my image took another nose dive. The June 1967 *Esquire,* in an article about Jackie Kennedy's great popularity, quoted her as saying that anyone who was against her would look like a rat unless she ran off with Eddie Fisher. We were pictured together on the cover, I dressed in a ski helmet and goggles, with Jackie behind me on a sled. I was amused, but it was the same kind of public pressure that had persuaded me to marry Debbie, and this time I was determined to resist. But the real pressure came from within myself. Was it right or wrong not to marry Connie? I didn't know. I only knew that I was torn between doing the "right" thing, the thing that my background and all my beliefs told me to do, and an inner voice that said, "Stop, stop. This marriage would be wrong"—for me, for Connie, and for our child.

The months we waited for the baby were one of the most difficult times of my life. Called callous and uncaring, I was just the opposite. I cared too much, knew all too well the pain of a bad marriage and the agony of divorce to go through them all over again, even after the New York *Daily News,* in Ocotber 1967, printed a picture on the front page with the caption: "Connie Stevens looking very pregnant at Eddie Fisher's opening at the Empire Room." Our daughter Joely was born two weeks later and her existence, her being, brought my confused emotions into focus. She was here, our daughter, and she didn't have a legal father. Connie and I *had* to get married. Buddy

Hackett offered us his Fort Lee house for the wedding. My family came from Philadelphia, Connie's family came from Queens, but at the last minute I couldn't go through with it and our wedding became an engagement party. It was embarrassing for everybody and I was beginning to feel very stupid and immature.

And guilty. I had painted myself into a corner and didn't know how to get out. A month or so later, leaving Connie and the baby in Los Angeles, I went to work at the Fontainebleau in Miami Beach. Frank Sinatra was following me in. He had the flu when he arrived and asked me to keep him company. We spent a lot of time together, talking. He was having his own problems. After an off-again on-again courtship, he had married Mia Farrow, who was half his age and completely unpredictable. At the moment, she was in India with her guru, Maharishi Mahesh Yogi.

I knew Mia. She was a beautiful little girl and very smart— even shrewd—with a charm and sense of humor that were completely unique. Frank was fascinated by her and so was I. When I first came to Hollywood, years ago, I had a crush on her mother, Maureen O'Sullivan, whom I used to see at Louella Parsons' house. Now I was just as enchanted by Mia, and we saw quite a lot of each other during one period. She and Frank were having a tiff, and ignoring his calls, she was going out with me, or anybody else, just to make him jealous. "Mia," I said, "what is all this nonsense? You know you're going to marry him." She just smiled her whimsical smile.

One night we were invited to dinner at George Hamilton's house. He was going with Lynda Bird Johnson, so we were chaperoned by his mother *and* the secret service—all very proper, even after the other guests left and the four of us sat around watching *An Affair to Remember*. Mia and I finally escaped to Polly Bergen's party at the Bistro and then Mia wanted to drive down to Mexico. She was always coming up with some crazy idea, so I said, "Why not?" Once we had crossed the border, she had another idea. "Let's get married," she said.

"Okay," I said, just to see how far she would go.

"I'll have to call Roddy for permission," she said.

"Roddy who?"

"Roddy McDowall."

Terrific.

It must have been three in the morning, but we found a phone and Mia tried to call Roddy. She couldn't reach him. "Does that mean we can't get married?" I said.

"I'm afraid so."

"Well, ask me again later," I said, turning the car around. We took our time driving back to Los Angeles.

By coincidence, I had also met the Maharishi. He was traveling with his manager on a flight from Los Angeles, where he was scheduled to make an appearance at the Hollywood Bowl, and I was with my friend Julie Chester, who, on a bet, persuaded the Maharishi's manager to change seats with me. "Oh, sir," I said, "I'm really very happy to meet you. I have some problems that maybe you can help me with."

"Yes, my son. Oh, yes, I know. You must come to see me."

"I'd like that. But couldn't you do something right here?"

"Oh, no, my son. There is too much noise, too much disturbance."

I persisted, half interested and half putting the Maharishi on, and he started telling me about transcendental meditation, reducing myself to nothingness and becoming one with the universe. As he spoke, I noticed that he was marking some figures on a corner of the menu, and when we reached Los Angeles I picked it up and took a look at it. I recognized some of the numbers: seating capacity, admission prices. The Maharishi was calculating his gross from the Hollywood Bowl.

I thought Mia and the Maharishi made a pretty funny pair. Sinatra, who was close to the end of his patience with Mia, was not amused. We talked together for hours, and I told him of my ambivalence about marrying Connie even if we did have a baby. In his opinion, there was only one thing to do. I had to live up to my "moral obligations." His remark came almost as a relief. In a way, that's what I had wanted him to say, because it reinforced my own feelings. I called Connie in Los Angeles and proposed.

She flew to Miami and I met her at the airport, where we boarded Sinatra's private plane for a flight to Puerto Rico. "There's something I've got to tell you," Connie said just as we were getting ready for takeoff.

"Well?"

"I can't tell you until we get to Puerto Rico."

"Come on, Connie," I said. "You can't set me up and then not tell me. What is it?"

"I had a dream," she said. "We were in a plane flying over water and we crashed."

I laughed, but I could see that Connie was very tense as we took off. A few minutes later I heard the pilot's voice over the loudspeaker: "Mr. Fisher, can we see you in the cabin for a moment?" I went forward and the pilots told me there was a red warning light flashing on the instrument panel. They weren't sure what the problem was. No cause for alarm, they said, but we had to turn around and go back to Miami.

I told Connie and for the next fifteen or twenty minutes she was completely hysterical. "I dreamed this!" she cried. "It's exactly like my dream!"

I tried to calm her and stay calm myself, even as we came down for a landing and I saw fire engines and ambulances tearing along both sides of the runway at exactly the same speed as the plane. There was a jolt when we touched down. The front landing gear had cracked and the plane bounced all over the runway. But somehow the pilots kept it under control and we came to a safe stop.

Connie had to have a drink and I decided we had to board another plane and fly to Puerto Rico immediately or she might never have the courage to fly again. That flight was uneventful, and soon after our arrival we were married by Doña Felisa de Gautier, the mayor of San Juan and an old and dear friend of mine, in a private ceremony in her office. I had lived up to my "moral obligations." Sinatra, my marriage counselor, took a different course of action. When Mia returned to the Fontainebleau, he refused to see her, and soon after, they were divorced.

Connie and I had a little argument just before our wedding ceremony, another little argument on our way back to the plane, and yet another before we got to Miami. I don't remember what any of them were about. But something happened to our relationship the moment we signed the marriage certificate. We argued perpetually. I can't explain why. Maybe marriage was something neither one of us really wanted and we both felt trapped. Maybe we were so used to going our separate ways that we couldn't compromise. Some friends told me that of all my marriages, Connie and I were the most suited to each other. We were not. She soon became pregnant again; that seemed to be one of the few things we could do well together.

Our daughter Trisha Leigh was born the day after Christmas in 1968. By an odd coincidence, all my children—Carrie, Todd, Joely, and now Trisha Leigh—were born at Saint Joseph's Hospital in Burbank. I was standing by her bed and Connie, in labor and groggy with medication, reached up and took my hand. "You can get me out of here," she said. "You've got pull." Then a curtain was drawn between us and when the doctor told me I had another daughter, I got dizzy all over again, just as I had when my other children were born. The doctor had to drive me home.

Much later, on *The Mike Douglas Show,* after Connie and I had been divorced, I summed up our marriage with the remark: "Connie Stevens is the nicest girl I know. We put two wonderful kids together, but we couldn't put two days together."

That was an exaggeration. Connie and I had some marvelous times. We went to parties, gave parties at our house, led a typical Hollywood life. One of our favorite pastimes was six-handed gin with Joey and Janine Forman and Willie Shoemaker and his wife, Babs. One day we all went to the track to watch Willie and placed two-dollar bets on a show parlay. Willie rode six winners that day and if we had been a little more daring, we could have made a fortune. But Babs said, "I never bet on William." And in a funny way, for different reasons, Connie and I did the same thing. We never seemed to be pulling for each other.

Somewhere in the back of my head there may have been the idea that I had let both of my previous wives walk all over me and it wasn't going to happen again. Connie wasn't going to be pushed around by me, either, just because I was her husband. Against my advice, she insisted on appearing on all the television game shows, which I thought was demeaning and unnecessary. I did try to do whatever I could to help her career. She wanted to play Vegas, and through Bill Miller, the former owner of Bill Miller's Riviera and now entertainment director of the Flamingo, I got her a job there. But when she was putting her act together, she resisted, with one or two exceptions, any suggestions I had to make. And I ignored her criticisms of my friends and the way I led my life. With different careers and different points of view about everything, the odds were against us from the start.

Even the way we argued was different. Connie was volatile and intensely emotional; she said whatever was on her mind. I was just the reverse. After years under the influence of meth, I was often withdrawn and sullen, and when Connie lit into me about something, I usually refused to fight back, replying with a sarcastic remark, or pretending indifference, which angered her even more. I really couldn't figure out what Connie wanted from me and our marriage. She could do whatever she pleased. I was faithful to her; I gave her everything. But she couldn't have me. I wasn't there. I was somewhere else, in my own private world.

Ironically, Connie was more suspicious of my friendship with Steve Brandt than of my association with Clyde. She may have thought Brandt was introducing me to girls, which he wasn't. But he was extremely jealous of Connie and picked fights with her until finally she refused to let him in our house. Clyde, whom she had met a few times, was a mystery to her. She didn't know he was my pusher and that keeping him happy was more important to me than almost anything else. Once, Clyde came up with a last-minute request: Sinatra, opening night at Caesar's Palace on a Saturday, and the best hotel accommodations for seven or eight people—what could be easier? I got on the phone and called everyone I knew: the president of the hotel, the entertainment director, even Sinatra's secretary. Then I realized that with all the pandemonium of a Sinatra opening, something might go wrong. I couldn't trust anyone but myself.

I hadn't intended to go to Vegas, but I did and checked with everyone to make sure Clyde and his friends were well taken care of. Just before the show began, there they were, all smiling and happy, so I decided to stay and watch. Sinatra gave a great performance and then the pandemonium began. I wanted to call Connie to tell her where I was, but I couldn't get a line out. Flights to Los Angeles were booked solid until morning. I stayed up all night and didn't get back home until early the next day.

There was a note from Connie on the pillow of our bed. "I'm in the park with Joely. Where have you been? You just disappeared. How could you do this to me?" I don't know where she thought I had gone, or what she thought I had been doing, but I was too exhausted to go to the park and explain. I left *her* a note and went to bed.

I found another note from Connie when I woke up and wrote her a note in return, telling her I had gone to Las Vegas to see Sinatra. Two or three more notes went back and forth. It was ridiculous and a little sad. Now my wife and I weren't even arguing; we were writing notes.

Our relationship was never quite the same after that, probably because Connie felt she could no longer trust me. On my closing night at the Frontier, she showed up unexpectedly, perhaps hoping to catch me doing something wrong. Even though my dressing room was full of people, she started an argument and I refused to reciprocate. Infuriated, she picked up a shot glass and threw it at me. It missed, and pointing to my cheek, I said, "Connie, if you want to get a story in the fan magazines, throw it here." She stormed out of the dressing room and went home.

I stayed over to watch Diana Ross. My friend Guy Marks was sitting next to me, and midway through the show, fuming at Connie's behavior, I took off my wedding ring and put it on Guy's finger. The moment I walked into the house, Connie noticed it was gone. And when I told her where it was, she called me every name in the book. It was the biggest fight we had ever had, and right in the middle of it, Marks phoned to say he still had my ring. Connie grabbed the phone and started calling him names too. I got the phone back and Marks said he was bringing the ring right over. He came, gave it to me, and then cleared out. Married four or five times himself, he knew enough not to get caught in somebody else's fight.

We had crossed Israeli and Italian flags over the fireplace in our bedroom. I was so mad at Connie that I crushed my wedding ring out of shape and stuck it up on the tip of the Italian flag. Then she walked in, demanding to know if Marks had returned the ring. I said yes, without even looking up from the book I was reading.

"Well, where is it?" Connie cried.

"Right in front of your nose."

She looked for it all over the room, and when she finally found it and saw what I had done to it, she said, "Get out of this house."

"It's my house, Connie."

"Then *I'm* leaving!"

I heard her on the living room phone, making reservations at every hotel in town. Putting down my book, I went out to talk to her, but as soon as she saw me, she ran over to the fireplace and picked up the poker. I followed her quickly and stood right beside her so she couldn't swing. "What are you going to do with that?" I said.

"I'm protecting myself."

"From who?"

"You!"

Both of us trembling with anger, we knew at that moment our marriage was over. And as we began making plans for a separation and divorce, those crossed Italian and Israeli flags over the bedroom fireplace, which were supposed to symbolize our happy union, seemed like a very bad joke.

My next move was predictable. I started looking at other women, something I had never done in all the time Connie and I had been together. And when she went to Las Vegas for an appearance at the Flamingo, taking Joely and Trisha with her, I saw one who rated more than just a passing glance. I will call her Ingrid. She was a beautiful Scandinavian of about twenty, who came to my house with a mutual friend one night for dinner. Someone had warned her she would fall in love with me; I would sweep her off her feet, she told me, and her description of the way I was supposed to operate made me laugh. What could I do but try to live up to that reputation? I pushed the button that closed the doors separating the dining room from the bedroom, and my guests had dinner without us.

By coincidence, my next engagement was at Caesar's Palace, directly across the street from the Flamingo. Connie and I had our pictures taken, hugging, in the middle of the Las Vegas Strip. I asked Ingrid to come with me, and invited four other female guests. Who knows what was going on inside my head? Maybe I wanted to prove to myself I would never be trapped in a one-woman relationship again. Maybe there was no reason, just the crazy ideas that come from using meth. It was all very carefully arranged, or so I thought. I was staying in a suite that Frank Sinatra had used—an entire floor—and my five guests were tucked away in rooms of their own. My plan was to visit each one in turn, without the others knowing about it, or even knowing anyone else was there. And that part worked beautifully. Things got complicated when Connie decided to leave her suite at the Flamingo and bring Joely and Trisha Lee to stay with me. But the night I intended to put my plan into action, I managed to elude her until she finally found me lying on the bed in Willard's room, reading a book. "Where have you been?" she cried angrily. "I've been looking for you everywhere. What are you doing?"

"As you can see, Connie," I said, "I'm reading a book." And it was true. I had made the rounds, but hadn't been able to perform with any of my five guests.

Something just as disturbing as my impotence occurred that night. I spotted some wires in one of the girls' rooms and pulled up the rug to see where they led. I found more wires in other rooms and discovered they were all connected to the main suite. I was being bugged! Furious, I began to rip out the wires, and tore a big gash in my hand. Then I called the president of the hotel and asked him to meet me somewhere in an unoccupied room. He came and I demanded to know what was going on.

"Calm down, Eddie. Calm down," he said. "You're not being bugged. Those wires are for a telephone intercom system Sinatra had installed and it's not in use."

I didn't believe him. And it was more than just the five women in my suite that I wanted to hide. There were the drugs. I had just signed an exclusive three-year contract to play Caesar's Palace, the best casino-hotel in Las Vegas, for six weeks a year at forty thousand dollars a week, and if the owners were looking for some reason to cancel that agreement, it wouldn't be hard to find. I was gambling with stakes higher than anything I had ever lost at the dice tables. I had lost my marriage. And now I was betting with my career.

Connie found a big house in Bel Air for her and the children, and Ingrid moved in with me. There was nothing complicated about our divorce once we decided to go through with it. We had filed in the Santa Monica Municipal Court and everything went smoothly until the eve of the hearing, when the judge called to tell me that Connie wanted to postpone it. "Is there anything I can do?" I asked. "No," he said, "unless you want to talk to her." I had an open invitation to spend time with Joely and Trisha, so I called Connie and said I was coming over. Ingrid was very upset. She didn't understand why I had to see Connie. I left her in tears, and she was still crying when

I returned home early the next morning. Connie and I had played with our little girls and then I just stayed. My feelings for Connie were still very deep, and our last night together may have been one of the most compatible of our entire marriage.

In court that morning, three hours later, Connie beckoned me over and whispered in my ear, "I still love you, Eddie. I really don't want to go through with this."

"Connie," I said, "you know we have to. I love you too, but we just can't live together. There's something wrong with me. Maybe I'm crazy, but I can't be married."

Fifteen minutes later we were divorced. On the surface, it seemed very painless, but underneath there was sadness and a deep traumatic experience. I felt empty. Another marriage had failed and again a certain distance would separate me from my children and the woman who was their mother even if she was no longer my wife. It had become a pattern in my life. But with Connie there were differences. We parted without bitterness, and there was no nonsense about Joely and Trisha. Unlike Elizabeth, Connie did not claim sole custody; unlike Debbie, she wouldn't make me feel guilty about our children. I was their father and Connie expected me to *be* their father.

I hadn't been a good father to Carrie and Todd, but even if I tried, Debbie would find fault. "We can't come and live with you, Daddy," Carrie once told me, "because Mommy says you ran away and left us." Nothing I did was right. Debbie criticized me for not visiting our children, and when I did, she criticized me for spoiling them or favoring one over the other. And on the day after my divorce from Connie, she made it very clear that I was setting them a bad example.

Carrie and Todd, now about eleven and twelve and a half, loved coming to my house. There were so many places to play and buttons to push, and Todd was fascinated by all my electronic equipment, a fascination that later became his career. They invited themselves over the day I divorced Connie. They thought Daddy would be sad and lonely, and I was very touched by their concern. They had met and liked Ingrid, and after dinner that night all four of us went to a movie. Debbie, with a coat thrown over her nightgown and a drink in her hand, was waiting for us in the living room when we got back. "I was worried," she said. "I called and there was no answer. I thought the house had burned down."

"Everything is fine, Debbie. We've been to a movie."

Ignoring me completely, Debbie started talking to Ingrid, until I finally offered to drive her home. She accepted and climbed into her Rolls without saying another word.

The next day, I took Carrie and Tood back home and found Debbie out by the pool. "I'm sorry," she said, "but the kids can't stay at your house anymore."

"May I ask why?"

"Because you have a woman living there."

"What do you want me to do, Debbie, get married?"

"You can do whatever you like, but Carrie and Todd can't stay overnight."

I was very angry. Why did Debbie always make me feel even more guilty than I already felt? No one knew better than I that I had neglected Carrie and Todd. And now if that pattern was repeated, Joely and Trisha would grow up without a father too. What kind of man was I? I wanted to change; I wanted to stay close to my children; I wanted them to love and be proud of me. But I was headed in another direction, toward the time when I would avoid having any contact with them at all, afraid they would see what their father had become.

23

Life was good again. I had everything I wanted: my beautiful house, lucrative contracts, a three-year deal with Caesar's Palace, Ingrid—and an overly generous supply of drugs from Clyde. Connie and I remained friends, and that was good too. But she was still capable of causing quite a commotion. One morning, as I was in bed with Ingrid, a panicky Willard woke us with the news that Connie had just arrived with Joely. Not knowing what to expect, I told Ingrid to hide by the pool and pushed the button that opened the doors to let her out. Then, thinking the coast was clear, I pushed another button to let Connie in. She was carrying Joely, both of them dressed in red, and the moment she entered she started screaming. Turning, I saw what she saw—Ingrid, naked, scampering around the pool.

Connie was enraged. "How could you do this to me?" she cried.

"Connie, for God's sake: We're *divorced!*" I said. But there was no way to calm her. I quickly told Willard to get Joely out of the room, and then he came back to help me. After breaking everything in sight, Connie was yanking the pictures off the walls. By the time her anger was spent, the room looked as if it had been hit by a tornado.

Connie eventually accepted the fact that I was living with another woman, although she referred to Ingrid contemptuously as my "blond Swede." She had black hair. Admitted to this country on a student visa to learn fashion design, she should have been going to school, which I urged her to do. Just to keep everything legal, I found a place where she could enroll without even going to classes. But Ingrid had other ideas. She was here to have a good time, not study. Unconcerned about either the immigration authorities or her family, which might have forced her to come home, she wanted to stay with me. Who was I to say no? In fact, I was afraid to let her out of my sight. If she spent an evening with friends, I waited up for her, and once when she came in late, I raced down the drive after a car, yelling, "Stop! Stop!" trying to find out who had brought her home. I became the possessive one in this relationship; Ingrid might find someone else, and I didn't want to lose her.

To keep her happy, I bought her everything she wanted, including a sewing machine, which we put in the children's room, and Ingrid spent hours pulling apart an old dress of Elizabeth's we found in storage, redesigning it for herself. She was a very talented if not very neat seamstress. All I had to do to find her was follow a trail of pins and needles through the house. At her insistence, the sewing maching was soon moved into our bedroom and the pins and needles turned up in bed. I didn't care. She was my first experience with a woman much younger than I was, a child really, or so she seemed to me, and I loved just watching her, whatever she did. She loved me too, and accepted whatever I did without question, even my drug routine, although I managed to conceal it from her for many months and always spared her the sight of me sticking needles in my arm. Ingrid was the first woman I allowed to glimpse that side of my life, but she was never tempted to try drugs herself. I wouldn't have permitted that.

My friends were worried about me. Remembering the early months of my marriage to Elizabeth, when I gave up everything just to be with her, they were afraid the same thing would happen. Ingrid was affecting my work, they told me; she was too young for me; I was always upset if she wasn't around. They wanted to get rid of her, and someone in my organization bought a ticket to send her back to Europe. I was furious when I found out. But they did talk me into sending her to Florida, where she had a brother. At the last minute, after Willard had her things all packed and she was ready to leave, I told her I didn't want her to go.

My friends' concern was justified. I wasn't performing well but it wasn't Ingrid's fault. The drugs had taken over. I forgot lyrics and missed cues. Making mistakes like that might have endeared me to my audiences when I was a young, inexperienced performer. Now they expected more from me and I wasn't giving it. All I looked for was my friend Clyde in the crowd; all I could think of was how many bottles I had left in my special case. Everything was there in my face—the tension, the anxiety. You cannot show a face like that to an audience you're supposed to be entertaining. And after I had divorced my third wife and abandoned two more babies, a lot of people came to my performances just to see what this person looked like—those who came at all.

Business was bad for my second appearance at Caesar's Palace in 1969. I tried to blame Slappy White and Steve Rossi, who were the opening act, or my competition on the Strip— anything but me. The owners saw it differently, and my fears that they might try to cancel my contract came true. I appeared once more at Caesar's Palace that year and then waited to be told when to come again. "We haven't worked out a schedule yet," I was informed. "We haven't decided." "We'll let you know as soon as we know." I finally got the message. I was being kept in limbo, and because my contract with Caesar's Palace was an exclusive, every other door in Vegas was shut in my face.

While I brought suit to settle my differences with Caesar's Palace, I found that not many other top clubs were interested in hiring me either. Word was getting around the business about my problems. After canceling engagements and missing performances, I was called arrogant, unpredictable, temperamental, too risky, too expensive, completely irresponsible— and worse, I couldn't bring in the customers. There were no television appearances, no records. But I had to work, I had to pay the bills. So I began to get bookings at suburban inns and what few clubs remained in smaller cities—the star attraction, but more than once I had to swallow my pride and lower my price. Still I refused to face the fact that my career was on a downward slide. I thought nothing had changed, nothing was wrong with me, even as I cheated my audiences, alienated friends, gambled compulsively, pumped my body full of drugs, and hung on to Ingrid for dear life.

What was wrong with me? Over forty now, if I wasn't yet afraid of growing old, I was afraid to grow up. My own worst enemy, I refused to face the negative image I was creating. I refused to face myself. And so the slide continued. It was a gradual process; my career didn't collapse overnight. It would take me just about as long to hit bottom as it had taken to climb to the top. But there was an important difference between those two journeys. I had worked hard on my way up. The way down was easier. All I did was let go.

Toward the end of 1969, I was booked on a tour of the Far East. With the exception of a trip to Vietnam in 1965 to entertain troops, I hadn't been in that part of the world since my army days. This wasn't exactly exile. After all, I had once been number four on a list of the most popular entertainers in the Far East. And I was being paid my price. But I had to play several different clubs in Tokyo, including one called the Copacabana—that's the way it was done there—and my three weeks in Sydney were spent in a rather broken-down cabaret in the Chevron Hilton. My audiences in Tokyo were very enthusiastic; in Sydney, even after rave reviews, nobody seemed to care.

Ingrid came with me, and knowing that once she left the country she might not be allowed back in, I went to a lawyer in Los Angeles, who, for a hefty fee, said he could fix it. He did somehow, and the American embassy in Sydney provided a new visa. The tour lasted several weeks and covered thousands of miles, but for all we saw of the cities we visited, including Hong Kong—where we stayed in the Marco Polo Suite at the Peninsula Hotel, on the Chinese side—we might as well have remained at home. Too tired to go anywhere or do anything, I performed at night and spent all day in bed to save what little energy I had left. I didn't attribute my condition to drugs and sleeping pills; I thought they were saving my life. I had a suitcase full of them in little prescription bottles, neatly labeled and signed by Max Johnson. Clyde had arranged all that, including forging Max's signature, and there was no problem getting them through customs. They were legitimate medications. The problems began when I ran out.

From Sydney, Ingrid and I went to a hotel in the Fiji Islands for a brief vacation. It was the rainy season and to get there we had to drive over muddy mountainous roads no better than trails. By that time I had used up my supply of drugs and pills and I began to hallucinate. The green of the jungle seemed to be closing in on me and I had terrifying visions of plunging over a steep cliff. Fixing my attention on the driver didn't work; closing my eyes, I still saw the jungle and the mud. At the hotel I couldn't sleep and at three or four in the morning, looking outside into the darkness, I saw people dancing around a fire. There were no people. There was no fire, except the fire in my head. And flying home on the plane, I stared down through the clouds to the empty sea and saw cities. Even if I blinked my eyes and shook my head, they wouldn't go away, and I thought, I'm seeing things that aren't there. This is the way I'm going to lead the rest of my life. As soon as we landed in Los Angeles, I headed straight for Clyde's.

Ingrid and I made another trip together, to France, Spain, and Israel. Buddy Ruskin, the creator of the popular television series *Mod Squad*, was with us for part of the trip. He wanted to put together an Israeli *Mod Squad*, which I was to produce. Ruskin, who was on some drug himself, was a crazy man; it was a crazy idea. We were both going to make a fortune, and all I did was spend a fortune. There was no money coming in because I wasn't working, but that didn't stop me from laying it out. People expected me to spend money. I tipped bell captains, headwaiters, and croupiers with hundred-dollar bills. Sales clerks with eager expressions converged on me whenever I entered a shop. In Hong Kong on my tour of the Far East, I brought 145 silk suits, 185 silk shirts, and fifty pairs of silk pajamas. George Unger of New York, known as the "jeweler to the stars," called on me regularly, knowing he could always make a sale. "Go to Cartier's, go to Tiffany's," he would say, "and I'll give it to you for half price." In fact, whatever he had to sell usually cost a lot more than it was worth. Once he offered me a seven-strand black pearl necklace, which I wanted to buy for Elizabeth, for seven thousand dollars a strand. Harry Winston appraised it at seven dollars a strand. It was paste. When I told Sam Giancana, he said, "It happened to me too. Forget about it." I did. Unger was convenient, and his assortment of genuine jewelry, if overpriced, was too tempting to resist as gifts for friends or the women of my life.

Spending money was a habit impossible to break. And what I didn't spend, I gave away—in cash if someone needed a loan (only one of which was ever repaid), or merchandise if anyone admired anything I owned. Greg Bautzer fell in love with my custom-made Bentley convertible, the last of its kind, so I gave it to him. Clothes, jewelry, a set of Irish china from the house— all a friend had to do was say he liked it and it was his. I gave Ingrid both the Cartier and the Piaget watches Elizabeth had given me, and the forty-thousand-dollar sapphire pendant I had worn at the Frontier. After so many years, I was still taking care of everybody, buying love. And in mid-1970 it finally caught up with me. The newspapers printed the story: "Eddie Fisher on the Rocks; Former Star Files for Bankruptcy."

It was my worst mistake in a long line of mistakes. After making something over twenty million dollars in my career, I believed I was broke, with debts of close to a million, a figure which included two lawsuits pending against me for $350,000 each. I had agreed to collaborate with Ketti Frings on an autobiography, but after reading a few outlined chapters, I thought it was fan magazine stuff and refused to go on with the book. Bitter at having her work rejected, Ketti sued. And I was being sued for a house I had considered buying and didn't. My actual debts were less and might have been taken care of if I got myself together and went back to work regularly. But unaware of what I really owned, I took my lawyers' advice when they said bankruptcy was the way—the smart way—out.

Whatever bankruptcy cost my creditors, it cost me my self-respect. Now, in addition to everything else, I was a loser, a man without credit who, no matter what other terrible things he had done in his life, couldn't even hang on to his money. I lost everything, including my house and all my assets. A Steinway piano, a gift with a gold plaque inscribed by the song pluggers and composers of Tin Pan Alley, thanking me for singing their songs, was sold for eight hundred dollars and I didn't even know about it. Probably all that was explained to me, but I wasn't listening. As usual, I trusted others to make an important decision. It was the wrong decision for me. My stock went down along with my price and I would never be able to command top dollar again, regardless of where or how well I performed. Eddie Fisher was a bankrupt; he came cheap.

For some legal reason, my bankruptcy was filed in Puerto Rico, and to establish residence, a hotel-apartment was rented in San Juan for my use. Ingrid and I went to Jamaica to visit my friend Ernie Smatt, and on my return to San Juan, I boarded a plane from Kingston carrying only a briefcase full of papers and a small amount of my medication: one hundred cc bottle with about five cc of Clyde's meth cocktail, six Seconal, and some Celestone, the very potent hormone I took to counteract any adverse reaction to the methamphetamine. I never worried about customs; wherever I went, I was usually recognized and waved through. I was stopped at the San Juan airport. The uniformed official was very polite. "Please come with me, Mr. Fisher," he said, and took me to a bare, brightly lit room, where he opened my briefcase and found the bottle and the pills. I told him what they were; he nodded and left the room. A few moments later, another official entered and said, "Do you have any other drugs on your person, Mr. Fisher?"

"No," I said, unable to believe this was happening to me.

"I'm sorry, sir, but I'll have to ask you to disrobe."

Too stunned to protest, I took off my clothes and stood naked in the bright lights, my hands covering my genitals, my face crimson with shame and embarrassment. The official didn't touch me. Walking around in a circle, he gave me a very careful visual examination and then left.

I waited, shivering with fear. Someone must have tipped off customs that I was carrying drugs, but who? Why? Were they illegal? Would I have to go to jail? It seemed like an eternity before two or three more customs officers came back into the room. They looked me over too, and then one of them said, "I'm the chief customs officer, Mr. Fisher. I'm sorry you had to wait, but I was at home when they called me. You can put your clothes back on, and then I'd like to ask you a few questions about the contents of this bottle and these pills."

Again I tried to explain what everything was: medication, a doctor's prescription. I listed the ingredients in the bottle and told them exactly what each drug was for. The chief officer listened attentively. "All right, Mr. Fisher," he said finally, "you're free to go. If you'll tell us where you're staying, we can take you there. But I'll have to keep your medication."

"Can I leave Puerto Rico?" I asked. "I had only planned to stay a day or so more."

"We would like you to remain available until we can have the contents of this bottle analyzed."

I remained "available" for eight days, and compared to the

drug search, the bankruptcy proceedings were a picnic. But the worst was yet to come. The San Juan papers carried a headline: "Eddie Fisher Bankrupt for $1,000,000," with the smaller headline: "Singer Suspected of Carrying Drugs." Reporters mobbed the hotel. Some of them got in and pounded on my door, demanding to see me; others shouted from below over loudspeakers. The police came. It was a nightmare. Without my medication and Seconal, I couldn't eat, sleep, or even think. Customs told me they had been unable to analyze the contents of the bottle and had sent a sample to Washington. There was another delay when Washington reported similar results. Desperate, I called Tommy Jacobson in Los Angeles. He wrote a letter describing the formula and I was finally allowed to leave Puerto Rico. Amazing what a doctor's signature can do.

Once back in Jamaica, I wanted to stay there forever. How could I sing again; how could I face an audience? People called to offer me jobs, but I turned them down. The humiliation was too great. My career was over. I had to retire.

I stayed in Jamaica for almost three months. Then, just for fun one night, I got up and sang at a party. I didn't sound too bad; people applauded and I thought to myself, I can't stop singing. I can't retire. I'll vegetate. I'll die. And I began to rationalize what had happened to me. Sure, I was having a lot of bad luck, but that could change. I could face it and make it change. There was one thing, however, that I wouldn't change. In Jamaica, my supply of drugs was regularly replenished by my friend Clyde through the mails. And back in Los Angeles, I picked them up in person.

My relationship with Ingrid was becoming very strained. She had been bored in Jamaica; she was bored by the way I had to live in Los Angeles. My house was gone, and although many of my possessions had been put in storage, I discovered that many more had just disappeared, stolen. A rented apartment was all I could afford even after I started getting jobs again. I didn't want to see people or go out very often, and Ingrid, at her age, wasn't ready to settle down with a man who spent all his time reading books. I really couldn't afford her either, and she began to nag me about money and never going out. Too preoccupied with my own problems to sympathize with hers, I grew impatient and then angry. She didn't understand me. We had nothing in common, really; we couldn't even talk. Here was another woman telling me what to do, trying to possess me, and I wouldn't put up with it.

The break came on New Year's Eve in 1970. Ingrid and I were going to a party at Clyde's house south of Los Angeles, and she was supposed to pick me up for the drive down. I waited two or three hours for her, seething. I was taking her out, damn it, and she didn't show up. I started out alone in my car and passed Ingrid on the road coming in the opposite direction. Not caring if she had seen me or not, I drove straight on.

Clyde's usual collection of oddballs was at the party. I was the star attraction; Clyde dragged me around, showing me off, introducing me to everybody. I wasn't in a party mood. Ingrid called, and kept calling, but I refused to speak to her. I just wanted to go off in a corner somewhere and forget all my troubles. A woman I will call Marcia seemed to understand. We sat down together and began to talk.

Marcia was an attractive blonde, much closer to my own age than Ingrid, and very intelligent, a woman who listened and had something to say. She told me we had met before, many years ago. Since then she had married and divorced, and living in a house in Los Angeles with custody of her child, she had gone back to school to work for a degree. She was very sympathetic when I told her about my problems with Ingrid. But it was hard to talk over all the noise of the party. We went into a bedroom, shut the door, and continued our conversation. Clyde wouldn't let us alone. "Hey, Jungle Boy, come on out," he shouted, pounding on the door. "I want you to meet somebody. What are you doing in there? How about singing us a song?" Finally he began slipping notes under the door. Ignoring them and the party, we didn't reappear until late afternoon of New Year's Day.

I made a date to have dinner with Marcia when we got back to Los Angeles. She invited me to her house and I met her child. Unlike most of Clyde's friends, she seemed so sane to me, a woman with both feet on the ground, someone I could confide in and trust, someone who wouldn't want to possess me. Ingrid and I were finished. I answered her phone calls, but on Marcia's advice refused to see her; once again I just walked away from a relationship that had become too difficult to handle. And when Marcia asked me to move in with her, I accepted willingly.

I had no place else to go, nothing else to do. And the answer to the one question I hadn't asked—how she happened to know a man like Clyde—came almost as a relief. Marcia was an old friend and knew all about my addiction: the meth formula, syringes, needles, everything. There was nothing for me to be ashamed of or try to hide. When I didn't want to see Clyde, Marcia was even willing to pick up whatever I needed from him, happy to take care of me, feeding my ego and tolerating my habit.

I think Marcia saw herself as my savior. She had rescued a poor, sick stray and was tenderly nursing him back to health. Proud of herself, she told everyone about my problems and how much she was doing for me. Her ex-husband called and advised me to marry her or move out. People were talking, and if what they said was true, she could be in danger of losing custody of her child. So for appearance' sake, I rented a small apartment and kept a few clothes and books there. I had an address and worked off and on, but I continued to spend almost all my time with Marcia. Maybe she was my savior after all.

Even though I was seeing much less of Clyde, he didn't let up on me. Tickets, reservations, introductions—he always had a list of favors a mile long, including one request to speak to Willie Shoemaker about riding a horse for a friend of his, the last thing I would do for anyone. I respected Willie too much. I don't know how much money I had given Clyde over the last five or so years, never in payment for drugs, of course, but always as "investments." On one occasion alone, a check for forty thousand dollars dwindled to twelve thousand dollars, and I could no longer afford losses like that. Even if I could, I had grown to hate the man. The last time I went to his house, I picked up one of the microphones he had hidden everywhere to tape-record his guests and told him exactly what I thought of him. He replied in one of his long, incoherent letters, chewing me out for my ingratitude. I saw him on only one more occasion, when I had to rush him to a hospital after he took an overdose of his own drugs. Thinking he was going to die, he apologized for all he had done to me, and begged me with tears in his eyes to call Max Jacobson, the only man who could save his life. Reluctantly I made the call, and then called another friend, who said he would take care of everything. With that, I walked out of Clyde's life. Who needed him? I had already found a replacement, a man with an unlimited supply of drugs who asked no favors from me in return. A real friend.

I will call him Bob Slick and I met him the same night I met Marcia, at Clyde's New Year's Eve party. About thirty, he was a self-made multimillionaire and offered to pay me $100,000 a year as a public relations man for him, as well as $10,000 every time I performed at one of his parties. Obviously he was an operator, and I had no interest in anything he had to offer, until I discovered he was even more generous than Clyde with meth. A heavyweight user of meth himself, he seemed able to make it materialize out of thin air, and he dangled it in front of me like candy for a kid. That offer I accepted, and my timing was perfect. Right after I finally shook Clyde off my back, Bob Slick climbed on.

Ties to my family began to disintegrate at about the same time everything else in my life was falling apart. With the exception of Bunny, who sometimes acted as my road manager, I saw very little of them anymore. For years I had been the head of the family, supporting my mother and father, helping my brothers and sisters if they needed it. As long as things were going smoothly for me, I tried to smooth things out for them. But there came a time when my generosity had to be reserved for my pusher and whatever woman was in my life. The money I sent my parents dwindled and then stopped; if my brothers and sisters had problems, there was nothing I was able to do for them. Sonny Boy had problems of his own.

Except for growing older, my father hadn't changed much over the years. He always took what I gave him without comment and came back for more. But when the money stopped, he finally felt free to tell me what he really thought. His list of criticisms and complaints was endless, and once over the phone, referring to my divorce from Connie, he said, "Sonny Boy, what did you do? You could have been a leading man in your community, a respectable citizen." That did it. He was proud to be "Eddie Fisher's father" only as long as I kept paying the bills. He didn't love me. He had never loved me, and I vowed never to speak to him again.

I couldn't keep that vow, of course. There were no fans, no autograph seekers or bobby-soxers hanging around the stage door of the Latin Casino when I arrived one night to begin an engagement there. Just one man, an old man, standing in the freezing cold with his coat collar turned up. It was my father.

I ran to him and we cried and embraced. But an hour later in my dressing room, we were arguing again. "So, Sonny Boy," he said. "What do you think about two Chinas in the U.N.?"

"Daddy, there's only one," I said. "Communist China."

He looked at me in disbelief. "What do you know about politics?" he asked. "What do you know about anything? You can't play poker. You can't play pinochle. A girl beat you playing marbles."

My father had a stroke in August 1972. The family phoned me with the news. Although she had been divorced from him for almost twenty years, my mother stayed by his bedside late at night and early in the morning, when his second wife and the rest of the family weren't there. Eight years before, my father had developed a serious kidney condition and I rushed him to California for an operation. He hadn't died then, I thought to myself; he won't die now. And I remembered what he once said when he got up and walked out in the middle of my act: "Don't worry, Sonny Boy. I'll be back."

I didn't want to go to Philadelphia to see my father or anyone else in the family, even my mother. Making up some excuse, I said I couldn't come, and the next phone call I received was from a doctor at the hospital, who said my father was on a heart machine. It was the only thing keeping him alive and my brothers had given their consent to pull the plug. Even then, I didn't react. So my father will die, I thought. He won't be back after all. There was nothing I could do about it.

I couldn't sleep that night. Dulled by pills that weren't working, my mind churned with memories of my father, not all of them bad. Once, just after I had married Connie, I was singing at the Empire Room of the Waldorf and introduced her to the audience. She was sitting with my father and my sister Miriam, and I called out, "What do you think of her, Daddy?" He called back, "Sonny Boy, I've loved them *all.*" Maybe he even loved me, I thought. He was my father; I couldn't let him die. Grabbing the phone at my bedside, I called the hospital in Philadelphia. It was three o'clock in the morning and I demanded to speak to somebody in charge. My words were barely coherent as I shouted into the phone. "Don't cut any fucking thing off! Leave that goddamn plug in there!" I don't know what happened after that. My father clung to life for three more days, and then he died.

I made up another excuse not to go to his funeral. After my

experience at Mike Todd's graveside, I had vowed never to go to a funeral again. But at the last minute, I changed my mind. I loved my father, and I was angry at my brothers, the doctors, the world, for letting him die. I flew to Philadelphia, and drove to the funeral parlor. Except for my mother, the whole family was there, along with other people I hadn't seen for years. Everybody looked so gray and old. My father was laid out in an open casket that seemed hardly big enough for a baby. I was late and a couple of people pushed me forward to look at him. Why did they do that? Why did I have to see him this way for the last time? I listened numbly as he was eulogized as a "great man" for bringing such a "great and talented son" into the world. That wasn't him. That wasn't me. People wailed all through the service. At the cemetery, my anger spent, I had nothing to say to anyone except my father. Staying behind the others for a moment at his grave, I whispered, "So long, Dad." Then I drove to the airport and took a direct flight back to Los Angeles.

Time was running out for a lot of my old friends. After a long illness, Jennie Grossinger died later in 1972. She had been a second mother to me and I felt her death very deeply. Too many of the people who had been important to my life and career were dead or dying. Eddie Cantor was dead. Skipper Dawes didn't have much longer to live. And in 1973, I attended the wedding reception of Max Jacobson and his third wife and looked directly into the face of death. Both Clyde and Bob Slick were closely involved with Max, but I hadn't seen him for years and was shocked by the way he looked: so bent, so old, a skeleton of the big, flamboyant, vital man he had once been. His new wife, who had been a nurse in his office, had to feed him during the reception and then helped him into another room to give him an injection.

Max and Milton were still inseparable and would stick together in spite of many difficulties in the years ahead. Using Milton's mental and physical decline as a reason, his brother Leo Schwartzstein had succeeded in taking control of his businesses. Milton lost everything. There were stories that he was living in cheap hotels and Bowery doorways, sleeping on park benches and begging for handouts on the street. Hospitalized, he insisted on being treated by Max, and both his brothers, Leo Schwartzstein and Daniel Blackstone, still unable to convince him to sever that relationship, sought to expose Max. Leo would soon die, but Daniel persisted, and in December 1972, *The New York Times* picked up their cause in a report that described in shocking detail every aspect of Max's unorthodox practice. Authorities had been gathering evidence against him for years and a full-scale investigation got under way.

I was named as only one of many of Max's famous patients, but I was never asked to testify or even appear for a deposition. Even if I had been, I wasn't ready to talk to anyone about what methamphetamines had done to me. With all the publicity surrounding Max's case, I could no longer kid myself that meth was "medication." The stuff could be lethal. It had destroyed my career and might very well destroy me, and the up and down of speed and sedatives was foolish and dangerous. I knew all that; or at least a part of me knew it. I knew I was killing myself. But I couldn't quit.

Maybe because I wasn't able to face up to my own weakness, I now saw Bob Slick as the villain. We often traveled together; he was my guest in Jamaica. And the more time I spent with him, the more I disliked him. He made no secret of his drug use. Sometimes he injected himself on a plane with syringes he kept in his breast pocket like fountain pens. A diabolical man, he was always plotting to harm someone in any way he could, and I discovered that many of his business ventures and associates operated outside the law. He and his friends were also very big drinkers, and the combination of drugs and alcohol at his parties turned them into bedlam. I couldn't handle it. We argued. I accused Slick of using me, just as Clyde had, and as a peace offering he would send me a dozen or so bottles of his special formula. There was no getting away from him.

There was no getting away from myself. And even though meth, after so many years of abuse, seemed to have the opposite effect on me—a down instead of an up—I couldn't get away from that either. During one appearance at the Century Plaza Hotel in Los Angeles, I performed like a zombie: no voice, no volume, a walking dead man. I was always tired, always angry, always bored.

Out of boredom, curiosity, or just to prove that at least one part of me was still alive, I began seeing hookers. A Los Angeles madam who specialized in "service to the stars" became my new supplier, her girls a new and very expensive recreation. For a long period of time I had a different girl almost every night, but there was something wrong, forbidden, about paying for sex, and more often than not we just talked. Young, some of them beautiful, they were very honest about themselves and the way they made their living. They told me where they came from and how they had got into the business; almost all of them had stories about the kinks of their other famous clients. Most of the money they made went to the madam and they spent the rest, so they were all broke and most of them on drugs. I became interested in these girls as human beings, fascinated by the stories they had to tell, so fascinated that I started making videotapes of them. Sounds and fuzzy pictures of prostitutes—time was running out for me too.

24

It was just a simple suggestion from a friend in Puerto Rico. Sympathizing with all my problems with meth, he said, "Eddie, what you need is a new habit." I thought he was kidding until he produced a plastic envelope full of fine white powder. "What the hell is that?" he asked.

"Cocaine."

I had heard about cocaine; I knew several musicians and performers who used it. But I had never used it myself, or even seen it before. How did you take it; what were its effects; how long did they last? My friend had the answers to all my questions. Better yet, why not find out for myself?

There were two ways you could take coke: by sniffing the powder or by mixing it with purified water and injecting it in a vein. Intravenous injections had become a way of life for me—I was addicted to the needle itself—so my friend prepared a syringe and gave me a shot in the forearm, the same place I injected meth. The effects were instantaneous. I heard a buzzing in my ears and began to feel light-headed. All my senses were mellowed. My whole body was suffused with a warm and happy feeling, a euphoria that lasted only a very few minutes but was a marvelous experience. I had discovered a beautiful new world.

A coke high was a very different sensation from the effects I was getting from meth. On meth I had become irritable, temperamental, full of false energy, and then depressed, always looking for a sense of well-being that wasn't there. Now I had found it. But I was wary; it was too easy, too good. There had to be a catch somewhere. After that first experience, I read every book on cocaine I could lay my hands on. Compared to meth, it seemed harmless. After all, Freud and Sherlock Holmes had used it. By the time I left Puerto Rico, I was off meth completely, hooked on my new habit.

I brought it back to Los Angeles—and there, if you had the right contacts, coke was easy enough to get. Again Marcia knew exactly what I was doing: my suppliers sometimes came directly to me and everything was done right out in the open. I sampled the goods, they weighed whatever amount I wanted to buy, and I paid them—a very businesslike transaction, and a very expensive one. That was the catch. I parted with five or ten thousand dollars every visit, always in cash. For the next two or three months, my new habit would cost me close to $200,000.

To pay for it I sang in second-rate hotels and small clubs, wherever I could get a job. I performed on coke only once, and as wonderful as that feeling was, I knew I wasn't under control and couldn't trust myself to do it again. I tried to recreate a coke high in my imagination, but it wasn't the same thing. My audience probably thought I was drunk, and before long I gave up performing altogether. My habit had escalated from three or four shots a day to sometimes as many as twenty. How could I sing when there was virtually no time, day or night, that I wasn't high? It was a miracle I didn't OD. I was never certain of the purity or the concentration of the coke I bought. I cared, but I had to have it.

In those rare moments when I could think straight, I knew I was in trouble, and that drove me to retreat even further from the real world into the blissful, carefree haze of coke. By this time Marcia had sold her house in Los Angeles, so I rented a house for us on Stone Canyon Road in Bel Air and hired a private detective to guard it. I seldom went out. I didn't have to. A steady stream of friends, and sometimes complete strangers, showed up at all hours to keep me company and enjoy a sniff or a snort. I had no trouble replenishing my supply of coke, and to make sure I could sleep, I bought ten thousand dollars' worth of Seconal, a dollar a pill. I didn't have to worry about food. I was repulsed by the sight of it. My weight began to drop, my face became haggard and drawn, as day after day, week after week, I tried desperately to hang on to my high. Dazed, lonely, I was a prisoner in my own house, a prisoner of my own mind. If this wasn't the sudden death of an overdose, I was dying all the same. And I didn't even know it.

Jack Kelly knew it. As a Deputy Commissioner of Narcotics and Dangerous Drugs, with a territory that covered California, Nevada, and Hawaii, he made it his business to know who was on drugs. He kept an eye on a lot of very famous people, including Elvis Presley. I had met Kelly when he and several other men, with their own special ways of enforcing the law, assembled in the kitchen of Marcia's house one night to confront a hood who had already shaken me down for fifteen thousand dollars and was coming back for more.

Jack Kelly cared about me. Handsome, white-haired, a former policeman from Atlantic City, he was tough but also the gentlest of men. We grew to be friends and he came to see me every once in a while, bringing sets of books he bought at garage sales because he knew I liked to collect them. I was very aware of what he did; he told me what was happening to Presley and why, but he never mentioned my problem until the day he turned up at my rented house. It wouldn't have taken an expert to see I was in serious trouble. My weight was down to 118 pounds; my complexion was the color of chalk. "Jack," I said, "how much do you know about me?"

It was the opening he had been waiting for. "More than you know about yourself, Eddie," he said. "I know what you're on. I know where you get it and how much they make you pay— more than twice as much as anybody else in town, by the way. What you do with your money is your business. But what you do with your life is mine. Keep it up, Eddie, and you've got about six more months."

I didn't want to believe him, until he took me to a mirror and made me look at myself. "No," he said. "I give you three."

It was as if he had slapped me in the face. My emotions reeling, I understood for the first time what I was doing to myself. I didn't want to die. Kelly's words shocked me back to reality. They saved my life. "Just tell me what I've got to do, Jack," I said, "and I'll do it. I want to live again."

He sent me to his own doctor, who was with the police

department and all too familiar with cases like mine. Treating a coke habit and the abuse of Seconal was like child's play in his practice, and when I asked him about withdrawing from coke, he said, "Forget withdrawal. Just quit. Now. All you need is the will and your body will take care of itself."

Next I went to a psychiatrist, who recommended gradually decreasing the Seconal and prescribed a drug to counteract any adverse withdrawal symptoms. It was going to be tough, I knew, but with Kelly offering me courage and support, I was determined to try. "Why not get out of this town?" he suggested. "Someplace away from temptation, Jamaica. I know you love it there. A few weeks, that's all it'll take. I'll go with you if you want me to."

The first step was the easiest, getting rid of the coke. I walked into the bathroom and flushed $25,000 worth of happy dust down the toilet. And I found that out of my lifetime supply of ten thousand Seconals, I had only a few left. Half of them had aroused my suspicions because they were manufactured in Mexico, and I gave them back to the pusher who sold them to me. The other half, five thousand pills, I had hidden somewhere around the house, and when I looked for them, they were gone. Either I had forgotten where I put them, which can happen on coke, or they had been stolen.

The next step was Jamaica, and I asked Marcia to come with me. I needed her help to get through this. In a friend's apartment, just an hour or so before we had to leave for the airport and our flight to Kingston, I made a little ritual of taking my final injection of coke. This was the last of my supply, the end. I was finished with it. If I wanted to live, there was no other choice.

My new habit ended as abruptly as it had begun. I would never use coke again. Where that kind of willpower came from I don't know. Maybe it was left over from the days when I let nothing stand in the way of my becoming a successful singer. Maybe it came from that part of my personality that knuckled under to authority and I obeyed without question the commands of men like Max Jacobson and Milton Blackstone. Or maybe it was a combination of both. In Jamaica, I put myself under a doctor's care and again did exactly as I was told. I was off coke and I wanted to lick the sleeping pill problem as quickly as possible. But there my newly found willpower got me into trouble. I tried to do too much too fast, and the medication I was taking was not effective in combating withdrawal symptoms. Alternately sweating and shivering with chills, I suffered a seizure, and trembling violently, collapsed in a coma.

I woke up terrified, the only white patient in the small local hospital in Saint Ann's Bay, not knowing where I was or how I had got there. I was being fed intravenously, but no one really knew what was wrong with me or how to treat it. I had to get to the hospital in Kingston, and a friend, General David Smith, head of the Jamaican army, provided the means. The first helicopter he sent was too small to accommodate a stretcher, but the second got me to Kingston, where, by another stroke of good luck, I was put under the care of a world renowned specialist in the treatment of drug problems, a black doctor who just happened to be visiting the hospital. Six days later, I was well enough to leave the hospital and return, with Marcia, to Los Angeles for further treatment.

But something happened to my willpower in that town. It vanished. Although I had kicked the coke habit, a couple of problems remained: the sleeping pills, which I had been able to decrease but not eliminate, and money. I went to see my good friend Bob Slick, hoping to get back at least some of the $100,000 I had once given him to invest. He didn't have the money, but he offered me a generous supply of something he did have. Meth. And like a damn fool I took it.

That was the last time I saw Slick, but I was hooked again and there were other pushers happy, for the right price, to supply my needs. But some instinct, some lucky intuition, warned me to be careful of the formula I got from one of them. I had a sample analyzed not once but twice and then called Max Jacobson to ask his advice. He came to my bungalow at the Beverly Hills Hotel and I showed him the analysis. A look of horror crossed his face. "There's enough cyanide in there to kill a horse," he said. Then, his head lowered and his hands covering his face, he murmured, "Oh, God, what have I done?"

Those were Max Jacobson's last words to me. I never saw him again. In 1975, a two-and-a-half-year investigation by New York State medical authorities culminated in the loss of his license to practice medicine on the grounds of "unprofessional conduct." A broken and humiliated man, he died three years later.

* * *

Jack Kelly soon found out I was back on meth. He had licked a problem of his own—cancer of the mouth from smoking—and again he came to my rescue. "Nobody said getting off any of that stuff is easy," he told me. "In Los Angeles, it's impossible." I knew he was right. After one close call with death on coke, I was on the way to a head-on collision and knew I had to do something about it. I had to find someplace to go. But where? Kelly suggested Switzerland and that made sense if I could only get there.

Willard Higgins wanted to help. He was still with me as my valet, but over the years he had become an intimate friend. Alarmed by my condition during the months I was on coke, he had tried to feed me milk shakes. And now that I was again using meth, he grew even more concerned, until one day, with tears in his eyes, he picked up the phone and called Ingrid. Although our relationship had ended badly, Ingrid had remained in touch with me during the two or so years I had been with Marcia, calling me from time to time to ask how I was and tell me what she was doing. In response to Willard's plea, she called again, using the pretext that her mother would be in Los Angeles for only one more day before flying home to Europe. "She would love to see you before she goes back," Ingrid said.

I didn't want to see her or her mother. But the moment Ingrid mentioned Europe, something clicked in my head. Knowing I had to get out of Los Angeles, I said, "I'm going to use you, Ingrid. You're going to help me. I've got to find a hospital in Switzerland and you've got to take me there."

Her reply was immediate. "Of course, Eddie. I'll do whatever I can." She made only one condition: Marcia couldn't come with us.

It was a perfectly normal demand. I had left Ingrid for Marcia and she couldn't forget that. But I pleaded with her. "I just can't walk out on her, Ingrid," I said.

Ingrid was adamant. "I won't help you if she comes with us, Eddie. It just won't work. This is something you've got to do by yourself.

In a way, she was right. My friends, doctors, everyone had told me that my relationship with Marcia was not a good one for either one of us. Marcia had become very demanding and too possessive of me; I had become too dependent on her. Our last few months together had drained us both emotionally. But forced to make a choice, reluctantly I chose to leave without Marcia.

Ingrid said she had heard of a place in Switzerland where they just put you to sleep and when you woke up, you were cured of whatever was wrong with you. It turned out there was no such place. But in Geneva, Ingrid found another hospital, The Bel Aire, and said that from the questions she was asked over the phone, I had to be pretty sick to get in. A doctor from the hospital came to our hotel suite and she told me to put on an act for his benefit. Ignoring him completely, I paced from room to room, yelling, slamming doors, behaving like a complete crazy man. It worked, another award-winning performance. I got in and spent exactly two nights there. Ingrid had made a mistake. The Bel Aire was a hospital for the criminally insane, which was very funny, almost hilarious, even if I *was* in desperate shape. We phoned everywhere, trying to locate another hospital, anyplace that could handle a case like mine, and finally found one, the Bircher-Benner Clinic in Zurich. I was skeptical. The clinical specialized in patients who wanted to lose weight, and dropping a few more pounds was the last thing I needed. But this time, we made the right choice.

First of all, the clinic was beautiful. Ingrid and I shared a pretty little cottage on the grounds with a breathtaking view of the Alps. No drugs were used in my treatment, the food we ate was grown right on the premises, and I was given herbs to help me sleep at night. The first few days were difficult, not because I suffered any dramatic physical or psychological withdrawal symptoms, but because I didn't. When would I start hallucinating, I wondered. When would I wake up in the middle of the night, screaming? Nothing like that happened, and gradually I began to relax. After a week, I was eating again and started putting on weight; the color returned in my face. I discovered I could still sing. And I thought, This is too easy. Jack Kelly had sold me a bill of goods. I wasn't dying; maybe I hadn't really been sick at all.

Who was I kidding? My memory wasn't that bad. I had come very close to killing myself for a lot of complicated reasons I didn't yet understand. But one of the things I feared most—that I wouldn't have the strength to *stop* killing myself—had been an illusion. I was doing it. How many millions of dollars had I wasted, how many years of my life? God, what a fool I had been!

I wasn't doing it by myself. Luck was on my side, the same kind of luck that had been with me all my life. I just happened to find myself in the right place at the right time. Ingrid was wonderful, and that was lucky too. In many ways, I was the child now, and she encouraged me to take the first wobbly steps toward recovery. She loved the clinic more than I did. After a couple of weeks, both of us had never felt better in our lives. Walking around together in the gardens, through the woods, even through the city, I rediscovered the world I had almost lost. We rediscovered each other as friends.

Ingrid couldn't stay. She had dropped everything to bring me here and had to resume her life. My recovery was so remarkably that there was no reason why she shouldn't leave. I wanted her to go; she had already done so much for me. And now that she was going, I thought of Marcia. The fresh air, the food, the exercise—the clinic had performed wonders for me and Ingrid; it could do the same for Marcia. I called her in Los Angeles and told her she had to come.

I thought Ingrid would be gone by the time Marcia arrived in Zurich, but she kept postponing her departure. I had to sneak out of the clinic to meet Marcia at the airport. I put her up at the Grand Hotel, and a day or two later, Ingrid still hadn't left. Finally I realized I had to tell her what I had done. Late one afternoon in our little cottage, I said, "I don't know how you're going to react to this, Ingrid, but Marcia is here. You know I wanted to bring her with us, and I thought it would be all right as long as you were going. It will be good for her."

Ingrid's reaction surprised me. "Oh, Eddie," she said. "Of course I understand. You're such a wonderful man, always thinking of other people." And then, in less than a second, her expression changed as she grasped the full implications of what I had said. "How could you do this to me?" she cried. "You are the worst son of a bitch in the world. I saved your life and this is how you thank me!"

That was the reaction I'd expected. "It has nothing to do with our friendship, Ingrid," I said. "This is for Marcia."

She didn't believe me and jealousy was not the only reason for her anger. She was afraid that everything I had done at the clinic would come undone. The drugs, the sleeping pills—it could all happen again. She said I should be completely sure of myself before I resumed any relationship.

She argued for hours, until I thought it would be better if

I just left and found someplace else to spend the night. But the doors of the clinic were locked at 10 P.M. and Ingrid and I were trapped together for the night, both of us fighting in different ways for the same thing—my life.

It was raining heavily the next morning when the doors were opened. This should have been the moment to express my love and gratitude to Ingrid, but she was still very angry and wouldn't let me tell her how I felt. I left without even saying goodbye, and for the next several hours walked the streets of Zurich, drenched to the skin, calling the clinic from time to time to find out if Ingrid had gone. Why did all my relationships end in tears and anger? What was wrong with me? Now that I was free of drugs and able to look at myself with some kind of objectivity, maybe I should try to find out. My life had been full of miracles—my voice, my success, and now my cure from dependence on drugs. Was it too much to ask for just one more?

I went back to the clinic and an empty cottage. Ingrid had gone. And the next day, Marcia left the Grand Hotel and moved in.

Bircher-Benner was a sanitarium, not a mental hospital. But Dr. Lichti, the head of the clinic, suggested that I see a psychologist, another woman, a pupil of Jung's who lived and practiced in the same house outside Zurich where Goethe had lived. Arriving for our first session, I thought I was in for some heavy intellectual analysis, until she pointed to the sandbox and a collection of little toys in her office and asked me to create something we could talk about. I was stumped; sand reminded me of sand and I remembered the time Mike Todd stuck me on top of a big pile of sand along the shore in Palm Beach. It was supposed to be a stage, I was the main attraction in some imaginary circus, and he was the barker: "Step right up, ladies and gentlemen, the one and only, the great Eddie Fisher!" "Here's me on stage," I told the psychologist, "and that's my friend Mike Todd, and out there is the ocean, only it's really the audience." I thought the whole thing was pretty silly. Audiences weren't like the ocean—or were they? And had I been standing on a pile of sand all my life, always in danger of being washed away unless I could find some piece of solid ground? I didn't think about that then. I had two or three more sessions with the psychologist and several conversations with Dr. Lichti. I loved talking to them and all the other doctors at the clinic. I got a lot off my chest, but I didn't discover any profound insights into myself. That final miracle of understanding would have to come from someplace else.

Maybe that wasn't the point. I was getting well. And Marcia seemed to like the place as much as I did. Dr. Lichti had advised me not to live with her at the clinic. She, too, understood my problems with relationships. But I did live with her and there were soon signs of trouble. For professional reasons, the doctors had tactfully suggested that I might become too friendly with fellow patients; they thought I might get involved with somebody else's problems when I still had problems of my own. But I couldn't help myself. I liked these people and cared about them, particularly a brilliant pianist just one day younger than I, whose talent had been compared to Rubinstein's. His career had been cut short by arthritis, and I used to push him around the grounds in his wheelchair. Marcia probably resented that I was paying more attention to the other patients than to her and picked a fight with me in front of them. Once we went to the movies with some friends from the clinic; it was raining when we came out and she accused me of deliberately forgetting to bring an umbrella. Another time, we were driving through Zurich to see my psychologist and I accidentally turned the wrong way into a one-way street. "You did that on purpose," Marcia said. "You did that to hurt me."

After I had been at the clinic four weeks, and Marcia had been there two, I was ready to go home. I was eating well, sleeping well, exercising. I wanted to go back to work. And now that I felt so much better, I thought Marcia and I would be able to straighten out the problems in our relationship. Dr. Lichti offered me a piece of advice. In one of our final conversations, she asked me, "Eddie, what do you think your main problem is?"

"Women," I answered immediately.

"You're right, but could you be more specific?"

"Well," I said, "I can't live with them and I can't live without them."

Dr. Lichti had the solution. Knowing how I felt about California, she recommended that I stay in Europe. "You can perform here," she said, "live in some nice place, and then when you're about sixty-five, find a nice girl, get married, and settle down for the rest of your life."

I smiled to myself. I couldn't take Dr. Lichti's advice. I had to go back where I came from, where I belonged. Her world wasn't my world, and my world never had been, and probably never would be, "nice." But I could handle it. My confidence was real now, not chemical, and I thought I could handle anything.

But in a matter of months, everything fell apart. If I felt like a new man when I got back from Switzerland, I returned to my old life. Jobs were few and far between, friends had drifted away, I was alone. There seemed to be no solution to the problems in my relationship with Marcia, and gradually, just as Ingrid had predicted, I again sank back into the old self destructive patterns. I started taking sleeping pills again. Only one thing had changed. I would have nothing more to do with needles—with meth. I had made one giant step toward regaining reality, regaining myself, and I would never go back. That part of my life was over, and even if I didn't know what to do with the part that was left, I soon realized that Marcia and I had to separate. She saw it coming and we began to argue. She had kept careful account of her expenditures in the years we had been together and claimed I owed her many thousands of dollars for all she had done for me. But somehow her records neglected to mention the more than half a million dollars I had spent on her, not including gifts of clothes, jewelry, a full-length white mink coat, a Jaguar, and a painting by Bonnard that Elizabeth had given me.

Then I went into the hospital for a routine medical checkup and discovered a growth on my chest that was painful to the touch. Sure it was cancer, and terrified of an operation, terrified of dying, I asked Marcia not to tell the doctors what I had found. She promised, and then told the next doctor who entered the room, which was the right thing to do, of course. I was taken to surgery, the growth proved to be nonmalignant, and I woke up to find Marcia at my bedside. We argued until she was finally asked to leave the room, while I became so agitated that I started to hemorrhage and the doctors rushed me back to surgery.

After I got out of the hospital, I went to Caracas for an engagement and took Marcia with me, but our arguments continued and we found it impossible to get along. She went back to Los Angeles while I went on to Jamaica with Kurt Frings, who had become my agent. One night, sprawled on the vicuña rug in the master bedroom of the house where we were staying, we smoked a little ganja with friends. Everybody began giggling, and Kurt, laughing so hard he was crying, announced, "Here we are, celebrating Eddie's liberation after twenty years on drugs."

That was an odd way to do it, I agreed, but I *had* been liberated from drugs—and my relationship with Marcia was over too. Still, I was concerned about her, and before leaving with a friend for a trip to Europe, I called her from New York. She said she was experiencing a numb feeling all over her body and something was wrong. I thought it was an act, a trick to make me come back. But a few weeks later, I called again from London and found out that she was in the hospital with Guillain-Barré syndrome, a rare, mysterious, and debilitating illness. I flew back to Los Angeles immediately, and for the next two or three weeks, living in a motel near the hospital, I went to see her every day. The disease had caused paralysis of her entire body and she was like a vegetable. It seemed to me that machines were the only thing keeping her alive, but the doctors told me the disease was rarely fatal and its victims almost always made a complete recovery. It was merely a matter of time.

Marcia did recover, although it was a long and painful process. The first time I saw her after she left the hospital, she was walking with a cane, but gradually almost all traces of the disease disappeared. To me it seemed like a miracle. But Marcia was bitter and brought suit against me for the money she said I owed her. Refusing to contest the claim, I made an out-of-court settlement. I hope that Willard was right. "Someday," he once told me, "you'll get involved with a woman who won't cause you aggravation."

I was still waiting for my own miracle. After returning from Switzerland, I found myself in a kind of personal and professional limbo. Anxious, alone, suffering bouts of depression, I lived on a steady diet of tranquilizers and sleeping pills, wondering what had become of my life. Every performance was labeled a "comeback," and on stage I was quick to make fun of myself and my past, telling jokes at my own expense before audiences did. During this period, I think I first became aware of how much I once had, and how much I had lost. I had seen other performers plunge from the top to the bottom, but I always thought it could never happen to me. I had too much talent; too many people loved me. It *had* happened and I felt very sorry for myself.

Something else had happened, almost without my realizing it. My children were growing up. Inexplicably, Connie had bought a house in Malibu, right next door to Debbie's; Carrie and Todd, Joely and Trisha, were getting to know each other. Debbie's waning movie career and divorce from Harry Karl had left her in financial troubles, or so she claimed, and she had embarked on a whole new career, starring on Broadway as well as Las Vegas. "It's because of you and Harry that I have to work Vegas!" she shouted at me angrily one night when I came to visit Carrie and Todd, and then she hit me with a shoe.

I went to see Debbie on closing night of her act at the Desert Inn. Both Carrie and Todd were performing with her and I was excited about seeing them on stage for the first time. Still a clown, always a trouper, Debbie hadn't changed. It was Carrie and Todd who astonished me. Telling jokes and kidding around, Todd was obviously having a great time on stage. And Carrie, at the age of fourteen, belted out Paul Simon's "Bridge over Troubled Water" with all the confidence in the world. My daughter could sing! Tears of joy began streaming down my cheeks, until she caught my eye and winked.

I heard myself singing when Carrie sang, saw myself at her age, and it was an inspiration. Whatever had happened in the past, I still had a name and a voice. I had to go back to work. And an opportunity came early in 1975, when Buddy Hackett asked me to appear with him again. There was no question now of who was the star—Hackett. Still, I had to be grateful. Of the many performers who were once much closer friends, he was the only one who hadn't forgotten me. It wasn't a question of charity. I could leave an audience cheering and he knew it. But he gave me a chance to prove it, especially to myself, and it worked. In June of that year, I was booked at the Riviera, for $30,000 a week, without Hackett. My contract dispute with Caesar's Palace had been settled in my favor with an award of $350,000, and Las Vegas welcomed me back.

Why had I felt so sorry for myself? All I had to do was get up on stage and sing. Even more remarkable, I was performing well without meth, something I once had thought impossible. I had almost forgotten that the high I got from an audience was better than any drug. But there was something else I had almost forgotten. A performer presents more than just a name or a voice to his audience; he must present himself. If that is missing, the stage might as well be empty.

25

I was on a roll, happy that this latest comeback could mean I was here to stay. But I wasn't happy about myself or the way I looked. Years of improper diet and lack of exercise, emotional stress and drug abuse, had finally caught up with me. Although I hated using it, I had learned a few tricks with makeup, and was able to get away with that on stage for a while. But there came a time, looking at myself in the mirror, even in makeup, when my face always caught me by surprise. That wasn't me. It was somebody else.

A man I met at Buddy Hackett's offered to help. Dr. Rudi Unterthiner was a plastic surgeon and after we were introduced and chatted for a while, he began to talk shop. "Eddie," he said, "you look wonderful but maybe there is just one little thing I could do around the eyes." I discounted the idea: plastic surgery was something a woman might do, not a man. I didn't want anyone messing around with my face. What if something went wrong? What guarantees did I have? Rudi could be another Max Jacobson, a doctor with a magic scalpel instead of magic needles.

He was, in fact, a remarkable man. Ten years younger than I, he was well educated and spoke many languages; he flew jets and helicpoters, went scuba diving and back packing, took an interest in a wide range of ideas and activities. We became great friends, perhaps my closest friendship since Mike Todd's death. We talked about books, philosophy, politics, and the better I got to know him, the better I liked and trusted him. I watched him operate, and reassured that he knew what he was doing, I agreed to let him perform an operation to remove the deep folds over my eyes and the bags underneath.

The procedure was a fairly simple one, and I went to Lancaster, northeast of Los Angeles, where Rudi had his practice. A local anesthetic was all that was required, and a few days later, when the stitches were removed and the swelling and discoloration subsided, I was so pleased with the results that I was more than receptive to the next step—a complete face lift. I was totally anesthetized for six and a half or seven hours and woke up to find my face wrapped in bandages with only narrow slits for my eyes, nose, and mouth. I looked like a mummy. And after the bandages were removed and I saw my face in a mirror for the first time, it was so bruised and swollen I thought I would never be able to appear in public again. For the next two or three weeks, I lived at the Desert Inn Motel, right next door to the hospital, and walked the streets of Lancaster with a contraption on my head that looked like a football helmet, cursing Rudi for what he had done to me, cursing myself for being dumb enough to have let him do it. But gradually, as the scars began to heal and my face took on its normal color, I liked what I saw. Maybe I didn't look like the kid from Philadelphia again, but the lines and wrinkles were gone and it was enough just to look like a man my own age. Rudi's scalpel *was* magic.

For the final stages of my recuperation, I stayed at Rudi's house, just outside Lancaster, with his wife, Linda, and their two children, Shane and Robin. I felt like a member of the family. Terry Richard came up from Los Angeles to see me every once in a while. I had met her at a friend's house in Beverly Hills when she got locked in a bathroom and I broke down the door to ler her out. After that romantic introduction we started going around together, no emotional entanglements. We just had fun, swimming, playing paddle tennis, doing things that were healthy for us.

At twenty, less than half my age, Terry had been Miss Louisiana in the Miss World beauty contest and came to Hollywood looking for a career as an actress and a singer. But she wasn't driven by ambition, like so many other young women

I had known. If it happened, it happened. Things were so
uncomplicated in her life. Sweet, simple, unaffected, she
seemed the perfect companion for someone trying to clear the
cobwebs out of his own head. She was almost in awe of me,
like the teenagers of a generation ago who had made me their
idol. Terry reminded me of those days; she reminded me of
what it was like to be young. And like Rudi's operation, I
thought she would be a way of erasing time.

    Eager to show off my new face, and the self-confidence that
came along with it, I arranged to appear on *The Mike Douglas
Show*, which was telecast from my hometown, Philadelphia.
The program, an entire week as Mike's cohost, was a near
disaster. The face was fine, the voice was fine; I thought I was
in great shape. But I was too anxious, too self-conscious, my
speech was slurred, my emotions too close to the surface. At
one point during the week, I began to thank all the people who
had been important in my life, including my mother, sitting
in the audience, and my face contorted painfully as I tried to
hold back tears. Sometimes I seemed to be trying to run the
show; other times, it was almost as if I wasn't there. At the
end of the week, Mike was so upset that he couldn't even say
goodbye.

    Friends were sympathetic. Thinking I had been sick, they
asked, "Are you all right? Are you better now?" I didn't know
what they were talking about until I saw tapes of the show and
realized how awful I had been. And it wasn't hard to figure
out the cause. If meth and cocaine were things of the past, I
had come to rely on a new "medication"—tranquilizers. My
collection of little bottles went wherever I went—pills to relieve depression, pills to relieve anxiety, pills to put me to
sleep. I had taken them singly and in combination during the
week of the show. All on doctors' prescriptions, of course.

    Terry Richard was becoming more than just a companion.
As usual, marriage was the farthest thing from my mind, but
Terry and I were seeing quite a lot of each other, both in Los
Angeles and as guests of the Unterthiners. Rudi, a very complex
man, was a believer in the "simple life" and tried to convert
me. On weekends we often hedge-hopped in his plane around
the lakes and deserts of southern California, or flew to a place
called Puerto Citos in Baja California, where Rudi had a
shack—which really was a shack—to swim, look for starfish

on the beach, and take the hot mineral baths. No telephones, the electricity went off at ten o'clock, or thereabouts, and rattlesnakes outnumbered the people. As much as I loved Rudi, I really didn't like sleeping on a cement floor.

That was not the only foolish thing I did in Puerto Citos. One night in October 1975, everybody got a little tipsy, joking, clowning around, and someone said that Terry and I were such a perfect couple, so ideally suited to each other, wouldn't it be wonderful if we got married? Right there in Puerto Citos, under the stars. What could be more romantic? And by the luckiest of chances, Paul Baxter, one of the largest distributors of airplane parts in the world and Rudi's neighbor, was a mail-order minister. He could perform the ceremony.

Getting married was no joke to me, not even a mock ceremony, but under the influence of one Gatorade and vodka, I went along with it. Why spoil everybody's fun? Terry draped herself in a white sheet, I was barefoot, naked to the waist, dressed only in a pair of jeans. Rudi's children acted as our ring bearer and flower girl until they fell asleep. And after Baxter led us through a ceremony very close to the real thing, I put a cigar band on Terry's finger. Then amid high-spirited shouts and laughter, we went on our honeymoon—a few steps away to the local cantina, where we were given the bridal suite, so called because the bed was so big it filled the entire room. Leaky plumbing was our wedding-night serenade, while outside our window scores of racing cars, preparing for the Baja 500, gunned their engines all night long. The next morning, a friend of Rudi and Linda's presented us with our wedding certificate, which she had painted on a piece of canvas. I wasn't entirely convinced the ceremony or the certificate was legal, but Terry and I went back to California as man and wife.

Our marriage was announced in the press, and I bought a handsome Spanish hacienda on the top of a hill in Palmdale, Lancaster's twin city, in order to be close to the Unterthiners. The house was an even thousand yards from the San Andreas Fault. I didn't want to live in Los Angeles or be a part of that scene, where I felt I no longer belonged. Terry and I talked about raising quarter horses. We went on tour in Australia as Mr. and Mrs. Fisher, but Palmdale was our home. I sported a beard. Terry wore feathers and white leather. This was our version of the simple life.

Who was I kidding? Our simple life quickly became very

complicated. First of all, I really couldn't afford the house. It was too big and expensive to maintain. And too isolated. Traveling the fifty-six miles back and forth to Los Angeles proved to me more than I bargained for. Then Rudi and Linda moved from Lancaster to Palm Springs, leaving us friendless in Palmdale. There was nothing to do, no place to go. Terry missed Los Angeles and started talking again about a career. Her voice teacher told her it would be a great idea if we went on tour together singing *Carousel*. "My teacher thinks I have a wonderful voice," she said.

"Terry," I said, "I've never even heard you hum."

After that remark, she never stopped humming, or talking about becoming a star.

We were both lonely and unhappy in Palmdale and my intake of tranquilizers began to increase, not decrease, as we led our "simple" life. My relationship with Terry was deteriorating, which troubled me, but that wasn't the only reason. There was something about me, my personality, that had always looked for a quick chemical fix to regulate the moods and emotions that seemed beyond my own control. But from my past experience with drugs, at least I knew I was headed for trouble and had to do something about it.

Through Rudi I found a psychiatrist, who told me that dependence on any one of the tranquilizers I took was bad enough; in combination, it could be deadly. Once again, on doctor's orders, I had come dangerously close to killing myself. The psychiatrist recommended hiring a nurse to watch me at home while I gradually withdrew from all but Valium, but Terry volunteered for the job. Not knowing what might happen or how long it would take, I was grateful for her offer.

A million questions raced through my mind that first day after I got rid of the pills with the exception of Valium. Would it never end, this business of hobbling along on chemical crutches? And if, at the last minute, I could always find the strength to give them up before I killed myself, why didn't I have the strength to avoid using them in the first place? There were no answers to those questions yet, only my determination to kick another habit. And that night, to my surprise, after taking only Valium, I slept like a baby. The next morning I woke up triumphant and even hungrier than I usually was in the mornings. "Terry," I said, shaking her. "I did it. I slept without all those damned pills! Let's have something to eat."

"Well, *I* didn't sleep a wink," she said, then buried her head in the pillow and refused to get up.

I was very angry at Terry, not knowing that the psychiatrist had told her to stay awake and watch me that night. She really hadn't slept a wink. I knew only that I hadn't yet licked tranquilizers, and I called Rudi to ask him to get me into a hospital. He didn't consider that necessary, but we made arrangements for me to stay at a nearby Holiday Inn with a private nurse until we were certain I had won my battle.

At the motel, I did little more than walk, eat, read, and sleep. The Holiday Inn in Palmdale was a far cry from the Bircher-Benner Clinic in Zurich, but the results were the same. After two weeks I had given up everything but Valium, and in much better shape, both physically and emotionally, I was ready to go home. It was Christmas. Terry, her family, and many of their friends were at the house to celebrate the holidays when I walked in. They were surprised, but happy, to see me. And I was happy to be there. The unhappiness lay ahead. At the Holiday Inn, I had decided that Terry and I should separate.

Terry didn't understand why and I couldn't explain it. We left Palmdale to return to Los Angeles, and for the next few months separated and reconciled time and time again. Neither one of us could make the break. Finally I went to my lawyer, who told me that romantic Mexican ceremony had probably been a charade. The woman who painted our wedding certificate on a piece of canvas had copied the seal from *Good Housekeeping*.

Terry and I were divorced on April 1, 1976, a necessary procedure, my lawyer told me. She didn't ask for alimony, and friends told me she would do just fine without me. But I cared about her and her future, and after the divorce we saw each other from time to time. Still waiting to be discovered, Terry took acting and singing lessons, had her teeth straightened. I got Kurt Frings to act as her agent. But like so many other young Hollywood hopefuls, she couldn't seem to make her dreams come true. We began to see less and less of each other as time passed and I went back to work. For once a relationship of mine didn't end abruptly, and if that was some kind of progress, it finally ended all the same.

A dream had eluded me too—the dream of erasing time, trying to live a life in Palmdale that wasn't me. I eventually lost the house. It was too remote, too expensive; no one was interested in property that close to the San Andreas Fault. Even so, Palmdale marked a turning point in my life, a gain that more than made up for anything I had lost. I was free, at last and forever, of all the potent mood-altering drugs I had taken for nearly twenty-five years. There was still the Valium, and I knew, like a recovering alcoholic, I would have to take my life one day at a time, walk before I could run. But I had made an important first step, and I would never go back.

Early in 1976, Buddy Hackett and I were again on tour together, including an appearance at the O'Keefe Center in Toronto, where we raised four and a half million dollars for Bonds for Israel, far and away the most money ever raised for Israel in Canada. At the Sahara in Las Vegas, the climax of the tour, we played to more than capacity crowds; customers were sitting in the aisles. There were problems. My relationship with Terry had not been resolved; I had trouble with my voice because of laryngitis and missed a couple of performances. But in August of that year, I was again sharing the bill with Buddy at the Sahara, glad to be working again, eager to repeat our earlier success. There was a lot at stake.

Although I didn't know it, there was a lot at stake for Buddy too. He had just returned from a disappointing tour of many of the theaters we had previously played together and was afraid his box office appeal was slipping. Our competition on the Strip was tough: Johnny Carson, Bob Newhart, Don Rickles, and Dean Martin were opening the same night. But Buddy had his pride, and when he learned that both Carson and Martin were playing on a "cocktails only" policy during their shows, he insisted on the same policy at the Sahara during ours. Opening night, the house was half full. In a panic, Buddy called the other hotels to check the competition, something he did regularly anyway. The story was the same all over town: everybody was doing better business than we were.

There had to be a reason, and to Buddy's way of thinking, I was it. Remembering that I'd come down with laryngitis and missed a couple of shows the last time we played the Sahara, Buddy began to tease me, predicting it would happen again—a convenient excuse to replace me. Determined to prove him wrong, I stayed in my dressing room between shows, talking to no one, and went to bed early to get plenty of rest. I had vaporizers *and* humidifers going night and day. But during one performance my voice did crack, and Buddy, just waiting in the wings for something like that to happen, walked on stage with the remark, "Hey, Ed, why don't we go back to that doctor who helped you the last time?"

"No," I said, "I'm taking care of it myself."

"Okay," Buddy said, and after some wisecracks, walked off.

He wanted to talk to me after the show. I refused to speak to him even on the phone, afraid I would get into an argument and hurt my voice. Buddy had already approached Charo to replace me on the bill, which I wasn't supposed to know. Then I discovered something else. As a favor to me, Buddy had got Terry's mother a job in the pit at the Sahara. Now she told me she had been fired.

I called Buddy to ask him to get her the job back. It was my forty-eighth birthday. "Buddy," I said, "she needs the money."

"Tell her to go back to Oklahoma and get a job with the Indians," Buddy said. "And by the way, you just saved me nine hundred dollars. I bought you a watch for your birthday, but I'm taking it back."

Laughing, hoping we could make peace, I told Buddy I really would like to have the watch. He brought it to my suite, and walking in, spotted a bottle of Tylenol on the bedside table. "Ah ha," he said, "you're on drugs again." It was the kind of remark Buddy often made and I ignored it. Then he presented me with the watch, which was engraved, "Dear Eddie: Fuck you on your birthday. Hate, Buddy Hackett." I thanked him and put on the watch.

Just before the first show that night, Buddy said, "Hey, Ed, could you do a little more time?" I was puzzled, because he usually asked me to do less time, but I added about twenty minutes to my act for the first show, only to be told by the Sahara's Jack Eglash, just after I walked off, to cut it again. "Jack," I said, even more puzzled now, "Buddy just asked me to do more time."

"I know," Eglash said. "We're having a hell of a time with him."

Buddy had a contract with the Sahara and had to be humored. "Okay," I said with exasperation. "I'll do anything you want. I'll do fifteen minutes."

"No," Eglash said. "Just do what you've been doing."

A few moments before the second show, Eglash came to my dressing room. "Look, Eddie," he said. "It's not going to work out. Buddy is going crazy in his demands. We'll give you two dates in December."

"Whatever you say, Jack," I said with a sad shake of my head. Buddy was firing me, the first time in my career that anything like that had happened. I was being humiliated, but there was nothing I could do about it. "You might at least have waited until I came off," I said to Eglash. That was the cruelest shot of all.

I knocked myself out for the second show and left the stage sweating and unbuttoning my shirt. Buddy followed me on, and as I walked up the steps to my dressing room, I heard him say to the audience, "He's going to see a doctor...." What kind of game was this man playing now? I walked angrily back on stage, still sweating, my shirt unbuttoned. Looking at me in surprise, Buddy handed me the microphone. "I don't need that, Buddy," I told him. "I don't need you to make excuses for me. I just want to tell the audience ... I just want to read the inscription on the watch you gave me for my birthday."

There was a gasp from the audience after I read the inscription, and then silence. I threw the watch at Buddy. "And you also gave me this," I said, taking off a Mexican antique silver belt and throwing it at Buddy's feet. "What are you trying to prove?"

"I'm just a little guy trying to make a buck," Buddy replied.

I walked off and Buddy started calling for Jack Eglash. "Mr. Entertainment Director, Mr. Entertainment Director..." Reluctantly Eglash came to the mike on stage and Buddy interrogated him. "Did I fire Eddie Fisher? Did I do this or the hotel?" Eglash gave all the right answers.

Back in my dressing room, I was close to tears, knowing I shouldn't have done what I did. The audience hadn't understood what was going on. The phone rang. It was Shecky Greene, calling from Lake Tahoe. "Bet you wish you were up here with me," he said, knowing how difficult Buddy could be. I told him what had happened and he immediately called Buddy. "You son of a bitch," he said, "I'm going to come down there and kill you for what you just did."

Shecky was laughing when he phoned later to tell me about his call and Buddy's reaction. To retaliate, he had called the police and said that Shecky had made a threat on his life. Then offering me some words of comfort, Shecky said, "Don't worry about it, Eddie. You got guts. I'm proud of what you did and so are a lot of other people."

Buddy couldn't wait to get on the phone and tell reporters his version of what happened that night. It was written that I had walked on stage half naked and after shouting obscenities at Buddy Hackett, had taken off even more of my clothes and thrown them at him. At best, I was sick; at worst, crazy. Neither was true. But far from being proud of what I had done, I was deeply sorry. It was unjustified, totally unprofessional. All too often in private I kept my emotions bottled up until they exploded, but this was the first time it had ever happened in public, and I had to pay for it. If I have guts, I didn't have a job, and it would be a long time before anyone in Las Vegas would hire me again. I had learned a valuable lesson.

Back in Los Angeles, I had plenty of time to brood about past mistakes, and working infrequently, worrying a lot, I began to eat compulsively and put on weight. I developed a pot belly, and in Amsterdam to do a special on Dutch television, I couldn't get into my suit. The wardrobe mistress had to slit the pants down the back and I did the whole show with my jacket open because I couldn't button it. At 170, thirty pounds over my normal weight, I suddenly had another battle on my hands.

I thought the problem was simply too much food. Ice cream, cookies, candy, junk food—I was shoveling them all in. My friend Rudi Unterthiner sent me to a specialist in nutrition and metabology, who, as a preliminary, asked me to fill out a questionnaire. I more than flunked. And after extensive physical tests, we discovered I was suffering from severe hypoglycemia, anemia, and high blood pressure. My health was in serious trouble. The doctor told me that if I didn't change my eating habits, I would be a candidate for a heart attack within six months.

Put on a high-protein, saltless, sugarless diet—which meant giving up the kind of food I had eaten all my life—as usual I tried to do too much too fast. I went into hypoglycemic shock, trembling, sweating, my head and my heart pounding. Certain it was a heart attack, I called the doctor, who told me to eat anything available. The attack subsided, and to prevent any recurrence, I supplemented my diet with high-protein snacks and liquids and vitamins. I also learned that my condition had strong emotional components. Not only had it probably affected my behavior for the past couple of years, when I had been so nervous, irritable, and quick to anger, but anxiety, stress, and tension could aggravate the problem. It was a vicious circle. And to break it, I had to work on my mind as well as my body.

Back to basics: proper diet, exercise, medical and psychiatric help, and for the first time in my life, singing lessons. My voice was no less important to me than my body and mind, part of the same package. If I had to do it all over again, I would start at the bottom, and this time do it right.

It was a lonely business, that kind of discipline and self-examination. But it seemed to pay off. At fifty, drug-free with the exception of Valium, I was in good shape in spite of everything I had been through. The proof came when I joined "Roy Radin's Vaudeville '78: A Tribute to the '50s," a month of one-night stands in twenty-seven cities coast to coast. I wasn't too happy playing a figure of nostalgia, a relic from the past. I had much more to offer than that, but audiences everywhere were very warm, and the grueling schedule put my physical and vocal stamina to the test. I passed with flying colors and joined the same show again later in the year. I couldn't make it a second time. Quitting in the middle of the tour, I returned to Los Angeles and checked into the Beverly Comstock, completely exhausted.

My physical problems were easy to diagnose: bronchitis, laryngitis, extreme fatigue. But there was also something wrong with my mental attitude. Sometimes I pushed myself too hard, sometimes not hard enough. I either cared too much or too little, and the Valium, which was supposed to even out my moods and emotions, didn't seem to help. Why bother with it? Already taking every vitamin and dietary supplement in the world, I could do without one more pill. The last of the long list of drugs I had used for years, I would be well rid of it. And so without asking a doctor, I stopped. Cold.

A day or so later I began to suffer a whole new set of symptoms, which seemed unrelated to the fatigue and stress caused by the tour. My skin began to prickle and burn; parts of my body suddenly started twitching. I couldn't focus my thoughts; I couldn't sit still. Alarmed, I called every doctor I knew in Los Angeles, and they either suggested I make an appointment, or offered to prescribe some pill. Finally I called Rudi Unterthiner in Palm Springs and described my symptoms. An hour or so later his Beverly Hills pharmacist delivered a package. Valium. I kept the bottle on my bedside table but never touched it.

When the symptoms got even worse, I again called Rudi, who found a doctor for me. I checked into Cedars-Sinai Hospital; the doctor met me at the front door and took me to my room. We talked, I told him about the burning sensation in my skin, the sudden twitches. He left and came back a moment later with two little pills in a paper cup. "What are they?" I asked after swallowing them with a glass of water.

"Valium," he said.

Within a very few moments all my mysterious symptoms vanished. I felt like a fool. Someone who had as much experience with drugs as I had should have recognized the symptoms of withdrawal. But I hadn't. If I had taken just one of the Valiums Rudi's pharmacist delivered, I would have been all right.

I stayed in the hospital for tests and a complete physical checkup. Unhappy, alone, I started calling up friends to tell them I was back in town, in the hospital. I called my son Todd. Friends sent cards and flowers, said they would try to find time to see me. Todd was at my bedside exactly half an hour after I hung up the phone.

He was twenty years old, a man. When had that happened? His big smile came from my side of the family, and I recognized myself at his age, shy and eager to please. He was an electronics and computer wizard, but that certainly didn't come from me. He could build a television set; I had trouble turning one on. On his own, he had assembled and equipped a very complex mobile sound unit, which he rented to film and recording companies.

Todd came to the hospital almost every day and invited me to stay with him at his house in Beverly Hills when I got out. I didn't want to intrude, but how could I resist an opportunity to get to know my son? We spent the next three months just "hanging out" together. We rode around Beverly Hills on his motorcycle. I learned a lot about the latest sound equipment; we both learned a lot about each other. Todd wanted to take care of me, to cleanse the poisons from my body and spirit.

We saw a holistic doctor in Malibu and went on a health food diet—with a few forbidden baked potatoes and ears of corn on the side. Along with many of his young friends, Todd had become a Born Again Christian, and, very sincere and earnest in his beliefs, he tried to convert me. I admired the change they had brought to his life. I was proud of his spirit and strength of character. But I was born a Jew and a Jew I would die.

One day I heard a loud crash from the garage and called out to Todd, "Are you okay?"

"Yes," came his reply, and then, "well...not really."

I raced out and found him sitting on the steps, bleeding profusely. He had tripped carrying a huge Sparkletts bottle, which shattered and cut severe gashes in his arm and abdomen. He tried to pretend it wasn't very serious; I thought he was going to bleed to death. "Don't pass out!" I cried. "I won't know what to do." He did pass out. Dressed only in a bathrobe, I carried him to the car and rushed to the emergency entrance of Cedars-Sinai. Todd was smiling weakly as he was wheeled into the operating room. Some sixty to a hundred stitches were required to close his wounds. I called Debbie, but she wanted to talk to the doctors, not to me. But Ray Reynolds phoned later and said, "Bravo, Eddie! You were in the right place at the right time."

For once, I thought to myself. But Todd did much more for me than I had done for him. Just being with him, talking about our ideas and feelings, was the best possible medicine. Making up for a lot of lost time, we achieved the father-and-son relationship I had always hoped for. With new confirmation of the love that had always been there, we were friends. But soon after Todd returned from the hospital, I knew it was time to move out. He had his own life, friends his own age; he was in love and planning to get married. We were both crying the day I left.

It was a mistake. I had put all my possessions in storage, and somehow in the confusion of changing addresses and going on tour, I overlooked notices of payment due. The bill was never paid and everything I owned was sold at auction. Todd heard about it, and very upset, rushed to the sale and bought things he thought I would want to keep. I didn't learn what had happened until it was too late. Everything I treasured was lost. Thousands of priceless books, records, and photographs, letters, plaques, and awards, my gold records, irreplaceable mementos of my career—all gone.

I was shocked and saddened. And as I thought about all the things I had lost, like a drowning man, I saw my whole life flash before my eyes. I had inhabited many worlds, not just the world of show business. Politics. I remembered Truman, Eisenhower, and Jack Kennedy, of course. I remembered a ten-state jet whistle-stop campaign for Lyndon Johnson in 1964. Someone called me Johnson's "secret weapon" on that tour because I was the only one who would leave the plane if it was raining, or circulate among the crowd passing the hat. In Arizona, the home state of Johnson's opponent, Barry Goldwater, I was told that all the Democrats needed to win was $25,000 to get voters to the polls, and when we were greeted at the airport by a number of well-heeled and bejeweled Democratic ladies, I told them in jest, "If one of you will contribute just one earring, we can carry this state." Apparently none of the ladies was willing to make the sacrifice. Johnson won the election by a landslide but he lost Arizona.

He invited me to his ranch to thank me for my help during the campaign. I flew to Austin on Governor Pat Brown's plane with Ruth and Milton Berle, George Stevens, Jr., and Gene Autry, among others. We played poker and Autry, as usual, picked up all the chips. Johnson gave us a barbecue, and although there were several celebrities present, I was the only one asked to entertain. Milton Berle stood behind a tree heckling me as I walked through the crowd singing my medley of Jolson songs. The mike cord got tangled, and I was pulled up short until the President himself jumped out of his seat and rushed forward a great distance to untangle it.

I remembered a weekend at Hickory Hill, rehearsing for a telethon to raise funds for retarded children. Ethel Kennedy had asked politicians, performers, athletes, everyone she knew, to participate and I suggested that Andy Williams, Perry Como, and I do a number together on the show. The telethon lasted six and a half hours, an hour longer than planned, and people were understandably tired and ready to leave. But the moment I walked on stage, they stood up and cheered. I sang for about twenty minutes and then, for the finale, Perry and Andy joined me for "Bye, Bye, Blackbird." Bobby and Ted Kennedy, both better politicians than singers, chimed in and we brought down the house. Reviewers later wrote that Perry Como and Andy

Williams could take a lesson from Eddie Fisher in the techniques of performing. No mention was made of the vocal abilities of Bobby or Ted.

The following day, back at Hickory Hill, I urged Bobby to run for the Presidency in 1968. "I wouldn't get one delegate vote," he said. Not content with that answer, I raced around buttonholing Pierre Salinger, Robert MacNamara, Senators Fulbright and Mansfield, everybody there, and they all backed me up, even if Johnson should decide to seek reelection. "Okay," Bobby said. "Let's say I did run and was nominated. The ticket would be split and Nixon would get in. You want to see Nixon in the White House?"

Bobby Kennedy did run and was close to nomination when he was shot. First Jack and then Bobby: like the rest of the world, I couldn't believe it had happened, and I remembered a meeting I once had with General Curtis LeMay, who, as head of the Strategic Air Command, had enough power at his fingertips to destroy the planet. My son Todd, then about ten, came along with me and had no idea who LeMay was, but was very impressed by the room in his Bel Air house crammed full of medals from practically every country in the world. Toward the end of our visit, I happened to mention that I was going to Bobby Kennedy's for his wife's telethon. "Bobby Kennedy?" LeMay said without expression. "He's going to be assassinated."

I campaigned for Hubert Humphrey in 1968 and sat next to Mayor Richard Daley at the Democratic National Convention, while outside the convention hall Chicago police brutally cracked the heads of antiwar demonstrators. I had been to Vietnam to entertain the troops in 1965 and like so many others, didn't realize then what kind of war it would become. General William Westmoreland gave me a plaque, but there would be no awards, not even honor, for the men who fought and died there. Both Humphrey and Nixon promised to end it; Nixon won the election and still the war went on. I loved my country and welcomed the opportunity to work for any just cause. I knew we had to find a way to eliminate all wars. But after the riots in the streets of Chicago, I lost my taste for politics and politicians.

How could I remember all the people I had known during my career, men and women I met not only because I was a celebrity. They were celebrities too, more famous than I was,

yet we called each other by our first names and became friends.
As a kid I had collected baseball cards. Ballplayers were my
heroes. I will never forget "Eddie Fisher Day" at Ebbets Field,
when I lined up with the Brooklyn Dodgers. And the day at
Fenway Park when I put on Ted Williams's uniform, number
9. It would have taken three of me to fill it. All my dreams
of glory as a ballplayer came true during an Old Timers vs.
Celebrities game at Yankee Stadium. Leo Durocher put me in
to pinch hit for Joe DiMaggio and Lonnie Stratton faced me
on the mound. The first ball came by so fast I didn't even see
it. "Lob it in, lob it in!" Durocher shouted to Stratton from the
dugout. He refused, and pitching with his one arm, burned the
ball in even faster. But I managed to get a piece of one of
them, a foul tip, before I fanned out. The crowd went wild and
I wondered what would have happened if I got a hit.

I sang the national anthem so often, particularly at ball
games, that I was called the "Star-Spangled Kid." I used to
pray that Lucy Monroe would come down with a sore throat.
And once I flew all the way from Philadelphia, where I was
performing, to sing the national anthem at the opening game
of the 1962 World Series at Dodger Stadium in Los Angeles.
A limousine met me at the airport, but it was stalled in traffic
as we approached the ball park. The radio was on and I realized
I couldn't possibly get there in time to sing. I jumped out of
the limousine, dodged around cars, vaulted over the turnstile,
and raced to the dugout, where the electric cart was waiting
to take me out to center field. "And now, ladies and gentlemen," the voice over the loudspeaker announced, "Mr. Eddie
Fisher singing our national anthem." I scrambled out of the
cart, took two steps, and stood panting in front of the microphone. "Oh, say can you see..." That was just a little too
close.

Books had opened up another world to me. I sometimes
think I spent more time reading than singing, and once I had
kicked the meth habit I read with greater comprehension. I
used to walk into bookstores and buy everything in sight; one
room in my house on Beverly Estate Drive was lined from floor
to ceiling with books. Science, psychology, and philosophy
fascinated me, and if I didn't always completely understand
or agree with the major writers in those fields, I wanted to be
exposed to their ideas, to learn. Reading was, at least in part,
an escape, a distraction from things that troubled me, but I was

also looking for explanations and answers, some way to make sense out of the confusions in my own mind and the world around me. Nothing gave me greater pleasure than finding someone—a dentist, a college professor, even a stranger at a party—who had read books that I had read and who could talk about them. My greatest pleasure was meeting the author himself. Bob Bandier, a friend of mine whom I first knew as a bartender at Grossinger's and who now owned a bookstore in Syracuse, introduced me to Thomas Szasz. His most famous book, *The Myth of Mental Illness,* had made a deep impression on me, and after spending five or six hours in conversation with Szasz, I found him to be just as humorous as he was profound.

I was in complete awe of playwrights and writers. Paddy Chayefsky a brilliant man, was a close friend for over twenty-five years. Henry Miller, whom I met at a dinner party in Beverly Hills, was astonished to hear that I had read almost all his books. We began to talk before dinner, and as we sat down at the table, I was eager to pursue our conversation, but Miller said in his gruff way, "Let's wait, Eddie. When I eat I don't like to talk." He recommended Isaac Bashevis Singer to me as "the greatest philosopher in the world today," and sent me many of his books. He also sent me copies of all his own books, including *Time of the Assassins,* his homage to Rimbaud, he inscribed "To my new idol"; and *The World of Sex,* in which he wrote, "And who should know more about it than you?"

Both of these books were gone now, sold at auction. And to me, at that moment in my life, the sale of everything I owned was profoundly symbolic. It was the end. Eddie Fisher was finished, washed up. I was a has-been, with a name that people recognized, but remembered more for the women I had married than for my career as a singer. My quotient of self-pity was high. I was the guy who had it all—and blew it. My only image now was of a man who had fucked up a career, fucked up his life. And the reasons why eluded me. I had been victimized by women, Milton, Max, drugs, bad luck, bad advice, bad publicity—the list was endless. But when I was through blaming others, I was forced to add another name to that list. I had been responsible. I was my own victim.

If that was true, I could still rationalize it. Fate. Good things and bad things happen to everyone. That's life and I had more of both than most men. Whatever pain and unhappiness I felt now, there had been years of great joy, love, and fulfillment. Why not settle for that? Maybe I was lucky after all. A lot of performers I knew had literally killed themselves with drugs and alcohol. Others had committed suicide. *I* was alive. And God knows, I wasn't unique. Los Angeles was a haven for has-beens. We were show business clichés, and whenever we met, the talk was all about comebacks, the big deal in the works—memories of the past and lies about the future. I had to get out of that town.

I knew there was only one way out—singing—but too proud to ask for help, powerless to help myself, I couldn't move. Without the elaborate organization that had supported me for years, the agents, managers, secretaries, conductors, arrangers—my entourage—I would have to handle both the business and the musical details of my performances virtually by myself, and how could I deal with some club owner who might agree to up my price if I agreed to settle for three violins instead of six? The trappings of stardom—air fares, limousines, suites, accommodations and reservations for family and friends—had become a habit with me. Now they were "negotiable." Did I really want to start all over again? Did I want to perform badly enough to work at it, settling for small victories and ignoring the defeats? I wasn't sure. I wasn't even sure people still wanted to hear me sing.

A few of my old friends stuck by me: Joey and Janine Forman, Lenny Gaines, Bob Abrams, Jim Mahoney, Warren Cowan, Gloria Luchenbill, Howard and Arlene Eisenberg, Linda Foster Winter, Bill Trowbridge and Rona Barrett. They tried to bring me out of myself, cheer me up, encourage me. Other friends I cut off myself, ashamed that I wasn't working, ashamed of the way I had to live. I didn't want to see anyone. I thought I deserved to suffer. And so, month after month, I sat on my tail in Los Angeles, that graveyard of hope, lost in the dark, waiting for some flash of light, a new miracle, unable to see that if a miracle was possible, it had to come from me.

"Sure it's crazy," Lenny said. "I've never heard of the Newport Hotel either. It was Lenny Bruce's mother's idea. What have you got to lose?"

The answer to that question was "Nothing." So I pulled myself together and flew to Miami. But after one look at the room where I would have to perform, I almost took the next flight back to Los Angeles. It was a disco. I didn't want people to come to a place like that to hear me sing. I thought of the Blackamoor Room in that same town, more than thirty years before, when I stood on the bar to sing. I had come full circle and couldn't start at the bottom all over again, with no hope of ever reaching the top. But I did, and the place was jam-packed on opening night. Thanks to the enthusiasm of my friends Bruce and Marilyn Schwartz and Vic Jarmel, my appearance made headlines in the Miami papers, I played to overflowing crowds for two weeks, and every night my audiences cheered. It was a love affair—but not quite the same love affair as that between me and the audiences of the early years of my career. Then people had rooted for a young kid because they wanted him to succeed. I wasn't a kid anymore; I had seen success and failure, and they were rooting for me now to get up off the canvas and fight. This was the flash of light, the miracle I had been waiting for. I had doubted my audiences, but most of all I had doubted myself, and here was all the proof I needed that I had to go on singing.

I returned to Los Angeles with renewed self-confidence, certain I could create a new kind of magic between me and my audiences—if I could only reach them. I needed help and asked for it, but a lot of people who owed me at least some small consideration in return for past favors didn't even bother to return my calls. A few seemed to take pleasure in kicking me while I was down. I had seen it happen to others, and knew that was the way the game was usually played, but I couldn't believe it was happening to me. I wanted to sing at Grossinger's and phoned Paul Grossinger every day for a week. Finally his sister Elaine called. One of the tabloids had printed an article claiming that Todd had converted me into a Born Again Christian. It wasn't true, of course, but Elaine said, "We're sorry, Eddie. We just can't handle a situation like that."

Grossinger's, which had been a second home to me for years, turned me away. With Milton gone and Jennie dead, Grossinger's wasn't Grossinger's anymore. So I sang at the Concord, Grossinger's chief competitor. Again there was magic and I played one whole show to my daughter Carrie, who was sitting in the audience and then came up on stage with me to sing "If I Loved You." It was one of the most memorable moments of my life. But no matter where I sang, I always returned to Los Angeles, and there it was all too easy to fall back into the old patterns of self-pity and resignation.

It was a little girl I used to know, Carrie Frances Fisher, who got me to my feet—and out of Los Angeles. She had become an actress, first playing a teenager in *Shampoo*. "Wait till you hear what I have to say, Daddy," she told me. I saw the movie and blushed beet red when my daughter propositioned Warren Beatty with the words, "You wanna fuck?" Movies had come a long way since Debbie and I made *Bundle of Joy*. Then Carrie appeared as Princess Leia in *Star Wars,* which was so successful that she could go on playing the same part in sequels until the day she died. But she didn't want to be stuck in outer space, she told me. She could sing, write, direct—there were so many things she wanted to do. Phoning me in Los Angeles, she said, "Hey, Daddy. You know, I think it would be a great idea for you and me to start all over. So why don't you come to New York? There's a movie script we can do together. We could do a fabulous nightclub act. And while you're at it, bring me the head of Beverly Hills."

I was amused by the idea of a twenty-two-year-old "starting over," but she said the words I wanted to hear. We *could* start over together as father and daughter. Why not come to New York? Why not take the plunge? I couldn't wait to get there when I was seventeen years old. So I was over fifty now and a lot had happened in the intervening years. But it had all started in New York. And I knew I had made the right decision the moment I walked into Carrie's apartment. She was entertaining friends. There was music, laughter. There was life. "Sing for us, Daddy," Carrie said. Someone sat down at the piano and I sang "Once Upon a Time," her favorite.

Carrie took me under her wing, just as Todd had done in Los Angeles. She was a marvelous daughter and made me feel as if I had always been the greatest father in the world. Through Carrie I met a whole new generation of performers, writers and musicians: her friends Paul Simon, Art Garfunkel, and Penny Marshall, Joan Hackett, Buck Henry, Mike Nichols, Richard Dreyfuss, Michael O'Donahue, Dan Aykroyd, John Belushi, Tom Schiller, and the rest of the crazy crowd whose talents made *Saturday Night Live* the funniest and most original show on television. They were all brilliantly inventive and their energy rubbed off on me. If they seemed a lot older than their years, they made me feel a lot younger than mine.

Carrie and I did the town together. We went to plays and movies and out-of-the-way clubs. We took a ride through Central Park in a hansom cab. Messengers were always arriving at my door with presents from her: movie magazines with my picture on the cover that she found in a Greenwich Village shop, silly things like chattering teeth and old sheet music, anything in purple—shirts, ties, socks, sweaters—because "my dad is royalty." For my birthday, she threw a surprise party for me at Paul Simon's house in the Hamptons. Carrie was an actress and made every moment we spent together a theatrical event. I marveled at her wit and intelligence; she had an endless supply of funny stories about what it was like to grow up in a Beverly Hills mansion with an army of servants. "Not one thing I dropped ever hit the floor," she told me. "And when I moved into my first apartment in New York, I suddenly discovered dust. And hair in the sink. I just couldn't handle it." But beneath all the jokes and laughter, there was a serious side and she sometimes came to me for advice about her problems. We got to know each other not only as father and daughter but as friends, and her love and concern gave me renewed confidence in myself.

Carrie and her friends brought me new songs and new ideas for my act. New York itself filled me with energy and ambition and I began working steadily. I sang in Philadelphia, of course, Chicago, Lake Geneva, Wisconsin. I made television appearances, sang at Brown's. Grossinger's welcomed me back, as did the Sahara in Las Vegas. I thought I had seen it all in my long career: I've been here before. But every performance was a new challenge, a new excitement, a new sense of accomplishment. As long as I could keep singing, giving myself as well as my voice to my audiences, anything was possible.

In a nostalgic mood one day, I found myself in Times Square looking around for the landmarks of thirty years ago. I remembered when I first came to New York with just pennies in my pocket and the dream of seeing my name on the marquee of the Paramount. That dream came true. And I remembered the thousands of teenagers who had waited in the rain to see me there the day I got out of the army in 1953. Audiences weren't quite so enthusiastic when my name appeared on other marquees, first with Debbie in *Bundle of Joy* and then with Elizabeth in *Butterfield 8*. But I wasn't an actor; I was a singer, and I won them back at the Winter Garden after my separation from Elizabeth in 1962, and again at the Palace in 1967. How many people, I wondered, had bought my records? How many people had heard me sing over the years, on *Coke Time,* the Chesterfield show, at Grossinger's, the Waldorf, the Plaza, in Philadelphia, Miami, Los Angeles, Las Vegas? Millions? Hundreds of millions? Would they remember me?

I remembered them—not individual names and faces, but the feelings that my audiences had always given me. I started out with nothing but a voice, a gift of God; all the rest had come from people who wanted to hear me sing. I had wasted their gifts. They came so easily, so abundantly, that I thought they would always be there. Now I knew better. Like the Paramount itself, they were gone. But why look back? Why regret the past? I was still here. I had my voice. I had a career. I had Carrie and Todd, Joely and Trisha—a family. I had a future. And I was going to work like hell to keep them.

The little kid with a big voice had taken a long time growing up. There was a lot left to do, a lot more to learn, and I hadn't stopped dreaming. I felt, at that moment, as I must have felt more than thirty years before. I can still make my dreams come true. Standing on the busy corner where the Paramount used to be, I said to myself, "Here I go again."

Epilogue

Toots Shor led a fabulous life. A very colorful character, he had an endless fund of stories about the people he knew—and as the owner of one of New York's most famous restaurants, he knew intimately people from every walk of life. "Toots," I said to him one night, "you've got to write a book."

"I can't write a book," he said.

"Why not?"

"Because I couldn't tell the truth."

In my book, it never occurred to me to tell anything but the truth. Each of us has his own truth, and this is mine. I have changed the names of a few people in the story of my life and omitted some truths about others, but I have been completely honest about myself. And I have tried to write as I sing—from my heart.

It wasn't always easy to do. There was something about writing an autobiography that implied my life was over—this was it, my farewell performance. Memories can be dead weight, dragging you down, and I wanted to move forward, not look back. But then I realized I had a story to tell, and I wanted to set the record straight. A future of promise is possible only when you have made peace with the past.

374

A gentleman, so the saying goes, does not "kiss and tell." But I couldn't write my autobiography without revealing the personal side of my life. Still, I wondered what effect my book would have on others—my family, my friends, my former wives, my children. My mother, of course, was happy to share her own memories with me. Her love and loyalty have always sustained me. And among my brothers and sisters, I have found a new understanding. Our lives have taken us in very different directions, but we are still a family. I discovered, too, that I had many good friends who helped me remember the past we shared. Their insight, humor and honesty have made me cherish their friendship even more.

"I really don't care what you write," Connie Stevens told me, and then added jokingly, "I've got the perfect title for your book: *Ballbreakers I Have Known.*" Our daughters Joely and Trisha have inherited both Connie's talent and her beauty. They have inherited my voice. "We sang on stage with George Burns," they told me excitedly over the phone. "You stole the show," I could hear Connie say in the background. "We wished you could have been there," Joely said. "Yes, we love you, Daddy," Trisha said. I love them, too, and will always be grateful to Connie for reserving my place in their lives. They aren't growing up without me, and someday soon we will sing on stage together.

Although I have seen Debbie Reynolds only two or three times in recent years, there remains a strong bond between us—our love for Carrie and Todd. One of the proudest moments of my life occurred recently when Debbie and I stood together as mother and father of the groom at Todd's marriage to Donna Freberg. Both Carrie and Todd know why I had to write about my life. To me they seem to have an understanding well beyond their years, and I'm sure that Joely and Trisha, when they have added a few more years to their lives, will have that same understanding. I couldn't have written my book without the love and support of all my children.

I met Elizabeth Taylor recently at Sardi's in New York. The maître d', perhaps intentionally, sat us facing each other only two tables apart. I sent her a bottle of Dom Perignon and she raised a glass to me with a *"Mazel tov."* We spoke a few friendly words, and looking into her eyes and her still beautiful face, I realized that the painful memories had gone long ago. We had both changed over the years and I wished her well.

We spoke again as I left the restaurant. *"Shalom,* Eddie," she said.

"Shalom, Elizabeth."

I also met Milton Blackstone in New York. I hadn't seen him for years, and after all we had both been through, neither of us knew quite what to expect. But in many ways, Milton hadn't changed at all. He was in charge of his life, making plans, his head full of new ideas, almost as energetic and innovative as he had been decades before. I saw in Milton what I had first seen years ago, and regretted that circumstances had driven us apart. But life and our experiences have brought us together again and we are good friends.

I could not have written my book without the help of Burton Beals, or finished it without the help of Lyn Davis. Burton had the difficult job of putting it all down on paper in a collaboration that has grown to include friendship. Lyn and I met and fell in love as I was working on the book, and because we came from very different worlds, my first reaction was, "I can't let her read this—not one word." I underestimated her intelligence. I underestimated her respect for the truth. From California with a background in psychology and philosophy, she is a teacher with a profound understanding of human nature. She put aside her studies and her plans for a career in television and a book of her own until I finished mine. In Lyn I have found a kind of love that was new to me; I have found many things in her that I have found in no other person. She is the most complete woman I have ever known: deeply spiritual yet practical, strong but still vulnerable, both serious and playful, a personification of every facet of love. I'm sure there is no other person in the world like her. Through her eyes, I have seen my past in a new light. She lights up my present. Because of our love there will be light in the future.

One evening, just after I had finished my book, I was relaxing, reading a magazine, when I heard a familiar sound. Lyn was in another room playing one of my old albums and a few moments later she asked me to come in and listen. Then, with my voice in the background, she began to read the last few pages of my book. I sat there filled with a complexity of emotions. My voice on a record, my voice from the pages of a book. My songs, my words—that evening they were the last things I wanted to hear.

Sensing my mood, Lyn said, "No, Eddie. Please listen. I want you to hear what you've done. You've always been willing to share yourself with others in your music, and now in your book. It's the greatest gift anyone can give. It's one of the highest expressions of love."

Yes, I thought, if I have been able to do that, then it's been worth it, every day of my life, and I felt a sense of accomplishment, a moment of peace. I also glimpsed a new faith, not only in myself and others but in a presence beyond us all. I don't know where it will lead, but I do know it begins with forgiveness. My life did have a purpose, a meaning after all.

I had searched for meanings as I wrote this book. And with the perspective that time always brings, I could look back and laugh at myself. I sometimes wanted to give myself a good, swift kick in the pants. But many of the things I did that raised so much ire at the time would scarcely raise an eyebrow now; stories about me that made headlines twenty-five years ago might make only a small item in the gossip columns today. I could see, too, in my life all the familiar elements of the Horatio Alger rags-to-riches story, a fairy tale about a poor boy who grows up to sing for a princess, dine with presidents and marry not one but three Hollywood stars. Then there is the darker side of that same story, the equally familiar tale of the man who couldn't handle sudden success, and wasting his talent and money went from riches back to rags. But beyond all that, I realized, my book is about the different kinds of love—the kind that nourishes, the kind that inspires, the kind that destroys and the kind that endures.

My first love, my love for singing, has endured. The world of show business is a world of extremes and it makes extreme demands on performers. I have lived a life of extremes. Yet I have always been, and always will be, happiest on stage. For even in that unreal world, the love I have for singing, the love exchanged between a performer and his audience, are real. They were the foundation on which I built my life. Singing is what I do, what I am.

But I am not only a performer. I am a man with needs for warmth, intimacy, sharing with one other person, and my experience with that kind of love has also been extreme, almost unreal. Because I was somehow unable to separate my private life from my public one, or because the public inevitably has a fascination with the private lives of performers, I always seemed to be on stage. The dramas in any man's life—love affairs, marriages, even divorces—I played out in glaring spotlights. But I myself sometimes permitted my need to *be* loved to dominate my life. And a love that feeds only on the self destroys.

For years I strove for perfection in my performances and expected perfection in myself and in the people I loved. I could not reconcile the differences between the ideal and the real. Image—the word haunts me even today. I was always disappointed when people I admired failed to live up to the image I had of them. And when I found that I could not live up to the image I had of myself, I destroyed the very thing I felt I could never achieve. I almost destroyed myself. And characteristically, I again went to extremes. There has always been something about me that had to take risks, flirt with danger. It may have been inevitable that I eventually flirted with death.

But now I am very much alive. And life, of course, is never a solo performance. There were many people who loved me even when I felt I could no longer love myself. I have found new strength in the love of my audiences, my family, my children. I am *in* love. And friends and associates have again gathered around me to help build my career. With that kind of support, I can step out on the stage of my life with confidence and self-respect. I am a very lucky man.

I have made mistakes. There are regrets. But I have had one hell of a life, and both success and failure have taught me valuable lessons. With age and experience comes wisdom, and I can now accept myself as I am. I can accept the realities and the responsibilities of the world of show business. My life has been a journey, not a destination. No one can stop moving, growing, changing as time and circumstances change. But there are things in myself I will not change. Creating music will always remain my greatest challenge, performing my greatest satisfaction. I will always take risks in my work. I will always take risks in love. And I will always share whatever gifts I have with others. That is what the life of any man is all about.

Index

Glittering lives of famous people!
Bestsellers from Berkley

★ ★ ★ ★ ★ ★ ★ ★ ★ ★ ★ ★ ★ ★ ★ ★ ★ ★ ★

MS READ-a-thon—
a simple way to start youngsters reading

Boys and girls between 6 and 14 can join the MS READ-a-thon and help find a cure for Multiple Sclerosis by reading books. And they get two rewards — the enjoyment of reading, and the great feeling that comes from helping others.

Parents and educators: For complete information call your local MS chapter. Or mail the coupon below.

Kids can help, too!